Predictability of 'Public Policy' in Article V of the New York Convention under Mainland China's Judicial Practice

Predictability of 'Public Policy' in Article V of the New York Convention under Mainland China's Judicial Practice

Helena Hsi-Chia Chen

Published by:
Kluwer Law International B.V.
PO Box 316
2400 AH Alphen aan den Rijn
The Netherlands
Website: www.wolterskluwerlr.com

Sold and distributed in North, Central and South America by:
Wolters Kluwer Legal & Regulatory U.S.
7201 McKinney Circle
Frederick, MD 21704
United States of America
Email: customer.service@wolterskluwer.com

Sold and distributed in all other countries by:
Quadrant
Rockwood House
Haywards Heath
West Sussex
RH16 3DH
United Kingdom
Email: international-customerservice@wolterskluwer.com

Printed on acid-free paper.

ISBN 978-90-411-6743-9

e-Book: ISBN 978-90-411-6744-6
web-PDF: ISBN 978-90-411-8828-1

© 2017 Kluwer Law International BV, The Netherlands

All rights reserved. No part of this publication may be reproduced, stored in a retrieval system, or transmitted in any form or by any means, electronic, mechanical, photocopying, recording, or otherwise, without written permission from the publisher.

Permission to use this content must be obtained from the copyright owner. Please apply to: Permissions Department, Wolters Kluwer Legal & Regulatory U.S., 76 Ninth Avenue, 7th Floor, New York, NY 10011-5201, USA. Website: www.wolterskluwerlr.com

Printed in the United Kingdom.

MIX
FSC® C103993

'To my parents, Chu-Chih and Ying-Jer'

Table of Contents

List of Abbreviations   xiii

Acknowledgements   xv

CHAPTER 1
Introduction   1
1.1   Why Re-examining Public Policy?   1
1.2   Objectives   4
1.3   Scope   5
1.4   Methodology and Limitations   6
      1.4.1   Methodology   6
      1.4.2   Limitations   7
1.5   Terminology and System   8

CHAPTER 2
The Meaning of Public Policy   11
2.1   Etymology   12
2.2   Public Policy and Public Order (or *Ordre Public*)   13
2.3   Historical Development of Public Policy Provisions in International Conventions   14
2.4   Meaning of 'Public Policy' in Article V(2)(b) of the New York Convention   16
      2.4.1   Objectives and Functions of New York Convention's Article V(2)(b)   16
      2.4.2   'Public Policy of That Country'   17
      2.4.3   International Standard for Public Policy   17
2.5   ILA's Reports on Public Policy   19
2.6   Examples of National Legislation Concerning Public Policy   23
      2.6.1   Reference to the New York Convention   23
      2.6.2   'Public Policy of This Country'   24

Table of Contents

	2.6.3	'Public Policy' Only	24
	2.6.4	'International Public Policy'	24
	2.6.5	Parallel Provisions of Public Policy (or Public Order) and Good Morals	25
	2.6.6	'Basic Principles of Legal System', 'Good Morals and Other Social Order' and Other Terms	26

CHAPTER 3
'Public Policy' and the Even More Unpredictable 'Social and Public Interest' in PRC Arbitration Law and Their Interrelationship   27

3.1 'Public Policy' in PRC Civil Law System Is Only Seen in Provisions Relating to the New York Convention   29
    3.1.1 Recognition and Enforcement of Foreign Arbitral Awards   30
        3.1.1.1 Before PRC's Accession to the New York Convention   30
        3.1.1.2 After PRC's Accession to the New York Convention   31
            3.1.1.2.1 From the PRC's 'Basic Principles of Law or National and Social Interest' to 'Public Policy'   31
            3.1.1.2.2 Criteria for Differentiating Between Domestic Arbitral Awards and Foreign Arbitral Awards   35
    3.1.2 Recognition and Enforcement of Arbitral Awards of Taiwan, Hong Kong and Macau   39
        3.1.2.1 Taiwan   39
        3.1.2.2 Hong Kong   39
        3.1.2.3 Macau   40
        3.1.2.4 Comparative Analysis   40
    3.1.3 Summary   48

3.2 'Social and Public Interest': The Usual Terminology in PRC Legal System   49
    3.2.1 Identical Procedural Provisions: Centralised Jurisdiction, Reporting System, Functions of the SPC's Fourth Civil Tribunal   53
        3.2.1.1 Centralised Jurisdiction   53
        3.2.1.2 Reporting System   54
            3.2.1.2.1 Validity of Foreign-Related Arbitration Agreements   55
            3.2.1.2.2 Enforcement of PRC Foreign-Related Institutional Arbitral Awards and Recognition and Enforcement of Foreign Institutional Arbitral Awards   55
            3.2.1.2.3 Revocation of Foreign-Related Arbitral Awards   55
        3.2.1.3 Functions of the SPC's Fourth Civil Tribunal   57
        3.2.1.4 Summary   58

	3.2.2	Inconsistencies Between Arbitration Law and Civil Procedure Law	60
		3.2.2.1 'Foreign-Related Arbitral Awards' and 'Foreign-Related Institutional Arbitral Awards'	60
		3.2.2.2 Social and Public Interest as a Ground for Revocation of Foreign-Related Arbitral Awards, Non-enforcement of Foreign-Related Arbitral Awards or Domestic Arbitral Awards?	70
	3.2.3	Mixed Use of Terms in PRC Cases	82
	3.2.4	'Social and Public Interest' as a Ground for Excluding the Application of Foreign Laws	82
3.3	Scholarly Opinions		83

CHAPTER 4
PRC's Convergence with International Consensus — 87

4.1 Public Policy Should Be the Public Policy of the State Where the Enforcement is Sought Rather Than Transnational Public Policy — 88
    4.1.1 International Consensus — 88
    4.1.2 PRC Judicial Practice — 88

4.2 Public Policy Should Be Limited by 'Internationality' — 89
    4.2.1 International Consensus — 89
    4.2.2 PRC Judicial Practice — 90
        4.2.2.1 Arbitral Tribunal's Error in Merits or Applicable Laws, or Unfair Outcomes — 90
        4.2.2.2 Violation of Mandatory Laws for Registering Foreign Debt Guarantees — 93
        4.2.2.3 Award's Violation of Other Mandatory Laws — 96

4.3 Joint Consideration of Merits and Arbitral Decisions — 98
    4.3.1 International Consensus — 98
    4.3.2 PRC Judicial Practice — 98

4.4 Public Policy is Applicable in 'Exceptional' Circumstances Only — 98
    4.4.1 International Consensus — 98
    4.4.2 PRC Judicial Practice — 99

4.5 Procedural Public Policy in Non-recognition and Non-enforcement of Foreign Arbitral Awards — 103
    4.5.1 International Consensus — 103
    4.5.2 PRC Judicial Practice — 104

4.6 Substantive Public Policy in Non-recognition and Non-enforcement of Foreign Arbitral Awards — 106
    4.6.1 International Consensus — 106
    4.6.2 PRC Judicial Practice — 106

4.7 Violation of Enforcement State's Mandatory Laws Is Not Necessarily Violation of Enforcement State's Public Policy — 106
    4.7.1 International Consensus — 106

Table of Contents

| | 4.7.2 | PRC Judicial Practice | | 107 |

CHAPTER 5
Mainland China's Departure from International Consensus — 147
5.1 Protection of Departmental or Local Interests — 148
    5.1.1 Before the Reporting System's Implementation: *Dongfeng* Case — 148
    5.1.2 After the Reporting System's Implementation: *Tom Hulett* Case, *Shin-Etsu* Case and *Baosheng* Case — 150
        5.1.2.1 *Tom Hulett* Case — 150
        5.1.2.2 *Shin-Etsu* Case — 152
        5.1.2.3 *Baosheng* Case — 155
5.2 Protection of PRC's Judicial Sovereignty and Jurisdiction: Arbitral Tribunal Cannot Violate PRC Courts' Jurisdiction — 156
    5.2.1 *Hemofarm* Case: Arbitral Tribunal's Violation of PRC's Judicial Sovereignty and PRC Courts' Jurisdiction — 156
        5.2.1.1 Case Summary — 156
        5.2.1.2 Comment — 158
        5.2.1.3 Reviewing the SPC's Reply Letter — 164
    5.2.2 *Louis Dreyfus* Case: Arbitral Tribunal's Misconception of Whether There Exists Significant Gaps Between PRC Laws and Their Practical Application — 167
        5.2.2.1 Case Summary — 167
        5.2.2.2 Comment — 168
    5.2.3 *Guangxia Culture* Case: Arbitral Tribunal's Disapproval of PRC Administrative Decisions — 168
        5.2.3.1 Case Summary — 168
        5.2.3.2 Comment — 171
    5.2.4 Summary — 172
5.3 Protection of PRC's Judicial Sovereignty and Jurisdiction: In Cases Without Foreign Elements, Parties' Agreements on Foreign Arbitration Institution or Foreign Arbitral Seat Are Invalid — 174
    5.3.1 *Liupanshui* Case, *Chao Lai Xin Sheng* Case and *Leaf Confectionery* Case — 174
    5.3.2 Substantive Differences Between Domestic Arbitration and Foreign-Related Arbitration — 176
        5.3.2.1 Parties to Domestic Arbitration Cannot Submit Disputes to Foreign Arbitration Institutions — 176
        5.3.2.2 Parties to Domestic Arbitration Cannot Seat Their Arbitration Outside the Territory of Mainland China? — 177
        5.3.2.3 Only Parties to Foreign-Related Arbitration Can Stipulate Foreign Laws to Govern Their Arbitration Agreements — 178

	5.3.2.4	The Law Governing Substantive Matters in Domestic Arbitration is PRC Law	179
	5.3.2.5	Parties to Foreign-Related Arbitration Have More Freedom in Choice of Arbitrators	180
	5.3.2.6	The Grounds for Revocation and Non-enforcement Differ Between Domestic Arbitral Awards and Foreign-Related Arbitral Awards	181
	5.3.2.7	Reporting System is Applicable to Foreign-Related Arbitration	182
	5.3.2.8	Different Court Levels for Determining Applications for Preservation of Evidence and Property	183
5.4	Summary		185

CHAPTER 6
Conclusion   187

Bibliography   193

Table of Cases   209

Index   225

List of Abbreviations

AQSIQ	Administration of Quality Supervision Inspection and Quarantine
ARATS	Association for Relations Across the Taiwan Straits
BAC	Beijing Arbitration Commission
CCOIC	China Chamber of International Commerce
CIETAC	China International Economic and Trade Arbitration Commission
CMAC	China Maritime Association Commission
ECOSOC	United Nations Economic and Social Council
FOSFA	Federation of Oils, Seeds and Fats Associations
HKIAC	Hong Kong International Arbitration Centre
HKSAR	Hong Kong Special Administrative Region
ICAC	The International Commercial Arbitration Court at the Chamber of Commerce and Industry of the Russian Federation
ICC	International Chamber of Commerce
ILA	International Law Association
JCAA	Japan Commercial Arbitration Association
JVC	Joint Venture Contract
KCAB	Korean Commercial Arbitration Board
LCIA	London Court of International Arbitration
NPCSC	Standing Committee of National People's Congress of the PRC
OECD	Organisation for Economic Co-operation and Development
PRC	People's Republic of China
SAL	Sugar Association of London
SCC	The Arbitration Institute of the Stockholm Chamber of Commerce

List of Abbreviations

SEF	Straits Exchange Foundation
SIAC	Singapore International Arbitration Centre
SPC	Supreme People's Court of the People's Republic of China
UNCITRAL	United Nations Commission on International Trade Law
US	The United States
VAM	Valuation Adjustment Mechanism
VCLT	Vienna Convention on the Law of Treaties
VIE	Variable Interest Entity

Acknowledgements

This book is an English updated version of my doctoral dissertation (in Chinese) at the College of Law of National Taiwan University, which has won the Outstanding Doctoral Dissertation Award of College of Law of National Taiwan University in 2015.

My sincere appreciation to the Honorable Justice Chang-fa Lo, for guiding me to write the dissertation. Special thanks to the former Honorable Justice Tze-chien Wang, for his continuous encouraging words and inspiration since I was a freshman at National Taiwan University.

I would like to thank Winnie Jo-Mei Ma and I-Ching Tseng for their assistance in translating the dissertation. I would wish to thank Jing Bei for her research on English titles of the Chinese literature and company names of the parties in the cases heard by the Chinese courts and cited in the book. Thanks to Alison Shih-Yun Chang, who have helped to read chapters in draft and given useful feedback.

This book is delicated to my parents, Chu-Chih and Ying-Jer, for loving and supporting me all the time.

CHAPTER 1
Introduction

1.1 WHY RE-EXAMINING PUBLIC POLICY?

The Convention on the Recognition and Enforcement of Foreign Arbitral Awards[1] was made in New York on 10 June 1958 and is therefore commonly referred to as the 'New York Convention' or 'New York Convention of 1958'. Its principal aim is that foreign and non-domestic arbitral awards will not be discriminated against and it obliges Contracting States to ensure such awards are recognised and generally capable of enforcement in their jurisdiction in the same way as domestic awards.[2] Article V of the New York Convention stipulates the grounds for the competent authorities (usually the courts) in the relevant country to refuse the recognition and enforcement of arbitral awards on their own ex officio or upon the parties' application. One of which is Article V(2)(b) – an arbitral award's recognition and enforcement may be refused if '[t]he recognition or enforcement of the award would be contrary to the public policy of that country'. As 'public policy' is an uncertain legal concept, its interpretation and application in each jurisdiction have always been the scholars' focus of attention.

As early as in the 1820s, Justice Burrough in *Richardson v. Mellish* already vividly described the uncertain concept of public policy as follows:[3]

> '[Public policy is]' a very unruly horse, and when once you get astride it you never know where it will carry you. It may lead you from sound law. It is never argued at all, but when other points fail.

---

1. The full text of the New York Convention is available at UNCITRAL's website: http://www.uncitral.org/pdf/english/texts/arbitration/NY-conv/New-York-Convention-E.pdf (accessed 4 May 2017).
2. *See* http://www.uncitral.org/uncitral/en/uncitral_texts/arbitration/NYConvention.html (accessed 4 May 2017).
3. *Richardson v. Mellish*, All ER 258, 266 [1824-24].

1

The Swiss Federal Court in *Tensaccia S.P.A v. Freyssinet Terra Armata R.L.*[4] also began its discussion of public policy as specified in Article 190(2)(e) of the Swiss Private International Law (concerning the grounds for revoking arbitral awards) by stating: '[t]he fleeting character of public policy may be inherent to the concept, due to its excessive generality; the wide scope of the almost countless opinions proffered in this regard would tend to prove it. As a commentator pointed out, all attempts to answer the numerous recurring questions raised by the interpretation of this concept merely resulted in raising further thorny or polemical questions.'[5] Yet the Court proceeded to elaborate on the differences between substantive public policy and procedural public policy in considerable length, explaining the circumstances which would be classified as violations of substantive public policy and violations of procedural public policy respectively. Accordingly, despite the difficulty (and even inability) to define public policy with precision, it is nevertheless necessary to examine the meaning of public policy at a particular time, so that the courts can apply the law correctly when adjudicating specific cases.

Premised on respecting national sovereignty and enabling national courts to have ultimate control over the outcomes of arbitration, Article V(2)(b) of the New York Convention expressly stipulates that public policy is the public policy of the enforcement State ('the country where recognition and enforcement is sought'). An in-depth study of the applicability of Article V(2)(b) in the People's Republic of China (PRC) is particularly worthwhile due to the following reasons.

First, 'public policy' is not a legal term inherent in the PRC's 'civil' law framework.[6] The PRC legislators and courts only began to use the term 'public policy' as specified in Article V(2)(b) of the New York Convention after the PRC acceded to the New York Convention in 1987. 'Social and public interest' was the traditional PRC legal term. Some scholars believe that 'social and public interest as specified in the PRC legislations is essentially public policy',[7] although the majority of scholars regard 'social and public interest' as a potentially even more uncertain legal concept than

---

4. *Tensaccia S.P.A v. Freyssinet Terra Armata R.L.*, 4P.278/2005, 24 ASA Bull. 500 (2006).
5. Original in French and English translation by Charles Poncet: 'Le caractère insaisissable de l'ordre public est peut-être inhérent à cette notion même, étant donné sa trop grande généralité; le large éventail des avis presque innombrables émis au sujet de celle-ci tendrait à le prouver. Et comme le souligne un auteur, toutes les tentatives de réponses aux nombreuses questions récurrentes posées par l'interprétation de ladite notion n'ont fait que soulever d'autres questions épineuses, voire polémiques.'
   For the full French and English text of this case, *see* http://www.swissarbitrationdecisions.com/violation-of-public-policy-notion-of-public-policy-exclusion-of- (accessed 4 May 2017).
6. *See* Ch. 3 s. 3.1 for detailed discussions.
7. Yifei Lin, *Recognition and Enforcement of Foreign Arbitral Award: 20 Years' Judicial Practice in China*, 16(1) Journal of International Economic Law 49 (2009). According to another scholar: '[T]he grounds for refusing to enforce a foreign-related award are set out in Article 260 of the CPL [Code of Civil Procedure]. Although slightly different to the New York Convention Article V grounds, the essence is very similar.' *See* Andrew Jefferies, *Arbitration in the PRC: Enforcement Issues*, in *Arbitration in China: A Practical Guide* 295, 327 (Daniel R. Fung & Shengchang Wang eds, Sweet & Maxwell 2004).

'public policy'.⁸ This has raised substantial interest in the interpretation and application of 'social and public interest' in the PRC's judicial practice. How have the PRC courts interpreted and applied 'public policy' as specified in Article V(2)(b) of the New York Convention following the PRC's accession to the New York Convention? Are such interpretation and application converging with international consensus, or are they specially flavoured with 'Chinese characteristics'? Have the interpretation and application of 'public policy' in the context of Article V(2)(b) of the New York Convention been influenced by the PRC's traditional concept of 'social and public interest'?

Second, public policy basically concerns the basic moral convictions and policies of a particular place and varies with each nation.⁹ Matters that are regarded as pertaining to public policy in one nation may not be so regarded in another nation with different economic, political, religious or social backgrounds.¹⁰ And even within the same nation or society, the meaning of public policy may change over time as that society's values and standards change and develop over time; so does the society's public policy, which derives from that society. As for arbitration, national public policy may change in accordance with the development of national politics and legal system, the degree of participation in the international economy, and policies for encouraging foreign investments, etc. Similarly, because of international developments over time, such as the New York Convention's coming into force, the extent of other states' growing acceptance and recognition of arbitration, the growing infrastructure and legal security of international arbitration which has made it more difficult for states to adopt or keep a negative approach to arbitration if they desire to participate in international trade and investment to the benefit of their own countries.¹¹ Over the past twenty years, the PRC experienced substantial social and economic changes, causing corresponding changes in the entire society's values and systems while driving the evolution and development of law, all of which make the PRC a very suitable object for studying and examining how the concept of 'public policy' changes with social, economic, cultural and other changes. As a long-time observer of the PRC's legal development, the author has detected the evolution of the PRC's legal system over time. At legislative levels, there is a growing focus among the PRC legislators on establishing legal norms and systems which converge with those at the international level; at all levels of judicial practice, there is also a growing focus on improving the quality of judicial decision-making. This period of time coincidentally and substantially overlaps with the period after the PRC's accession to the New York Convention in 1987. Thus it is worth examining whether the meanings of 'the basic principles of national law and social and public interest' in the PRC's legal tradition have changed in correspondence with

---

8. Nigel Blackberry et al., *Redfern and Hunter on International Arbitration* 660 (5th ed., Oxford University Press 2009).
9. Albert Jan van den Berg, *The New York Arbitration Convention of 1958 – Towards a Uniform Judicial Interpretation* 376 (Kluwer Law International 1981).
10. Karl-Heinz Böckstiegel, *Public Policy and Arbitrability*, in *Comparative Arbitration Practice and Public Policy in Arbitration* 177, 179 (Pieter Sanders ed., Kluwer Law International 1987).
11. Karl-Heinz Böckstiegel, *Public Policy as a Limit to Arbitration and its Enforcement*, 2(1) Dispute Resolution International (IBA Journal of Dispute resolution, Special Issue 2008, The New York Convention – 50 Years) 123, 125 (2008).

changes in time and social circumstances, as well as examining whether the PRC courts' application and interpretation of the New York Convention in the past twenty years have also changed in correspondence with social and economic changes. Is the concept of 'public policy' becoming more predictable in the PRC's judicial practice? If so, how and why? Is further improvement possible?

Third, when comparing civil litigation in the PRC courts with arbitration outside the PRC's territory (including institutional arbitration and ad hoc arbitration outside the PRC),[12] most foreign parties (including those from Taiwan, Hong Kong and Macau) trust the latter more. The 'Cross-Strait Bilateral Investment Protection and Promotion Agreement' signed between Straits Exchange Foundation (SEF) and Association for Relations Across the Taiwan Straits (ARATS) on 9 August 2012 specifically stipulates the mechanisms for resolving commercial disputes between investors across the Taiwan Straits (with Article 14 being the main provision). This shows the degree of importance attached to using arbitration to resolve commercial disputes between cross-strait private parties. Such regulation of commercial disputes resolution between private parties is extremely rare, because investment protection agreements in general regulate issues between nations and between investors and host nations, but not commercial disputes between private parties. The smooth enforcement of arbitral awards is one of the major concerns for the parties to arbitration. The most uncertain grounds for the PRC courts to refuse recognition ('Cheng-Ren' (承認)) and enforcement of foreign arbitral awards or to refuse recognition ('Ren-ke '(認可)) and enforcement of awards made in Taiwan, Hong Kong or Macau are 'public policy' and 'social and public interest', depending on the specific circumstances of each case. A deeper understanding of both concepts' predictability in the PRC legal system is therefore beneficial and necessary.

1.2 OBJECTIVES

Beginning with the theories and judicial practices concerning 'public policy' in Article V(2)(b) of the New York Convention, this book attempts to illustrate the features and meanings of public policy in accordance with the commonly and internationally accepted views, together with recent and noteworthy theoretical developments of international arbitration law, specifically the concept of 'transnational public policy (also called 'truly international public policy' or 'really international public policy'[13]). Its respective discussions on the features and meanings of different concepts such as 'domestic public policy', 'international public policy' and 'transnational public policy',

---

12. 'Ad hoc arbitration' means arbitration which is neither managed nor supervised by any arbitration institution: *see* Gary B. Born, *International Arbitration: Law and Practice* 28 (Kluwer Law International 2012).
13. For the meaning of 'transnational public policy, 'truly international public policy' or 'really international public policy', *see* Ch. 2 s. 2.5. *See also* W. Michael Reisman, *Law, International Public Policy (So-called) and Arbitral Choice in International Commercial Arbitration*, in *International Arbitration 2006: Back to Basics?* 849–856 (Albert Jan van den Berg ed., Kluwer Law International 2007); Catherine Kessedjian, *Transnational Public Policy*, in *International Arbitration 2006: Back to Basics?* 857–870 (Albert Jan van den Berg ed., Kluwer Law International 2007); Michael Pryles, *Reflections on Transnational Public Policy*, 24(1) Journal of International Arbitration 1–7 (2007).

etc., illustrate in-depth understanding of 'public policy' in the context of Article V(2)(b) of the New York Convention, before summarising the core consensus and majority views of this uncertain legal concept. This book then explains the PRC's relevant legal systems while examining and analysing the relevant PRC cases in depth. Its comparison and contrast clarify the similarities and differences between the PRC's judicial practice and the international consensus. Its examination of 'public policy' in Article V(2)(b) of the New York Convention within the development of the PRC's judicial practice together with its observation of judicial interpretation and application in specific cases attempts to depict relatively clearer contours.

1.3 SCOPE

The term 'public policy' may appear in different contexts; its meaning and weighting may also differ in these different contexts. This book centres around the PRC's interpretation and application of 'public policy' in Article V(2)(b) of the New York Convention. Accordingly, all references to 'public policy' mean public policy in the context of Article V(2)(b) of the New York Convention unless otherwise specified. In addition, although the issue of 'arbitrability' is often related to public policy, it is nevertheless an independent issue separately provided for in Article V(2)(a) of the New York Convention, and is therefore outside the scope of this book whose core discussions are about public policy in Article V(2)(b) of the New York Convention.

On the one hand, this book explores the majority views on the international level about 'public policy' in Article V(2)(b) of the New York Convention from a comparative law perspective, before examining the PRC courts' interpretation and application of 'public policy' in Article V(2)(b) of the New York Convention to clarify the similarities and differences between the international approach and the PRC approach, as well as to illustrate the predictability of public policy in the PRC's legal system. On the other hand, this book's analysis of PRC cases also considers and compares whether and how the PRC's traditional concept of 'social and public interest' has influenced the PRC courts' interpretation and application of 'public policy' in Article V(2)(b) of the New York Convention, thereby tracking the dynamic development of 'public policy' in the PRC's legal system and demonstrating how this concept has progressed in the PRC's legal system from being highly uncertain to becoming predictable to a certain degree. In this regard, the PRC's legal system categorises four types of cases, i.e., concerning 'the validity of foreign-related arbitration agreements', 'non-enforcement of foreign arbitral awards', 'revocation of foreign-related arbitration awards' and 'recognition and enforcement of foreign arbitral awards' as pertaining to the same 'group', which is subject to 'centralised jurisdiction', 'Reporting System' and other regulations. Additionally, the Fourth Civil Tribunal of the Supreme People's Court of the People's Republic of China (SPC) adjudicates all of these cases as part of the SPC's internal allocation of function. Examining the PRC courts' views on 'public policy' and 'social and public interest' in cases concerning 'the validity of foreign-related arbitration agreements', 'non-enforcement of foreign arbitral awards' and 'revocation of foreign-related arbitration awards' should therefore assist with understanding the PRC court's interpretation and application of 'public policy' in cases concerning 'the recognition and enforcement of foreign arbitral awards'. Accordingly these types of cases are also within the scope of this book.

1.4 METHODOLOGY AND LIMITATIONS

1.4.1 Methodology

As the author is a legal researcher, this book is in principle based on legal analysis, meaning that it conducts analysis and interpretation in basic legal context while observing the circumstances of their application in specific cases. Yet it must be acknowledged that law is essentially the superstructure of social life, which must respond to actual economic and social conditions. Confining the thinking to the ivory tower of legal reasoning without considering economic, social and many other factors would substantially limit the contributions to society by this book's research and conclusions. This especially applies to 'public policy', the topic of this book. As the meaning of public policy in various nations may differ, matters which are characterised as pertaining to public policy in one nation may not be so characterised in other nations with different economic, political, religious, social or other circumstances.[14] Thus, this book must, within possible range, also consider the economic and social factors which may be involved. Its methodology, while using legal thinking and reasoning as the core, also takes such economic and social factors into consideration.

In view of internationally renowned scholar, Albert Jan van den Berg's clear statement that 'what constitutes a violation of public policy is largely a question of fact and is to be decided on an ad hoc basis',[15] Professor Exiang Wan (Deputy President of the SPC in 2009) also stated during an international academic symposium on the New York Convention's fiftieth anniversary commemoration and judicial challenges:[16] 'Observing the international application of the principle of public policy and then characterising and concretising such principle through individual judicial practices is the judicial trend. In practice the PRC courts are also confirming the potential scope of application of "social and public interest" through adjudicating concrete cases.' As such, scholars studying the implications of public policy not only research the potential doctrinal and theoretical interpretations and implications, but should also investigate related cases to concretely delimit the meaning and applicability of 'public policy' in specific jurisdictions through the judicial views expressed in those cases. In spite of the PRC's incomplete publication of court judgments, the author has endeavoured to collect the available court judgments to ensure that the presentation and analysis of PRC-related circumstances are as complete as possible.

---

14. Karl-Heinz Böckstiegel, *Public Policy and Arbitrability*, in *Comparative Arbitration Practice and Public Policy in Arbitration* 177, 179 (Pieter Sanders ed., Kluwer Law International 1987).
15. Albert Jan van den Berg, *The New York Arbitration Convention of 1958 – Towards a Uniform Judicial Interpretation* 376 (Kluwer Law International 1981).
16. Exiang Wan, *Judicial Practice with Regards to the New York Convention in China*, 276 Journal of Law Application 4, 6 (2009).

Chapter 1: Introduction

Moreover, theoretical exploration must integrate with empirical analysis, as theories detached from practical experiences may be illusory and unrealistic. Thus, this book also examines non-PRC courts' related practice from the perspective of comparative law in addition to exploring academic discussions.

1.4.2 Limitations

As stated above, one of this book's research methods is to examine the PRC's court cases. Owing to the selective disclosure of PRC's court judgments, the proportion of published cases is extremely small in contrast with the enormous caseload of the PRC courts. According to the statistics published on the SPC's website, in 2014 only there were already 142,464 arbitration-related enforcement cases, and 50,513 cases concerning judicial assistance and other enforcement.[17] Although most of the arbitration-related enforcement cases concerned labour arbitration and included some arbitration of contractual and management disputes over rural land, the proportion of published cases is still very small in any event. Consequently, any glimpse of the PRC court cases is inevitably incomplete despite the author's endeavour to exhaustively ascertain the PRC's court judgments.

Fortunately, according to the statistics of Justice Honglei Yang from the SPC's Fourth Civil Tribunal, 610 was the total number of cases heard by seventeen higher people's courts (including Beijing, Shanghai, Jiangsu, Guangdong, Tianjin, etc.) between 2002 and 2006, comprising four types of cases: judicial review of foreign-related arbitration (i.e., recognition and enforcement of arbitration agreements), revocation of foreign-related arbitral awards, non-enforcement of foreign-related arbitral awards and recognition and enforcement of foreign arbitral awards, etc.[18] This figure is significantly less than the above-mentioned numbers of arbitration-related enforcement cases and of judicial assistance and other enforcement cases. It can thus be seen that the above-mentioned approximation of more than 140,000 arbitration-related cases per year were mostly domestic arbitration cases. Furthermore, according to the statistics of the former President Guixiang Liu and Justice Hongyu Shen from the SPC's Fourth Civil Tribunal, fifty-six was the total number of cases reported by the lower courts to the SPC from 2000 until September 2011 concerning the application of the New York Convention to non-recognition and non-enforcement of foreign arbitral awards.[19] Justice Hongyu Shen calculated that thirty-four cases concerning the recognition and enforcement of foreign arbitral awards were concluded and published on the

---

17. Cited from 'Resolving Difficulties in Enforcement and Enhancing Public Faith in Enforcement – 2014 Analysis of Judicial Enforcement Cases', People's Daily (5th ed., 28 May 2015), http://rmfyb.chinacourt.org/paper/images/2015-05/28/05/2015052805_pdf.pdf or http://www.chinacourt.org/article/detail/2015/05/id/1637270.shtml (accessed 4 May 2017).
18. Honglei Yang, *Report on the Judicial Review of International Arbitration in Chinese Courts*, 9(1) International Law Review of Wuhan University 304, 306 (2009).
19. Guixiang Liu & Hongyu Shen, *Recognition and Enforcement of Foreign Arbitral Awards in China: A Look Back on a Decade of Court Practices*, 79 Beijing Arbitration 1, 4 (2012).

Internet in 2014.[20] Most of these cases have been published in the 'Supreme People's Court Gazette',[21] 'Guide on Foreign-Related Commercial and Maritime Trial'[22] and other periodicals. The 'Guide on Foreign-Related Commercial and Maritime Trial' specifically publishes the full text of the lower courts' reporting documents and the SPC's reply letters regarding non-recognition and non-enforcement of foreign arbitral awards, thereby effectively enhancing transparency in this area.[23] Although these published cases are the SPC's specific replies to specific cases, the recorded opinions and reasons 'have representative significance' and 'provide certain guidance'.[24] Consequently, although it is impossible to ascertain all relevant PRC cases and the scale of the research is limited by objective conditions, examining the cases actually found and collected can still enable considerable grasp of the PRC's judicial practice.

1.5 TERMINOLOGY AND SYSTEM

Each of Mainland China, Hong Kong, Macau and Taiwan has its own distinctive laws, regulations and court systems. The public policy in each of the above four legal jurisdictions might be different. Laws in Mainland China are generally titled as the 'laws of the PRC', for example, the Arbitration Law of the PRC. The complete official name of the Supreme People's Court in Mainland China is 'the Supreme People's Court of the People's Republic of China.' The terms 'public policy of this country' or 'public policy of the People's Republic of China' are commonly used in the court judgments or rulings of the people's courts in Mainland China to refer to public policy of Mainland China. Likewise, the Chinese literature generally refers to laws, regulations or courts of Mainland China as the PRC or Chinese laws, regulations or courts.

This book refers to laws and regulations respectively promulgated by the authorities in Mainland China, Hong Kong, Macau and Taiwan as well as jurisprudence of the courts in Mainland China, Hong Kong, Macau and Taiwan. In order to be consistent with the titles of laws promulgated by the authorities in Mainland China and the terms generally used in judgments and rulings of people's courts in Mainland China, laws or regulations promulgated by the authorities in Mainland China are referred to in this book as 'the laws or regulations of the People's Republic of China',

---

20. Study Group of the Annual Report on International Commercial Arbitration in China (2014), *Annual Report on International Commercial Arbitration in China (2014)* 65 (China Academy of Arbitration Law 2015).
21. The Supreme People's Court Gazette is the SPC's official bulletin which publishes important laws, judicial interpretations and cases, etc. (edited by the General Office of the Supreme People's Court and published by People's Court Press).
22. Edited by the Fourth Civil Tribunal of the People's Supreme Court and published by People's Court Press. The first issue was published in October 2001 and named 'Guide and Research on China Foreign-Related Commercial and Maritime Trial'. It was renamed to 'Guide on Foreign-Related Commercial and Maritime Trial' since its seventh issue in 2004.
23. Guixiang Liu & Hongyu Shen, *Recognition and Enforcement of Foreign Arbitral Awards in China: A Look Back on a Decade of Court Practices*, 79 Beijing Arbitration 1, 4 (2012).
24. According to Art. 2 para. 2 of the Administrative Measures for the Proclamation of Document of Judgment by the Supreme People's Court, 'court documents with representative significance and provide certain guidance are published in the People's Court Daily or Gazette from time to time': *see* Fa-Ban-Fa (2000) No. 4, promulgated and implemented on 15 June 2000.

'the Chinese laws or regulations' or 'the PRC's laws or regulations'. The people's courts in Mainland China are referred to in this book as the Chinese courts, PRC's courts, the courts of the PRC or the courts of the People's Republic of China. The 'public policy of Mainland China' is referred to in this book as 'public policy of this country' or 'public policy of the People's Republic of China', as how it is generally referred to in the judgments or rulings of the people's courts in Mainland China. Likewise, the 'judicial practice in Mainland China' is referred to in this book as the 'Chinese judicial practice' or 'PRC's judicial practice'. All such references are for the purpose of keeping the original wording used in laws, regulations, jurisprudence and Chinese literature when translating those from Mandarin Chinese to English and do not carry any political implication.

Bilingual (English-Chinese) citations of the titles of the main PRC cases and Chinese literature referred in this book are appended to this book for readers' ease of reference. This book adopts the English translation provided by the original authors of the Chinese literature. The Chinese literature without such original English translation has been translated by the author of this book. Similarly, the content of all the PRC legislative and judicial documents and Chinese literature has been translated by the author of this book unless otherwise specified.

Furthermore, the italicised words are emphasis added by the author of this book unless otherwise specified (e.g., 'emphasis original').

CHAPTER 2
The Meaning of Public Policy

According to Article V(2)(b) of the New York Convention, one of the grounds for a country to refuse recognition or enforcement of a foreign arbitral award is if the 'recognition or enforcement of the award would be contrary to the public policy of that country'. 'Public policy' serves as a 'safety valve' as it is an uncertain legal concept (*see* section 2.4 of this chapter). However, there is a broadly accepted international consensus on this concept's core meaning. In order to facilitate international enforcement of arbitral awards, internationally renowned scholars have repeatedly explained the meaning of 'public policy' as specified in Article V(2)(b) of the New York Convention, while the International Law Association (ILA) have also presented the initial research in the report of Rapporteur Sheppard at the Taiwan Conference in 1998 and published its 'Interim Report on Public Policy as a Bar to Enforcement of International Arbitral Awards' and 'Final Report on Public Policy as a Bar to Enforcement of International Arbitral Awards' in 2000 and 2002 respectively (*see* section 2.5 of this chapter). Prior to examining the PRC's interpretation and application of 'public policy' in Article V(2)(b) of the New York Convention, it is therefore necessary to explore the international consensus or majority views on this concept in order to establish a benchmark for comparative reference.

Despite the difficulty of defining 'public policy' with precision, this chapter endeavours to present a complete illustration of the core concept of 'public policy' through various perspectives such as etymology, the history of relevant provisions in international conventions (especially the New York Convention), academic interpretations of Article V(2)(b) of the New York Convention, ILA's Interim Report and Final Report on public policy, examples of national legislation.

Some commentators use Articles 31–33 (on Interpretation of Treaties) of the Vienna Convention on the Law of Treaties (VCLT)[1] to interpret 'public policy' in Article

---

1. Vienna Convention on the Law of Treaties, *see* the United Nations' website, http://legal.un.org/avl/ha/vclt/vclt.html (accessed 4 May 2017). The PRC government deposited the instrument of accession on 3 September 1997, effective from 27 January 1980.

V(2)(b) of the New York Convention. Indeed, the issue of treaty interpretation is not merely encountered by the ILA, but also increasingly encountered by national courts.[2] For instance, national courts may need to address the issue of interpreting 'public policy' as specified in Article V(2)(b) of the New York Convention in cases concerning the recognition and enforcement of foreign arbitral awards. Nevertheless, it is generally considered that Articles 31-33 of the VCLT reflect 'universal custom' and are 'universally binding as customary international law'.[3] Consequently, some scholars directly use the principles of customary international law[4] (namely the rules laid down in customary international law that are identical to the contents of Articles 31-33) instead of the text of Articles 31-33 'to determine the meaning of an interpreted treaty provision'.[5] This book also adopts the same approach.

2.1 ETYMOLOGY

Black's Law Dictionary defines 'public policy' as '1. Broadly, principles and standards regarded by the legislature or by the courts as being of fundamental concern to the state and the whole of society. Courts sometimes use the term to justify their decisions, as when declaring a contract void because it is "contrary to public policy". – Also terms policy of the law... 2. More narrowly, the principle that a person should not be allowed to do anything that would tend to injure the public at large.'[6] It cites page 286 of 'Principles of the Law of Contract' (edited by Arthur L. Corbin):

> The policy of the law, or public policy, is a phrase of common use in estimating the validity of contracts. Its history is obscure; it is most likely that agreements which tended to restrain trade or to promote litigation were the first to elicit the principle that courts would look to the interests of the public in giving efficacy to contracts.[7]

However, this book's concern and research topic are not public policy as considered by the courts when determining validity of contracts, but public policy as considered by the courts when deciding whether or not to recognise and enforce foreign arbitral awards. In general, public policy is traditionally a criterion for determining the recognisability and enforceability of foreign arbitral awards, the

---

2. Anthony Aust, *Modern Treaty Law and Practice* 230 (2nd ed., Cambridge University Press 2007).
3. Oliver Dörr & Kirsten Schmalenbach eds, *Vienna Convention on the Law of Treaties* 524-525 (Springer 2007).
4. The so-called customary international law is a pattern of behaviours established by long-term interaction between members of the international community, with some degree of binding force established through continuous emulation and compliance by many countries. Accordingly, the formation of customary international law needs to satisfy the two pre-conditions of temporal continuity and spatial universality. It requires the international community's acceptance and recognition that it is legally binding in order to become '*opinio juris*'. Please *see* Chu-Cheng Huang, *Right of Passage over Indian Territory, Merits, Judgment of 12 April, 1960, ICJ Reports 1960* p. 6, 169 Taiwan Law Journal 93, 95-96 (2011).
5. Ulf Linderfalk, *On the Interpretation of the Law of Treaties. The Modern International Law as Expressed in the 1969 Vienna Convention on the Law of Treaties* 11 (Springer 2007).
6. Quoted cited from Black's Law Dictionary (9th ed., 209).
7. *Ibid.*

recognisability and enforceability of foreign court judgments, as well as the applicability of foreign laws. Almost all international treaties and agreements have provisions relating to public policy.[8]

2.2 PUBLIC POLICY AND PUBLIC ORDER (OR *ORDRE PUBLIC*)

'Public policy' is the common law terminology whereas the civil law terminology is 'public order' or '*ordre public*'. The New York Convention has five equally authentic official language versions: the English version uses 'public policy' while the French version uses '*ordre public*' for Article V(2)(b) respectively. Here it can be presumed that the drafters of the New York Convention considered that public policy in the English version and *ordre public* in the French version as having equivalent meaning. Internationally renowned arbitration scholar Albert Jan van den Berg also expressed the same view in his important book *The New York Arbitration Convention of 1958 – Towards a Uniform Judicial Interpretation*. In particular, he stated that among the three preliminary explanations for interpreting Article V of the New York Convention, the first one is the common understanding that '*ordre public*' in civil law has a wider scope of application than that of 'public policy' in common law; yet these two terms are often used interchangeably and should therefore be understood as having identical meaning in the context of Article V.[9] The ILA also adopted the same view in its Interim Report and Final Report (*see* section 2.5 of this chapter).[10]

Similarly, some PRC scholars also believe that 'these two terms are interchangeable in today's practice' even though the civil law term of '*ordre public*' was broader in its meaning than the common law term of 'public policy' in the past.[11] Yet it should be noted that the Chinese version of the New York Convention as published on United Nations Commission on International Trade Law's (UNCITRAL's) website uses the term 'public policy'[12] in Article V(2)(b) of the New York Convention, which contrasts with the term '*ordre public* (public order)'[13] used by the Standing Committee of National People's Congress of the PRC (NPCSC) in the Chinese translation of the New

---

8. Albert Jan van den Berg, *The New York Arbitration Convention of 1958 – Towards a Uniform Judicial Interpretation* 360 (Kluwer Law International 1981).
9. *Ibid.* at 359.
10. ILA's *Interim Report on Public Policy as a Bar to Enforcement of International Arbitration Awards*, n. 35 provides: 'We consider that the two terms are now synonymous', 19 Arbitration International 217 (2003) (ILA's Interim Report); ILA's *Final Report on Public Policy as a Bar to Enforcement of International Arbitration Awards*, n. 7 provides that 'Public policy' and 'ordre public' are now 'considered to be synonymous'.19 Arbitration International 249 (2003) (ILA's Final Report).
11. Hang Song, *Recognition and Enforcement of International Commercial Arbitral Awards* 170 (Law Press 2000). Guanghui Li and Han Wang also stated in similar terms: 'In current practice the differences between the two are gradually narrowing, and in today's common practice these two terms are interchangeable.' Please *see* Guanghui Li & Han Wang, *Arbitration Law* 340 (University of International Business and Economics Press 2011).
12. UNCITRAL's website, http://www.uncitral.org/pdf/chinese/texts/arbitration/NY-conv/1958_NYC_CTC-c.pdf (accessed 4 May 2017).
13. Decision of the Standing Committee of National People's Congress on Accession to the 'Convention on the Recognition and Enforcement of Foreign Arbitral Awards', promulgated and implemented on 2 December 1986.

York Convention annexed to the PRC's decision on accession to the New York Convention. Yet the SPC has subsequently and consistently used the term 'public policy' in its reply letters to specific cases. Accordingly the author believes that use of *'ordre public* (public order)' in 1986 by the PRC's Standing Committee of National People's Congress ('NPCSC') was merely a separate and an one-off translation term: the use of 'public *order*' (instead of 'public *policy*') should not have special effect on the PRC courts' interpretation and application of Article V(2)(b) of the New York Convention in the future. At the same time, this indicates that the PRC's NPCSC, at least in 1986, did not consider to think that there was any difference between 'public order' and 'public policy'.

The Taiwan Arbitration Law also uses the term 'public order': Article 49 paragraph 1 stipulates that the court 'shall issue a dismissal with respect to an application submitted by a party for recognition of a foreign arbitral award' where 'the recognition or enforcement of the arbitral award is contrary to the public order or good morals' of Taiwan.[14] However, since this book discusses Article V(2)(b) of the New York Convention through the prism of the PRC's judicial practice, it adopts, in principle, the term 'public policy' used in the Chinese version of the New York Convention as published on UNCITRAL's website.

2.3 HISTORICAL DEVELOPMENT OF PUBLIC POLICY PROVISIONS IN INTERNATIONAL CONVENTIONS

As early as in 1927, the Geneva Convention (Convention on the Execution of Foreign Arbitral Awards)[15] already contained provisions regarding public policy. According to its Article 1(2), '[t]o obtain such recognition or enforcement, it shall, further, be necessary:… (e) That the recognition or enforcement of the award is not contrary to the public policy or to the principles of the law of the country in which it is sought to be relied upon'.

Subsequently the International Chamber of Commerce (ICC) in 1953 deleted the reference to 'principles of the law' so that the draft Article IV(1)(a) merely referred to 'public policy'.[16]

---

14. Additionally, Taiwan's Code of Civil Procedure Art. 402 provides: 'A final and binding judgment rendered by a foreign court shall be recognized, except in case of any of the following circumstances… 3. Where the performance ordered by such judgment of its litigation procedure is contrary to R.O.C. public policy or moral.' English translation from the Taiwan Laws & Regulations Database, http://law.moj.gov.tw/Eng/LawClass/LawAll.aspx?PCode = B0010001 (accessed 4 May 2017). Similarly, Art. 8 of Taiwan's Act Governing the Choice of Law in Civil Matters Involving Foreign Elements provides: 'Where this Act provides that the law of a foreign State is applicable, if the result of such application leads to a violation of the public order of boni mores' of Taiwan, that law of the foreign State is not applied. English translation from the Taiwan Laws & Regulations Database of, http://law.moj.gov.tw/Eng/LawClass/LawAll.aspx?PCode = B0000007 (accessed 4 May 2017). Thus it can be seen that Taiwan uses the term 'public order' for the purposes of determining the recognisability and enforceability of foreign judgments as well as the applicability of foreign laws.
15. Convention on the Execution of Foreign Arbitral Awards (26 September 1927).
16. Reprinted in 9(1) ICC Bull. 32, 35 (1998).

Chapter 2: The Meaning of Public Policy

Article IV(h) of the Draft Convention on the Recognition and Enforcement of Foreign Arbitral Awards proposed by the United Nations Economic and Social Council (ECOSOC) used the wording 'the recognition of the award, or the subject matter thereof, would be clearly incompatible with public policy or with fundamental principles of the law ("ordre public") of the country in which the award is sought to be relied upon'.[17] The ECOSOC intended to use terms such as 'clearly', 'fundamental', etc. to restrict this ground, so that such ground only applied to cases in which the recognition or enforcement of foreign arbitral awards 'would be distinctly contrary to the basic principles of the legal system of the country where the award is invoked'.[18]

Some countries requested the deletion (or at least clarification) of the phrase 'incompatible with fundamental principles of law', as such phrase in addition to public policy was unnecessary and may cause perplexity. Other countries proposed revisions during the first week of the conference, such as the draft versions proposed by the Netherlands ('if the award would have the effect of compelling the parties to act in a manner contrary to the public policy in the country of enforcement'[19]), Germany,[20] as well as the joint draft by France, Federal Republic of Germany and Netherlands which narrowed the wording to 'incompatibility with the public policy of the State in which the award is sought to be relied upon'.[21] The versions proposed by other countries were similar to those of UNCITRAL.

During the discussions on the various draft proposals in the fourteenth meeting on 29 May 1958, the majority of the representatives suggested keeping the wording used in the Geneva Convention and UNCITRAL's draft,[22] while some representatives endorsed Germany's proposal and the joint proposal by France, Federal Republic of Germany and Netherlands.[23] Japan's representative cautioned that an excessively wide interpretation of public policy would 'defeat the purpose' of the New York Convention.[24]

The summary record of the seventeenth UNCITRAL meeting on 3 June 1958 records that 'the Working Party felt that the provisions allowing refusal of enforcement on grounds of public policy should not be given a broad scope of application'.[25] Accordingly, the Working Party recommended the deletion of references to 'the subject matter of the award and to fundamental principles of the law'.[26] Representatives from Peru and Iran commented that the mere reference to 'public policy' was inadequate

---

17. For the full text of ECOSOC's 1955 draft New York Convention, see UN Doc. E/2704 and E/AC.42/4Rev.1, *Report of the Committee on the Enforcement of International Arbitral Awards*, p. 2 (28 March 1955).
18. *Report of the Committee on the Enforcement of International Arbitral Awards*, E/AC.42/4Rev.1, p. 13, para. 49.
19. UN Doc. E/CONF.26/L.17, p. 2.
20. UN Doc. E/CONF.26/L.34, p. 1, Art. IV(c).
21. UN Doc. E/CONF.26/L.40, p. 2, Art. IV(e).
22. Examples include Iran (UN Doc. E/CONF.26/SR.14, p. 3), Israel (UN Doc. E/CONF.26/SR.14, p. 5), and Peru (with suggested deletion of the word 'clearly': UN Doc. E/CONF.26/SR.14, p. 9).
23. For example, Bulgaria (UN Doc. E/CONF.26/SR.14, p. 10).
24. *Ibid.* at 7.
25. Cited from the speech of the Chairperson of the Working Group, Mr de Sydow, UN Doc. E/CONF.26/SR. 17, p. 3 (12 September 1958).
26. *Ibid.*

and suggested adding the phrase 'or with the fundamental principles of the law';[27] Brazil's representative also proposed adding 'or with the fundamental principles of the law' after 'public policy' – yet these were rejected.[28] Moreover, Italy's representative stated that contravention of the res judicata principle would contravene public policy, specifically if the arbitral award 'was incompatible with a judgment applying to the same parties and the same subject matter'.[29] Israel's representative proposed that the words 'illegal or' should be inserted before 'incompatible', explaining that such amendment 'did not purport to prevent recognition or enforcement of an award because it was not in accordance with the civil law of the country in which the award was sought to be relied upon but only when it involved violation of the criminal law'.[30] Nonetheless, Israel's proposal was also rejected.[31]

Ultimately the Drafting Committee adopted the following text on 6 June 1958 (which is the current text of Article V(2)(b) of the New York Convention),[32] 'Recognition and enforcement of an arbitral award may also be refused if the competent authority in the country where recognition and enforcement is sought finds that:... (b) the recognition or enforcement of the award would be contrary to the public policy of that country.'

2.4 MEANING OF 'PUBLIC POLICY' IN ARTICLE V(2)(B) OF THE NEW YORK CONVENTION

2.4.1 Objectives and Functions of New York Convention's Article V(2)(b)

Understanding the objectives and functions of 'public policy' in the New York Convention is necessary for proper understanding of the meaning of 'public policy' in Article V(2)(b) of the New York Convention. On the one hand, 'public policy' in this Article serves as a safety-valve mechanism in the New York Convention through which the Contracting States may avoid intrusion by arbitral awards that are incompatible with their legal systems. Article V(2) stipulates that, apart from 'non-arbitrability', 'public policy' is the only ground for non-recognition and non-enforcement of foreign arbitral awards that the courts can consider ex officio, thereby reflecting the importance of 'public policy' in this provision to the Contracting States. In the absence of such public policy ground for non-recognition and non-enforcement of foreign arbitral awards, it may not be possible for the New York Convention to achieve its current success through the participation and accession by the vast majority of nations. Pursuant to this understanding, the ambiguity and uncertainty of the term 'public policy' happen to be in line with its function as a safety-valve mechanism.[33]

---

27. *Ibid.* at 15.
28. *Ibid.* at 16–17: twenty-one votes against twelve votes and four abstentions.
29. *Ibid.* at 15.
30. *Ibid.* at 16.
31. *Ibid.* at 16–17: twenty-seven votes against eight votes and four abstentions.
32. UN Doc. E/CONF.26/L.61, p. 3.
33. Reinmar Wolff ed., *The New York Convention: Convention on the Recognition and Enforcement of Foreign Arbitral Awards of 10 June 1958 – Commentary* 406 (Hart Publishing 2012).

On the other hand, 'public policy' in Article V(2)(b) may also become a 'gateway for undesirable obstructions', meaning that, through a broad definition (which may possibly be even wider than the scope of ambiguity and uncertainty inherent in the term 'public policy'), Contracting States may effectively refuse recognition and enforcement of any undesirable foreign arbitral awards, thereby impeding the pro-enforcement policy of the New York Convention through the 'back door' of public policy.[34] As stated in the ILA's Final Report, although Article V(2)(b) of the New York Convention 'has not given rise to any serious mischief and attempts to resist enforcement on grounds of public policy have rarely been successful', uncertainty and inconsistency in the interpretation and application of public policy have 'encouraged losing parties to rely on public policy to resist, or at least delay, enforcement'.[35] To avoid or reduce such risks, many scholars and experts attempt to interpret the concept of public policy narrowly so as to increase its predictability. The tension between the appropriate use of public policy in Article V(2)(b) of the New York Convention as a safety valve and avoidance of its abuse as an obstruction to the New York Convention's pro-enforcement policy seems 'unlikely to be ever fully resolved'.[36]

2.4.2 'Public Policy of That Country'

Viewing public policy in Article V(2)(b) of the New York Convention from its function as a safety valve entails respecting the public policy recognised by every Contracting State and allowing Contracting States to interpret the meaning of such public policy themselves. The text of Article V(2)(b) expressly requires determination according to the public policy of 'that country' (namely, the enforcement State where recognition and enforcement is sought).

2.4.3 International Standard for Public Policy

Nonetheless, in order to prevent 'public policy' in Article V(2)(b) from hampering the New York Convention's pro-enforcement policy, it is commonly recognised that every Contracting State should interpret and understand 'public policy' in the context of Article V(2)(b) as 'international public policy'. From a purely literal viewpoint, there are three different approaches for understanding the meaning of the term 'international public policy'.[37]

The first approach is to understand the meaning of international public policy by directly viewing from the word 'international' through the sources of international law rather than a particular nation's sources of law. Here the meaning of 'international public policy' is equivalent to that of the so-called transnational public policy or truly international public policy. Professor Pierre Lalive has already discussed the existence

---

34. Ibid.
35. ILA's Final Report, *supra* n. 10, at para. 23, Recommendation 1(c).
36. Wolff, *supra* n. 33, at 406.
37. Gary B. Born, *International Commercial Arbitration* 3657 (2nd ed., Kluwer Law International 2014).

and implications of 'transnational public policy' or 'truly international public policy' in considerable detail.[38] However, if 'public policy' in Article V(2)(b) of the New York Convention is understood as transnational public policy, then Article V(2)(b) may no longer function as an escape mechanism and may become another form of uniform international standard.

The second approach is that 'international public policy' means the court of the country in which recognition and enforcement is sought may consider the public policy of 'that country', but only where such public policy is consistent with important public policies constituted by international principles as recognised by most countries. Such international principles originate from international sources and are applicable as limits on national laws.[39]

The third approach is that 'international public policy' refers to public policy applicable to the cases with international character or element in the enforcement State. This understanding demands ascertaining the enforcement State's legislative purpose and intent rather than directly exploring international sources of law. This view has been adopted by Albert Jan van den Berg, etc.[40]

If 'public policy' in Article V(2)(b) of the New York Convention were to be understood from the first or the second of the above-mentioned three approaches to international public policy, then 'public policy' in Article V(2)(b) would not function as an escape mechanism. Thus only the third approach would accord with the nature of 'public policy' as 'an exceptional escape device' by enabling the enforcement court to apply and enforce the enforcement State's local laws in exceptional circumstances, and therefore accord with the wording 'of that country' in Article V(2)(b) of the New York Convention.[41] Article 36(1)(b) of UNCITRAL Model Law on International Commercial Arbitration also expressly stipulates 'the recognition or enforcement of the award would be contrary to the public policy of this State' as a ground for refusing an arbitral award's recognition or enforcement.[42] In light of further analysis by some commentators, the above-mentioned first and second approaches to understanding international public policy do not comply with the text and purpose of the New York Convention's Article V(2)(b) because they replace a national standard with 'supranational' standard and 'international' standard respectively. Only the third approach to international public policy complies with the text and purpose of the New York Convention's Article V(2)(b), namely, 'international public policy' is 'a national standard for the recognition

---

38. Pierre Lalive, *Transnational (or Truly International) Public Policy and International Arbitration*, in *Comparative Arbitration Practice and Public Policy in Arbitration* 257–318 (Pieter Sanders ed., Kluwer Law International 1987); ILA's Final Report, *supra* n. 10, at 251–252.
39. ILA's Final Report, *supra* n. 10, at 251–252.
40. Albert Jan van den Berg, *Why Are Some Awards Not Enforceable?*, in *New Horizons in International Commercial Arbitration and Beyond* 309 (Albert Jan van den Berg ed., Kluwer Law International 2005).
41. Born, *supra* n. 37, at 3657–3658.
42. UNCITRAL Model Law on International Commercial Arbitration (1985), with amendments adopted in 2006, UNCITRAL's website: http://www.uncitral.org/pdf/english/texts/arbitration/ml-arb/07-86998_Ebook.pdf (English version); http://www.uncitral.org/pdf/chinese/texts/arbitration/ml-arb/07-86997_Ebook.pdf (Chinese version).

and enforcement of international awards' as opposed to 'national public policy' (i.e., 'the national standard for the recognition and enforcement of domestic awards').[43]

In addition, although it is common for commentators to differentiate between 'international public policy' and 'national public policy', Article V(2)(b) of the New York Convention does not expressly require such a distinction. The New York Convention acknowledges its Contracting States' freedom to shape their own public policy; therefore, in terms of public policy, Contracting States can apply either different standards or the same standard to international arbitral awards and domestic arbitral awards. Yet the best approach in consideration of international comity is to apply a more lenient standard to foreign arbitral awards.[44]

With respect to the interpretation of Article V(2)(b), one of the most authoritative publications on the New York Convention, Albert Jan van den Berg's *The New York Arbitration Convention of 1958 – Towards a Uniform Judicial Interpretation*, specifically states:

> It may suffice to draw the attention to the important *distinction between domestic and international public policy*... According to this distinction what is considered to pertain to public policy in domestic relations does not necessarily pertain to public policy in international relations. It means that the number of matters considered to fall under public policy in international cases is smaller than that in domestic cases. The distinction is justified by the differing purposes of domestic and international relations.[45]
>
> It may be added that certain French and Swiss authors maintain that there also exists a third category of public policy, the so-called truly international public policy' (*'ordre public reellement international*'). The rules of this public policy would comprise fundamental rules of natural law, the principles of universal justice, *jus cogens* in public international law and the general principles of morality accepted by what is referred to as 'civilized nations'.[46]

2.5 ILA'S REPORTS ON PUBLIC POLICY

The ILA's Committee on International Commercial Arbitration[47] conducted a six-year study on public policy issues to be considered by courts during enforcement proceedings involving arbitral awards (rather than by arbitral tribunals during arbitration proceedings). They began after the Helsinki conference in 1996, presenting the initial report in the Taiwan conference in 1998, the 'Interim Report' in the London conference in 2000 ('The Interim Report on Public Policy as a Bar to Enforcement of International Arbitral Awards'), and finally the 'Final Report' in the New Delhi conference in 2002 ('The Final Report on Public Policy as a Bar to Enforcement of International Arbitral

---

43. Wolff, *supra* n. 33, at 409.
44. *Ibid.*
45. Albert Jan van den Berg, *The New York Arbitration Convention of 1958 – Towards a Uniform Judicial Interpretation* 360–361 (Kluwer Law International 1981).
46. *Ibid.* at 361.
47. The International Law Association (ILA) is a non-governmental international organisation established in 1873 in Brussels.

Awards').[48] The Final Report should be read together with the Interim Report,[49] both of which are internationally important documents for using public policy in refusing recognition and enforcement of international arbitral awards.

According to the ILA's Committee on International Commercial Arbitration in the Final Report, the term 'public policy' can be understood from three categories with varying scope:[50] 'domestic public policy', 'international public policy' and 'transnational or truly international public policy'.

Among these three categories, 'domestic public policy' has the widest scope of meaning, followed by 'international public policy' and then by 'transnational or truly international public policy' with the narrowest scope of meaning. Figure 2.1 is a Taiwanese scholar's diagrammatic representation of the interrelationship between these three categories of public policy.[51]

Figure 2.1 Domestic Public Policy, International Public Policy and Transnational Public Policy

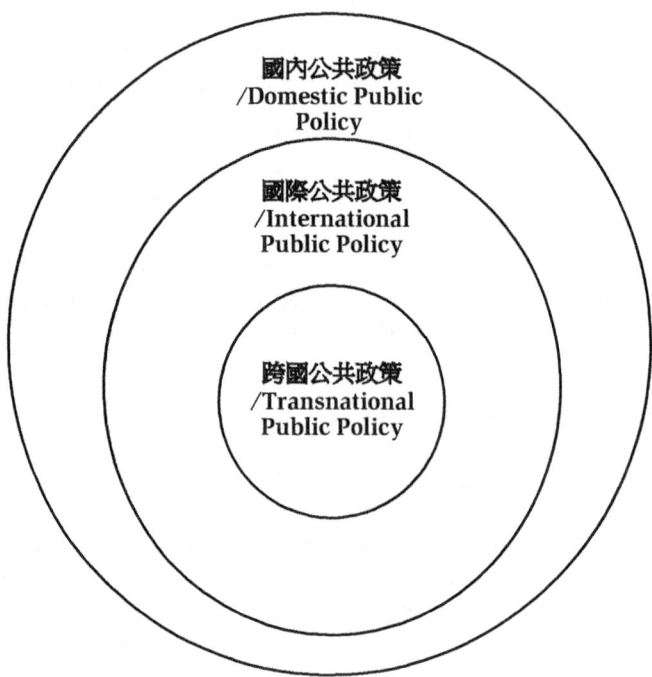

---

48. For the Chinese translation of the ILA's Final Report, *see* Huanfang Du, *Final Report on Public Policy as a Ground for Refusing to Enforce International Arbitral Awards*, in *Judicial Practice of New York Convention and International Commercial Arbitration* (CIETAC ed., Law Press 2010).
49. ILA's Final Report, *supra* n. 10, at para. 2.
50. *Ibid*.
51. Chang-fa Lo, *Principles and Criteria for International and Transnational Public Policies in Commercial Arbitration*, 1(1) Contemporary Asia Arbitration Journal 67, 86 (2008).

Chapter 2: The Meaning of Public Policy

In light of the three categories of public policy, the ILA's Committee on International Commercial Arbitration endorses the standard of 'international public policy' to be used by the courts when determining whether to refuse enforcement of international arbitral awards on public policy ground.[52] Such international public policy is 'that part of the public policy of a State which, if violated, would prevent a party from invoking a foreign law or foreign judgment or foreign award'.[53]

It is particularly noteworthy that 'international public policy' as defined in the Final Report does not mean public policy common to many countries. In the Final Report's definition, public policy that is common to many countries is known as 'transnational or truly international public policy', whose fairly narrow scope includes 'fundamental rules of natural law; principles of universal justice; *jus cogens* in public international law; and the general principles of morality accepted by what are referred to as "civilised nations"'.[54]

In contrast, the so-called international public policy is still part of a particular nation's public policy, namely that particular nation's public policy for matters involving international elements. Yet some scholars regard 'international public policy' as a 'misnomer', as such term may cause misunderstanding about international public policy being common to every nation's public policy.[55] Nonetheless this book still follows the terminology and the above-mentioned categorisation in accordance with the Final Report and other international literature.

Furthermore, 'international public policy' as defined in the Final Report does not mean public policy in the sense of public international law – it should be understood in the sense given to it in the field of private international law.

With respect to the ILA's Committee on International Commercial Arbitration's detailed discussion in the Final Report on using 'international public policy' as the test for determining the enforceability of foreign arbitral awards, the following highlights the essential points. In particular, the three categories of international public policy ('fundamental principles', '*lois de police*' and 'international obligations'[56]) warrant separate elaboration.

First Category: Fundamental Principles

Fundamental principles are the basic principles of justice or morality that the relevant country wishes to protect. It can be sub-categorised as 'substantive fundamental principles' and 'procedural fundamental principles'. One of the examples of fundamental principles is the principle of good faith and prohibition of abuse of rights (especially

---

52. ILA's Final Report, *supra* n. 10, at para. 10.
53. *Ibid.* at para. 11.
54. Albert Jan van den Berg, *The New York Arbitration Convention of 1958 – Towards a Uniform Judicial Interpretation* 316 (Kluwer Law International 1981); *see also* ILA's Final Report, *supra* n. 10, at para. 43, Recommendation 2(a).
55. *Transnational (or Truly International) Public Policy and International Arbitration*, in ICCA Congress Series No. 3, 258 para. 3 (1986); Winnie (Jo-Mei) Ma, *Public Policy in the Judicial Enforcement of Arbitral Awards: Lessons For and From Australia* 77 (2005) (SJD thesis, Bond University): http://epublications.bond.edu.au/cgi/viewcontent.cgi?filename=0&article=1023&context=theses&type=additional (accessed 4 May 2017).
56. ILA's Final Report, *supra* n. 10, at para. 25 and Recommendation 1(d).

in civil law countries). Other examples cited by the courts or commentators include: *pacta sunt servanda*, prohibition against uncompensated expropriation and prohibition against discrimination. Prohibition of activities that are *contra bonos mores* such as piracy, terrorism, genocide, slavery, smuggling, drug trafficking and paedophilia, also belong to this category.[57]

One of the examples of procedural public policy is the requirement of arbitral tribunal's impartiality. Other cited examples of violations of procedural public policy include: fraud or corruption inducing or affecting award making, violation of rules of natural justice, appointment of arbitrators by parties who were on unequal footing. In addition, enforcing an award that is inconsistent with a court judgment or arbitral award with res judicata effect in the enforcement State would also violate procedural public policy. It is commonly accepted that procedural public policy should not include manifest disregard of law or facts. Rules of procedural public policy overlap with the due process requirements prescribed in Article V(1)(b) of the New York Convention.[58]

Second Category: *Lois de Police* or Public Policy Rules

Rules which aim to safeguard the relevant country's essential political, social or economic interests are known as '*lois de police*' or 'public policy rules'. An award's inconsistency with a mandatory rule per se does not constitute a ground for its non-recognition or non-enforcement – only the violation of mandatory rules which are '*lois de police*' or 'public policy rules' can be a ground for non-recognition or non-enforcement of arbitral awards.[59] An example of public policy rule is anti-trust law (specifically including European Union competition law, Article 81 EC). Other commonly cited examples include currency controls; price fixing rules; environmental protection laws; measure of embargo, blockade or boycott; tax laws; and laws protecting parties presumed to have inferior bargaining position (such as consumer protection laws).[60]

Third Category: International Obligations

International obligations are the relevant country's obligations towards other countries or international organisations. An example of international obligations is United Nations Security Council resolutions imposing sanctions, which are directly binding on United Nations' Member States (pursuant to Chapter V Article 25 of the United Nations Charter). The relevant country must also fulfil obligations in international conventions ratified by it.

Some international public policies may fall within more than one category. For instance, bribery and corruption are generally regarded as *contra bonos mores*, so that most courts would refuse to uphold agreements tainted by corruption even when the parties and the conduct of corruption are unrelated to their country. Corruption may also assume the status of '*lois de police*' through legislative enactment. In addition, the

---

57. *Ibid.* at para. 28.
58. *Ibid.* at para. 29.
59. *Ibid.* Recommendation 3(a).
60. *Ibid.* at para. 30.

relevant country may assume an obligation to other countries to prohibit corruption as a result of signing the Organisation for Economic Co-operation and Development (OECD) 1997 Convention on Combating the Bribery of Foreign Officials in International Transactions.[61]

2.6 EXAMPLES OF NATIONAL LEGISLATION CONCERNING PUBLIC POLICY

The main types of legislative examples of national provisions concerning public policy in refusing recognition or enforcement of foreign arbitral awards are as follows.[62]

2.6.1 Reference to the New York Convention

Without referring to concepts such as 'public policy' and 'public order', some national legislations directly require that recognition and enforcement of foreign arbitral awards subject to the New York Convention be governed by the New York Convention. Examples include the United States (US) Code: Title 9 – Arbitration § 201,[63] German Code of Civil Procedure Article 1061(1),[64] English Arbitration Act 1996 section 100,[65] Korean Arbitration Act Article 39(1)[66] and the Chinese Civil Procedure Law Article 269.[67]

---

61. *Ibid.* at para. 32.
62. Xianchu Zhang, *New Developments in the Theory and Practice of 'Public Policy' in Judicial Review of Foreign Commercial Arbitral Awards*, in *Judicial Review of the Foreign-Related Arbitration* 363–365 (CIETAC South China-Sub-Commission ed., Law Press 2006). *See also* Audley Sheppard, Kuenchen Fu (translated), *Public Policy as a Ground for Refusing Enforcement of Foreign Arbitral Awards*, 56 Arbitration 38–45 (2000).
63. 9 U.S.C. § 201 provides: 'The Convention on the Recognition and Enforcement of Foreign Arbitral Awards of June 10, 1958, shall be enforced in United States courts in accordance with this chapter.'
64. The Tenth Book of the German Code of Civil Procedure contains provisions relating to arbitration.
65. English Arbitration Act 1996 s. 100.
66. Korean Arbitration Act, Act No. 10207 (revised on 31 March 2010). Article 39(1) stipulates: 'Recognition or enforcement of a foreign award which is subject to the Convention on the Recognition and Enforcement of Foreign Arbitral Awards, shall be governed by that Convention.'
67. Chinese Civil Procedure Law Art. 269 provides: 'If an award made by a foreign arbitration agency requires the recognition and enforcement by a people's court of the People's Republic of China, the party concerned shall directly apply to the intermediate people's court in the place where the party subject to execution has its domicile or where its property is located. The people's court shall deal with the matter in accordance with the relevant provisions of the international treaties concluded or acceded to by the People's Republic of China or on the principle of reciprocity.' English translation from the website of the Supreme People's Court of the People's Republic of China, http://en.chinacourt.org/public/detail.php?id = 2694 (accessed 4 May 2017).

2.6.2 'Public Policy of This Country'

The provision 'public policy of this country' is constituted by adopting the concept of public policy in domestic legislation and by adding a modifying term of 'this country', which can also be found in the New York Convention and UNCITRAL Model Law. Examples include Article 36 of Law of the Russian Federation on International Commercial Arbitration:[68] 'Recognition or enforcement of an arbitral award, irrespective of the country in which it was made, may be refused only:... (2) if the court finds that:... the recognition or enforcement of the award would be contrary to the public policy of the Russian Federation.'

2.6.3 'Public Policy' Only

This adopts the concept of public policy without specifically adding the term 'this country'. For instance, Article 1721(1) of the recently revised Belgian Judicial Code merely stipulates 'public policy' without expressly stipulating public policy of 'this country':[69] 'The Court of First Instance may only refuse to recognize or enforce an arbitral award, irrespective of the country in which it was made, in the following circumstances:... (b) if the Court of First Instance finds that... the recognition or enforcement of the award would be contrary to public policy.'

2.6.4 'International Public Policy'

Some national legislations specifically differentiate between the concepts of 'domestic public policy' and 'international public policy' by expressly specifying that one of the grounds for refusing recognition or enforcement of foreign arbitral awards is 'where the recognition or enforcement is contrary to international public policy' (French Code of Civil Procedure Article 1502(5)[70]). The French Court of Appeal in *Intrafor Cofor v Gagnant*[71] clearly stated that 'international public policy' and 'domestic public policy' are two different concepts, and clarified that violation of domestic public policy (assuming its establishment in this case) does not constitute a ground for appealing against the judicial enforcement of foreign arbitral award in France, because Article 1502(5) stipulates that 'the recognition or enforcement is contrary to international public policy' (and not domestic public policy). Likewise, Article 56 of Portuguese Law

---

68. English translation cited from the website of the International Commercial Arbitration Court at the Chamber of Commerce and Industry of the Russian Federation (ICAC), https://mkas.tpprf.ru/en/documents/ (accessed 4 May 2017).
69. English translation cited from the website of the Belgian Centre for Arbitration and Mediation, http://www.cepani.be/en/arbitration/belgian-judicial-code-provisions (accessed 4 May 2017).
70. Original version in French: 'L'appel de la decision qui accorde la reconnaissance ou l'execution n'est ouvert que dans les cas suivants:...5. Si la reconnaissance ou l'execution sont contraires a l'ordre public international.' *See* the website of the Government of France, http://www.legifrance.gouv.fr/affichCode.do?cidTexte = LEGITEXT000006070716&dateTexte = 20050514 (accessed 4 May 2017).
71. 1985 Rev. Arb. 299, 12 March 1985.

on Voluntary Arbitration Law (which became effective in 2012) provides:[72] 'Recognition or enforcement of an arbitral award made in a foreign country may be refused only:... (b) if the court finds that:... (ii) The recognition or enforcement of the award would lead to a result incompatible with the international public policy of the Portuguese State.'

2.6.5 Parallel Provisions of Public Policy (or Public Order) and Good Morals

Some national legislations provide the concept of 'public policy' (or public order) in parallel with good morals. An example is Japanese Arbitration Law. Article 45 paragraph 2 of the Japanese Arbitration Law states that Article 45 paragraph 1 (concerning arbitral awards having the same legal effect as court judgments) does not apply if 'the content of the arbitral award would be contrary to the public policy or good morals of Japan'.[73] Similarly, Article 235(2) of the UAE Civil Procedure Code stipulates:[74] 'Execution may not be ordered unless the following was verified:... (e) It... does not include any violation of public policy or *bonos mores* as understood in the UAE.'

Article 49 paragraph 1 of Taiwan's Arbitration Law also adopts this legislative approach:[75] 'The court shall issue a dismissal with respect to an application submitted by a party for recognition of a foreign arbitral award,... Where the recognition or enforcement of the arbitral award is contrary to the public order or good morals' of Taiwan. In addition, Article 74 paragraph 1 of Taiwan's Act Governing Relations Between Peoples of the Taiwan Area and the Mainland Area provides for recognition and enforcement of awards made in the Mainland China:[76] 'To the extent that an irrevocable civil ruling or judgment, or arbitral award rendered in the Mainland Area is not contrary to the public order or good morals of the Taiwan Area, an application may be filed with a court for a ruling to recognize it.' As for recognition and enforcement of awards made in Hong Kong or Macau, Article 42 paragraph 2 of the Act Governing Relations with Hong Kong and Macau provides:[77] 'Article 30 through Article 34 [currently Articles 47 to 51] of the Commercial Arbitration Act shall apply to the validity, petition for court recognition, and suspension of execution proceedings in cases involving civil arbitral awards made in Hong Kong or Macau.'

---

72. Portuguese Law on Voluntary Arbitration, Law No. 63/2011 of 14 December 2012 (effective from 14 March 2012).
73. Japanese Arbitration Law, Law No. 138 of 2003 (promulgated on 1 August 2003, effective from 1 March 2004).
74. The UAE Civil Procedure Code, Federal Law No. 11 of 1992.
75. Revision dated 2 December 2015. English translation from the Taiwan Laws & Regulations Database, http://law.moj.gov.tw/Eng/LawClass/LawAll.aspx?PCode=I0020001 (accessed 4 May 2017).
76. Revision dated 17 June 2015. English translation from http://www.mac.gov.tw/ct.asp?xItem=51261&ctNode=5915&mp=3 (accessed 4 May 2017).
77. Revision dated 11 January 2016. English translation from the Taiwan Laws & Regulations Database, http://law.moj.gov.tw/Eng/LawClass/LawAll.aspx?PCode=Q0010004 (accessed 4 May 2017).

2.6.6 'Basic Principles of Legal System', 'Good Morals and Other Social Order' and Other Terms

This stipulates other corresponding concepts instead of directly using the term 'public policy'. For example, Article 55 of the Swedish Arbitration Law provides:[78] 'Recognition and enforcement of a foreign award shall also be refused where a court finds:… (2) that it would be clearly incompatible with the basic principles of the Swedish legal system to recognize and enforce the award.' Another example is Article 39 paragraph 2 of Korean Arbitration Law, which, by reference to Article 217 of Korean Civil Procedure Law, provides that in terms of an arbitral award not subject to the New York Convention, one of the conditions to recognise such award is that the award 'does not violate good morals and other social order of the Republic of Korea'.[79]

---

78. Swedish Arbitration Law (SFS 1999:116).
79. Article 217 of Korean Civil Procedure Law, Act No. 10373 (revision dated 23 July 2010) provides: 'A final and conclusive judgment by a foreign court shall be acknowledged to be valid, only upon the entire fulfillment of the following requirements: … 3. That such judgment does not violate good morals and other social order of the Republic of Korea.' In contrast, Art. 39 para. 1 of Korea's Arbitration Law expressly stipulates that recognition and enforcement of arbitral awards which are subject to the New York Convention are governed by the New York Convention.

CHAPTER 3
'Public Policy' and the Even More Unpredictable 'Social and Public Interest' in PRC Arbitration Law and Their Interrelationship

Understanding the interpretation and application in the PRC of 'public policy' in Article V(2)(b) of the New York Convention should be concurrent with examining the concept of 'social and public interest' for the following reasons.

First, in the past and in principle the PRC's civil law did not have any provisions concerning 'public policy' (the author only found one exception).[1] It was only after the PRC's implementation of the New York Convention since 1987 that the term 'public policy' entered into the PRC's civil law system, and that the PRC courts gradually began to consider whether the recognition and enforcement of specific foreign arbitral awards would violate the PRC's 'public policy' in cases concerning recognition and enforcement of foreign arbitral awards. Yet this does not mean that concepts similar to 'public policy' did not exist within the PRC's civil law system before the New York Convention entered into force in the PRC. In actual fact, Article 204 of the PRC Civil Procedure Law (For Trial Implementation) of 1982 already stipulated:[2]

---

1. The only exception found by the author is the Opinion of the Law Commission of the Government Administration Council of the Central People's Government Concerning Marriage Issues between Chinese Nationals and Foreign Nationals as well as between Foreign Nationals. This Opinion indicates that the PRC's marriage law not only applies to marriages and divorces in the PRC between Chinese nationals and foreign nationals as well as between foreign nationals, but also accommodates, within appropriate limits, the parties' own marriage laws, such limits being that 'the application of the parties' own marriage laws do not violate the *public order, public interest* and current basic policies of the People's Republic of China' (emphasis added): cited from Yifei Lin, *Law and Practice of Challenges to Arbitral Awards* 263, n. 1 (Wuhan University Press 2008).
2. Enacted on 8 March 1982 and implemented on 1 October 1982.
    For an example of the full English translation, *see* the website of Worldlii, http://www.asianlii.org/cn/legis/cen/laws/cplti422/ (accessed 4 May 2017).

> When a people's court of the People's Republic of China is entrusted by a foreign court with the enforcement of a final judgment or *award*, the people's court shall examine it in accordance with any international treaty concluded or acceded to by the People's Republic of China or the principle of reciprocity. If the court deems that the judgment or award does not violate the *basic principles of the laws of the People's Republic of China or national and social interest*, it shall recognize the validity of the judgment or award and enforce it according to the procedures specified in this Law (emphasis added).

Therefore it can be seen that the concept of the PRC's 'basic principles of the law' or 'national and social interest' already existed at that time. Subsequently Articles 7 and 150 of the General Principles of the Civil Law of the PRC (promulgated in 1986) both contained provisions concerning 'social and public interest'. Consequently, examining the PRC courts' interpretation and application of both 'social and public interest' and 'public policy' can assist with observing and tracking the dynamic development of the concept of 'public policy' in the PRC's legal system over time.

Second, through systemic establishments such as centralised jurisdiction, the Reporting System and the allocation of the Fourth Civil Tribunal of the SPC's function, etc. within the PRC's current system, the same procedures apply to cases involving the interpretation and application of 'public policy' and 'social and public interest' in the PRC's arbitration law. All these cases are ultimately centralised in the SPC's Fourth Civil Tribunal in order to improve the consistency of judicial approaches (*see* section 3.2.1 of this chapter). Hence, examining the SPC's interpretation and application of 'social and public interest' can assist with understanding the SPC's interpretation and application of 'public policy'.

This chapter begins by analysing the PRC's arbitration-related legislative provisions concerning 'public policy', explaining the provisions about the recognition and enforcement of foreign arbitral awards together with comparing and contrasting the provisions about the recognition and enforcement of arbitral awards made in Taiwan, Hong Kong and Macau. It then explains 'social and public interest' as stipulated in the PRC Arbitration Law and Civil Procedure Law. On the one hand, it can be seen from procedural regulations that the PRC's provisions relating to civil procedure deem four types of cases concerning 'the validity of foreign-related arbitration agreements', 'non-enforcement of foreign-related arbitral awards', 'revocation of foreign-related arbitration awards' and 'recognition and enforcement of foreign arbitral awards' as belonging to the same 'group', which is subject to centralised jurisdiction, the 'Reporting System' and other regulations. Moreover, the SPC's Fourth Civil Tribunal reviews all of these cases as part of SPC's internal allocation of function in order to facilitate uniform approaches. Yet on the other hand, the inconsistencies between the PRC Arbitration Law and Civil Procedure Law have engendered disagreements, which will be explained in detail. Finally, this chapter cites various academic opinions to explain 'public policy' and 'social and public interest' in the PRC's legal system of arbitration.

Chapter 3: 'Public Policy' and the Even More Unpredictable

3.1 'PUBLIC POLICY' IN PRC CIVIL LAW SYSTEM IS ONLY SEEN IN PROVISIONS RELATING TO THE NEW YORK CONVENTION

Within the PRC's current civil law system, the term 'public policy' is mainly seen in legislative provisions relating to the New York Convention, as well as in the statements issued by the SPC concerning the enforcement of arbitral awards made in Hong Kong and Macau (*see* section 3.1.2 of this chapter). However, the PRC's legislative provisions relating to the Constitution and public order had already used the term 'public order' a long time ago. For instance, as early as in 1954, Article 100 of the first version of the PRC's Constitution stipulated:[3] 'Citizens of the People's Republic of China shall comply with the Constitution and the law, observe labour discipline, *comply with public order*, and respect social ethics (emphasis added).' Article 53 of the current PRC Constitution also requests its citizens to '*comply with public order*'.[4] In addition, Chapter 3 section 1 of the PRC's Public Security Administration Punishments Law (revised in 2012)[5] provides for 'Acts Disrupting Public Order and Punishment', in which Article 25 expressly stipulates the following three types of behaviour as disturbing public order:[6] 'intentionally disturbing public order by spreading rumour, giving false information about any danger, epidemic disease or emergency, or by other means'; 'disrupting public order by spreading any fictitious explosive, toxic, radioactive or corrosive substances, or infectious pathogens and other dangerous substances'; and 'disrupting public order by threatening to set fire, explosion or spread dangerous substances'. Article 13 of the PRC's Tourism Law (proclaimed in 2013) further provides that 'tourists shall comply with *social public order* and social morality, respect local customs, cultural traditions and religions, preserve travel resources, protect the ecological environment, and comply with the regulations of civilised tourist behaviour (emphasis added)', etc. However, in light of the context and content of the above-mentioned legislative provisions, the use of the terms 'public order' and 'social public order' by these provisions focuses on maintaining 'order' and may not necessarily relate to the basic principles of law. These provisions differ from the subject matter of this book and therefore fall outside the scope of this book.

---

3. Constitution of the People's Republic of China of 1954 enacted and implemented on 20 September 1954.
4. The current Constitution of the People's Republic of China as amended on 14 March 2004.
   For an English version, *see* the website of China's Leader in Online Legal Research: http://www.lawinfochina.com/display.aspx?id = 3437&lib = law&SearchKeyword = constitution &SearchCKeyword = (accessed 4 May 2017).
5. As amended on 26 October 2012 by Order of the President No. 67.
   For an English version of this legislation, *see* the website of China's Leader in Online Legal Research: http://www.lawinfochina.com/display.aspx?lib = law&id = 4549&CGid = # (accessed 4 May 2017).
6. *Ibid. See* Art. 25 of the PRC's Public Security Administration Punishments Law.

3.1.1 Recognition and Enforcement of Foreign Arbitral Awards

3.1.1.1 Before PRC's Accession to the New York Convention

Before the PRC acceded to the New York Convention, a clearer provision concerning the enforcement of foreign arbitral awards was seen in the first version of the PRC's Civil Procedure Law (For Trial Implementation) of 1982, specifically Article 204:

> When a people's court of the People's Republic of China is entrusted by a foreign court with the enforcement of a final judgment or *award*, the people's court shall examine it in accordance with any international treaty concluded or acceded to by the People's Republic of China or the principle of reciprocity. If the court deems that the judgment or award does not violate the basic principles of the laws of the People's Republic of China or national and social interest, it shall recognise the validity of the judgment or award and enforce it according to the procedures specified in this Law (emphasis added).

This provision has several noteworthy points. First, its reference to 'entrusted by a foreign court with the enforcement of a final judgment or award' simultaneously regulated the enforcement of both foreign court judgments and foreign arbitral awards. Second, the parties could not directly apply to the PRC courts to enforce a foreign arbitral award. They must do so through firstly applying to foreign courts. Third, since the PRC was yet to accede to the New York Convention at the time, the reference to judicial determination 'in accordance with international treaties concluded or acceded to by the People's Republic of China' was yet to include the New York Convention. Finally, the criteria for the PRC courts' determination included violation of 'national' and 'social' interest, a term capable of considerably broad interpretation and inevitably raising concern that the PRC courts may accordingly refuse enforcement of foreign arbitral awards recklessly.

The Arbitration Research Institute of China Chamber of International Commerce (CCOIC) forwarded questionnaires to a total of 310 intermediate courts and maritime courts during August and September of 1997. According to its report compiled by the responses from forty-three courts, there were no cases concerning the enforcement of foreign arbitral awards before 1990.[7] Although the response rate of this questionnaire was not high and therefore cannot completely reflect the circumstances of the cases concerning the enforcement of foreign arbitral awards before 1990, one can still speculate that such cases, if any, were rare. As expressed by one scholar:[8] 'In practice, the parties applied directly to the competent courts of the PRC for recognition and enforcement of foreign arbitral awards and the PRC courts then decided on such applications. Foreign courts had never requested the PRC courts to assist with the

---

7. The content of the research report of September 1997 by the Arbitration Research Institute of China Chamber of International Commerce was cited from Shengchang Wang, *Enforcement of Foreign Arbitral Awards in the People's Republic of China*, in *Improving the Efficiency of Arbitration Agreements and Awards: 40 Years of Application of the New York Convention* 480, 482 (Albert Jan van den Berg ed., Kluwer Law International 1999).
8. Xiangquan Qi, *Study on the Recognition and Enforcement of Foreign Arbitral Awards* 325 (Law Press 2010).

Chapter 3: 'Public Policy' and the Even More Unpredictable

enforcement of foreign arbitral awards.' Here it may be inferred that court decisions concerning the enforcement of foreign arbitral awards might not exist at the time. Furthermore, court decisions of this particular era could not be found despite the author's research efforts. In the absence of any specific cases available for examination, it is difficult to ascertain the specific circumstances surrounding the practical interpretation and application of Article 204 at that time.

3.1.1.2 After PRC's Accession to the New York Convention

3.1.1.2.1 From the PRC's 'Basic Principles of Law or National and Social Interest' to 'Public Policy'

The Sixth National People's Congress Standing Committee (NPCSC) approved the decision of the PRC's accession to the New York Convention during its Eighteenth Conference on 2 December 1986.[9] The PRC government deposited the instrument of accession on 22 January 1987 and the New York Convention became effective in the PRC from 22 April 1987. According to the PRC's 'reciprocity reservation' and 'commercial reservation' at its time of accession,[10] '[t]he People's Republic of China will apply the Convention, only on the basis of reciprocity, to the recognition and enforcement of arbitral awards made in the territory of another Contracting State', and '[t]he People's Republic of China will apply the Convention only to differences arising out of legal relationships, whether contractual or not, which are considered as commercial under the national law of the People's Republic of China'.[11]

When the New York Convention became effective in the PRC on 22 April 1987, Article 204 of the PRC's Civil Procedure Law (For Trial Implementation) was not revised immediately and accordingly. Consequently there were inconsistent criteria for determining contravention of the enforcement State's 'public policy' under Article V(2)(b) of the New York Convention and contravention of the PRC's 'basic principles of the law or national and social interest' under Article 204 of the PRC's Civil Procedure Law (For Trial Implementation). Nevertheless on 10 April 1987 (which was slightly more than ten days before the New York Convention became effective in the PRC on 22 April 1987), the SPC issued a notification to all higher people's courts and intermediate

---

9. In its decision on acceding to the New York Convention, the PRC simultaneously declared both the 'reciprocity reservation' and 'commercial reservation'.
10. See United Nations Treaty Collection, https://treaties.un.org/Pages/showActionDetails.aspx?objid=080000028002a637 (accessed 4 May 2017).
11. The so-called contractual or non-contractual commercial legal relationships specifically refer to the economic rights and obligations arising from contracts, torts or according to relevant legal provisions. Examples include sale of goods, property leasing, engineering contracting, processing, technology transfer, joint venture, joint management, exploration of natural resources, insurance, financing, services, agency, consulting, carriage of goods or passengers by air, sea, rail or road, product liability, environmental pollution, maritime accidents and ownership disputes, but do not include disputes between foreign investors and host governments: see Art. 2 of the SPC's Notification concerning the PRC's accession to the New York Convention, Fa-(Jing)-Fa (1987) No. 5, issued and implemented on 10 April 1987.

people's courts concerning the PRC's accession to the New York Convention:[12] 'the Convention [i.e. the New York Convention] applies to the recognition and enforcement of arbitral awards made in the territory of another Contracting State. *The Convention's provisions apply where they differ from those of the Civil Procedure Law* (emphasis added)' and 'with respect to the recognition and enforcement of arbitral awards made in the territory of non-Contracting States, Article 204 of the PRC's Civil Procedure Law (For Trial Implementation) should apply'. The author speculates that the SPC's issuance of the notification to the lower courts may be a temporary interim measure before any amendment to the Civil Procedure Law.

The PRC's subsequent amendment to the Civil Procedure Law in 1991 provided for the recognition and enforcement of foreign court judgments and foreign arbitral awards in Articles 268 and 269 respectively. Some commentators believe that the PRC's legal system in the recognition and enforcement of foreign arbitral awards had thereby been perfected.[13]

Article 269 of the 1991 version of the Civil Procedure Law stipulated:

> If an arbitral award of a foreign arbitration institution requires recognition and enforcement by a people's court of the People's Republic of China, the party shall apply directly to the intermediate people's court located in the place where the party subject to the enforcement is domiciled or where its property is located, and the people's court shall act in accordance with international treaties concluded or acceded by the People's Republic of China or the principle of reciprocity.

The two subsequent revisions of the Civil Procedure Law in 2007 and 2012 did not amend the content of this provision but merely renumbered Article 269 to Article 267 in 2007 and then to Article 283 in 2012, the content of which remains the same.

It is worth noting the following points when comparing the previous Article 204 of the Civil Procedure Law in the 1982 version and the subsequent Article 269 in the 1991 version (which is Article 283 in the current 2012 version) concerning the recognition and enforcement of foreign arbitral awards.

First, Article 204 of the 1982 version of the Civil Procedure Law stipulates:

> When a people's court of the People's Republic of China is entrusted by a foreign court with the enforcement of a final judgment or award, the people's court shall examine it in accordance with any international treaty concluded or acceded to by the People's Republic of China or the principle of reciprocity. If the court deems that the judgment or award does not violate the basic principles of the laws of the People's Republic of China or national and social interest, it shall recognize the validity of the judgment or award and enforce it according to the procedures specified in this Law, otherwise the people's court shall return the judgment or award to the foreign court.

---

12. *See* Art. 1 of the SPC's concerning the PRC's accession to the New York Convention, *ibid*.
13. Jian Han, *Theory and Practice of Modern International Commercial Arbitration* 474 (Law Press 2000); Qiaofa Liu, *Recognition and Enforcement of Foreign Arbitral Awards in the PRC*, 7 Guide on Foreign-Related Commercial and Maritime Trial 178, 180 (People's Court Press 2004).

Accordingly, a party cannot directly apply to the PRC court to enforce a final court judgment or arbitral award and must entrust a foreign court to do so, thereby causing inconvenience to the parties. This led to the revision of the Civil Procedure Law in 1991, whereby Article 269 provides:[14]

> If an arbitral award of foreign arbitration institution requires recognition and enforcement by a people's court of the People's Republic of China, *the party shall apply directly to the intermediate people's court located in the place where the party subject to the enforcement is domiciled or where its property is located*, and the people's court shall act in accordance with international treaties concluded or acceded by the People's Republic of China or the principle of reciprocity (emphasis added).

This enables the parties to submit applications to the PRC courts rather than via the foreign courts and, therefore, is beneficial to the parties' direct claims to rights. Thus it has been said that the 1991 amendment to the Civil Procedure Law has perfected the PRC's legal system in the recognition and enforcement of foreign arbitral awards.[15]

Second, the Civil Procedure Law deleted the old review criteria concerning the PRC's 'basic principles of the law or national and social interest' and instead merely referred to 'international treaties concluded or acceded by the People's Republic of China or the principle of reciprocity', thereby resolving the previously mentioned inconsistency between the criteria in the old Article 204 of the Civil Procedure Law and Article V(2)(b) of the New York Convention.

Third, the recognition and enforcement of arbitral awards made in the territory of non-Contracting States to the New York Convention would depend on whether or not the PRC has any relevant bilateral treaties with these non-Contracting States. If yes, the relevant bilateral treaties would govern; if not, the 'principle of reciprocity' would apply. Although Article 269 of the 1991 version of the Civil Procedural Law (which is Article 283 of the current version) merely requires the PRC courts to decide on enforceability 'in accordance with... the principle of reciprocity', this does not mean that the PRC courts need not examine whether enforcing the relevant foreign arbitral award would 'violate the basic principles of the laws of the People's Republic of China or national and social interest'. In this regard, the SPC's Fourth Civil Tribunal has specifically clarified in the answer to the ninety-second question in 'Answers to Practical Questions on Foreign-Related Commercial and Maritime Trials (I)', which it elaborated:[16]

> For arbitral awards which are not made in the territory of the New York Convention's Contracting States, the people's court should consider whether the relevant country and the PRC have a relationship of reciprocity. *Where such*

---

14. Article 269 of the PRC Civil Procedure Law of 1991.
15. Qiaofa Liu, *Recognition and Enforcement of Foreign Arbitral Awards in the PRC*, 7 Guide on Foreign-Related Commercial and Maritime Trial, 178, 180 (People's Court Press 2004).
16. Exiang Wan (editor-in-chief), the Fourth Civil Tribunal of the Supreme People's Court (ed.), *Answers to Practical Questions on Foreign-Related Commercial and Maritime Trial (I), in* 7 *Guide on Foreign-Related Commercial and Maritime Trial*, 2004(1), 66 (People's Court Press 2004).

> *relationship of reciprocity exists, the people's court may recognize and enforce the relevant arbitral award if the recognition and enforcement of the relevant arbitral award would not violate the PRC's national sovereignty and dignity, basic principles of law and social and public interest.* Where such relationship of reciprocity does not exist, the people's court shall refuse recognition and enforcement (emphasis added).

Here it is worth noting that the above answer to the ninety-second question not only refers to the PRC's basic principles of law or national and social interest as specified in the original Article 204 of the Civil Procedure Law, but also refers to 'national sovereignty and dignity' which possibly has a broader meaning.

Finally, while the phrase 'arbitral award of foreign arbitration institution' in the revised Civil Procedure Law seems to confine to 'institutional arbitral awards' and does not include 'ad hoc arbitral awards', the SPC nevertheless issued a Notification concerning the PRC's accession to the New York Convention on 10 April 1997.[17] Article 1 of this Notification explicitly states: 'According to the declaration of reciprocity reservation made by the People's Republic of China upon its accession to this Convention, China will apply this Convention to the recognition and enforcement of arbitral awards made in the territory of another Contracting State. In case of any discrepancy between the provisions of this Convention and the provisions of China's Civil Procedure Law (Trial Implementation), this Convention prevails.' Thus the New York Convention applies to 'arbitral awards made in the territory of another Contracting State' regardless of whether such awards are institutional or ad hoc. Consequently, as expressed in the answer to the eighty-eighth question in the 'Answers to Practical Questions on Foreign-Related Commercial and Maritime Trials (I)' of 2004: 'The People's Republic of China has acceded to the New York Convention, which expressly imposes obligations to recognize and enforce ad hoc arbitral awards made in the territory of other Contracting States. Accordingly, if the relevant parties have agreed on ad hoc arbitration in the territory of a Contracting State and that Contracting State does not prohibit such agreement, then the people's court should recognize the validity of such agreement concerning ad hoc arbitration.' The content of this answer corresponds with Article 1 of the above-mentioned SPC's Notification concerning the PRC's accession to the New York Convention issued on 10 April 1987.[18]

Yet a question worthy of further discussion is whether the PRC courts would recognise ad hoc arbitral awards made in the territory of nations which are not the New York Convention's Contracting States. If the answer is affirmative, what would be the basis of such answer? The New York Convention does not apply, nor does the current Article 283 of the PRC Civil Procedure Law apply in this context as it refers to 'arbitral award of foreign arbitration institution'. Thus the recognition and enforcement of ad hoc awards made in non-Contracting States seem to be lawless and in a state of legal vacuum. In practice, the author has not seen any precedents in this regard. Apart from ad hoc awards made in non-Contracting States, even for arbitral awards made in non-Contracting States regardless of whether they are ad hoc or institutional (both of

---

17. Fa-(Jing)-Fa (1987) No. 5, 10 April 1987.
18. *Ibid.*

which are subject to the principle of reciprocity rather than the New York Convention), Justice Guixiang Liu and Justice Hongyu Shen of the SPC's Fourth Civil Tribunal stated in 2012 that 'currently available circumstances indicate that the PRC courts are yet to apply the principle of reciprocity to the recognition and enforcement of foreign arbitral awards'.[19]

3.1.1.2.2 Criteria for Differentiating Between Domestic Arbitral Awards and Foreign Arbitral Awards

There is a major difference between the New York Convention and the PRC Civil Procedure Law with respect to the recognition and enforcement of foreign arbitral awards, namely the different criteria for differentiating between domestic awards and foreign awards. The New York Convention adopts the theory of territoriality in relation to foreign arbitral awards. This is evident from the phraseology of the New York Convention's Article I(1): 'arbitral awards made in the territory of a State other than the State where the recognition and enforcement of such awards are sought'. The PRC's reciprocity reservation upon acceding to the New York Convention also declares: 'The People's Republic of China will apply the Convention, only on the basis of reciprocity, to the recognition and enforcement of arbitral awards made in the territory of another Contracting State.'[20] In addition, the SPC's Notification to the PRC's lower courts concerning the PRC's accession to the New York Convention issued on 10 April 1987 (which was slightly more than ten days before the New York Convention became effective in the PRC on 22 April 1987) also states: '[a]ccording to the declaration of reciprocity reservation by the People's Republic of China when acceding to the New York Convention, the Convention applies in the People's Republic of China in the recognition and enforcement of arbitral awards made *in the territory of another Contracting State* (emphasis added)'.[21] Thus it can be seen from this SPC's Notification that the theory of territoriality is the applicable criterion for differentiating between domestic awards and foreign awards.

Nevertheless the PRC Civil Procedure Law uses 'arbitration institution' as a criterion for distinguishing between domestic awards and foreign awards, which is self-evidently different from the theory of territoriality as adopted by the New York Convention. As Article 283 stipulates:[22] 'If an arbitral award of foreign arbitration institution requires recognition and enforcement by a people's court of the People's Republic of China,...the people's court shall act in accordance with international treaties concluded or acceded to by the People's Republic of China or the principle of reciprocity.' This difference highlights the question of whether arbitral awards made by foreign arbitration institutions in the PRC's territory should be regarded as domestic

---

19. Guixiang Liu & Hongyu Shen, *Recognition and Enforcement of Foreign Arbitral Awards in China: A Look Back on a Decade of Court Practices*, 79 Beijing Arbitration 2 (2012).
20. *See* United Nations Treaty Collection, http://treaties.un.org/pages/ViewDetails.aspx?src=TREATY&mtdsg_no=XXII-1&chapter=22&lang=en#EndDec (accessed 4 May 2017).
21. Fa-(Jing)-Fa (1987) No. 5, issued and implemented on 10 April 1987.
22. Article 283 of the current PRC Civil Procedure Law is comparable to Art. 269 of the 1991 version and Art. 267 of the 2007 version.

awards or foreign awards. From the perspective of the reciprocity reservation, awards made by foreign arbitration institutions in the PRC's territory are not 'awards made in the territory of another Contracting State' and are therefore not governed by the New York Convention. Yet such awards are also 'award of foreign arbitration institution' as stipulated in Article 283 of the PRC Civil Procedure Law and should arguably be governed by the New York Convention.

In theory some scholars consider that such type of arbitral awards should pertain to 'non-domestic awards' within the meaning of the latter part of the New York Convention's Article I(1) (i.e., 'arbitral awards not considered as domestic awards in the State where their recognition and enforcement are sought'), and therefore their recognition and enforcement should be determined in accordance with the New York Convention.[23] Other scholars believe that 'non-domestic awards are not parallel with foreign awards, as non-domestic awards are merely foreign awards resulting from different criteria of determination'; awards made by the ICC International Court of Arbitration in the PRC's territory are foreign awards pursuant to the characteristics and criteria for arbitration institutions in the PRC Civil Procedure Law, so the New York Convention can apply to such awards.[24] Yet scholars with differing views have stated that, although such awards are 'non-domestic awards', the PRC does not bear any obligation to enforce 'non-domestic awards' pursuant to the New York Convention.[25] This is because, while Article I(1) of the New York Convention stipulates that the Convention applies to two types of arbitral awards, namely 'foreign arbitral awards' and 'non-domestic awards', the PRC's reservation with regards to a convention should apply to the entire convention and not merely a part of it (i.e., foreign arbitral awards). According to general interpretation, the PRC's reciprocity reservation means that the New York Convention only applies to the recognition and enforcement of 'arbitral awards made in the territory of another Contracting State' and therefore excludes 'non-domestic awards'. It follows that the PRC does not bear any obligation to enforce 'non-domestic awards' in accordance with the New York Convention.

In the opinion of the PRC's leading law scholar Zongyi Fei, if foreign arbitration institutions select the PRC as the arbitral seat, then such awards should be regarded as the PRC's awards capable of revocation.[26] Scholars with similar opinion have stated that, 'although the nationality of such type of awards are yet to be clearly defined due to the imperfection of the PRC legislation, after exploring the trend in the PRC's judicial

---

23. Xiuwen Zhao, *The Research of the Opening of China Arbitration Market*, 27(6) Tribune of Political Science and Law June 69–78 (2009); Xiuwen Zhao, *Recognition and Enforcement of an ICC Arbitral Award in the PRC*, 6 The Jurist 67–72 (2005); Xiuwen Zhao (ed.), *International Commercial Arbitration Law* 157–159 (3rd ed. China Renmin University Press 2012); Yaying Huang, *Foreign Arbitral Award: In Perspective of the New York Convention and the Judicial Practice of China*, 2007(1) Modern Law Science 124, 130 (2007).
24. Ling Yang, *Recognition and Enforcement of Arbitral Awards in China – Based on 'Guide on Foreign-Related Commercial and Maritime Trial' from 2001 to 2011*, 218 The Taiwan Law Review 133, 143 (2013).
25. Bing-bin Lv, *Reflection on Foreign Arbitral Institution to Arbitrate in Our Country – Reservations Made by the PRC When Acceding to the New York Convention*, 2010 (10) Research on Rule of Law 71, 74 (2010).
26. Zongyi Fei, *Comment on the Revision of the Arbitration Act by Fei Zong Yi*, 62 Beijing Arbitration 1, 4 (2007).

Chapter 3: 'Public Policy' and the Even More Unpredictable

practice under the SPC's guidance, such type of awards should, according to the arbitral seat's criteria, be regarded as the PRC's foreign-related awards and be governed by the PRC's regulations concerning the revocation and enforcement of foreign-related awards'.[27] Thus there are considerable disparities in academic opinions.

In practice, the arbitration clause in a case concerning an application by Züblin International GmbH for recognition and enforcement of a foreign arbitral award (the *Züblin* case)[28] was 'Arbitration: 15.3 ICC Rules, Shanghai shall apply'. The ICC International Court of Arbitration made an award in Shanghai pursuant to this arbitration clause. In its decision in 2006 on Züblin's application for this award's recognition and enforcement, the Jiangsu Wuxi Intermediate People's Court held that the award made by the ICC International Court of Arbitration and approved by the Headquarter Secretariat under seal should be viewed as a 'non-domestic award'. Since the relevant party had applied to the people's court for a declaration on the validity of the arbitration agreement and the Court in Technology Development Zone of Jiangsu Province Wuxi City also held such arbitration agreement to be invalid,[29] consequently the award was refused recognition and enforcement under Article V(1)(a) of the New York Convention (namely, the said agreement is not valid under the law to which the parties have subjected it or, failing any indication thereon, under the law of the country where the award was made). By comparison, the award in the *Duferco* case[30] was made by the ICC International Court of Arbitration in Beijing and Zhejiang Ningbo Intermediate People's Court ruled in 2009 that such award was not a PRC's domestic award and should be governed by the New York Convention. The Court also considered that the objection to the relevant arbitration agreement's validity by the relevant party (Ningbo Arts & Crafts Import & Export Co., Ltd.) could not be established due to that party's failure to raise such objection within the statutory period after receiving legal notice.[31]

---

27. Lianbin Song & Jun Wang, *On Authorization, Nationality and Enforcement of ICC Awards Made in Mainland China: Reflections from the Ningbo Intermediate Court's Ruling*, 41(3) Journal of Northwest University (Philosophy and Social Sciences Edition) 154–161 (2011).
28. Jiangsu Wuxi Intermediate People's Court Civil Ruling (2004) Xi-Min-San-Zhong-Zi No. 1, 19 July 2006.
29. The arbitration agreement was held to be invalid by the Court in the Jiangsu Province Wuxi City Technology Development Zone (Xin-Min-Zr-Chu-Zi No. 154, 2 September 2004). The 'Reporting System' applies to this case involving foreign-related arbitration agreement. Upon reporting to the SPC the SPC replied: 'The parties in this case have an arbitration clause in their contract stating 'Arbitration: ICC Rules, Shanghai shall apply'. In circumstances where the parties have not agreed on the law applicable to the validity of arbitration clause and pursuant to the general principles about the law applicable to confirming the validity of arbitration clause, the law of the arbitral seat should apply, as such the law of the People's Republic of China should apply to determine the validity of this arbitration clause.' 'Literally, although the arbitration clause in this case has a clear reference to arbitration, arbitration rules and place of arbitration, however it does not have a clear reference to arbitration institution. Accordingly, this arbitration agreement should be invalid.' *See* (2003) Min-Si-Ta-Zi No. 23, 8 July 2004.
30. Zhejiang Ningbo Intermediate People's Court Civil Ruling (2008) Yong-Zhong-Jian-Zi No. 4, 22 April 2009.
31. Article 13 of the Interpretation of the Supreme People's Court concerning Some Issues on Application of the Arbitration Law of the People's Republic of China stipulates: 'Pursuant to Article 20 para. 2 of the Arbitration Law, if the parties do not object to the validity of arbitration agreement before the arbitral tribunal begins its first hearings but apply to a people's court for declaration of the arbitration agreement's invalidity, the court may refuse to hear such

Thus the Court granted recognition and enforcement of the award as none of the grounds for refusing recognition and enforcement in the New York Convention was applicable. The adjudicating people's courts in both cases regarded awards made by foreign arbitration institutions in the PRC's territory as 'non-domestic awards' and subject to the New York Convention. In the *Züblin* case, the relevant party successfully applied for judicial ruling that the arbitration agreement was invalid, leading to the adjudicating court's refusal to recognise the award pursuant to Article V(1)(a) of the New York Convention. In the *Duferco* case, the relevant party failed to object to the validity of arbitration agreement within the statutory period and consequently could not establish such objection, thereby leading to the award's recognition and enforcement in the absence of any applicable grounds in Article V of the New York Convention.

Nonetheless some judges in the SPC hold opinions different from the opinions of the intermediate courts in the above-mentioned *Züblin* case (Jiangsu Wuxi Intermediate People's Court) and *Duferco* case (Zhejiang Ningbo Intermediate People's Court). In the opinion of Justice Guixiang Liu and Justice Hongyu Shen of the SPC's Fourth Civil Tribunal,[32] the New York Convention should not apply to 'non-domestic awards' in the absence of clear provisions about 'non-domestic awards' in the PRC's legislation. Furthermore: 'from the perspective of maintaining the PRC's judicial sovereignty and jurisdiction, the traditional theory of deciding an award's nationality in accordance with the arbitral seat should apply to incorporate awards made by foreign arbitration institutions in the PRC's territory into the scope of PRC awards, thereby subjecting such awards to revocation, enforcement (or non-enforcement) and other supervision by the PRC. Viewing such awards as "non-domestic awards" is very likely to render such awards stateless or anational. None of the courts would have appropriate jurisdiction to revoke such awards, which is unfavourable to the supervision of arbitration, as well as unfavourable to the protection of the parties' legitimate rights and interest'. On the other hand, Justice Honglei Yang of the SPC's Fourth Civil Tribunal has expressed that currently there are no clear provisions about whether awards made by foreign arbitration institutions in the PRC's territory should pertain to foreign awards or domestic awards.[33] In 2009 the Vice President and Justice of the SPC, Exiang Wan, also opined that 'currently there are no clear provisions' in this regard and indicated that 'this will inevitably cause trouble in enforcing awards'.[34]

---

application. If the parties apply to a people's court for confirmation of the arbitration agreement's validity or revocation of the arbitral decision after the arbitration institution has made a decision on the arbitration agreement's validity, the court may refuse to hear such application'. See Fa-Shi (2006) No. 7, issued on 23 August 2006.

32. Guixiang Liu & Hongyu Shen, *Recognition and Enforcement of Foreign Arbitral Awards in China: A Look Back on a Decade of Court Practices*, 79 Beijing Arbitration 1, 6–8 (2012).
33. Honglei Yang, *Report on the Judicial Review of International Arbitration in Chinese Courts*, 9 (1) International Law Review of Wuhan University 304, 318 (2009).
34. Exiang Wan, *Judicial Practice with Regards to the New York Convention in China*, 276 Journal of Law Application, 6 (2009). Exiang Wan was elected as the Vice Chairman of the Standing Committee of the National People's Congress since March 2013 and consequently relieved from his judicial obligations: *see* the 'Dismissal List of Standing Committee of the National People's Congress' passed by the first meeting of the Twelfth Standing Committee of the National People's Congress on 19 March 2013.

Thus the current PRC legal system does not have any clear provisions and experts have various opinions. The academia is appealing for legislative solutions to this problem[35] in order to urge the PRC to become an attractive arbitral seat in the international society.[36]

3.1.2 Recognition and Enforcement of Arbitral Awards of Taiwan, Hong Kong and Macau

Although the New York Convention does not apply to the recognition and enforcement of arbitral awards of Taiwan, Hong Kong and Macau, as discussed below, the relevant legislative provisions also refer to 'public order' or 'social and public interest'.

3.1.2.1 Taiwan

Article 14 paragraph 2 of the Provisions of the Supreme People's Court on Recognition and Enforcement of the Arbitral Awards of the Taiwan Region (effective from 1 July 2015) stipulates that,[37] '[w]here the relevant dispute is not capable of settlement by arbitration pursuant to PRC law, or recognition of the arbitral award would violate the One China policy or other basic principles of law or damage social and public interest', a people's court shall refuse recognition of an arbitral award made in Taiwan.

3.1.2.2 Hong Kong

Pursuant to Article 7 item 3 of the SPC's Arrangement Concerning Mutual Enforcement of Arbitral Awards Between the Mainland and the Hong Kong Special Administrative Region, the enforcement of the award may be refused if the court of the Mainland holds that the enforcement of the arbitral award in the Mainland would be contrary to the public interest of the Mainland, or if the court of the Hong Kong Special Administrative Region (HKSAR) decides that the enforcement of the arbitral award in Hong Kong would be contrary to the public policy of the HKSAR.[38] It is noted that the phrase 'be contrary to the public interest of the Mainland' is used when addressing the Mainland people's courts' non-enforcement of arbitral awards made in the HKSAR, whereas the phrase 'contrary to the public policy of the HKSAR' is used when addressing the Hong Kong courts' non-enforcement of arbitral awards made in the Mainland.

---

35. Kun Fan, *Prospects of Foreign Arbitration Institutions Administering Arbitration in China*, 28(4) Journal of International Arbitration 353 (2011); Xiaohong Liu (ed.), *A Monographic Study on International Commercial Law* 426–428 (Law Press 2009).
36. Kun Fan, *ibid.*
37. Fa-Shi (2015) No. 14, issued on 29 June 2015 and implemented on 1 July 2015.
38. Fa-Shi (2000) No. 3, issued on 24 January 2000 and implemented on 1 February 2000. English text available at: http://www.doj.gov.hk/eng/mainland/intracountry.html (accessed 4 May 2017).

3.1.2.3 Macau

The latter part of Article 7 paragraph 1 of the SPC's Arrangement Concerning Mutual Recognition and Enforcement of Arbitral Awards Between the Mainland and Macau Special Administrative Region stipulates:[39] 'An application for the recognition and enforcement of an arbitral award may be refused at the request of the party subject to the application if that party furnishes proof about one of the following circumstances (which are considered and verified by the relevant court)... (v)... a competent court of the Mainland finds that the recognition and enforcement of the arbitral award would violate *the Mainland's basic principles of law or social and public interest*, or a competent court of Macau Special Administration Region finds that the recognition and enforcement of the arbitral award in Macau Special Administration Region would violate that Region's basic principles of law or *public order*' (emphasis added).

3.1.2.4 Comparative Analysis

A comparison of the various provisions cited above reveals some subtle differences in terminology. Such differences are worth noting, as they may cause doubts in interpretation and perplexity in application during the practical application of these provisions. The following elaborates on the important differences.[40]

First, before the implementation of the Provisions of the Supreme People's Court on Recognition and Enforcement of the Arbitral Awards of the Taiwan Region on 1 July 2015 ('the New Provisions'), Article 19 of the SPC's Provisions on the People's Courts' Recognition of Taiwan Courts' Civil Judgments (repealed on 1 July 2015 and hereinafter referred to as 'Old Provisions'[41]) governed the applications to the people's courts for 'recognition of Taiwan Region's relevant civil courts' judgments and Taiwan Region's institutional arbitral awards'. The reference to 'Taiwan Region's institutional arbitral awards' only in the Old Provisions may be interpreted as excluding awards made by ad hoc or non-institutional arbitration,[42] as well as seemingly excluding awards made in Taiwan by foreign arbitration institutions (such as the ICC

---

39. Fa-Shi (2007) No. 17, issued on 12 December 2007.
40. *See also* Xianchu Zhang, *The Contribution of the Macau SAR to the Developments of Regional Judicial Assistance in Civil and Commercial Matters and its Characteristics*, 2010(3) Journal of Comparative Law 93, 96–98 (2010) for the detailed differences between the SPC's Arrangement on the Mutual Enforcement of Arbitral Awards Between the Mainland and Hong Kong Special Administrative Region and the Arrangement Concerning Mutual Recognition and Enforcement of Arbitral Awards Between the Mainland and Macau Special Administrative Region. Such detailed discussions are omitted as they are less relevant to topic of this book.
41. Fa-Shi (1998) No. 11, issued on 22 May 1998 and implemented on 26 May 1998. Article 23 of the Provisions of the Supreme People's Court on Recognition and Enforcement of the Arbitral Awards of the Taiwan Region (effective from 1 July 2015) provides that the Old Provisions would be repealed on the same date when the New Provisions became effective.
42. For instance, some PRC scholars have expressed that the Old Provisions 'clearly exclude Taiwan Region's ad hoc arbitral awards': *see* Xiaohong Liu, *Scheme of Mutual Recognition and Enforcement of Cross-Strait Arbitral Awards: Examination & Revision*, 12 Law Science 86, 89 (2011). Yet other scholars adopt different view that, in terms of interpretation, ad hoc arbitral awards made in Taiwan can still be approved and enforced pursuant to the Old Provisions: *see*

International Court of Arbitration, etc.), as such foreign arbitration institutions are not Taiwan Region's arbitration institutions. Such terminology is not equivalent to the term 'civil arbitral awards made in Mainland China' used in Article 74 paragraph 1 of the Act Governing Relations Between the People of Taiwan Area and the Mainland Area.

Further comparison with the arrangements for enforcing the arbitral awards of Hong Kong and Macau indicates that the 'theory of territoriality' applies to these awards, as can be seen in the terminology 'arbitral awards made in Hong Kong Special Administrative Region pursuant to the Arbitration Act of Hong Kong Special Administrative Region' and 'civil and commercial arbitral awards made in Macau'. Here the criterion is the place where the award is made, which includes institutional awards and ad hoc awards made in Hong Kong and Macau. The first part of Article 1 paragraph 1 of the SPC's Arrangement Concerning Mutual Recognition and Enforcement of Arbitral Awards Between the Mainland and Macau Special Administrative Region provides for the 'recognition and enforcement of civil and commercial arbitral awards made in Macau by arbitration institutions and arbitrators of Macau Special Administrative Region pursuant to Macau Special Administrative Region's arbitration laws and regulations', which clearly includes institutional awards and ad hoc awards.[43] With respect to arbitral awards made in Hong Kong, the SPC's Notice of the Supreme People's Court on Issues concerning the Execution of Hong Kong Arbitral Awards in the Mainland specifically clarifies:[44] 'Where the relevant party applies to a people's court for the enforcement of ad hoc arbitral awards made in Hong Kong Special Administrative Region, or arbitral awards made in Hong Kong Special Administrative Region by the ICC International Court of Arbitration or other foreign arbitration institutions, the people's court shall examine in accordance with the Arrangement. If none of the circumstances in Article 7 of the Arrangement applies, the relevant arbitral award may be enforced in the Mainland.'

In comparison, the SPC's Old Provisions had different and seemingly unbalanced provisions about the enforcement of arbitral awards of Taiwan, Hong Kong and Macau. In practice, ad hoc arbitral awards are rare[45] but not non-existent in Taiwan.[46]

Lianbin Song, *A Probe into Some Issues on Recognition and Enforcement of Taiwan's Arbitral Awards in Mainland China*, 2 Chinese Yearbook of Private international and Comparative Law 399–408 (1999).

43. One of the questions raised during the press conference on 30 October 2007 about the Arrangement Concerning Mutual Recognition and Enforcement of Arbitral Awards Between the Mainland and Macau Special Administrative Region was whether or not this Arrangement 'recognizes ad hoc arbitration'. The SPC's Vice President, Song Huang, replied: 'According to the laws of the Macau Special Administrative Region, Macau has ad hoc arbitration system, and it is understood that there are more ad hoc arbitral awards than institutional arbitral awards in Macau. Although the current Mainland laws do not provide for ad hoc arbitration, however the mutual recognition and enforcement of arbitral awards between the Contracting States pursuant to the New York Convention should include ad hoc arbitral awards. As a Contracting State, the People's Republic of China should recognize ad hoc arbitral awards of Contracting States, and should recognize and enforce ad hoc arbitral awards of other law jurisdictions within the state'. *See* the website of China News, http://www.chinanews.com/ga/kong/news/2007/10-30/1063837.shtml (accessed 4 May 2017).
44. Fa (2009) No. 415, 30 December 2009.
45. According to Nigel Li & Joyce Fan: 'An alternative to institutional arbitration is ad hoc arbitration. Ad hoc arbitration in Taiwan may be conducted by following the procedure agreed

Moreover, there have been arbitral awards made in Taiwan by foreign arbitration institutions (such as the ICC International Court of Arbitration, etc.).[47] Hence the discriminatory treatment of only recognising 'Taiwan Region's institutional arbitral awards' cannot be said to have no effect in practice.

Following the practitioners' repeated requests for addressing the issues mentioned above,[48] the SPC implemented the New Provisions (Provisions on Recognition and Enforcement of the Arbitral Awards of the Taiwan Region) and at the same time repealed the Old Provisions from 1 July 2015. Articles 1 and 2 of the New Provisions have resolved these issues by providing for application to the people's courts for the recognition and enforcement of 'the arbitral awards concerning civil or commercial disputes made by permanent arbitration institutions or ad hoc arbitral tribunals in Taiwan Region pursuant to the Taiwan's arbitration laws, including arbitral awards, settlement agreements and mediated settlement agreements reached during arbitration proceedings'.

Second, the Old Provisions did not have specific provisions for the recognition and enforcement of Taiwan's arbitral awards, as Article 19 of the Old Provisions merely stipulated that these Provisions apply to the application for recognition of 'Taiwan Region's institutional arbitral awards'. This approach was imperfect, a clear example being that many of the circumstances for refusing recognition of court judgments specified in Article 9 of the Old Provisions were inapplicable to arbitral awards. By contrast, there are specific provisions for the enforcement of arbitral awards made in

---

upon by the parties, subject to the provisions of the Arbitration Law. However, ad hoc arbitration is very rare in the R.O.C.' *See* Nigel N.T. Li & Joyce C. Fan, *Taiwan* Chapter in *Dispute Resolution in Asia* 337, 343 (Michael Pryles ed., Kluwer Law International 2002).

46. A widely discussed case in recent years was the case concerning disputes arising from a construction contract between Jinchengfeng Construction Co., Ltd. and National Taiwan University Hospital Bei-Hu Branch. The arbitral award was made by a tribunal consisting of En-Fong Lan, Sen-Hsiung Tai and James L Yu. *See* Helena Hsi-Chia Chen, *A Review of the Taiwanese Court's Ruling on Ad Hoc Arbitral Awards*, 20(1) Asian Pacific Law Review 89 (2012); Helena Hsi-Chia Chen, *A Review of the Taiwanese Court's Ruling on Ad Hoc Arbitral Awards – Comment on Taiwan High Court' s Ruling: 99 Fei-Kang-Zi No. 122 and Its Possible Impacts*, 93 Arbitration 26–41 (2011); Chin-Yen Wang, *Has Taiwan Only Institutional Arbitration But No Ad Hoc Arbitration? A Serious Mistake behind Formosan Supreme Court Case 2010-Tai-Kang-Zi No. 358*, 171 Taiwan Law Journal 193, 198 (2011).

47. An example is Taiwan Shilin District Court Civil Ruling 97 Zhong-Zhi-Zi No. 2 (9 March 2009) concerning ICC Case No. 14876/JEM with Taipei, Taiwan as the arbitral seat. Although this case was subject to two appeals by the respondent, the two appellate courts both upheld the decision of the first instance court, please *see* Taiwan Shilin District Court Civil Ruling 98 Kang-Zi No. 67 (31 December 2009); Taiwan High Court Civil Ruling 99 Fei-Kang-Zi No. 24 (26 February 2010).

48. *See*, e.g., Helena Hsi-Chia Chen, *The Current Status and Future Possible Developments with Regards to Cross-Strait Mutual Recognition and Enforcement of Arbitration Awards and Mediated Settlement Agreements*, 17 Chinese Yearbook of Private International Law and Comparative Law 188–206 (April 2016). An earlier version of this book manuscript was presented at the Third Law Forum for the Peaceful Development Across the Taiwan Strait on 25 August 2014, during which Justice Zhonglin He, Deputy Director of the SPC's Research Office and Director of the SPC's Hong Kong, Macau and Taiwan Task Force indicated that the SPC was revising the relevant regulations and would refer to the author's opinion. Subsequently in June 2015 the SPC issued the new Provisions on Recognition and Enforcement of Taiwan Courts' Civil Judgments and the new Provisions on Recognition and Enforcement of the Arbitral Awards of the Taiwan Region (effective from 1 July 2015). The author is especially pleased to see that these New Provisions have resolved several practical issues.

Hong Kong and Macau (in the two Arrangements mentioned above). The New Provisions have addressed this problem by specifically providing for the recognition and enforcement of Taiwan's arbitral awards, and Article 14 of the New Provisions stipulates the grounds for refusing the recognition of such arbitral awards.

Third, under the Old Provisions, Article 4 of the SPC's Notification concerning the conscientious and consistent enforcement of the Old Provisions stipulated:[49] 'In the current period of time, when the party applies for the approval of Taiwan Region's civil court judgments, a people's court must, before deciding whether to allow or refuse approval, submit to the higher people's court of its jurisdiction for review. The higher people's court must provide timely reply about agreeing or disagreeing with such opinion and report to the Supreme People's Court for filing.' This raises a possible practical question of whether Article 4 also applies to cases concerning applications for recognising Taiwan Region's institutional arbitral awards, so that reporting to the SPC for filing purposes would suffice, as opposed to adhering to the 'Reporting System'[50] whereby the SPC must 'reply'. The author raised this question with a judge of the SPC's Fourth Civil Tribunal,[51] who replied that applications for approval of Taiwan Region's institutional arbitral awards, enforcement of Hong Kong's arbitral awards, approval and enforcement of Macau's arbitral awards, as well as for recognition and enforcement of foreign arbitral awards, are all subject to the Reporting System, thereby pending the SPC's 'reply' before their determination. The above-mentioned Article 4 of the SPC Notification applies to provisions of the Old Provisions concerning 'Taiwan Region's relevant civil court judgments' but does not fit well with arbitral awards.

The implementation of the New Provisions has also addressed this question because the explicit abolition of the Old Provisions in the New Provisions entails that the above-mentioned SPC's Notification about the enforcement of the Old Provisions has lost its basis of attachment and should therefore expired. At the same time, Article 13 of the New Provisions is sufficient proof of the Reporting System's applicability, as it stipulates that 'the people's court shall promptly review the application for approval of Taiwan Region's arbitral award..., if it decides to refuse approval or reject the application, it shall, before making such decision, report to the Supreme People's Court within two months from the date the application was registered with the court in accordance with relevant provisions'.

As seen from the previous three points of discussion, the Old Provisions did not meet actual demands and required overall adjustment by providing individual specifications. The SPC's implementation of the New Provisions since 1 July 2015 has resolved these practical issues. In particular, Article 14 paragraph 4 of the Cross-Strait Bilateral Investment Protection and Promotion Agreement expressly provides that '[t]he parties to a commercial dispute may designate an arbitration institution of either side of the strait and agree on the seat of arbitration'.[52] This provision about dispute

---

49. Fa (1998) No. 54, issued and implemented on 17 June 1998.
50. See s. 3.2.1.2 of this chapter for detailed discussions of the 'Reporting System'.
51. Cited from the reply to the author's email by Justice Xiaoli Gao of the SPC's Fourth Civil Tribunal dated 9 January 2014.
52. For the possible issues encountering the interpretation, application and practice of Art. 14 para. 4 of the Cross-Strait Bilateral Investment Protection and Promotion Agreement, *see* Helena

settlement mechanism for commercial disputes between private parties is rare in investment protection agreements. The New Provisions' implementation is indeed praiseworthy as it assists with enhancing the parties' willingness to submit their disputes to arbitration by Taiwan's arbitration institution or agree on using Taiwan (or a Taiwanese city) as the seat of arbitration.

Fourth, although cases involving Taiwan, Hong Kong and Macau are generally dealt with as foreign-related cases in the PRC, different terminologies apply to the recognition and enforcement of extra-territorial arbitral awards depending on whether they are foreign awards or awards of Taiwan, Hong Kong and Macau. For the recognition and enforcement of foreign arbitral awards, the PRC courts apply Article V(2)(b) of the New York Convention to consider whether such recognition and enforcement would be contrary to the PRC's 'public policy'. For the enforcement of arbitral awards made in Taiwan, Hong Kong or Macau, the previously mentioned Provisions and Arrangements do not use the term 'public policy' as specified in Article V(2)(b) of the New York Convention and instead requires the PRC courts to consider whether the enforcement of such awards would violate the PRC's 'social and public interest'.

It should also be noted that the terminology used in the two above-mentioned Arrangements has certain directionality. Pursuant to these two Arrangements, for the enforcement in the PRC of arbitral awards made in Hong Kong or Macau, the question for the PRC courts is whether such enforcement would violate 'social and public interest of the Mainland'. On the contrary, for the enforcement in Hong Kong or Macau Special Administrative Region of arbitral awards made in the PRC, the question for the courts in these two Regions is whether such enforcement would violate the 'public policy' of Hong Kong or Macau Special Administrative Region. Such inconsistent terminologies have raised concerns among scholars in Hong Kong. For instance, the law professor of Hong Kong University, Xianchu Zhang, stated in 1999 (before the SPC's Arrangement Concerning Mutual Enforcement of Arbitral Awards Between the Mainland and the Hong Kong Special Administrative Region was signed on 24 January 2000):[53]

> [S]ocial public interest in China can be much broader and more flexible. It includes not only adopted rules, expressed state commitments and social morality, but also less transparent state interest and unstable short-term policies. Invocation of the doctrine may not only deny the application of any possibly conflicting foreign laws, but also international practice. It has been characterized as not only a legal institution, but also a political means to implement current domestic policy.

Hsi-Chia Chen, *Commercial Arbitration after the Cross-Strait Bilateral Investment Protection and Promotion Agreement – Focused on the Interpretation and Application of Article 14.4 of the Cross-strait Bilateral Investment Protection and Promotion Agreement*, 92 NTPU Law Review 137–185 (2014).

53. Xianchu Zhang, *The Agreement Between Mainland China and the Hong Kong SAR on Mutual Enforcement of Arbitral Awards: Problems and Prospects*, 29 Hong Kong Law Journal 463, 476 (1999). *See also* Xianchu Zhang, *Establishing the System for Mutual Enforcement of Arbitral Awards Between Hong Kong and Mainland China and Related Questions*, in *Judicial Practice of New York Convention and International Commercial Arbitration* (CIETAC ed., Law Press 2010).

Despite this, from the cases available to the author, in more than ten years since the implementation of the SPC's Arrangement Concerning Mutual Enforcement of Arbitral Awards Between the Mainland and the Hong Kong Special Administrative Region, it cannot be observed that the SPC has used different criteria for determining the recognition and enforcement of 'arbitral awards made in Hong Kong of Macau' and 'foreign arbitral awards' because of the above-mentioned different terminologies. Internationally, scholars have commented in 2004 that there 'appears in fact to be no difference in practice' despite the difference in terminology.[54] Similarly, according to Hong Kong scholars:[55] 'Article 7 of the SPC's Arrangement Concerning Mutual Enforcement of Arbitral Awards Between the Mainland and the Hong Kong Special Administrative Region actually shifts and applies the grounds and criteria in Article V(2)(b) of the New York Convention to Hong Kong and Mainland China. This provides a firm foundation for integrating the general direction of the criteria of arbitration judicial review in both places, as such integration is gradually emerging since implementing the Arrangement.'

To date the author has not seen any cases in which a people's court has refused recognition and enforcement of Taiwan Region's institutional arbitral awards on the basis of 'violation of social and public interest'.

Fifth, the phrase 'violate the One China policy or other basic principles of law or damage social and public interest' in Article 14 paragraph 2 of the Provisions of the Supreme People's Court on Recognition and Enforcement of the Arbitral Awards of the Taiwan Region is similar to the phrase 'violate the Mainland basic principles of law or social and public interest' in the Arrangement concerning the recognition and enforcement of arbitral awards made in Macau. Yet these differ from the phrase 'contrary to the public interest of the Mainland' in the Arrangement concerning the enforcement of arbitral awards made in Hong Kong, namely, the omission of national or 'Mainland basic principles of law'. Since 'social and public interest' is generally considered to be wider than and inclusive of 'national or Mainland basic principles of law', there should be no substantial effect in practice regardless of whether 'national or Mainland basic principles of law' is used in parallel with 'social and public interest'. It is noteworthy that Article 14 paragraph 2 of the New Provisions also specifically states that 'violation of the One China policy' is one type of violation of basic principles of law.

Finally, in Chinese, a term with a subtle distinction, 'Ren-ke (认可)', is used for recognition with respect to the recognition and enforcement of arbitral awards between Taiwan and Mainland China (*see* Article 74 of the Act Governing Relations between the People of Taiwan Area and the Mainland Area, Article 19 of the Old Provisions and the New Provisions), whereas the term 'Cheng-Ren (承認)' is used for recognition with respect to the recognition and enforcement foreign arbitral awards in Taiwan (*see* Articles 47–51 of Taiwan Arbitration Law) as well as the recognition and enforcement of foreign arbitral awards in Mainland China (*see* Article 283 of the PRC

---

54. Andrew Jefferies, *Arbitration in the PRC: Enforcement Issues*, in *Arbitration in China: A Practical Guide* 295, 343 (Daniel R. Fung & Shengchang Wang eds, Sweet & Maxwell 2004).
55. Weixia Gu, *Judicial Review of Arbitral Awards in Hong Kong and the Mainland: Lessons and Convergence Between Two Jurisdictions in China*, The Jurist 106, 117 (2009).

Arbitration Law). While we usually do not distinguish these terms in English, the author would like to give an in-depth analysis on this nuance below.

Why is there such differentiation in terminology? Does such differentiation have specific meaning? A Taiwanese scholar has stated that 'Ren-ke (認可)' is the procedure through which arbitral awards made in the PRC become effective in Taiwan, and this differs from the 'Cheng-Ren (承認)' procedure for recognising foreign arbitral awards.[56] In speculation of legislative intent, another Taiwanese scholar commented that the approach of using 'Ren-ke (認可)' (approval) instead of 'Cheng-Ren (承認)' (recognition) in order to avoid the 'recognition' (namely 'Cheng-Ren (承認)) and 'application' of PRC laws is truly correct.[57] The author's thorough reading of the parliamentary proceedings and drafts of the Act Governing Relations between the People of Taiwan Area and the Mainland Area (as detailed below) did not uncover any explanation for using the term 'approval'. Since the distinction between 'approval' and 'recognition' is not within the scope of this book, the following paragraphs simply explain the legislative history without further in-depth discussions.

Legislative examples concerning the mutual recognition/approval and enforcement of arbitral awards between Mainland China and Taiwan were first seen in 1992 in Article 74 of Act Governing Relations between the People of Taiwan Area and the Mainland Area. In the Executive Yuan's written proposal for deliberation by the Legislative Yuan in 1990, Article 62 of the Draft Act Governing Relations between the People of Taiwan Area and the Mainland Area (which is comparable to Article 74 of the current Act) already used the term 'approval',[58] even though the Draft Act and its explanatory notes did not specifically explain any reason for using the term 'approval' instead of the term 'recognition'.

Subsequent draft proposals submitted to joint views by the Judiciary, Internal Administration and Organic Laws and Statutes Committees are as follows:

---

56. Lillian Chu, *Chapter 7: Foreign Arbitral Awards*, in *New Study on Arbitration Act* 399 (Chung-Sen Yang et. al., 3rd ed, CAA, Taipei 2012).
57. *See* the relevant discussions in John Huan-Wen Chen, *Cross-Strait Commercial Disputes and Arbitration Practice* 276 (Perennial Publishing 1993): 'Article 74 paragraph 2 of the Act Governing Relations between the People of Taiwan Area and the Mainland Area states that if the judgments or awards recognized/'Ren-ke (認可)' by a court ruling in the preceding paragraph require performance, the ruling may serve as a writ of execution. This paragraph deliberately avoids the terms 'a ruling to recognize/Cheng-Ren(承認)' and 'a ruling to enforce' and instead use the term 'Ren-ke (認可)' and even delete the procedures for enforcement rulings. *The legislative intent speculated by this author of the approach of using 'Ren-ke (認可)' instead of 'Cheng-Ren(承認)' so as to avoid the 'recognition', namely 'Cheng-Ren (承認)' and 'application' of PRC laws is truly correct* (emphasis added).'

    In addition, Justice Jiun-Yi Lin has investigated the arbitration laws across the Taiwan Strait for many years but has not commented on such differences in terminology, please *see* Jiun-Yi Lin, *Collection of Taiwan's Court Judgments Concerning Recognition of Arbitral Awards Made in Mainland China and Hong Kong* 1–25 (CAA, Taipei 2008); Jiun-Yi Lin, *Practice of Arbitration Act* 386–387 (Yung-Ran Culture Publishing Inc. 2001).
58. Publication Department of the Legislative Yuan, 79(98) Legislative Yuan Official Gazette 46–83 (1990), especially pp. 55 and 77.

Chapter 3: 'Public Policy' and the Even More Unpredictable

- 'Draft Act Governing Relations between Taiwan and Mainland China' proposed by S. K. Chao and other twenty-two committee members (abbreviated as the 'Chao proposal');
- 'Draft Act Governing Relations between the People of Taiwan Area and the Mainland Area' proposed by Lien-Hui Chou and other twenty committee members (abbreviated as the 'Chou proposal');
- 'Draft Act Governing Relations between the People of Taiwan Area and the Mainland Area' proposed by Kuei-Miao Chen and other twenty committee members (abbreviated as the 'Chen proposal');
- 'Draft Act Governing Relations between the People of Taiwan Area and the Mainland Area' proposed by Shou-chung Ting and other thirty-four committee members (abbreviated as the 'Ting proposal');
- 'Draft Act Governing Relations between the People of Taiwan Area and the Mainland Area' proposed by the Executive Yuan for deliberation by the Legislative Yuan (abbreviated as the 'Executive Yuan proposal'); and
- Amendment to the 'Draft Act Governing Relations between the People of Taiwan Area and the Mainland Area' by the Joint Committees.

In the various proposals listed above, only the Chao proposal used the term 'recognition' whereas the term 'approval' was used in the Chen proposal, Ting proposal, the Executive Yuan proposal and the amendment by the Joint Committees. The Chou proposal merely contained provisions for 'recognition of PRC court judgments' but not for arbitral awards.[59] Yet none of the proposals specifically explained the reasons for using the term 'approval' (or 'recognition'). The Executive Yuan proposal was ultimately adopted by the Legislative Yuan, and the Minister of Justice at the time, Yu-wen Lu, also did not specifically explain the use of the term 'approval' instead of the term 'recognition' in Article 74 of the Draft Act during his presentation of the Executive Department Yuan's proposal before the Legislative Yuan.[60] Nor were there any specific explanations for using the term 'approval' in the second and third reading of the Draft Act.[61]

Subsequently the term 'approval' was still used in the regulations issued by the SPC of the PRC: the Old Provisions (concerning the people's courts' approval

---

59. 'Comparison Chart of Draft Provisions of the Joint Committee's amendment to the Draft Act Governing Relations between the People of Taiwan Area and the Mainland Area, Draft Act Governing Relations between Taiwan and Mainland China proposed by S.K. Chao et al., Draft Act Governing Relations between the People of Taiwan Area and the Mainland Area proposed by Lien-Hui Chou et al., Draft Act Governing Relations between the People of Taiwan Area and the Mainland Area' proposed by the Executive Yuan, Draft Act Governing Relations between the People of Taiwan Area and the Mainland Area proposed by Kuei-Miao Chen et al., and Draft Act Governing Relations between the People of Taiwan Area and the Mainland Area proposed by Shou-chung Ting et al.', Publication Department of the Legislative Yuan, 81(51) Legislative Yuan Official Gazette 161–162 (1992).
60. For the explanation by Yu-wen Lu, see Legislative Yuan Official Gazette, ibid. 59–65.
61. For the clause-by-clause discussions during the Second Reading at the Legislative Yuan, please see Publication Department of the Legislative Yuan, 81(58) Legislative Yuan Official Gazette 346. For the Third Reading and relevant records, see Publication Department of the Legislative Yuan, 81(58) Legislative Yuan Official Gazette 367–368.

of Taiwan Region's relevant civil court judgments)[62] in 1998 and the Supplementary Provisions[63] in 2009, as well as the New Provisions (concerning the approval and enforcement of Taiwan Region's arbitral awards) in 2015. Again the SPC has not specifically explained the reasons for using the term 'approval'.

3.1.3 Summary

As summarised below, the PRC has been basically following certain principles in its choice of terminology when prescribing regulatory provisions:

(1) 'Social and public interest' is used in legislative provisions for domestic arbitral awards (including foreign-related arbitral awards and domestic arbitral awards without any foreign elements).
(2) 'Public policy' is used in relation to the recognition and enforcement of foreign arbitral awards in the PRC.
(3) 'Social and public interest' is used in relation to the approval and enforcement of arbitral awards of Hong Kong, Macau and Taiwan in the PRC. Yet 'public policy' is still used for the enforcement by the Hong Kong courts and Macau courts of arbitral awards made in the PRC (as seen in the SPC's Arrangement Concerning Mutual Enforcement of Arbitral Awards Between the Mainland and the Hong Kong Special Administrative Region, as well as the Arrangement Concerning Mutual Recognition and Enforcement of Arbitral Awards Between the Mainland and Macau Special Administrative Region).

In other words, the PRC's regulatory provisions in principle use the term 'public policy' in relation to the New York Convention. The use of the same term 'public policy' (as specified in Article V(2)(b)) of the New York Convention) in the two SPC's Arrangements concerning the enforcement by the Hong Kong courts and Macau courts of arbitral awards made in the Mainland, arose from the consideration that Hong Kong Arbitration Ordinance uses the term 'public policy',[64] while in 2007 Macau Chief Executive Notice No. 3/2007 promulgated the PRC's notification concerning the application of the New York Convention to Macau Special Administrative Region together with the official Chinese version of the New York Convention.[65]

In light of the PRC's legal evolution, and the continuous use of violation of 'social and public interest' (rather than 'public policy') in the current PRC law as a ground for refusing the enforcement of arbitral awards made in Taiwan, Hong Kong or Macau, it is evident that the term 'social and public interest' plays a certain important role in the

---

62. *Supra* n. 41.
63. Fa-Shi (2009) No. 4, issued on 24 April 2009 and implemented on 14 May 2009.
64. Article 40E(3) of Hong Kong Arbitration Ordinance of 1 February 2000 stipulated the grounds for refusing the enforcement of domestic arbitral awards to include 'the enforcement of that award would be contrary to public policy'. Article 95(3)(b) of Hong Kong Arbitration Ordinance of 2014 also uses the same terminology.
65. Jianguo Lai, *Amendment of the Macao Arbitration System*, 95 Administracao: Revista de Administracao Publica de Macau 63, 64 n. 5 (2012).

Chapter 3: 'Public Policy' and the Even More Unpredictable

legal system for enforcing 'extra-territorial' arbitral awards (including foreign arbitral awards and arbitral awards of Taiwan, Hong Kong and Macau) in the PRC.

3.2 'SOCIAL AND PUBLIC INTEREST': THE USUAL TERMINOLOGY IN PRC LEGAL SYSTEM

As discussed in the previous section, the PRC arbitration-related legal system did not use the term 'public policy' before the PRC acceded to the New York Convention. The provision concerning 'public policy' in Article V(2)(b) of the New York Convention only began to apply after the PRC became a Contracting State. Yet this does not mean that similar concepts did not exist in the PRC legal system. According to the previously mentioned Article 204 of the PRC Civil Procedure Law (For Trial Implementation) of 1982: 'When a people's court of the People's Republic of China is entrusted by a foreign court with the enforcement of a final judgment or *award*, the people's court shall examine it in accordance with any international treaty concluded or acceded to by the People's Republic of China or the principle of reciprocity. If the court finds that the judgment or award does not violate the basic principles of the laws of the People's Republic of China or national and social interest, it shall recognise the validity of the judgment or award and enforce it according to the procedures specified in this Law' (emphasis added). The terminology 'the basic principles of the laws of the People's Republic of China or national and social interest' already existed at that time.

It is generally considered that the concept closest to 'public policy' in the PRC legal system is 'social and public interest'. In the field of PRC civil commercial and economic law, the term 'social and public interest' first appeared in the PRC Economic Contract Law in 1982 (which has expired).[66] According to Article 4 of that Law at that time: '[w]hen concluding an economic contract, the parties shall comply with national laws, and conform to the demands of national policies and plans. Any entity or individual shall not use the contract to conduct illegal activities, disrupt economic order, destroy national plans, damage national interest and social and public interest, or obtain illegal income'. This Law of 1982 has been repealed by the PRC Contract Law, although Article 7 of the new (and current) Contract Law is similar: 'In concluding and performing a contract, the parties shall comply with the laws and administrative regulations, respect social ethics, and shall not disrupt social and economic order or damage social and public interest.' The PRC Contract Law also expressly specifies damage to social and public interest as one of the circumstances for invalidating a contract (*see* Article 52 paragraph 1. item 4). Simultaneously Article 150 requires that 'the applicable foreign law or international customs shall not violate the social and public interest of the People's Republic of China'. Subsequently in 2009 the National People's Congress Standing Committee (NPCSC) slightly revised Article 7 of the PRC Civil Law, which currently reads: 'civil activities shall respect social ethics and shall not

---

66. Order No. 12 of the Chairman of the Standing Committee of the National People's Congress of the People's Republic of China, issued on 13 December 1981, subsequently repealed by the PRC Contract Law: *see* Art. 428 of the PRC Contract Law.

damage social and public interest or disrupt social and economic order'.[67] Furthermore, the PRC laws about corporations, negotiable instruments, insurance, etc. all contain provisions relating to 'social and public interest'.[68]

With respect to arbitration-related regulations, the PRC Arbitration Law and the PRC Civil Procedure Law both provide for 'social and public interest', the content of which is shown in the Table 3.1 below.

Table 3.1 Comparison of Provisions Concerning 'Social and Public Interest' in PRC Arbitration Law and Civil Procedure Law

	Domestic Arbitral Awards	Foreign-Related Arbitral Awards
Revocation of arbitral awards	Article 58 of Arbitration Law: Paragraph 1: Where a party furnishes proof that the arbitral award involves one of the following circumstances, the party may apply to the intermediate people's court of the arbitration institution's location to set aside the award: (1) There was no arbitration agreement. (2) The award deals with matters beyond the scope of the arbitration agreement or the authority of the arbitration institution. (3) The composition of the arbitral tribunal or the arbitral procedure was contrary to the applicable legal procedures. (4) The evidence on which the award is based was forged. (5) The other party withheld evidence which is sufficient to affect the impartiality of arbitration. (6) During the arbitration the arbitrator(s) demanded or accepted bribes, engaged in favouritism or malpractice for personal gain, or perverted the law. Paragraph 2: The people's court shall set aside the award after its relevant panel examined and verified that the award involves	Article 70 of Arbitration Law: Where a party furnishes proof that the *foreign-related arbitral award* involves one of the circumstances specified in *Article 260 paragraph 1 of the Civil Procedure Law*, the people's court shall, upon examination and verification by its relevant panel, set aside the award. (Here the reference to Article 260 pertains to the 1991 version of the Civil Procedure Law, which was renumbered to Article 258 in 2007 and Article 274 in 2012 without any changes to content. In addition, it should be specifically noted that Article 70 of Arbitration Law only cites paragraph 1 but not paragraph 2 of Article 260 of Civil Procedure Law.)

---

67. Decision of the Standing Committee of the National People's Congress concerning modification of laws, Order of the President No. 18, issued and implemented on 27 August 2009.
68. Please *see* Qilin Fu & Jinjing Luo, *Social Public Interests and Economic Law*, 2007(7) Hebei Law Review 23–24 (2007).

Chapter 3: 'Public Policy' and the Even More Unpredictable

	Domestic Arbitral Awards	*Foreign-Related Arbitral Awards*
	one of the circumstances specified in the preceding paragraph. Paragraph 3: The people's court shall set aside the award if it finds that the award violates social and public interest.	
Non-enforcement of arbitral awards	Article 237 of the current Civil Procedure Law: Paragraph 2: Where the respondent furnishes proof that the arbitral award involves one of the following circumstances, the people's court shall, upon examination and verification by its relevant panel, refuse enforcement: (1) The parties' contract did not have an arbitration agreement or the parties did not reach any arbitration agreement in writing after the dispute arose. (2) The award deals with matters beyond the scope of the arbitration agreement or the authority of the arbitration institution. (3) The composition of the arbitral tribunal or the arbitral procedure was contrary to the applicable legal procedures. (4) *The evidence on which the award is based was forged* [amended in 2012]. (5) *The other party withheld evidence which is sufficient to affect the impartiality of arbitration* [amended in 2012]. (6) During the arbitration the arbitrator(s) demanded or accepted bribes, engaged in favouritism or malpractice for personal gain, or perverted the law. Paragraph 3: The people's court shall refuse enforcement if it finds that the award's enforcement would violate social and public interest. Article 213 of the 2007 version of Civil Procedure Law:	Article 274 of the current Civil Procedure Law (renumbered from Article 260 in 1991 and Article 258 in 2007 without substantive amendment): Paragraph 1: Where the respondent furnishes proof that an *arbitral award made by foreign-related arbitration institution* involves one of the following circumstances, the people's court shall, upon examination and verification by its relevant panel, refuse enforcement: (1) The parties' contract did not have an arbitration agreement or the parties did not reach any arbitration agreement in writing after the dispute arose. (2) The respondent was not given proper notice of the arbitrator appointment or the arbitral proceedings, or was otherwise unable to present his/her case for reasons not attributable to him/her. (3) The composition of the arbitral tribunal or the arbitral procedure was contrary to the applicable arbitration rules. (4) The award deals with matters beyond the scope of the arbitration agreement or the authority of the arbitration institution.

	Domestic Arbitral Awards	*Foreign-Related Arbitral Awards*
	Paragraph 2: Where the respondent furnishes proof that the arbitral award involves one of the following circumstances, the people's court shall, upon examination and verification by its relevant panel, refuse enforcement: (1) The parties' contract did not have an arbitration agreement or the parties did not reach any arbitration agreement in writing after the dispute arose. (2) The award deals with matters beyond the scope of the arbitration agreement or the authority of the arbitration institution. (3) The composition of the arbitral tribunal or the arbitral procedure was contrary to the applicable legal procedures. (4) The main evidence for finding the facts was insufficient. (5) There was an error in the application of law. (6) During the arbitration the arbitrator(s) demanded or accepted bribes, engaged in favouritism or malpractice for personal gain, or perverted the law. Paragraph 3: The people's court shall refuse enforcement if it finds that the award's enforcement would violate social and public interest. Article 63 of Arbitration Law: Where the respondent furnishes proof that the arbitral award involves one of the circumstances specified in *Article 217 paragraph 2 of the Civil Procedure Law (i.e. Article 237 paragraph 2 of the current version)*, the people's court shall, upon examination and verification by its relevant panel, refuse to enforce the award.	Paragraph 2: The people's court shall refuse enforcement if it finds that the award's enforcement would violate social and public interest. Article 71 of Arbitration Law: Where the respondent furnishes proof that the *foreign-related arbitral award* involves one of the circumstances specified in *Article 260 paragraph 1 of the Civil Procedure Law (Article 274 paragraph 1 of the current version)*, the people's court shall, upon examination and verification by its relevant panel, refuse to enforce the award.

Table 3.1 reveals the inconsistencies in the relevant provisions of the PRC's Arbitration Law and Civil Procedure Law, resulting in different practice opinions and academic discussions. In terms of judicial review process, however, the same regulations concerning 'centralized jurisdiction' and the 'Reporting System' apply to both the revocation and non-enforcement of foreign-related arbitral awards, whereby these cases are reported to the SPC and reviewed by the SPC's Fourth Civil Tribunal. The same procedural requirements apply to cases concerning the recognition and enforcement of foreign arbitral awards. The following sections explain the identical procedural requirements and then the differences.

3.2.1 Identical Procedural Provisions: Centralised Jurisdiction, Reporting System, Functions of the SPC's Fourth Civil Tribunal

It can be observed from the PRC provisions relating to civil procedure that the PRC legal system uses 'centralized jurisdiction', the 'Reporting System' and the SPC's internal allocation of function, etc., and categorises the four types of cases concerning 'the validity of foreign-related arbitration agreements', 'non-enforcement of foreign-related arbitral awards', 'revocation of foreign-related arbitration awards', and 'recognition and enforcement of foreign arbitral awards' into the same 'group' subject to the same procedural regulations. The following explains each of these features respectively.

3.2.1.1 Centralised Jurisdiction

Pursuant to Article 3 of the Provisions of the Supreme People's Court on Some Issues Concerning the Jurisdiction of Civil and Commercial Cases Involving Foreign Elements, the jurisdiction of cases involving applications for 'revocation, recognition and compulsory enforcement of international arbitral awards' and 'reviewing the validity of foreign-related civil and commercial arbitration clauses' are 'centralized' to certain courts, meaning that the following people's courts have jurisdiction in the first instance:

(1) People' courts in economic and technological zones approved by the State Council.
(2) People's courts located in provincial capitals, capitals of autonomous regions and municipalities directly under the central government.
(3) People's courts in special economic zones or cities designated in the state economic plan.
(4) Other intermediate people's courts designated by the SPC.
(5) Higher people's courts.

The reference in Article 3 of the above SPC's Provisions to 'international arbitral awards' (in the context of applications for recognition, revocation and enforcement of international arbitral awards) is commonly understood to mean arbitral awards made by territorial (domestic) or extra-territorial (foreign) arbitration institutions in relation to foreign-related commercial disputes. The test for determining 'international arbitral awards' should be whether the relevant disputes decided in the arbitral award involved any foreign elements, rather than whether the arbitration institution was extra-territorial (foreign).[69] This type of cases mainly includes:[70]

(1) Applications for recognition of arbitral awards made by foreign arbitration institutions.
(2) Applications for recognition and enforcement of arbitral awards made by foreign arbitration institutions, and
(3) Revocation of foreign-related arbitral awards made by domestic arbitration institutions.

The reference in Article 3 of the Provisions of the Supreme People's Court on Some Issues Concerning the Jurisdiction of Civil and Commercial Cases Involving Foreign Elements to 'reviewing the validity of foreign-related civil and commercial arbitration clauses' mainly includes the following:[71]

(1) the parties to foreign-related commercial cases merely object to the arbitration agreement's validity and apply for the people's court's declaration ruling on this issue; and
(2) the parties to foreign-related commercial cases raise jurisdictional objections and also object to the arbitration agreement's validity and therefore require the people's court's declaration ruling on the arbitration agreement's validity.

3.2.1.2 Reporting System

As detailed below, the SPC has established the 'Reporting System' for cases concerning the 'validity of foreign-related arbitration agreements', 'enforcement of PRC foreign-related institutional arbitral awards', 'recognition and enforcement of foreign institutional arbitral awards' and 'revocation of foreign-related arbitration awards', etc. through the SPC's Notification of Certain Issues Relating to the People's Courts'

---

69. An example of such interpretation is Art. 7 para. 1 of Guangdong Higher People's Court's Notification about Publication of 'Opinions Concerning Further Implementation of Centralizing Foreign-Related Cases': please see Yue-Gao-Fa-Fa (2004) No. 35, issued on 20 December 2004 and implemented on 1 January 2005.
70. Ibid., Art. 7 para. 2; Art. 8 of Zhejiang Higher People's Court's Regulation Concerning Jurisdiction over Foreign-Related Cases, Zhe-Gao-Fa (2008) No. 78, issued on 31 March 2008 and implemented on 1 April 2008.
71. Article 8 of Guangdong Higher People's Court's Notification about Publication of 'Opinions Concerning Further Implementation of Centralizing Foreign-Related Cases' (ibid.); Art. 9 of Zhejiang Higher People's Court's Regulation Concerning Jurisdiction over Foreign-Related Cases (ibid).

Chapter 3: 'Public Policy' and the Even More Unpredictable

Dealing with Foreign-Related and Foreign Arbitration[72] and the SPC's Notification of Certain Matters Relating to the People's Courts' Revocation of Foreign-Related Arbitral Awards.[73]

3.2.1.2.1 Validity of Foreign-Related Arbitration Agreements

According to Article 1 of the SPC's Notification of Certain Issues Relating to the People's Courts' Dealing with Foreign-Related and Foreign Arbitration:

> In cases commencing in a people's court concerning *economic and maritime disputes involving foreign elements, Hong Kong, Macau or Taiwan*, where the parties either have an arbitration clause in their contract or have reached an arbitration agreement after their disputes arose, and the people's court finds such an *arbitration clause or arbitration agreement to be void or invalid or unenforceable because of uncertainty*, the people's court shall report to the higher people's court in its locality before accepting the case. The higher people's court shall report its review opinions to the SPC if it agrees to accept the case, and may temporarily withhold acceptance pending the SPC's reply (emphasis added).

3.2.1.2.2 Enforcement of PRC Foreign-Related Institutional Arbitral Awards and Recognition and Enforcement of Foreign Institutional Arbitral Awards

According to Article 2 of the SPC's Notification of Certain Issues Relating to the People's Courts' Dealing with Foreign-Related and Foreign Arbitration:

> Where a party applies to a people's court for the enforcement of foreign-related institutional arbitral awards or for the recognition and enforcement of foreign institutional arbitral awards, if the people's court finds that the foreign-related institutional arbitral award falls within one of the circumstances specified in *Article 260 of the Civil Procedure Law* [Article 274 of the current version], or that the recognition and enforcement of the foreign arbitral award is incompatible with *international conventions acceded to by the People's Republic China or the principle of reciprocity*, the people's court shall, before deciding to refuse recognition or enforcement, report to the higher people's court in its locality for review. The higher people's court shall report its review opinion to the SPC if it agrees with refusing recognition or enforcement. The court may refuse recognition or enforcement after the SPC's reply (emphasis added).

3.2.1.2.3 Revocation of Foreign-Related Arbitral Awards

According to Article 1 of the SPC's Notification of Certain Matters Relating to the People's Courts' Revocation of Foreign-Related Arbitral Awards:

---

72. Fa-Fa (1995) No. 18, issued and implemented on 28 August 1995.
73. Fa (1998) No. 40, issued and implemented on 23 April 1998.

Where a party applies to a people's court to set aside a foreign-related arbitral award pursuant to Arbitration Law, and if the people's court upon its review finds that the foreign-related arbitral award falls within one of the circumstances specified in *Article 260 paragraph 1 of the Civil Procedure Law* [Article 274 paragraph 1 of the current version], the people's court shall, before deciding to revoke the award or notify the arbitral tribunal about re-arbitration, report to the higher people's court in its locality for review. The higher people's court shall report its review opinion to the SPC if it agrees with revoking the award or notifying the arbitral tribunal about re-arbitration, and the court may decide to do so after the SPC's reply (emphasis added).

The above-mentioned 'Reporting System' effectively centralises in the SPC the four types of cases concerning the 'validity of arbitration agreements', 'non-enforcement of foreign-related arbitral awards', 'revocation of foreign-related arbitral awards' and 'recognition and enforcement of foreign arbitral awards' respectively. This prevents the lower courts from reckless denial of arbitration agreement's validity, non-enforcement of foreign-related awards, non-recognition and non-enforcement of foreign awards, and revocation of foreign-related awards before receiving the SPC's reply in agreement. Some scholars have expressed that such a system 'actually abolished the local courts' discretion in refusing recognition and enforcement of foreign arbitral awards, and conferred the right of final decision on the SPC, thereby enabling certain procedural supervision by the SPC and higher people's courts over every local court's strict implementation and correct application of the legal system for the recognition and enforcement of arbitral awards, as well as controlling and regulating every local court's conduct in refusing to enforce arbitral awards'.[74] Since its implementation, the Reporting System has substantially increased the enforceability of foreign-related and foreign arbitral awards.[75] Thus 'it cannot be denied that such centralized report and review system has significantly bolstered the confidence of foreign investors who feared that local protectionism might unduly influence the enforcement of arbitral awards in China'.[76]

Criticisms nevertheless exist. For instance, according to some scholars: 'the Reporting System is only applicable to the non-recognition and non-enforcement of foreign arbitral awards by the intermediate people's courts; the intermediate people's courts can directly make effective rulings on the recognition and enforcement of foreign arbitral awards and execute against the respondents' assets without the multi-tiered reporting. This is obviously unfair to the respondent;…because the internal reporting system is neither fair nor regulated, and it should be replaced by an appeal system'.[77]

---

74. Xiaohong Liu (ed.), *A Monographic Study on International Commercial Law* 507 (Law Press 2009).
75. Weixia Gu, *In Arbitration We Trust…Not? – A Review of English Literatures on the Study of Arbitration in China*, 72 Beijing Arbitration 1, 16 (2010).
76. Jingzhou Tao, *Arbitration Law and Practice in China* 205 (3rd ed., Wolters Kluwer 2012).
77. Fanglong Sun & Chuxu Zhao, *Procedural Discussions in the PRC Cases Concerning Recognition and Enforcement of Foreign Arbitral Awards*, in *Judicial Practice of New York Convention and International Commercial Arbitration* 207 (CIETAC ed., Law Press 2010).
    Scholars have different suggestions for the specific content of the appeal system. For instance, Xianming Shi suggests 'appeal to the next upper level of court': *see* Xianming Shi, *Studies on the Remedies for the Parties' Rights Injured in International Commercial Arbitration*

Other scholars believe that the Reporting System 'provides more favourable treatment to foreign parties' and 'neglects the PRC's interest'.[78] Despite its awareness of the problem of unfairness to the parties arising from the existence of the Reporting System, the SPC has nevertheless indicated that, 'if the internal reporting system expands to all cases of judicial supervision of arbitration, one can imagine the objective difficulties arising from the rapidly expanding workload of the higher people's courts and the SPC'.[79] Furthermore, some scholars even believe that the higher courts' intervention in the lower court's rulings through this system of multi-tiered reporting is 'outright violation of the requirements of due process and the principle of judicial independence'.[80]

3.2.1.3 Functions of the SPC's Fourth Civil Tribunal

On the other hand, Article 1(9) of the SPC's Functions of Internal Organization and Newly Established Institutions provides that reviewing 'applications for revocation, recognition and enforcement of international arbitral awards and foreign court judgments' as well as 'cases concerning the validity of foreign-related arbitration clauses' are within the functions of the SPC's Fourth Civil Tribunal.[81] These cases are centralised in SPC's Fourth Civil Tribunal for review after being reported to the SPC, thereby avoiding the situation where the lower courts do not know who to follow or what to do because of inconsistent judicial opinions. Indeed Justice Honglei Yang of the SPC's Fourth Civil Tribunal issued a research report in 2009 on the people's courts' review of foreign-related arbitration covering these four types of cases.[82]

404–405 (Renmin Press 2011). By contrast, Xiuwen Zhao suggests: 'On the one hand, the court level for hearing international arbitration cases should be elevated, such as elevating the courts with jurisdiction at first instance from the intermediate people's courts to the higher people's courts of every province, self-governing regions and municipalities through legislative means. On the other hand, the current Reporting System should be abolished and replaced with an appeal system. The parties should be permitted to appeal to the SPC within prescribed timeframe if they are dissatisfied with the decisions of the courts at first instance on the validity of arbitration agreements, or judicial revocation, non-recognition or non-enforcement of international commercial arbitral awards, and the SPC's decisions should be final.' See Xiuwen Zhao, *International Commercial Arbitration Modernization Research* 350 (Law Press 2010).

78. Weixia Gu, *In Arbitration We Trust...Not? – A Review of English Literatures on the Study of Arbitration in China*, 72 Beijing Arbitration 1, 16 (2010).
79. Exiang Wan & Xifu Yu, *The Latest Development of Judicial Supervision over Arbitration in the PRC – Comment on the Supreme People's Court's Judicial Interpretations Concerning the Application of Arbitration Law*, 141 Law Review 73, 73–79 (2007).
80. Weixia Gu, *supra* n. 78. For detailed criticisms of the Reporting System and the necessity for an appeal system, *see also* Xiangquan Qi, *Study on the Recognition and Enforcement of Foreign Arbitral Awards* 402–414 (Law Press 2010).
81. Fa-Fa (2000) No. 30, issued and implemented on 4 December 2000.
82. Honglei Yang, *Report on the Judicial Review of International Arbitration in Chinese Courts*, 9(1) International Law Review of Wuhan University 304–321 (2009). The subject matter of this research report concerns the issues arising from the people's courts dealing with foreign-related and foreign arbitration cases, and the main types of such cases are as follows: (1) applications for confirmation of validity of arbitration agreements; (2) applications for revocation of foreign-related arbitral awards; (3) cases where one party applies for enforcement of foreign-related arbitral awards and the other party applies for non-enforcement; (4) applications for

3.2.1.4 Summary

It can be seen from the above observation of the PRC procedural regulations that 'validity of foreign-related arbitration agreements', 'non-enforcement of foreign-related arbitral awards', 'revocation of foreign-related arbitral awards' and 'recognition and enforcement of foreign arbitral awards' are categorised as the same 'group' in the PRC. Pursuant to the regulations concerning centralisation, the designated courts will hear these cases in the first instance. If the court at first instance finds that the arbitration clause or agreement is void, invalid or unenforceable because of uncertainty, or the foreign-related arbitral award should be set aside or refused enforcement or the arbitral tribunal should be notified about re-arbitration, or the foreign arbitral award should be refused recognition and enforcement, then the court at first instance must report to the higher people's court in its locality for review. The higher people's court must then report to the SPC if it agrees with the court at first instance, and must wait for the SPC's reply before making any ruling. Furthermore, the SPC's Fourth Civil Tribunal reviews these types of cases in order to unify legal opinions and prevent inconsistent judicial approaches. This demonstrates that the PRC legal system regards these types of cases as possessing a certain commonality and therefore requiring common procedural regulations. Hence a comparative examination of the PRC court's opinions in these types of cases would be quite helpful to examine the PRC courts' interpretation and application of 'public policy' in Article V(2)(b) of the New York Convention.

For instance, 'violation of public policy' is not an explicit legal ground for invalidating arbitration agreements in the PRC. Yet in the *Liupanshui* case of 2010 (a non-foreign-related case concerning the validity of agreement for arbitration by extra-territorial arbitration institution – jurisdictional objection to the contract for transfer of mining rights between Liupanshui Hidili Industrial Co., Ltd. and Hongxing Zhang),[83] Hongxing Zhang was a PRC citizen while Liupanshui Hidili Industrial Co., Ltd. remained a PRC corporate entity despite its establishment in the PRC as a wholly foreign-owned enterprise of Hidili Industrial International Co., Ltd. (a company listed on the Hong Kong Stock Exchange).[84] This case did not involve any foreign elements, yet the parties agreed for arbitration by Hong Kong International Arbitration Centre (HKIAC). Considering that the focal issue of this case was whether or not the agreement between parties to non-foreign-related civil dispute for institutional arbitration outside the PRC's territory is valid, the SPC opined:

> *The issue of resolving civil and commercial disputes which arose within a nation's territory concerns that nation's judicial sovereignty and should therefore pertain to*

---

recognition and enforcement of foreign arbitral awards (including applications for recognition as well as applications for recognition and enforcement).

83. Objection to the Jurisdiction over Disputes arising from the Mining Right Transfer Agreement between Liupanshui Hidili Industry Co., Ltd. and Zhang Hongxing, Supreme People's Court Civil Ruling (2010) Min-Er-Zhong-Zi No. 86, 26 August 2010.
84. *See* the website of Hidili Industrial International Co., Ltd. (for registering a limited company in the Cayman Island and listing on the Hong Kong stock exchange): http://www.hidili.com.cn (accessed 4 May 2017).

Chapter 3: 'Public Policy' and the Even More Unpredictable

that nation's categories of public policy. The parties can only make agreement within the permitted scope of that nation's current law, and any agreement evading or exceeding such permitted scope of that nation's law should be regarded as invalid by virtue of public policy violation (emphasis added).

Although this case involved an arbitration institution of Hong Kong, in the SPC's opinion, 'considerations of public policy also exist between different law jurisdictions within one sovereign nation', only the parties to foreign-related civil cases can select arbitration by institutions outside the PRC's territory in accordance with the legislative intent of Article 271 of the PRC Civil Procedure Law[85] and Article 128 paragraph 2 of the PRC Contract Law. The parties in this non-foreign-related civil case agreed to arbitrate their disputes by an arbitration institution outside the PRC's territory, such arbitration agreement exceeds the permitted scope of the PRC law and is therefore invalid. In addition, the Beijing Second Intermediate People's Court also adopted the same view in the *Case concerning the application of Beijing Chao Lai Xin Sheng Sports and Leisure Co., Ltd. for recognition and enforcement of a foreign arbitral award*.[86] In that case the Beijing Second Intermediate People's Court held that the two Chinese companies' arbitration agreement of submitting their dispute to 'Korean Commercial Arbitration Board' was invalid and it led to the arbitral award's non-recognition and non-enforcement.

Another court adopting the same view was the Shanghai Second Intermediate People's Court in 2009 in the *Leaf Confectionary* case (concerning the application by Leaf Confectionary (Shanghai) Co., Ltd. for the recognition and enforcement of foreign arbitral award against Shanghai Lianfu Food Co., Ltd.).[87] The basic facts of this case were quite similar to those of the *Liupanshui* case and *Chao Lai Xin Sheng* case. Leaf Confectionary (Leaf Confectionary (Shanghai) Co., Ltd.) was established in Shanghai as a wholly foreign-owned enterprise of CSM N.V., a Dutch company. Leaf Confectionary remained a PRC legal person despite being wholly owned by the Dutch CSM N.V. The other party involved in this case, Lianfu (Shanghai Lianfu Food Co., Ltd), was a PRC company funded by a PRC natural person. Lianfu alleged that Leaf Confectionary and Lianfu had contravened the PRC's law and infringed the PRC's judicial sovereignty by submitting their dispute arising under a non-foreign-related asset purchase contract to arbitration by Singapore International Arbitration Centre (SIAC), consequently the recognition and enforcement of the resulting arbitral award would be contrary to the PRC's public policy within the meaning of Article V(2)(b) of the New York Convention. However, the Shanghai Second Intermediate People's Court found that Hanguang Huang, a Malaysian citizen, was also a party to the asset purchase contract in addition to Leaf Confectionary and Lianfu. Accordingly the asset purchase contract was foreign-related, and Lianfu's claim that the asset purchase contract lacked foreign elements was inadmissible for lacking factual and legal bases. Thus it can be seen that

---

85. The original text of the *Liupanshui case* refers to Art. 255 of the 2007 version of the PRC Civil Procedure Law, which is comparable to Art. 271 of the current version.
86. Shanghai Second Intermediate People's Court Civil Ruling (2013) Er-Zhong-Min-Te-Zi No. 10670, 20 January 2014.
87. Shanghai Second Intermediate People's Court Civil Ruling (2008) Hu-Er-Zhong-Min-Wu-Shang-Chu-Zi No. 19, 24 June 2009.

the Shanghai Second Intermediate People's Court considered this case as foreign-related from a fact-finding perspective, namely one of the contracting parties, Hanguang Huang, had Malaysian citizenship. Otherwise the Court may possibly allow Lianfu's claim.

It is evident from the *Liupanshui* case, *Chao Lai Xin Sheng* case and *Leaf Confectionary* case that the PRC courts have applied the concept of 'public policy' in actual cases even though the PRC law does not expressly stipulate that the parties' submission of non-foreign-related civil disputes to arbitration by institutions outside the PRC's territory as being contrary to 'public policy'. Examining the PRC court's application of 'public policy' or 'social and public interest' in this group of cases should substantially assist with understanding the PRC court's application of interpretation of 'public policy' as specified in Article V(2)(b) of the New York Convention. Accordingly the following tables are annexed to the end of Chapter 4:

- Table 4.1: Cases concerning non-recognition and non-enforcement of foreign arbitral awards;
- Table 4.2: Cases concerning non-enforcement of arbitral awards made in Hong Kong;
- Table 4.3: Cases concerning non-enforcement of foreign-related arbitral awards; and
- Table 4.4: Cases concerning the validity of foreign-related arbitration agreements.

Before further exploring these cases, it is necessary to explain the differences between the PRC's Arbitration Law and Civil Procedure Law as the foundation for follow-up discussions.

3.2.2 Inconsistencies Between Arbitration Law and Civil Procedure Law

The PRC's legislative provisions concerning arbitration are primarily seen in the PRC Arbitration Law and the PRC Civil Procedure Law. Inconsistencies between these legislations nevertheless raise doubts in application (please *see* Table 3.1 in this chapter). As discussed below, these inconsistencies still exist in the current PRC law as they have not been addressed despite the revision of the Civil Procedure Law in 2012.

3.2.2.1 'Foreign-Related Arbitral Awards' and 'Foreign-Related Institutional Arbitral Awards'

The PRC's arbitration legislation adopts the 'dual-track' or 'bifurcated' system of 'domestic arbitration' and 'foreign-related arbitration'.[88] With respect to the criteria for

---

88. Binsheng Zhang (ed.), *Arbitration Law and Practice* (4th ed., Xiamen University Press 2010).
    Other terms used by scholars include 'separate track system' (Xiaohong Liu (ed.), *A Monographic Study on International Commercial Law* (Law Press 2009)), 'dual-track regime' or 'bifurcated arbitration system' (Nadia Darwazeh & Michael J. Moser, *Arbitration Inside China* in

Chapter 3: 'Public Policy' and the Even More Unpredictable

differentiating between 'domestic arbitration' and 'foreign-related arbitration', the traditional terminology in the PRC Civil Procedure Law is 'foreign-related institutional arbitral awards' (for instance, 'awards made by foreign-related arbitration institutions' in Article 274 of the PRC Civil Procedure Law).[89] Previously, especially before the implementation of the PRC Arbitration Law, China International Economic and Trade Arbitration Commission (CIETAC) and China Maritime Association Commission (CMAC) accepted foreign-related cases only and were traditionally known as 'foreign-related arbitration institutions'.[90] Consequently scholars at that time believed that 'the PRC's foreign-related arbitration' actually referred to arbitration conducted by CIETAC and CMAC.[91]

By contrast, the PRC Arbitration Law uses the terminology 'foreign-related arbitration' and specifically provides for it in chapter VII. Examples include Article 65 of the PRC Arbitration Law, which states: '[t]he provisions of this Chapter shall apply to the arbitration of *foreign-related* disputes arising from economic, trade, transportation and maritime activities. For matters not covered in this Chapter, the other relevant provisions of this Law shall apply (emphasis added)'. Article 70 provides for revocation of arbitral awards:[92] '[w]here a party furnishes proof that the *foreign-related arbitral award* involves one of the circumstances specified in Article 260 paragraph 1 of the Civil Procedure Law, the people's court shall, upon examination and verification by its relevant panel, set aside the award (emphasis added)'. There were different views on the meaning of 'foreign-related arbitration' when the PRC Arbitration Law began its implementation on 1 September 1995. At that time some scholars still followed the traditional view that 'foreign-related arbitration is arbitration of foreign-related economic, trade, transportation or maritime disputes by the PRC's foreign-related arbitration institutions',[93] and that 'the terminology of both the PRC Civil Procedure Law of

---

Managing Business Disputes in Today's China-Duelling with Dragons 60 (Michael J. Moser ed., Kluwer Law International 2007). For historical development of foreign-related arbitration, *see* Jingzhou Tao, *Arbitration Law and Practice in China* 8–12 (3rd ed., Kluwer Law International 2012).

89. As another example, Art. 280 para. 2 of the PRC Civil Procedure Law stipulates: 'Where a party applies for the enforcement of a *legally effective arbitral award made by a foreign-related arbitration institution* of the People's Republic of China and the party or property subject to the enforcement or its property is not within the territory of the People's Republic of China, the applicant shall directly apply for the recognition and enforcement of the arbitral award to the foreign court that has jurisdiction over the case (emphasis added).'

90. For examples, Art. 2 para. 1 of the 1988 version of the CIETAC Arbitration Rules (revised and adopted on 12 September 1988, implemented on 1 January 1989) refers to 'disputes arising from *international* economic trade), while Art. 2 para. 1 of the 1994 version of the CIETAC Arbitration Rules (revised and adopted on 17 March 1994, implemented on 1 June 1994) refers to 'disputes arising from *international or foreign-related* contractual or non-contractual economic trade' (emphasis added). Both indicate acceptance of 'international or foreign-related' disputes only.

91. Dejun Cheng, Shengchang Wang & Ming Kang, *International Practice and Foreign-Related Arbitration* 163 (China Youth Press 1993).

92. For commentary on Art. 70 of PRC Arbitration Law, *see* Lianbin Song, *A Study of Jurisdictional Problems*, in *International Commercial Arbitration* 220 (Law Press 2000).

93. Yan Gao & Lu Liu, *Understanding and Application of Arbitration Law and Case Analysis* 170 (People's Court Press 1996).

    Other scholars also adopt the same view that the differences between foreign-related arbitration and domestic arbitration include the different administering institutions, 'foreign-

1991 and the PRC Arbitration Law of 1994 uses the award-making arbitration institution as the defining standard pursuant to which arbitral awards made by the PRC's foreign-related arbitration institutions or foreign-related arbitration commissions are regarded as foreign-related arbitral awards'.[94]

Yet the PRC Arbitration Law does not expressly specify whether or not newly established arbitration institutions can accept foreign-related cases, even though such institutions are highly interested in accepting foreign-related cases. To remove this doubt, the General Office of the State Council of the PRC issued Circular Regarding Some Problems Which Need to be Clarified for the Implementation of the Arbitration Law of the PRC on 8 June 1996. Article 3 of this Circular states: 'While the main responsibility of the newly-established arbitration institutions is to arbitrate domestic disputes; where the parties to foreign-related arbitrations voluntarily select arbitration by the newly-established arbitration institutions, such arbitration institutions may also accept and arbitrate such cases.'[95] This clear basis prompted the newly established arbitration institutions of all areas to accept foreign-related cases one after another. CIETAC also revised its arbitration rules in 2000, expressly extending its scope of cases to all domestic disputes, and, for the first time, specifying the procedures for domestic arbitration in a designated chapter.[96] Since then the traditionally 'foreign-related arbitration institutions' have been dealing with both foreign-related and domestic arbitration cases while the newly established arbitration institutions have also been dealing with both foreign-related and domestic cases at the same time, such that the so-called foreign-related arbitration institutions in the past has lost its meaning.

The views of all sectors on the definition of 'foreign-related arbitration' are converging nowadays, using 'foreign elements' in specific cases as the distinguishing criterion instead of 'arbitration institutions'. In practice, the people's courts commonly refer to the following two SPC regulations on judicial interpretation as the basis of their rulings:

(1) Article 304 of the Opinions of the Supreme People's Court on Some Issues Concerning the Application of the Civil Procedure Law of the PRC defines 'foreign-related civil cases' as civil cases where one party or both parties are a foreigner, stateless person, foreign enterprise or organisation; or where the

---

related arbitration institutions are China International Economic and Trade Arbitration Commission and China Maritime Association Commission' whereas '[d]omestic arbitration institutions should only accept and hear cases concerning disputes between domestic companies, enterprises, other economic organizations and individuals': *see* Bing Tan (ed.), *Research on Chinese Arbitration Legal System* 274 (Law Press 1995).

94. Jian Han, *Theory and Practice of Modern International Commercial Arbitration* 470 (Law Press 2000).
95. Guo-Ban-Fa (1996) No. 22, issued on 8 June 1996.
96. Article 2 of the 2000 version of the CIETAC Arbitration Rules (revised and adopted on 5 September 2000, implemented on 1 October 2000) expressly stipulates its scope of cases as including 'other domestic disputes that the parties have agreed to submit to arbitration by [CIETAC]'.

Chapter 3: 'Public Policy' and the Even More Unpredictable

legal facts that lead to the creation, change or termination of the parties' civil relationship occurred in a foreign country; or where the subject matter is located in a foreign country.[97]

(2) Article 178 paragraph 1 of the Notice of the Supreme People's Court on Issuing the Opinions on Several Issues concerning the Implementation of the General Principles of the Civil Law of the PRC (For Trial Implementation) defines 'foreign-related civil relationships' as civil relationships where one party or both parties are a foreigner, stateless person or foreign legal person; or where the subject matter of the civil relationship is within a foreign territory; or the legal facts that lead to the creation, change or termination of the civil relationship occurred in a foreign country.[98]

The above provisions about judicial interpretation use the same criteria despite slight differences in terminology. Addressing the issue of how to define foreign-related arbitration, Point 6 of the Shanghai Higher People's Court's Opinion on Several Issues Concerning the Implementation the Implementation of the Arbitration Law of the PRC issued in 2001 also states that such determination should be made in accordance with of Article 178 of the Notice of the Supreme People's Court on Issuing the Opinions on Several Issues concerning the Implementation of the General Principles of the Civil Law of the PRC (For Trial Implementation).[99]

Academics also adopt the same view.[100] An example is Professor Xiuwen Zhao's statement that 'foreign-related arbitral awards are arbitral awards with foreign elements made in the PRC's territory, which possess PRC nationality, and may be set aside by the PRC courts in accordance with PRC laws'.[101] The author agrees.[102]

---

97. Fa-Fa (1992) No. 22, issued and implemented on 14 July 1992.
98. Fa-Ban-Fa (1988) No. 6, issued and implemented on 2 April 1988.
99. The Shanghai Higher People's Court's Opinion on the Various Issues Concerning the Enforcement of the PRC Arbitration Law was discussed and adopted by the Judicial Committee of the Shanghai Higher People's Court during the first meeting on 3 January 2001 and implemented on 1 February 2001. As stipulated in Art. 6: 'With respect to the issue of how to define foreign-related arbitration, Article 65 of the Arbitration Law provides that '[t]he provisions of this Chapter shall apply to the arbitration of disputes arising from economic, trade, transportation and maritime activities involving a foreign element' but without any corresponding provisions for the specific meaning of foreign-related arbitration. At present, reference should be made to Article 178 of the SPC's Opinion on the various issues concerning the consistent application of the PRC Civil Law, namely, one or both of the contracting parties is a foreigner, stateless person, foreign legal person or other economic organization; or where the subject matter of the civil relationship is within a foreign territory; or the civil relationship commenced, changed or ended in a foreign country. These should be deemed as involving foreign elements and belonging to the category of foreign-related arbitration. Arbitration involving Hong Kong, Macau and Taiwan should also be dealt with by reference to foreign-related arbitration.'
100. Honglei Yang, *Report on the Judicial Review of International Arbitration in Chinese Courts*, 9(1) International Law Review of Wuhan University 304, 316 (2009); Lianbin Song (ed.), *Theory and Practice of Commercial Arbitration* 361 (Hunan University Press 2005).
101. Xiuwen Zhao (ed.), *International Commercial Arbitration Law* 444 (3rd ed., China Renmin University Press 2012).
102. Helena Hsi-Chia Chen, *A Comparative Study on the Arbitration Law on Both Sides of the Taiwan Strait (Part I)*, 96 Arbitration 73, 76–77 (2012).

The following elaboration by the enforcement ruling of Zhejiang Taizhou Intermediate People's Court ((2013) Zhe-Tai-Zhi-Cai-Zi No. 2)[103] demonstrates that the people's courts have completely renounced the so-called foreign-related arbitration institutions as a determining criterion and adopted 'foreign elements' instead:

> In this Court's opinion, where the party against whom enforcement is sought applies for non-enforcement of an arbitral award made by foreign-related arbitration institution, the people's court should adjudicate and apply different laws depending on whether or not the case involves foreign element. Whether or not foreign element is involved should be determined in accordance with Article 178 of the Notice of the Supreme People's Court on Issuing the Opinions on Several Issues concerning the Implementation of the General Principles of the Civil Law of the People's Republic of China (For Trial Implementation). In this case, *although the arbitral award was made by a foreign-related arbitration institution, the China International Economic and Trade Arbitration Commission, Shanghai Sub-Commission, the case does not involve the foreign element as specified above*, and the arbitration institution used its arbitration rules specifically set forth for domestic arbitration. Consequently the award in this case should belong to *domestic arbitral award*, LDK Solar Hi-Tech company's submission that Article 274 of the PRC Civil Procedure Law is applicable cannot be established. Article 237 of the PRC Civil Procedure Law should apply (emphasis added).

The following four points are worth noting with respect to determining the existence of foreign element.

First, according to the long-standing view on whether the parties have foreign element, subsidiaries established in the PRC pursuant to PRC laws by companies in foreign countries, Taiwan, Hong Kong or Macau, even if wholly owned foreign subsidiaries, are still 'Chinese' corporate entities registered in the PRC rather than foreign enterprises and are therefore without foreign elements.[104] A case illustration is the application by China International Engineering Consulting Corporation to enforce a CIETAC award.[105] At that time CIETAC only accepted foreign-related cases and considered that 'Lido Hotel is a joint venture between Mainland China and Hong Kong with foreign element' and made an award. After China International Engineering Consulting Corporation applied for this award's enforcement, Beijing Lido Hotel Company (the party against whom enforcement was sought) applied to the Beijing Intermediate People's Court for non-enforcement. It submitted that China International Engineering Consulting Corporation and Lido Hotel were both Chinese legal persons, the dispute arising from the parties' engineering contract was purely a domestic economic contractual dispute which is outside CIETAC's scope of jurisdiction and therefore CIETAC had no authority to arbitrate. Upon review, the Beijing Intermediate

---

103. Ruling issued on 29 July 2013.
104. Michael Moser & Peter Yuen, *Arbitration Outside China*, in *Managing Business Disputes in Today's China Duelling with Dragons* 88 (Michael Moser ed., Kluwer Law International 2007); Adam Li & George Wang, *Conflict of Law Issues in Ascertaining Validity of an Arbitration Agreement*, in *Arbitration in China: A Practical Guide* 101–102 (Daniel R. Fung & Shengchang Wang eds, Sweet & Maxwell 2004).
105. Dated 23 December 1992, cited from Chinese Institute of Applied Jurisprudence (ed.), *Selection of People's Courts' Cases (Civil Cases) (Part II) (1992–1999 combined)* 20182021 (China Legal Publishing House 2000).

Chapter 3: 'Public Policy' and the Even More Unpredictable

People's Court refused to enforce the award, holding that Lido was jointly funded by China Travel Service and Hong Kong Yihe Co., Ltd. and was registered in the PRC's State Administration for Industry and Commerce; the parties' dispute arising from their engineering contract was a domestic economic contractual dispute without any foreign element. Both the *Liupanshui* case and *Chao Lai Xin Sheng* case were also held to be without any foreign elements, even though the party in the former case (Liupanshui Hidili Industry Co., Ltd.) established in the PRC was wholly owned by a company listed on Hong Kong Stock Exchange (Hidili Industrial International Co., Ltd), and the party in the latter case (Beijing Suowangzhixin Investment Consulting Co., Ltd.) established in Beijing was wholly owned by a foreign natural person (a Korean citizen).

Nationality is not the only factor of consideration for natural persons. A case illustration is the SPC's Reply in 2003 concerning the application by Tsinghua Tongfang Co. Ltd and Tsinghua Tongfang Optical Memory JSLD for revocation of an arbitral award).[106] One of the parties in that case, Uotani Yuka, is a Chinese expatriate in Japan. In the SPC's opinion, Japan is Uotani Yuka's habitual residence, this case is in essence similar to cases involving parties from Hong Kong, Macau and Taiwan, namely the parties' nationality is Chinese but the cases should be treated as foreign-related in consideration of the objective existence of foreign elements.

Second, there are two important cases with respect to the interpretation and application of the term 'the subject matter is in a foreign country'. One case in 2008 concerned a sales contract dispute between Shandong Hengdian Grass and Animal Husbandry Co., Ltd. and John Deere (Tianjin) International Trading Co., Ltd.[107] The Shandong Dongying Intermediate People's Court in this case held that the goods located in a customs bonded area in Mainland China also possessed foreign element for the following reasons:

> Pursuant to the Procedures on Customs Control over Bonded Areas issued by General Administration of Customs of the People's Republic of China, a customs bonded area is a special area which is within borders but outside customs and under special supervision by Customs. Trade in goods or services between enterprises and foreign enterprises within the customs bonded area is deemed and managed as import and export trade. As this case involved goods processed and manufactured overseas and the delivery of goods began overseas, its categorization in the arbitral award as a foreign-related case was not inappropriate. This Court does not support the applicant's claim due to lack of legal basis.

Another case concerned an application to set aside an arbitral award. Here the Beijing Fourth Intermediate People's Court held:[108] '[t]he two contracts in this case both specified delivery method as spot delivery in Shanghai customs bonded area, goods yet to be cleared by customs in a customs bonded area are classified as goods yet to be entered pursuant to the customs management system, consequently this case

---

106. Supreme People's Court (2003) Min-Si-Ta-Zi No. 2, 28 February 2003.
107. Shandong Dongying Intermediate People's Court Civil Ruling (2008) Dong-Ming-San-Chu-Zi No. 55, 2 November 2008.
108. Beijing Fourth Intermediate People's Court Civil Ruling (2015) Si-Zhong-Min-(Shang)-Te-Zi No. 00152, 19 June 2015.

possesses foreign element. Based on this analysis this Court considers that this case should be deemed as foreign-related arbitration case'.

Third, recent legislative trends and judicial practice are developing towards a broader interpretation and recognition of 'foreign elements'. In 2012 the SPC issued Interpretations of the Supreme People's Court on Several Issues Concerning Application of the Law of the PRC on Choice of Law for Foreign-Related Civil Relationships (I), Article 1 of which stipulates:[109]

> A civil relationship involving any of the following circumstances may be held by a people's court to be a foreign-related civil relationship:
> (1) One party or both parties are foreign citizen, foreign legal person or other organisation, stateless person;
> (2) One party or both parties have habitual residence outside the territory of the People's Republic of China;
> (3) The subject matter is located outside the territory of the People's Republic of China;
> (4) The legal facts that leads to the creation, change or termination of the civil relationship occurred outside the territory of the People's Republic of China;
> (5) Other circumstances under which a civil relationship may be identified as foreign-related civil relationship.

Here it can be seen that the additional criterion for determining foreign-related civil relations is 'other circumstances under which a civil relationship may be identified as foreign-related civil relationship'. As to what may constitute such circumstances, one may refer to a civil ruling of the Shanghai First Intermediate People's Court dated 27 November 2015 (2013) Hu-Yi-Zhong-Min-Ren(Wai-Zhong)-Zi No. 2). The parties in that case, Siemens International Trading (Shanghai) Co., Ltd. and Shanghai Golden Landmark Co., Ltd. were both Chinese companies registered in the PRC. The delivery place specified in the contract and the location of the facilities (the subject matter of the contract) are both within the PRC's territory. This case does not have the typical foreign elements according to the traditional view. However, for the two reasons stated below, the Shanghai First Intermediate People's Court held the contractual relationship in this case fell within the above-mentioned 'other circumstances which may be identified as foreign-related civil relations' and therefore possessed foreign elements:[110]

> Firstly, the subject matter of the contracts in this case all had certain foreign elements. Although Siemens and Golden Landmark are both Chinese legal persons, their places of registration are both within the Shanghai Pilot Free Trade Zone, and they are both wholly-owned foreign enterprises in nature. Since the capital sources, ultimate ownership of profits, management decisions of this type of companies are all closely related to their foreign investors, therefore such companies have more obvious foreign elements in contrast with ordinary domestic companies. Necessary attention should be given to these foreign elements in light of the pilot free trade zone's reform background of advancing convenience in investment and trade. Secondly, the performance characteristics of the contracts in

---

109. Fa-Shi (2012) No. 24, issued on 28 December 2012 and implemented on 7 January 2013.
110. Shanghai First Intermediate People's Court Civil Ruling (2013) Hu-Yi-Zhong-Min-Ren-(Wai-Zhong)-Zi No. 2, 27 November 2015.

this case have foreign elements. Although the facilities (the subject matter of the contract) were to be ultimately delivered to a domestic construction site, however in light of these contracts' process of execution and performance, the relevant facilities were transported from somewhere outside the PRC territory into the pilot free trade zone (previously known as Shanghai Waigaoquiao customs bonded area) for bonding supervision, followed by timely processing of customs clearance and tax payment in accordance with the contracts, transferring from within to outside the zone, until completion of import procedures. It follows that the transfer process of these contracts' subject matter possesses certain characteristics of international sale of goods. Accordingly the performance of contracts in this case can be more obviously distinguished from the common domestic sales contract disputes because it involved the use of a pilot free trade zone's special customs regulatory measures.

Furthermore, on 19 January 2015 the PRC's Ministry of Commerce issued the Foreign Investment Law of the PRC (Draft for Comments). Article 11 provides for foreign investors, introduces the criterion of 'actual control' and deems domestic enterprises controlled by foreign investors as foreign investors.[111] This is merely a draft for public consultation and is yet to complete the legislative process. Nonetheless, whether and how this legislative direction will affect and expand the determination of foreign elements in the laws concerning foreign-related civil relations is especially worthy of follow-up observation.

The fourth noteworthy point is that the PRC basically and usually treats cases involving Hong Kong, Macau and Taiwan as foreign-related cases.[112] In terms of the applicable laws to cases involving Hong Kong and Macau, Article 19 of the Interpretations of the Supreme People's Court on Several Issues Concerning Application of Law of the PRC on Choice of Law for Foreign-Related Civil Relationships (I) expressly stipulates that this Law applies to issues about the applicable laws for civil relations involving Hong Kong Special Administrative Region or Macau Special Administrative Region. This Law also provides a citing basis for judges dealing with issues about the applicable laws for civil relations involving Taiwan. The Provisions of the Supreme People's Court on the Application of Law in the Trial of Taiwan-Related Civil and Commercial Cases is a judicial interpretation specifically developed for cases involving

---

111. Article 11 para. 1 of the PRC Foreign Investment Law (Draft for Consultation) stipulates: 'Foreign investors referred to in this Law means the following bodies investing within the territory of China: (1) natural persons without Chinese citizenship; (2) enterprises established in accordance with the laws of other countries or law areas; (3) other national or regional governments and their associated departments or institutions; (4) international organizations.' Paragraph 2 deems the enterprises within China controlled by the bodies prescribed in para. 1 as foreign investors. *See* http://tfs.mofcom.gov.cn/article/as/201501/20150100871010.shtml (accessed 4 May 2017).
112. Please *see* the response by the representative of the SPC's Fourth Civil Tribunal during a press conference on 6 January 2013 about the Interpretation of various issues concerning the PRC Law on the Applicable Laws for Foreign-Related Civil Relations (Part 1), website of the PRC, http://www/court.gov.cn/zixun-xiangqing-4966.html (accessed 4 May 2017). *See also* Wei Jiang (ed), *Arbitration Law* 217 (China Renmin University Press 2011).

Hsi-Chuan Hsueh indicated that 'treating awards involving Hong Kong, Macau and Taiwan by reference to foreign-related awards is the consensus of PRC scholars': Hsi-Chuan Hsueh, *Cross-Strait Arbitration Law: Theory and Practice* 457 (Hong-Yang Publishing 2011).

Taiwan.[113] Article 1 stipulates: '[a] people's court hearing Taiwan-related civil or commercial case shall apply the relevant provisions of laws and judicial interpretations. Where, according to the principle of selecting the applicable laws as specified in laws and judicial interpretations, the civil law of Taiwan region are determined as the applicable law, the people's court shall apply that law'.

In terms of jurisdiction, Article 5 of the Provisions of the Supreme People's Court on Some Issues Concerning the Jurisdiction of Civil and Commercial Cases Involving Foreign Elements expressly provides that 'the jurisdiction over civil and commercial cases involving parties from the Special Administration Regions of Hong Kong, Macau and Taiwan Region shall be dealt with by reference to this Regulation'.[114]

In terms of arbitration, the last sentence of Point 6 of the previously mentioned Shanghai Higher People's Court's Opinion on Several Issues Concerning the Implementation of the Arbitration Law of the PRC issued in 2001 specifically states that 'arbitration involving Hong Kong, Macau and Taiwan should be dealt with as foreign-related arbitration'.[115] Article 10 of the Jiangsu Higher People's Court's Opinion on Several Issues Concerning Judicial Review of Civil and Commercial Arbitration also stipulates that 'judicial review of arbitral awards of Hong Kong, Macau or Taiwan shall be dealt with as judicial review of foreign arbitration cases, and shall apply the specific provisions of legal and judicial interpretation'.[116]

In addition, for commercial cases involving Hong Kong and Macau, paragraph 1 of Article 2 of the Notice of the Supreme People's Court on Issuing the Minutes of the Symposium on the Trial of Commercial Cases involving Hong Kong or Macao by Courts Nationwide provides that, in commercial cases involving Hong Kong and Macau, if the competent people's court finds that the arbitration agreement is void, invalid or unenforceable because of uncertainty, the court shall, before making its decision, follow the multi-tiered reporting system in accordance with the SPC's Notification of Certain Issues Relating to the People's Courts' Dealing with Foreign-Related and Foreign Arbitration. Cases involving Taiwan are also dealt with by reference to the provisions for foreign-related cases.[117] For instance, in a case concerning the enforcement of an arbitral award involving Career Technology (Mfg.) Co., Ltd. and Wujiang Jinhong High-Tech Co., Ltd.,[118] the court found that 'because the applicant Career Technology is a Taiwanese corporate entity, whether or not to enforce the arbitral award in this case should therefore be determined in accordance with and in modification of the legal provisions and procedures concerning foreign-related arbitral awards'. Another example is the case concerning application for cancellation of a cooperative contract between Landai International Entertainment Co., Ltd. and

---

113. Fa-Shi (2010) No. 19, issued on 27 December 2010 and implemented on 1 January 2011.
114. Fa-Shi (2002) No. 5, issued on 25 February 2002 and implemented on 1 March 2002.
115. *Supra* n. 99.
116. Su-Gao-Fa-Shen-Wei (2007) No. 4, issued and implemented on 30 March 2007; Jiangsu Higher People's Court's Opinion on the Various Issues concerning Judicial Review of Civil and Commercial Arbitration, Su-Gao-Fa-Shen-Wei (2010) No. 11, 13 August 2010 (the 2010 revision did not amend this article).
117. Fa-Fa (2008) No. 8, issued and implemented on 21 January 2008.
118. Jiangsu Suzhou Intermediate People's Court Civil Ruling (2008) Su-Zhong-Min-San-Zhong-Shen-Zi No. 003, 5 September 2008.

Chapter 3: 'Public Policy' and the Even More Unpredictable

Shanghai Sanmao Textile Co., Ltd.,[119] in which the Shanghai Second Intermediate People's Court also found that, because Landai (the respondent against whom enforcement is sought) is an enterprise registered in Taiwan Province, the revocation of the arbitral award made by CIETAC Shanghai Sub-Commission (2004) Hu-Zhong-Cai-Zi No. 011 should therefore be 'dealt with in reference to the procedures and laws for foreign-related arbitral awards'. Furthermore, some arbitration rules also expressly provide that the specific provisions concerning international commercial arbitration should apply to cases involving Hong Kong Special Administrative Region, Macau Special Administrative Region and Taiwan Region (e.g., Article 54 paragraph 2 of the Beijing Arbitration Commission (BAC) Arbitration Rules[120]).

However, there is a noteworthy possible exception to the principle of treating cases involving Hong Kong, Macau and Taiwan as foreign-related cases, namely Article 29 paragraph 2 of the Implementing Rules for the Implementation of the Law of the PRC on the Protection of Investments of Taiwan Compatriots: 'the parties unwilling or unable to negotiate or mediate may, pursuant to the arbitration clause in their contract or subsequent arbitration agreement in writing, submit to arbitration by *arbitration institutions of China*. The *Mainland arbitration institutions* may engage Taiwanese compatriots as arbitrators in accordance with relevant national legal provisions (emphasis added).'[121] Pursuant to this provision, if one of the parties to the arbitration involving Taiwan is a Taiwanese company, enterprise, other economic organisation or individual, then the parties can only submit their dispute to arbitration by 'arbitration institutions of China', and cannot agree to submit their dispute to arbitration by 'foreign arbitration institutions' (such as SIAC and ICC International Court of Arbitration, etc.).[122] This differs from the usual view that in foreign-related arbitrations, the parties can agree to select any arbitration institutions outside the territory of Mainland China. Moreover, there are different views on how to interpret 'arbitration institutions of China'. Some interpret it as 'arbitration institutions established pursuant to the PRC Arbitration Law' and exclude the arbitration institutions of Taiwan, Hong Kong and Macau from the 'arbitration institutions of China' stipulated in the Implementing Regulations as such institutions are not established pursuant to the PRC Arbitration Law. Yet other scholars believe that, in light of the basic 'One China policy' adopted by the PRC, the interpretation of 'arbitration institutions of China' in this provision should include arbitration institutions of Taiwan, Hong Kong and Macau. Upon closer observation of this provision, such interpretation is also more in line with the successive and simultaneous references to 'arbitration institutions of China' and

---

119. Shanghai Second Intermediate People's Court Civil Ruling (2004) Hu-Er-Zhong-Min-Wu-(Shang)-Chu-Zi No. 66, 15 June 2004.
120. Discussed and adopted by the Sixth Beijing Arbitration Commission during the Fourth Meeting on 9 July 2014; implemented on 1 April 2015.
121. Order No. 274 of State Council of the People's Republic of China, issued and implemented on 7 December 1999.
122. John Huan-Wen Chen, *Cross-Strait Commercial Disputes and Arbitration Practice* 5–6 (Yung-Ran Culture Publishing Inc. 1993); Kuan-Ming Wu & Hong-Lin Yu, *Theories and Development of International Commercial Arbitration* 367 (Hanlu Publishing 2013).

'Mainland arbitration institution' in this provision. From the perspective of systematic interpretation, it can infer that the above two are different.[123]

Finally and incidentally, it should be stated that 'arbitral awards involving Hong Kong, Macau and Taiwan' differ from 'arbitral awards made in Hong Kong, Macau and Taiwan'. The so-called arbitral awards involving Hong Kong, Macau and Taiwan are made in the PRC's territory but with elements involving Hong Kong, Macau or Taiwan, such as one of the parties being a corporation of Hong Kong, Macau or Taiwan, etc. In summary, Figure 3.1 represents the classification of arbitral awards under the PRC's arbitration legal system.

Figure 3.1 Categorisation of Arbitral Awards

3.2.2.2 Social and Public Interest as a Ground for Revocation of Foreign-Related Arbitral Awards, Non-enforcement of Foreign-Related Arbitral Awards or Domestic Arbitral Awards?

Table 3.1 clearly shows the inconsistent provisions for the revocation and non-enforcement of domestic arbitral awards in the PRC's Arbitration Law and Civil Procedure Law. Only Article 58 item 3 of the PRC Arbitration Law stipulates that '[t]he people's court shall set aside the award if it finds that the award violates social and

---

123. Helena Hsi-Chia Chen, *Commercial Arbitration after the Cross-Strait Bilateral Investment Protection and Promotion Agreement - Focused on the Interpretation and Application of Article 14.4 of the Cross-strait Bilateral Investment Protection and Promotion Agreement*, 92 NTPU Law Review 137, 161 (2014).

Chapter 3: 'Public Policy' and the Even More Unpredictable

public interest'. The PRC Civil Procedure Law does not have any related provisions for domestic arbitral awards and consequently questions about how to resolve and interpret any differences between the PRC Arbitration Law and Civil Procedure Law do not arise. The remainder requires interpretation and examination, which includes the following three questions:

(1) Can the courts set aside foreign-related arbitral awards on the ground of 'violation of social and public interest'?
(2) Can the courts refuse to enforce foreign-related arbitral awards on the ground of 'violation of social and public interest'?
(3) Can the courts refuse to enforce domestic arbitral awards on the ground of 'violation of social and public interest'?

These are discussed below.

(1) Can the Courts Set Aside Foreign-Related Arbitral Awards on the Ground of 'Violation of Social and Public Interest'?

Since Article 70 of the PRC Arbitration Law merely refers to Article 260 paragraph 1 but not paragraph 2 about 'violation of social and public interest', there are two views (affirmative and negative) on the issue of whether 'violation social and public interest' is a ground for revoking foreign-related arbitral awards. Proponents of the affirmative view include Justice Xingjun Ge and Shengchang Wang, etc.,[124] who believe that violation of social and public interest should also be one of the grounds for revoking foreign-related arbitral awards. In the opinion of Lianbin Song and Jian Zhao, the Arbitration Law should fully apply Article 261 of the PRC Civil Procedure Law of 1991 to this issue and not merely apply paragraph 1 of Article 261; such loopholes in Articles 70 and 71 of the Arbitration Law should require the addition of public order reservation clause for the revocation of foreign-related arbitral awards in future legislative amendments.[125] According to the supporters of the affirmative view,[126] although Chapter 7 of the PRC Arbitration Law (Special Provisions for Foreign-related Arbitration) does not

---

124. Xingjun Ge, *Issues Arising from Enforcement of Arbitral Awards – Talk by Justice Xingjun Ge, the Chair of the Enforcement Division of the Supreme People's Court at Arbitrators' Seminar on Practical Issues 2003*, 89 Arbitration and Law 18, 23 & 26 (2003) ('If the enforcement court finds that the arbitral award being enforced violates social and public interest, the court may order non-enforcement or revocation. This is because in the strict legal sense, social interest is not a legal term but a concept of political category which embodies social and public interest for domestic arbitral awards and embodies the interest of national sovereignty for foreign-related or foreign arbitral awards'; 'the omission of "violation of social and public interest" from the grounds for revocation and non-enforcement in Articles 70 and 71 of the Arbitration Law is a serious defect which should be remedied.'); Shengchang Wang, *Lectures on Chinese Arbitration Law*, Arbitration and Law Communication 23 (November 1999) ('According to the spirit of Article 65 of the Arbitration Law, the people's courts may also revoke foreign-related arbitral awards which they find to violate social and public interest'); Guanghui Li & Han Wang, *Arbitration Law* 279 (University of International Business and Economics Press 2011).
125. Lianbin Song & Jian Zhao, *Analysis on Amendments to Arbitration Act 1994*, 4 Journal of International Economic Law 597, 611–612 (2001).
126. Xiang Yin, *The Recognition and Enforcement of the Arbitral Award Manifested in the New York Convention by the Courts in China*, 27(7) Hebei Law Review 19, 22 (2009).

Helena Hsi-Chia Chen

contain specific provisions about this issue, Article 65 of this chapter stipulates that '[f]or matters not covered in this Chapter, the other relevant provisions of this Law shall apply', while the last sentence of Article 58 stipulates that, '[i]f the people's court finds that the arbitral award violates social and public interest, it shall set aside the award'. Thus the court should also set aside foreign-related arbitral awards which violate social and public interest.

The logical basis for adopting the negative view in practical cases is that Article 70 of the PRC Arbitration Law merely refers to Article 260 paragraph 1 of the PRC Civil Procedure Law, without expressly referring to paragraph 2, which provides that the people's court may refuse enforcement if it finds that the award's enforcement would violate social and public interest. Consequently 'violation of social and public interest' cannot be a ground for setting aside foreign-related arbitral awards. According to the supporters of the negative view,[127] Article 1 of the SPC's Notification of Certain Matters Relating to the People's Courts' Revocation of Foreign-Related Arbitral Awards also refers to paragraph 1 of Article 260 of the PRC Arbitration Law (currently Article 274) without referring to paragraph 2, which also evidences that the grounds for revoking foreign-related arbitral awards do not include 'violation of social and public interest'.

In addition, Table 3.2 below compares Article 1 of the SPC's Notification of Certain Matters Relating to the People's Courts' Revocation of Foreign-Related Arbitral Awards and Article 2 of the SPC's Notification of Certain Issues Relating to the People's Courts' Dealing with Foreign-Related and Foreign Arbitration.

Table 3.2 Comparison Between Article 1 of the SPC's Notification of Certain Matters Relating to the People's Courts' Revocation of Foreign-Related Arbitral Awards and Article 2 of the SPC's Notification of Certain Issues Relating to the People's Courts' Dealing with Foreign-Related and Foreign Arbitration

SPC's Notification of Certain Matters Relating to the People's Courts' Revocation of Foreign-Related Arbitral Awards[128]	SPC's Notification of Certain Issues Relating to the People's Courts' Dealing with Foreign-Related and Foreign Arbitration[129]
Article 1: Where a party applies to a people's court to *revoke* a foreign-related arbitral award pursuant to Arbitration Law, and if the people's court upon its review finds that the foreign-related arbitral award falls within one of the circumstances specified in *Article 260 paragraph 1* of the Civil	Article 2: Where a party applies to a people's court for the *enforcement* of a foreign-related institutional arbitral award or for the recognition and enforcement of a foreign institutional arbitral award, if the people's court finds that the foreign-related institutional arbitral award falls

---

127. Xianming Shi, *Studies on the Remedies for the Parties' Rights Injured in International Commercial Arbitration* 385 (China Renmin University Press 2011).
128. Fa (1998) No. 40.
129. Fa-Fa (1995) No. 18.

Chapter 3: 'Public Policy' and the Even More Unpredictable

SPC's Notification of Certain Matters Relating to the People's Courts' Revocation of Foreign-Related Arbitral Awards[128]	SPC's Notification of Certain Issues Relating to the People's Courts' Dealing with Foreign-Related and Foreign Arbitration[129]
Procedure Law, the people's court shall, before deciding to revoke the award or notify the arbitral tribunal about re-arbitration, report to the higher people's court in its locality for review. The higher people's court shall report its review opinion to the SPC if it agrees with revoking the award or notifying the arbitral tribunal about re-arbitration. The court may decide to revoke the award or notify the arbitral tribunal about re-arbitration only after the SPC's reply.	within one of the circumstances specified in *Article 260* of the Civil Procedure Law, or that the recognition and enforcement of the foreign arbitral award is incompatible with international conventions acceded to by the PRC or the principle of reciprocity, the people's court shall, before deciding on *non-enforcement* or refusing recognition and enforcement, report to the higher people's court in its locality for review. The higher people's court shall report its review opinion to the SPC if it agrees with non-enforcement or refusing recognition and enforcement. The court may decide on non-enforcement or refuse recognition and enforcement only after the SPC's reply.

It can be seen that Article 1 of the SPC's Notification of Certain Matters Relating to the People's Courts' Revocation of Foreign-Related Arbitral Awards merely refers to 'paragraph 1' of Article 260 of the PRC Civil Procedure Law (currently Article 274) with respect to 'revocation' of foreign-related arbitral awards, whereas Article 2 of the SPC's Notification of Certain Issues Relating to the People's Courts' Dealing with Foreign-Related and Foreign Arbitration refers to Article 260 of the PRC Civil Procedure Law (currently Article 274) without specifying any paragraph with respect to 'non-enforcement' of foreign-related institutional arbitral awards.[130] According to the general literal interpretation, such reference means reference to the entirety of Article 260 of the PRC Civil Procedure Law (currently Article 274), including both paragraph 1 and paragraph 2 (namely, the people's court may refuse enforcement of an award if it finds that the enforcement would violate social and public interest). The contrast between these two provisions also sufficiently evidences that the grounds for judicial revocation of foreign-related arbitral awards should not include 'violation of social and public interest'.[131]

---

130. According to its context, Art. 2 of the SPC's Notification of Certain Issues Relating to the People's Courts' Dealing with Foreign-Related And Foreign Arbitration concerning incompatibility with 'international conventions acceded to by the People's Republic of China or the principle of reciprocity' should pertain to the criteria for determining the parties' applications for 'recognition and enforcement of foreign arbitral awards' which are unrelated to the enforcement or non-enforcement of 'foreign-related arbitral awards' and therefore omitted from discussion.
131. According to some scholars: '[b]oth the SPC's Notification of Certain Issues Relating to the People's Courts' Dealing with Foreign-Related and Foreign Arbitration and the SPC's Notification of Certain Matters Relating to the People's Courts' Revocation of Foreign-Related Arbitral Awards merely refer to reporting to the SPC when deciding on non-enforcement or revocation of foreign-related arbitral awards under Art. 260 para. 1 of the Civil Procedure Law, this also

Some proponents of the negative view further suggest legislative reform of expressly providing 'violation of social and public interest' as a ground for revoking foreign-related arbitral awards that the PRC courts can invoke ex officio.[132] At the same time they reiterate the need to prevent and control the tendency to abuse 'social and public interest' when including violation of social and public interest as a ground for revoking foreign-related arbitral awards. Accordingly, the law should provide a workable definition of 'social and public interest' by confining it to the range of fundamental national interest, social interest, basic principles of law and moral ethics, by prohibiting merits review of foreign-related arbitral awards in the name of social and public interest, as well as prohibiting the revocation of foreign-related arbitral awards owing to violation of specific regulations of national law rather than basic principles.[133]

In practice the affirmative view and the negative view co-exist. An example of the negative view can be found in the case relating to an application for setting aside an award between a limited company and Mr Huang. In this case, the Guangdong Shenzhen Intermediate Court held that: 'the grounds for the company's application for setting aside the arbitral award also include:... 3. the arbitral award violates Mainland China's social and public interest. As none of these grounds are specified in Article 258 of the PRC Civil Procedure Law, this Court will not review those grounds'.[134] In the case concerning the application by Liya Trading Company, a Canadian company, to set aside an arbitral award made by Nanjing Arbitration Commission ((2007) Ning-Cai-Zi No. 266-35), although one of the applicant's grounds for revocation was the award's violation of social and public interest, the Jiangsu Nanjing Intermediate People's Court held that this was a foreign-related arbitral award which, pursuant to Article 70 of the PRC Arbitration Law, should be determined in accordance with Article 258 paragraph 1 (currently Article 274 paragraph 1) of the PRC Civil Procedure Law; here the applicant's alleged violation of social and public interest by the award is not one of the circumstances specified in Article 258 paragraph 1 (currently Article 274 paragraph 1) of the PRC Civil Procedure Law and therefore this Court will not adjudicate it.[135] In addition, the Shanghai Second Intermediate People's Court also held in an application for revocation of arbitral award concerning disputes over outstanding debts under a lift equipment contract between China Hefei Run'an (International) Development Co. Ltd and Dover Elevator (Far East) Ltd that, because one of the parties, Dover Elevator (Far East) Ltd, was a Hong Kong company, the arbitral award was therefore foreign-related

---

explains that only para. 1 (and not para. 2) of Art. 260 of the Civil Procedure Law can be cited when deciding on non-enforcement or revocation of foreign-related arbitral awards.' (Xianming Shi, *Studies on the Remedies for the Parties' Rights Injured in International Commercial Arbitration* 385 (China Renmin University Press 2011)).

132. *Ibid.*, at 398; Huanfang Du, *The Reform of the Revocation of Foreign-Related Arbitral Awards in China: From a Practice Perspective*, 100 Arbitration and Law 95, 104 (2006).
133. Xianming Shi, *ibid.*
134. Guangdong Shenzhen Intermediate Court Civil Ruling (2011) Shen-Zhong-Fa-Min-Si-Chu-Zi No. 1, 20 May 2011.
135. Jiangsu Higher People's Court Civil Ruling (2009) Ning-Min-Wu-Chu-Zi No. 38, 23 March 2009.

Chapter 3: 'Public Policy' and the Even More Unpredictable

and subject to the provisions of both Article 70 of the PRC Arbitration Law and paragraph 1 of Article 260 (currently Article 274) of the PRC Civil Procedure Law. The applicant sought revocation on the grounds of violation of social and public interest by directly citing Article 58 paragraph 3 of the PRC Arbitration Law, which is contrary to Article 65 of the PRC Arbitration Law. The Court did not adopt this view and rejected the application for revocation.[136] In the two arbitration cases in 2011 involving Shanghai Nanshi Development Sports Business Division and Imagine International Limited,[137] the applicant (Imagine International Limited) alleged that significant errors in the arbitral award essentially violated the PRC's social and public interest and should be set aside. The Shanghai Second Intermediate People's Court in both cases held that such ground for revocation did not pertain to the legal grounds for revoking arbitral awards, and therefore the Court did not support such application. The Shanghai Second Intermediate People's Court again adopted the same view in an application to set aside an arbitral award between Landai International Entertainment Co., Ltd. and Shanghai Sanmao Textile Co., Ltd. concerning Joint Venture Contract (JVC) disputes.[138]

It is worth noting that the same trial judges in the previously mentioned application by Liya Trading Company to revoke an arbitral award made by Nanjing Arbitration Commission (Award No. 266-35) also decided another application to revoke an award made by Nanjing Arbitration Commission (Award No. 222-31)[139] on the same day. Both cases were heard in the same court of Jiangsu Nanjing Intermediate People's Court, by Presiding Judge Feng Xue, Judge Liang Sun and Acting Judge Hanqing Zhang, with 23 March 2009 as the judgment date. However, unlike the application to revoke Award No. 266-35, the Jiangsu Nanjing Intermediate People's Court in the application to revoke Award No. 222-31 did not explain that 'the applicant's alleged violation of social and public interest by the award is not one the circumstances specified in Article 258 paragraph 1 of the PRC Civil Procedure Law' and that therefore the Court 'will not adjudicate it'. Instead, the Court stated in the last paragraph of its ruling that 'the arbitral award did not violate social and public interest' without detailed reasoning. This raises possible inferences that the Jiangsu Nanjing Intermediate People's Court recognised 'violation of social and public interest' as a ground for revoking foreign-related arbitral awards; the Court proceeded to determine whether the award would violate social and public interest and further found that the award did not violate social and public interest, etc. However, from a joint observation of a similar case with the same parties and judgment date of 23 March 2009 (application by Liya Trading Company to revoke Award No. 266-35) in which the Court's detailed discussions have been cited above, the same judges deciding the two cases on the same

---

136. Shanghai Second Intermediate People's Court Civil Ruling (2002) Hu-Er-Zhong-Min-Wu-(Shang)-Chu-Zi No. 55, 9 July 2002.
137. Shanghai Second Intermediate People's Court Civil Ruling (2011) Hu-Er-Zhong-Min-Si-(Shang)-Che-Zi No. S17, 15 September 2011; and Shanghai Second Intermediate People's Court Civil Ruling (2011) Hu-Er-Zhong-Min-Si-(Shang)-Che-Zi No. S18, 15 September 2011.
138. Shanghai Second Intermediate People's Court Civil Ruling (2002) Hu-Er-Zhong-Min-Wu-(Shang)-Chu-Zi No. 66, 15 June 2004.
139. Jiangsu Higher People's Court Civil Ruling (2009) Ning-Min-Wu-Chu-Zi No. 37, 23 March 2009.

day seemingly adopted different views. It may be inferred that the Court's statement in the application to revoke Award No. 222-31 that 'the award did not violate social and public interest' should be superfluous and insufficient to infer an affirmative view.

In a case in 2007 concerning an application by Central China (Asia) Investment Limited for revocation of an arbitral award, the Beijing Second Intermediate People's Court adopted the negative view that whether or not an arbitral award is contrary to social and public interest is not within the scope of review by the people's courts in cases concerning the revocation of foreign-related arbitral awards.[140] However, in a case in 2014 the applicant argued the arbitral award's violation of social and public interest as one of the grounds for revoking foreign-related arbitral awards;[141] the Beijing Second Intermediate People's Court on the one hand expressed that violation of social and public interest 'does not belong to the grounds for revoking arbitral awards in Article 274 of the PRC Civil Procedure Law', while on the other hand proceeded to adjudicate the issue of social and public interest violation and held that 'the disputes arising from the performance of the share transfer agreement and supplementary agreement by the various parties in this case belong to civil disputes between equal entities and do not involve social and public interest'.[142]

A case adopting the affirmative view that violation of social and public interest can be a ground for revoking foreign-related arbitral awards can be found in the Beijing Second Intermediate People's Court's rejection in 1996 of an application by Shanghai Dental Instrument Factory to revoke an award made by the CIETAC Shanghai Sub-Commission.[143] In that case, the Court was of the view that violation of 'social and public interest' can be a ground for revoking foreign-related arbitral awards, and such violation indeed existed in that case. The applicant (Shanghai Dental Instrument Factory) alleged that the 'joint venture's profits of 1994' acknowledged in the award actually arose from smuggling by the respondent (Junxiong Hu) during his appointment as General Manager of the joint venture. It was subsequently confiscated by customs, and that therefore the award's finding violated social and public interest. In response, the Beijing Second Intermediate People's Court held:[144] 'according to the documentary evidence submitted by the applicant (Shanghai Dental Instrument Factory) in relation to the alleged illegal business conducted by the respondent (Junxiong Hu), the joint venture company and the person appointed by the joint venture company's board of directors should be legally liable for such illegal business, which do not have any direct legal relationship with the scope of the arbitration agreement and the arbitral award, and therefore there is no legal basis for the applicant's allegation that the award violates social and public interest.' Thus it can be seen that

---

140. Beijing Second Intermediate People's Court Civil Ruling (2006) Er-Zhong-Min-Te-Zi No. 16175, 15 February 2007.
141. Beijing Second Intermediate People's Court Civil Ruling (2014) Er-Zhong-Min-Te-Zi No. 07648, 18 December 2014. One of the parties to this arbitral award was a company registered in Hong Kong; thus there was a foreign-related element.
142. *Ibid.*
143. Beijing Second Intermediate People's Court Civil Ruling (1996) Er-Zhong-Jing-Chu-Zi No. 83, 20 May 1996. Cited from Chinese Yearbook of Foreign-Related Arbitration (1995–1997) 54–55 (CIETAC, 1998).
144. *Ibid.*

the court ultimately found the award did not violate social and public interest and rejected the application to set aside the award.

Recently the Beijing Third Intermediate People's Court adopted the affirmative view in the case concerning arbitral award No. 1 regarding Shenyun Chen and Beijing Jiali Heng De Real Estate Development Co., Ltd.[145] as well as the case concerning arbitral award No. 2 regarding Shenyun Chen and Beijing Jiali Heng De Real Estate Development Co., Ltd.[146] After finding that the applicant Shenyun Chen is a Taiwanese resident and therefore the cases involve foreign elements, the Court clearly stated that the entire Article 274 of the Civil Procedure Law (which is Article 260 of the 1991 version) and not just paragraph 1 should apply to these cases. After hearing the alleged violation of social and public interest by the relevant arbitral awards as the ground for revocation, the Beijing Third Intermediate People's Court held in both cases that such ground for revocation was not established, as 'the relevant arbitral awards merely adjudicated on the private rights arising from the contracts between Shenyun Chen and Jiali Heng De and do not involve social and public interest'.

The text of some other practical rulings also refers to phrases such as 'the circumstances of violating the basic principles of law or social and public interest do not exist in this arbitral award' (e.g., the case between Zhejiang Materials Industry International Co., Ltd. and NOVO Commodities LIMIXXX[147]), leading to a possible inference that the judge in that case adopted the affirmative view. Another example is the Reply of the Supreme People's Court to the Request for Instructions Concerning Whether to Revoke the Arbitral Award of CIETAC South China Sub-Commission, where the SPC stated in its Reply to the Guangdong Higher People's Court:[148] 'the China International Economic and Trade Arbitration Commission South China Sub-Commission made an arbitral award (2005) Shen-Zhong-Cai-Zi No. 37, in relation to the JVC dispute between Electricity Supply Bureau of Luoding City and Huien (China) Investment Co., Ltd. Luoding Bureau applied to the Shenzhen Intermediate People's Court to set aside this award on the grounds that the arbitrated matters exceeded the scope of the parties' arbitration agreement, that the arbitral proceedings violated the arbitration rules and that the award's enforcement would violate social and public interest, etc. Because the tribunal has the authority to decide whether to accept the amendment to counterclaims and Electricity Supply Bureau of Luoding City takes responsibility as a civil body participating in civil activities, therefore the grounds that the arbitral proceedings violated the arbitration rules and that the enforcement of the award would violate social and public interest cannot be established according to law'. This demonstrates that the SPC did not refuse adjudication directly on the basis that 'violation of social and public interest' is not a ground for revoking foreign-related arbitral awards, but instead stated, after its adjudication, that Luoding Bureau's alleged

---

145. Beijing Third Intermediate People's Court Civil Ruling (2014) San-Zhong-Min-(Shang)-Te-Zi No. 10476, 15 December 2014.
146. Beijing Third Intermediate People's Court Civil Ruling (2014) San-Zhong-Min-(Shang)-Te-Zi No. 10475, 15 December 2014.
147. Shanghai Second Intermediate People's Court Civil Ruling Civil Ruling (2010) Hu-Er-Zhong-Min-Si-(Shang)-Che-Zi No. 22, 20 October 2010.
148. Supreme People's Court (2005) Min-Si-Ta-Zi No. 47, 1 March 2006.

'violation of social and public interest by the award's enforcement cannot be established according to law'. This seems to adopt the affirmative view.

(2) Can the Courts Refuse to Enforce Foreign-Related Arbitral Awards on the Ground of 'Violation of Social and Public Interest'?

It can be seen from Table 3.1 that Article 274 of the PRC Civil Procedure Law and Article 71 of the PRC Arbitration Law both provide for the non-enforcement of foreign-related arbitral awards, yet the two differ slightly. Article 274 paragraph 2 of the PRC Civil Procedure Law stipulates that the people's court may refuse to enforce a foreign-related arbitral award if it finds that the award's enforcement would violate *social and public interest*. Yet Article 71 of the PRC Arbitration Law merely refers to paragraph 1 of Article 260 (currently Article 274) of the PRC Civil Procedure Law but not paragraph 2 concerning violation of social and public interest. Hence it cannot be said without a doubt that violation of social and public interest is a ground for non-enforcement of foreign-related arbitral awards.

In this respect the majority view is affirmative, as endorsed by Justice Xingjun Ge, Yifei Lin, Hu Li, Lianbin Song and Jian Zhao, etc.[149] Several cases have also adopted the affirmative view, an early example is a court's refusal to enforce a foreign-related arbitral award on the ground of 'violation of social and public interest' in 1992. In an application by Dongfeng Clothing Factory of Kaifeng for enforcement of arbitral award, the applicant (Dongfeng Clothing Factory of Kaifeng) requested enforcement from Henan Zhengzhou Intermediate People's Court on 28 May 1992. The respondent pleaded against enforcement. In its decision dated 28 September 1992 the Zhengzhou Intermediate People's Court held:[150] 'Pursuant to the current national policies and legal regulations, the enforcement of this award would severely damage national economic

---

149. Xingjun Ge, *supra* n. 124; In Yifei Lin's opinion, although Art. 71 of the PRC Arbitration Law merely cites the four procedural grounds for non-enforcement in Art. 258 para. 1 of the PRC Civil Procedure Law with respect to foreign-related arbitral awards, 'however the court can certainly decide on non-enforcement *ex officio* if it finds that the award violates public policy' (Yifei Lin, *International Commercial Arbitration Law and Practice* (Citic Publishing House 2005). Additionally Hu Li states: 'Article 71 of the Arbitration Law 1995 does not authorize the courts to refuse arbitral awards on the basis of violation of social and public interest. Nevertheless this does not mean that the circumstances of "violation of social and public interest" are excluded... The Civil Procedure Law 1991 and Arbitration Law 1995 are not mutually incompatible. The courts can invoke the ground of violation of social and public interest in circumstances they find necessary, because safeguarding a country's social and public interest should be the rights and obligations reserved for the courts of that country.' See Hu Li, *Enforcement of the International Commercial Arbitral Award, with Special Reference to the Enforcement of Arbitral Awards in the P. R. China* 136–137 (Law Press 2000); Lianbin Song & Jian Zhao, *supra* n. 125; Philip McConnaughay & Thomas B. Ginsburg (eds), *International Commercial Arbitration in Asia* 45–46 (2nd ed., JurisNet 2006).
150. Shengchang Wang, *Enforcement of Foreign Arbitral Awards in the People's Republic of China*, in *Improving the Efficiency of Arbitration Agreements and Awards: 40 Years of Application of the New York Convention* 461, 491 (Albert Jan van den Berg ed., Kluwer Law International 1999) ('Without much logical or reasoned analysis, the Zhengzhou Intermediate People's Court simply rejected enforcement of the award, by stating...'); Xiuwen Zhao (ed.), *International Commercial Arbitration Law* 381 (3rd ed. China Renmin University Press 2012); Dejun Cheng, Shengchang Wang & Ming Kang, *International Practice and Foreign-Related Arbitration* 258–260 (China Youth Press 1993).

Chapter 3: 'Public Policy' and the Even More Unpredictable

interest and social and public interest as well as affect national foreign trade order, and should be refused enforcement under Article 260 paragraph 2 (currently Article 274 paragraph 2) of the PRC Civil Procedure Law.' This case has caused extensive concerns and discussions in the academia (see section 5.1.1 of Chapter 5). Subsequently in 1997 the SPC, in its Reply of the Supreme People's Court on the Non-enforcement of an Arbitral Award on Dispute over the Performance Contract among USA Productions, Tom Hulett & Associates and China Women Travel Service,[151] also invoked 'violation of social and public interest of this country' and agreed with the Beijing Higher People's Court's opinion in refusing to enforce a foreign-related arbitral award – another case engendering extensive concerns and academic discussions (see section 5.1.2 of Chapter 5). Furthermore, in its decision dated 30 December 1998, the Guangdong Zhanjiang Intermediate People's Court also refused to enforce an arbitral award made by the Shenzhen Sub-commission of CIETAC on the basis of 'violation of social and public interest' pursuant to Article 260 paragraph 2 of the Civil Procedure Law of 1991.[152]

According to Article 2 of the SPC's Notification of Certain Issues Relating to the People's Courts' Dealing with Foreign-Related and Foreign Arbitration:[153] '[w]here a party applies to a people's court for the enforcement of foreign-related institutional arbitral awards, if the people's court finds that the foreign-related institutional arbitral award falls within one of the circumstances specified in *Article 260 (currently Article 274) of the Civil Procedure Law*, the people's court shall, before deciding to refuse recognition or enforcement, report to the higher people's court in its locality for review. The higher people's court shall report its review opinion to the SPC if it agrees with refusing recognition or enforcement. The court may refuse recognition or enforcement only after the SPC's reply (emphasis added)'. It seems that the grounds for non-enforcement of foreign-related arbitral awards are 'Article 260 (currently Article 274) of the Civil Procedure Law' without specifying any provisions. According to the general literal interpretation, this should refer to the entirety of Article 260 (currently Article 274) of the Civil Procedure Law, including paragraphs 1 and 2 (paragraph 2 provides that the people's court shall refuse enforcement if it finds that the award's enforcement would violate social and public interest). Consequently violation of social and public interest should be a ground for non-enforcement of foreign-related arbitral awards.

In addition, the SPC also adopted the affirmative view and considered whether the relevant foreign-related arbitral awards would violate social and public interest in its Reply in 2011 on the Non-enforcement of an Foreign-Related Arbitral Award on Dispute Over the Cooperative Contract between Turbo (Fareast) Ltd. and Hubei Province Yingtai Economic Development Company[154] and its Reply in 2006 to Anhui Higher People's Court's Request for Instruction Concerning Whether to Revoke the

---

151. Reply of the Supreme People's Court on the Non-enforcement of an Arbitral Award on Dispute over the Performance Contract among USA Productions, Tom Hulett & Associates and China Women Travel Service, Ta (1997) No. 35, 26 December 1997.
152. Guangdong Zhanjiang Intermediate People's Court Civil Ruling (1996) Zhan-Zhong-Fa-Zhi-Zi No. 1, 30 December 1998.
153. Fa-Fa(15) No. 18.
154. Supreme People's Court (2011) Min-Si-Ta-Zi No. 62, 14 December 2011.

Arbitral Award (2003) Mao-Zhong-Cai-Zi No. 0138 of CIETAC.[155] Other three recent cases are: the case concerning sale of goods contract between applicant Touhou Bussan & Co. Ltd and respondent Suzhou Hengliang Import & Export Co. Ltd (2008),[156] the case concerning ship repair and modification contract between applicant Goldsun International Shipping Limited and respondent Zhenjiang Yong'an Shipbuilding Co., Ltd. (2010),[157] and the case concerning the sale of international technology and engineering contract between applicant Sumitomo Mitsui Finance and Leasing Co., Ltd and respondents Suzhou Xiqi Electronic Technology Co., Ltd. and Jiangsu Overseas Group Corporation (2010).[158] Although in all three cases the respondents failed to raise defences within the prescribed timeframe, the trial courts nevertheless considered ex officio and determined that the enforcement of the relevant arbitral awards would not damage the PRC's public interest and therefore granted enforcement. Furthermore, the court also granted the application for enforcement in a case involving Career Technology (Mfg.) Co. Ltd. and Wujiang Jinhong High-Tech Co. Ltd. after considering and concluding that 'the award's enforcement would not damage this state's public interest'.[159]

(3) Can the Courts Refuse to Enforce Domestic Arbitral Awards on the Ground of 'Violation of Social and Public Interest'?

Domestic arbitral awards are also in the same situation. From Table 3.1 it can be seen that Article 237 of the PRC Civil Procedure Law and Article 63 of the PRC Arbitration Law both provide for non-enforcement of domestic arbitral awards, yet the two differ slightly. Article 237 paragraph 3 of the PRC Civil Procedure Law stipulates that the people's court 'shall refuse to enforce the award if it finds that the award's enforcement would violate *social and public interest*' (emphasis added), whereas Article 63 of the PRC Arbitration Law simply cites paragraph 2 of Article 217 (currently Article 237) of the PRC Civil Procedure Law but not paragraph 3 concerning violation of social and public interest. Thus it cannot be said without a doubt that violation of social and public interest can be a ground for non-enforcement of domestic arbitral awards.

In this respect most scholars adopt an affirmative view, stating that, firstly, although Article 63 of the PRC Arbitration Law merely cites paragraph 2 but not paragraph 3 of Article 217 (currently Article 237) of the PRC Civil Procedure Law, however, as the most basic law for civil proceedings the Civil Procedure Law can also apply to arbitration. Second, violation of social and public interest is already a ground for revoking domestic arbitral awards under the Arbitration Law.[160] Both revocation

---

155. Supreme People's Court (2005) Min-Si-Ta-Zi No. 45, 23 January 2006.
156. Jiangsu Suzhou Intermediate People's Court Civil Ruling (2008) Su-Zhong-Min-San-Zhong-Shen-Zi No. 0004, 24 September 2008.
157. Jiangsu Suzhou Intermediate People's Court Civil Ruling (2008) Su-Zhong-Shang-Wai-Zhong-Shen-Zi No. 0004, 1 March 2010.
158. Jiangsu Suzhou Intermediate People's Court Civil Ruling (2008) Su-Zhong-Shang-Wai-Zhong-Shen-Zi No. 0005, 18 May 2010.
159. Jiangsu Suzhou Intermediate People's Court Civil Ruling (2008) Su-Zhong-Min-San-Zhong-Shen-Zi No. 0003, 5 September 2008.
160. As stipulated in Art. 58 para. 3 of the PRC Arbitration Law: 'If the people's court determines that the arbitral award violates social and public interest, it shall set aside the award'.

Chapter 3: 'Public Policy' and the Even More Unpredictable

and non-enforcement of arbitral awards will lead to re-arbitration or litigation. Since 'violation of social and public interest' has the same content and legal consequences, it is sufficient to specify it in the provision for revocation (with more direct effect), rather than specifying it again in the provision for non-enforcement.[161] The first (former) view seems more sensible and worthy of adoption.

In practice, the courts in many cases have already considered whether the arbitral awards would violate social and public interest in applications for non-enforcement of domestic arbitral awards. Examples include the application for enforcement concerning disputes arising from a contract on sale of commercial real estate, shop management and profit sharing between Miandong Xia, etc. and Yueyang Jinhong Real Estate Co., Ltd.,[162] the application for enforcement concerning disputes over confirmation of rights to homestead land use between Da Huang and Wei Huang,[163] the application for enforcement concerning disputes over confirmation of rights to land between Hainan Haocheng Real Estate Co., Ltd. and Junpeng Ma,[164] as well as the application for enforcement concerning project transfer agreement between Hainan Jinghe Decoration Co., Ltd. and Bo Wang, etc.[165]

---

161. Jingyi Liu & Shiming Qiao, *Arbitration Law: Theory and Application* 237 (People's Court Press 1997).
162. Upon review the Court held that this case did not involve any violation of social and public interest: Hunan Yueyang Intermediate People's Court Enforcement Ruling (2011) Yue-Zhong-Zhi-Zi No. 73-1, 2 September 2011.
163. The Court ruled on the non-enforcement of arbitral award pursuant to Art. 213 (currently Art. 237) para. 3 of the Civil Procedure Law, *see* Hainan First Intermediate People's Court, (2011) Hai-Nan-Yi-Zhong-Zhi-Zi No. 54 dated 8 August 2011.

   The PRC term of 'disputes over confirmation of rights' means disputes associated with confirming the ownership of various rights and interest. An example is Art. 41 of the SPC's Opinions Concerning the Regulation of the Cause of Action in Intellectual Property Disputes (for Trial Implementation), which provides: '[p]atent right ownership disputes means cases concerning disputes over confirmation of patent rights between legal persons, citizens and other organizations after the invention and grant of such patent rights, as well as which legal persons, citizens or other organizations should be entitled to such patent rights.' Cited from: Beijing Higher People's Court's Notification of Issuing the Opinions Concerning the Regulation of the Cause of Action in Intellectual Property Disputes (for Trial Implementation), Jing-Gao-Fa-Fa (1999) No. 149, issued and implemented on 24 May 1999. Other examples include: 'disputes over confirmation of maritime claims' as stipulated in Part VII, Item 19 (227) of the SPC's Cause of Action in Civil Cases (latest revision issued on 18 February 2011 and implemented on 1 April 2011); and 'disputes over confirmation of shareholder's rights' as stipulated in Art. 2.1.3 of the Jiangsu Higher People's Court's Opinion on the Certain Issues Concerning the Application of the Company Law (for Trial Implementation), adopted by the Jiangsu Higher People's Court's Judicial Committee during the twenty-first meeting on 3 June 2003): 'In disputes over confirmation of shareholder's rights arising between the shareholders and the company, the parties to the court proceedings should be the shareholders and the company; in disputes between shareholders, between shareholders and third parties external to the company, the parties to the court proceedings should be the disputing parties and the company may participate as a party when necessary'.
164. The Court ruled on the non-enforcement of arbitral award pursuant to Art. 213 (currently Art. 237) para. 3 of the Civil Procedure Law, *see* Hainan First Intermediate People's Court Enforcement Ruling (2009) Hai-Nan-Yi-Zhong-Zhi-Zi No. 26-4, 3 May 2011.
165. The Court ruled on the non-enforcement of arbitral award pursuant to Art. 213 (currently Art. 237) para. 3 of the Civil Procedure Law, *see* Hainan Haikou Intermediate People's Court Enforcement Ruling (2011) Hai-Zhong-Fa-Zhi-Zi No. 121, September 2011.

3.2.3 Mixed Use of Terms in PRC Cases

As illustrated in section 3.1.3 of this chapter, the PRC has been basically following certain principles quite cautiously in its choice of terminology when enacting relevant laws and regulations as well as issuing the SPC's judicial interpretations. In principle, the term 'public policy' is used only when the New York Convention applies. On the contrary, the term 'social and public interest' is used in the following circumstances:

(1) Enforcement of arbitral awards made in Taiwan;
(2) Enforcement of arbitral awards made in Hong Kong;
(3) Enforcement of arbitral awards made in Macau;
(4) Revocation and non-enforcement of domestic arbitral awards; and
(5) Non-enforcement of foreign-related arbitral awards.

Although the SPC in most of its replies has been mindful of such distinction by using the term 'public policy' in cases concerning the recognition and enforcement of foreign arbitral awards while using the term 'social and public interest' in the five categories of cases listed above, the mixed use of terms can still be seen in some cases, which is generally more commonly seen in the documents of lower courts.

3.2.4 'Social and Public Interest' as a Ground for Excluding the Application of Foreign Laws

The SPC has not directly given general judicial interpretation on 'public policy' as specified in Article V(2)(b) of the New York Convention, nor has it given general judicial interpretation on 'social and public interest' as stipulated in the PRC's Civil Procedure Law and Arbitration Law. Nonetheless the SPC's Fourth Civil Tribunal has replied to the question of 'in what circumstances does the public order reservation apply' in its edited 'Answers to Practical Questions on Foreign-Related Commercial and Maritime Trials (I)' of 2004:[166] 'when hearing foreign-related commercial cases, if the law of a foreign country or related region is applicable, the people's court should consider whether that foreign law would violate our nation's social and public interest. If that foreign law would violate our nation's social and public interest, then the court should exclude the application of that foreign law. In general the public order

---

166. Exiang Wan (editor in chief), the Fourth Civil Tribunal of the Supreme People's Court (ed.), *Answers to Practical Questions on Foreign-Related Commercial and Maritime Trials (I)*, in 7 *Guide on Foreign-Related Commercial and Maritime Trial*, 54 (People's Court Press 2004).
    Subsequently in 2010 the PRC proclaimed the PRC Law on the Applicable Laws for Foreign-Related Civil Relations (Order of the President No. 36, issued on 28 October 2010 and implemented on 1 April 2011), Art. 5 of which stipulates: 'the law of the People's Republic of China applies in the event of violation of the social and public interest of the People's Republic of China'. The original text of this question uses the term 'public order' which is different from the term 'public policy' used in this book, even though their intention should be the same. Here the citation uses the original text 'public order' as it refers to the original text of the questions and answers in the Foreign-Related Commercial or Maritime Trial Practice Questions and Answers (Part 1).

reservation can apply to violations of our nation's basic principles or national sovereignty, security, good morals and basic code of ethics'. Although this answer to the forty-third question in 'Answers to Practical Questions on Foreign-Related Commercial and Maritime Trials (I)' concerns whether or not to exclude the application of foreign law, some scholars nevertheless believe that the explanation about the 'public order reservation' (namely, 'violations of our nation's basic principles or national sovereignty, security, good morals and basic code of ethics') also has considerable reference value for examining the PRC courts' application of 'public policy' in Article V(2)(b) of the New York Convention.[167]

Subsequently the Law of the PRC on Choice of Law for Foreign-related Civil Relationships was proclaimed in 2010 and implemented from 1 April 2011,[168] Article 5 of which uses the term 'social and public interest': 'the law of the People's Republic of China applies if the otherwise applicable foreign law would violate the *social and public interest* of the People's Republic of China' (emphasis added).

3.3 SCHOLARLY OPINIONS

In relation to whether or not the term 'social and public interest' equates with 'public order', some scholars are of the view that 'social and public interest' as traditionally stipulated in the PRC laws is indeed 'public order and good morals' as stipulated in other country's legislations.[169] For instance, according to Jian Zhao:[170] 'the PRC's laws do not use terms such "public order", "public policy", "public order reservation" or "reservation clause" and instead use the term "social and public interest". Article 260 (currently Article 274) paragraph 2 of the PRC Civil Procedure Law stipulates that the people's court can, ex officio, refuse enforcement of a foreign-related arbitral award if that award's enforcement would violate "social and public interest". Here the "social and public interest" is equivalent or similar to "public order" or "public policy".' Similarly, Yifei Lin has also stated:[171] 'As two separate expressions, one cannot see which is broader or more uncertain; as two uncertain concepts, it is unnecessary to argue which is broader or narrower. In terms of context, any public interest can become public policy; conversely, any public policy involves public interest... Social

---

167. Friven Yeoh & Yu Fu, *The People's Courts and Arbitration – A Snapshot of Recent Judicial Attitudes on Arbitrability and Enforcement*, 24(6) Journal of Arbitration International 635, 647 (2007); Lanfang Fei, *Public Policy as a Bar to Enforcement of International Arbitral Awards: A Review of the Chinese Approach*, 26(2) Journal of Arbitration International 301, 304 (2010).
168. Order of the President No. 36, issued on 28 October 2010 and implemented on 1 April 2011.
169. Jingyi Liu & Shiming Qiao, *Arbitration Law: Theory and Application* 218 (People's Court Press 1997).
170. Jian Zhao, *On the Public Order and the Recognition and Enforcement of International Commercial Arbitral Awards*, 6 Arbitration and Law Communication 14, 23 (1998). *See also* Andrew Jefferies, *Arbitration in the PRC: Enforcement Issues*, in *Arbitration in China: A Practical Guide* 295, 327 (Daniel R. Fung & Shengchang Wang eds, Sweet & Maxwell 2004): 'The grounds for refusing to enforce a foreign-related arbitral award are set out in Article 260 of the CPL [Code of Civil Procedure]. Although slightly different to the New York Convention Article V grounds, the essence is very similar'.
171. Yifei Lin, *Recognition and Enforcement of Foreign Arbitral Award: 20 Years' Judicial Practice in China*, 16(1) Journal of International Economic Law 30, 49 and fn. 46 (2009).

and public interest as specified in PRC laws is public policy in substance.' In Lianbin Song's opinion:[172] 'the so-called social and public interest, or known as public policy or public order, refers to the all members of society's fundamental interest, basic policies, basic concepts of morality or basic principles of law. Social and public interest, on the one hand, harmonises with individual interest or partial interest; while on the other hand, contradicts with individual interest or partial interest. It is difficult to exhaustively list the many forms of violation of social and public interest. Common examples include violating the basic system and principles of the PRC law, violating the basic values of social and economic life, and violating the PRC's basic moral standards etc.' Yet another similar statement comes from Haibo Mao:[173] 'the PRC legislations have not adopted the concept of public policy and have used "social and public interest' instead; however both are recognized as the same in essence by both scholars and practitioners".'

Many scholars adopting different views nevertheless regard the two as having different meanings. These scholars agree that the meaning of 'social and public interest' is wider and more flexible than that of 'public policy'. As stated by Xianchu Zhang, 'social and public interest' not only includes the 'expressed state commitments and social morality', but also includes the 'less transparent state interests and unstable short-term policies.[174] Some PRC scholars have even stated bluntly that the excessively uncertain status of 'social and public interest' may exclude the commonly accepted international customs and practices and thereby disable it from performing its functions similar to that of 'public policy' in judicial practice.[175] In Hu Li's opinion,[176] 'the interpretation of social and public interest in PRC law is wider than that of the comparable public policy in civil law or common law'. One of the PRC judges (Hang Song) has also stated:[177] '[t]he PRC law does not use terms such as "public policy" or "public order" and uses "social and public interest" instead. The term 'social and public interest' is actually more likely to cause controversy; its meaning is also uncertain and is even wider than that of "public policy" or "public order".' Many English literatures also express the same concerns. For instance: '[r]ather than refer to "public policy", Chinese law refers to the "social and public interest" which is potentially an even more oblique concept'.[178] Another example is that '[t]he concept of

---

172. Lianbin Song (ed.), *Theory and Practice of Commercial Arbitration* 293 (Hunan University Press 2005).
173. Haibo Mao, *Understanding and Application of Public Policy in International Commercial Arbitration in the Context of Chinese Judicial Practice*, 26 Arbitration Study 52, 54 (2011).
174. Xianchu Zhang, *The Agreement between Mainland China and the Hong Kong SAR on Mutual Enforcement of Arbitral Awards: Problems and Prospects*, 29 Hong Kong Law Journal 463, 476–477 (1999).
175. Shuangyuan Li & Guojian Xu (ed.), *Construction of the Theory of a New International Civil and Commercial Order –Repositioning and Changing the Function of Private International Law* 268–270 (Wuhan University Press 1998).
176. Hu Li, *Enforcement of the International Commercial Arbitral Award, with Special Reference to the Enforcement of Arbitral Awards in the P. R. China* 161 (Law Press 2000).
177. Hang Song, *Enforcement of Foreign-Related Arbitral Awards in China – Issues in Practice*, 4 Arbitration and Law Communication 7, 12 (1999).
178. Nigel Blackaby et al., *Redfern and Hunter on International Arbitration* 660 (5th ed., Oxford University Press 2009).

"social and public interest" in the Mainland is by its very nature broad and ill-defined'.[179] Simon Greenberg, Christopher Kee and J. Romesh Weeramantry also agree with these views in their book *International Commercial Arbitration: An Asia-Pacific Perspective* published in 2011.[180]

It is particularly noteworthy that, even if one adopts the first view that the term 'social and public interest' equates with 'public order', one can still notice that in judicial practice, some rulings demonstrate the PRC court's excessively broad interpretation of the term 'social and public interest', the extent of such breadth exceeds the international consensus on 'public policy'. For instance, as stated by Jian Zhao:[181] '[t]he PRC laws have neither interpreted nor defined "social and public interest". In judicial practice, some people's courts arbitrarily interpret "social and public interest" widely, even to the extent of using the economic interest of a department or region to replace "social and public interest", or using the violation of such departmental or local interest as the measure for determining violation of "social and public interest", thereby severely damaging the finality of arbitral awards'.' As another example, Lianbin Song's statement that 'the so-called social and public interest is also called public policy and public order'[182] is immediately followed by this clarifying statement that: 'in practice, the absence of any legal interpretation or restriction on 'social and public interest' together with the uncertainty of the concept itself have caused disparity in the people's court's understanding, and even made it convenient for a few people's courts to protect localism or other behaviours under the guise of 'violation of social and public interest'.[183]

With respect to the relationship between 'social and public interest' and 'local protectionism', Justice Hang Song made a candid statement in 1999 that 'the most prominent manifestation of the inconsistent understandings of "social and public interest" is the prevalence of local protectionism'.[184] As for the reason, Justice Hang Song indicated:[185] 'The reason is not merely legislative defects, but it also relates to the long-standing lack of clear distinction between law and policy in the PRC. Furthermore, as the current Chinese social and political life values individual relationships, the Party's intervention in the judiciary and some narrow economic and cultural concepts and other elements may rise above the law to a certain degree. Undoubtedly the influence from these extra-judicial elements may also create substantial pressure for the local courts in their impartial enforcement of arbitral awards and assistance with arbitration, resulting in the non-enforcement of certain arbitral awards.'

---

179. Robert Pé & Michael Polkinghorne, *Two Steps Forward, One Step...Sideways – Recent Developments in Arbitration in China*, 25(3) Journal of International Arbitration 407, 411 (2008).
180. Simon Greenberg, Christopher Kee & J. Romesh Weeramantry, *International Commercial Arbitration: An Asia-Pacific Perspective* 465 (Cambridge University Press 2011).
181. Jian Zhao, *On the Public Order and the Recognition and Enforcement of International Commercial Arbitral Awards*, 6 Arbitration and Law Communication 14, 23 (1998).
182. Lianbin Song (ed.), *Theory and Practice of Commercial Arbitration* 293 (Hunan University Press 2005).
183. Ibid.
184. Hang Song, *Enforcement of Foreign-Related Arbitral Awards in China – Issues in Practice*, 4 Arbitration and Law Communication 7, 12 (1999).
185. Ibid.

Given that some PRC courts have interpreted and applied 'social and public interest' too widely, Professor Xinli Du specifically pointed out that 'public policy does not equate with public interest',[186] followed by a clear reminder: 'when reviewing foreign arbitral awards, judges should apply the New York Convention ('public policy' in Article V(2)(b) of the New York Convention) and not the Chinese domestic law, and should not be influenced by the term 'social and public interest' in Chinese domestic law in their interpretation... If the PRC court interprets 'public policy' in the New York Convention from the perspective of protecting national economic interest, then this would damage the international credibility of the PRC courts' fulfilment of international obligations'.

---

186. Xinli Du, *Theory on the Recognition and Enforcement of Foreign Arbitral Award in China – Theory on Applying the New York Arbitration Convention of 1958 to China*, 2005(4) Journal of Comparative Law 98, 107 (2005).

CHAPTER 4
PRC's Convergence with International Consensus

As discussed in Chapter 2, although it is difficult to depict clear contours of public policy, internationally there are several majority views or consensus on the core meaning of public policy. Such majority views or international consensus form the basis for the author's in-depth study of the interpretation and application of 'public policy' in Article V(2)(b) of the New York Convention in Mainland China. In terms of methodology, the author collects and reviews as many PRC's precedents as possible to explain the similarities and differences between the PRC's judicial practice and the international consensus or majority views. This chapter illustrates the similarities while Chapter 5 explains the differences.

The summation of the majority of international opinions reveals the following common characteristics of 'public policy' as stipulated in Article V(2)(b) of the New York Convention:

(1) Public policy should be the public policy of the state where the enforcement is sought rather than transnational public policy.
(2) Public policy should be limited by 'internationality'.
(3) The merits of the parties' claims should be considered together with the arbitral tribunal's decisions in the arbitral award.
(4) Public policy should be applicable in 'exceptional' circumstances only.
(5) Procedural public policy may be a ground for refusing recognition and enforcement of foreign arbitral awards.
(6) Substantive public policy may be a ground for refusing recognition and enforcement of foreign arbitral awards.
(7) Violation of the enforcement state's mandatory laws is not necessarily violation of that state's public policy.

The following sections in this chapter will explain each of the above common characteristics in detail, using the relevant cases in the PRC's judicial practice to explain which PRC cases are in common or resonating with the majority of international opinions.

4.1 PUBLIC POLICY SHOULD BE THE PUBLIC POLICY OF THE STATE WHERE THE ENFORCEMENT IS SOUGHT RATHER THAN TRANSNATIONAL PUBLIC POLICY

4.1.1 International Consensus

Article V(2)(b) of the New York Convention expressly stipulates that '[t]he recognition or enforcement of the award would be contrary to the public policy of that country' (i.e., 'the country where recognition and enforcement is sought') while Article 36 of UNCITRAL Model Law on International Commercial Arbitration[1] closely follows the New York Convention as Article 36(1)(b)(ii) expressly provides that 'the recognition or enforcement of the award would be contrary to the public policy of *this State*' (emphasis added). It is thus evident from these provisions that the prescribed 'public policy' refers to the enforcement State's public policy rather than transnational public policy or truly international public policy.

At the same time, private international law usually regards public policy as an 'escape mechanism, permitting national courts and other authorities, exceptionally, to deny effect to foreign laws, judgments, or awards when local law and policy demand'.[2] In light of this view, 'public policy' in Article V(2)(b) of the New York Convention can only be understood as the enforcement State's public policy in order to accord with the function of public policy as an 'escape mechanism'.

4.1.2 PRC Judicial Practice

In all the SPC's replies concerning the applicability of public policy in Article V(2)(b) of the New York Convention ascertained by the author (*see* Table 4.1 at the end of this chapter), the subject matter of discussion or concern for the SPC had been whether the relevant arbitral awards would violate the so-called our nation's public policy (meaning the PRC's public policy). Thus it can be seen that the SPC clearly understands public policy in Article V(2)(b) of the New York Convention as the enforcement State's public policy.

---

1. United Nations Commission on International Trade Law's Twenty-First Session, 11–22 April 1988, New York, *UNCITRAL Model Law on International Commercial Arbitration: Note by the Secretariat* (A/CN.9/309) para. 45 states that the rules for the recognition and enforcement of arbitral awards 'should follow closely the 1958 New York Convention'.
2. Gary B. Born, *International Commercial Arbitration* 3657–3658 (2nd ed., Kluwer Law International 2014).

4.2 PUBLIC POLICY SHOULD BE LIMITED BY 'INTERNATIONALITY'

4.2.1 International Consensus

'Public policy' in Article V(2)(b) of the New York Convention is not unrestricted even though it should be understood as the enforcement State's public policy. The purpose and structure of the New York Convention impose certain restrictions on the application of 'public policy' as specified in that provision. Article 3 of the New York Convention requires each Contracting State to 'recognize arbitral awards as binding and enforce them...', while Article V lists each of the grounds for refusing recognition and enforcement in accordance with the New York Convention's basic purpose of promoting international unification and recognition of arbitral awards. Consequently, the more satisfactory interpretation according to an internationally renowned scholar Gary B. Born is to derive international limitations for 'public policy' in Article V(2)(b) from the New York Convention's constitutional status and basic objectives. In other words, the requirement of 'internationality' (as derived from the New York Convention's objectives and structure) restricts the Contracting States' use of their own laws to refuse recognition and enforcement of foreign arbitral awards. Such restriction precludes the Contracting States from using their unique local contract law to determine arbitration agreements as invalid, as well as from using their distinction local procedural regulations to determine the arbitration procedures agreed by the parties as invalid.[3] This accords with the common opinion that public policy, as understood from an international viewpoint, has a narrower scope than that of domestic public policy.[4]

For instance, the Celle High Court of Germany adopted a view similar to that of Gary B. Born (as mentioned above) in a dispute between seller and buyer.[5] In that case, the seller alleged that the relevant arbitral award's enforcement would violate public policy because of procedural defects in the arbitral proceedings on the one hand and excessive damages for breach of contract imposed by the award on the other hand. However, in the Celle High Court's view: 'the question is not whether or not the German judges would reach different conclusions in accordance with the mandatory laws of Germany. Relatively speaking, violation of international public policy occurs only if the application of foreign law in a specific case would violate German law to an unacceptable degree according to German principles'.[6]

According to the above, the New York Convention's Contracting States apply 'public policy' in Article V(2)(b) to refuse recognition and enforcement of foreign arbitral awards only in exceptional circumstances where the fundamental and mandatory policies are expressly stipulated in laws or judicial documents. Pursuant to this understanding, the courts cannot deny recognition and enforcement of foreign arbitral

---

3. Born, *supra* n. 2, at 3661–3662.
4. ICCA (ed.), *ICCA's Guide to the Interpretation of the 1958 New York Convention* 106–107 (ICCA 2011).
5. *Seller v. Buyer*, No. 99. Oberlandesgericht, Celle, 6 October 2005, cited from Albert Jan van den Berg (ed.), *Yearbook Commercial Arbitration XXXII* 322–327 (Kluwer Law International 2007).
6. ICCA (ed.), *ICCA's Guide to the Interpretation of the 1958 New York Convention* 108–109 (ICCA 2011).

awards 'where the arbitral tribunal's interpretation of a contract is putatively wrong, unfair, or contrary to local laws, or all awards which damage local commercial interest'.[7]

To guard against unwarranted national law intrusion upon the transborder regime of arbitration, many national courts have devised the notion of a 'international' public policy that applies under Article V(2)(b) of the New York Convention and which replaces the application of the domestic notions public policy.[8] Although not all countries in the world differentiate between 'domestic public policy' and 'international public policy', this does not matter, as a narrow interpretation of 'public policy' in accordance with the New York Convention's purposes and the non-inclusion of all mandatory laws should suffice. Courts which do not have a clear distinction between 'domestic public policy' and 'international public policy' usually opt for a narrow interpretation of the 'public policy' exception when applying Article V(2)(b) of the New York Convention.[9]

By contrast, the courts can only apply 'public policy' in Article V(2)(b) to refuse recognition and enforcement of foreign arbitral awards by using public policies that are specifically protected by the enforcement State's laws as well as consistent with the New York Convention's basic purpose and structure. Based on this, where the arbitral award 'required criminal or anticompetitive conduct, was an element of a criminal scheme, unacceptably violated fundamental civil or property rights, or violated fundamental and mandatory national laws that safeguard particular rights or classes of parties', the courts may apply 'public policy' in Article V(2)(b) to deny recognition and enforcement of such foreign arbitral awards.[10]

4.2.2 PRC Judicial Practice

A comparison of the PRC courts' practice concerning 'social and public interest' in the 'revocation and non-enforcement of domestic arbitral awards' with the PRC courts' practice concerning 'public policy' in the 'recognition and enforcement of foreign arbitral awards' reveals that the PRC courts indeed apply different standards for these two types of cases.

4.2.2.1 *Arbitral Tribunal's Error in Merits or Applicable Laws, or Unfair Outcomes*

There is no shortage of cases in which the PRC courts set aside or refuse to enforce domestic arbitral awards on the grounds of 'social and public interest' violation

---

7. Born, *supra* n. 2, at 3663.
8. Thomas E. Carbonneau, *The Law and Practice of Arbitration* 611 (5th ed, JurisNet 2014).
9. Bernard Hanotiau & Olivier Caprasse, *Public Policy in International Commercial Arbitration*, in *Enforcement of Arbitration Agreements and International Arbitral Awards: The New York Convention in Practice* 787, 791 (Emmanuel Gaillard & Domenico Di Pietro (eds), Cameron May Ltd. 2008).
10. Born, *supra* n. 2, at 3663.

Chapter 4: PRC's Convergence with International Consensus

because of the arbitral tribunal's errors in the merits or applicable laws or because of 'unfair outcomes'. First of all, with respect to cases concerning revocation of domestic arbitral awards, in an application for revoking arbitral awards made by Kunming Arbitration Commission involving Kunming Xinyi Real Estate Developing Co., Ltd. and Guoguang Wen, etc. Disputes arose between the buyers and the developer Kunming Xinyi Real Estate Developing Co., Ltd. over the same community. Yongsheng Shi and other sixty-four buyers claimed damages for breach of contract due to overdue housing delivery. The Kunming Arbitration Commission found, in the arbitration requested by Yongsheng Shi, etc., that the standard for pre-conditions to housing delivery was 'achieving qualification for fire control inspection'; whereas the standard for pre-conditions to housing delivery was found to be 'achieving qualification for all fire control, environmental protection, planning and air defense inspections' in some arbitrations requested by the other buyers. Considering that the arbitral tribunal's standard for pre-conditions to housing delivery should not be different for the same houses, the same environment and the same laws, Yanping Yang and others applied to revoke the arbitral awards. The Yunnan Kunming Intermediate People's Court held: 'The arbitral award in this case and the arbitral awards made by Kunming Arbitration Commission involved the same category of contracts, the same category of case facts and the same category of claims for damages for breach of contract, and because of disagreement on the pre-conditions to housing delivery, significant differences exist in the implementation of different buyers' rights and interests in the same community. This is contrary to the civil law principle of fairness about equal protection of all parties to the contract. Consequently the arbitral award has violated social and public interest and should be set aside.'[11] For the same reason the Yunnan Kunming Intermediate People's Court made more than twenty final decisions on the same day (16 June 2006) to revoke domestic arbitral awards with basically the same case details except for the different parties.[12]

In addition, in an application by China Cinda Asset Management Co., Ltd. Shanghai Office for revoking an arbitral award, (2007) Jing-Zhong-Cai-Zi No. 0185, made by BAC, the Beijing Second Intermediate People's Court determined that the arbitral award violated social and public interest and should be revoked on the basis that its outcomes were unfair. In that case, China Cinda Asset Management Co., Ltd., Shanghai Office (Cinda Asset) used an integral price to 'package' and transfer five non-performing loans to Shanghai Huayue International Trading Co., Ltd. (Shanghai Huayue), and accordingly the parties signed a contract for assignment of non-performing loans. Subsequently Shanghai Huayue submitted request to BAC to arbitrate and set aside part of the debts in the contract for assignment because of major misunderstanding and manifest unfairness. The arbitral tribunal severed the non-performing loans (which were subject to an integral transfer as agreed by both parties) and made an award to cancel the transfer of one of the non-performing loans. In

---

11. Yunnan Kunming Intermediate People's Court Civil Ruling (2007) Kun-Min-Yi-Chu-Zi No. 111, 16 June 2006.
12. Yunnan Kunming Intermediate People's Court Civil Ruling (2007) Kun-Min-Yi-Chu-Zi No. 112 to No. 135, all with the same judgment date of 16 June 2006.

response to the application by Cinda Asset to revoke this arbitral award, the Beijing Second Intermediate People's Court held:[13]

> Through the means of 'packaging', Cinda Asset transferred non-performing loans to Shanghai Huayue and made an integral price for such transfer. Accordingly the five non-performing loans were indivisible under these trading conditions. The arbitral tribunal's severance of the non-performing loans (which were subject to an integral transfer as agreed by both parties) together with its cancellation of the assignment of one of the non-performing loans changed the rules for trading non-performing loans by packaging which should be complied with, producing unfair results as well as impairing the interests of other trading parties, and at the same time causing negative impact on the trading order of non-performing loans. Thus this Court supports this application by Cinda Asset to revoke the arbitral award as the grounds of social and public interest violation has been established. This domestic arbitral award should be set aside pursuant to Article 58 paragraph 3 of the Arbitration Law: 'The people's court shall set aside the award if it finds that the award violates social and public interest.'

In Hainan Yixing Municipal Construction Investment Co., Ltd. ('Yixing')'s application with Hainan Haikou Intermediate People's Court against the sixth Engineering Bureau of China City Construction Holding Group Company for the revocation of a domestic arbitral award rendered by the Hainan Arbitration Commission, (2014) Hai-Zhong-Zi No. 368, the arbitral tribunal considered that the parties' affixing their respective corporate seals on the 'Final Account Signature Sheet' constitute the parties' confirmation of the total construction price for the work completed by the respondent, namely the sixth Engineering Bureau of China City Construction Holding Group Company, and thus, awarded that Yixing was to pay the remaining construction price of RMB 2,220,646.10. The Hainan Haikou Intermediate People's Court held that the impacts of the award are that the construction payment for municipal construction work is to be paid directly without the government's audit. This would damage the social and public interest. The award evading the government audit proceedings as required by law violates the social and public interest. It can be established that the award violates the social and public interest. Accordingly, Hainan Haikou Intermediate People's Court revoked the award.[14]

Second, with respect to cases concerning non-enforcement of domestic arbitral awards, Hainan Arbitration Commission made an award, (2010) Hai-Zhong-Zi No. 314, concerning a transfer contract. Part of the dispositive required the respondent (Bo Wang) together with another respondent (a Pickles Plant) to transfer the building project property located on 197 Wenming East Road, Haikou City to the claimant in the arbitration (Hainan Jinghe Decoration Co., Ltd.). Yet some floors of the building had already been seized and some other floors had been transferred to third parties as ordered by the Meilan District People's Court. Consequently, the Hainan Haikou

---

13. Beijing Second Intermediate People's Court Civil Ruling (2007) Er-Zhong-Min-Te-Zi No. 07204, 21 August 2007.
14. Hainan Haikou Intermediate People's Court Civil Ruling (2015) Hai-Zhong-Fa-Zhong-Zi No. 10, 11 June 2015.

Chapter 4: PRC's Convergence with International Consensus

Intermediate People's Court held that:[15] The arbitral award infringed the public law order of judicial enforcement by transferring property ownership without ascertaining the fact that some of the property had already been seized and some of the property had already been transferred to third parties pursuant to previous court orders. The arbitral award (2011) Hai-Zhong-Zi No. 314 'omitted important facts and erred in the applicable law'. Enforcing this award would infringe the interested parties' legitimate rights and interests and thereby violates social and public interest. Thus the arbitral award was refused enforcement under Article 213 paragraph 3 of the PRC Civil Procedural Law.

By contrast, the author has not seen any cases concerning the recognition and enforcement of foreign arbitral awards in which the SPC has found that the award's recognition and enforcement would violate the PRC's public order because of the arbitral tribunal's error in the merits or the applicable law. In terms of 'unfair arbitration results', the SPC clearly stated in its reply to a request concerning an application by GRD Minproc Limited to recognise and enforce an award made by the Arbitration Institute of the Stockholm Chamber of Commerce (SCC) (the *GRD Minproc* case):[16] 'In circumstances where Shanghai Flyingwheel Industry Co. Ltd requested arbitration of equipment quality disputes pursuant to a valid arbitration clause, the arbitral tribunal's judgment on equipment quality was within the arbitral tribunal's authority. Parties resolving their disputes through arbitration should bear the results. Whether or not the substantive results of arbitration are fair and reasonable should not be the criterion for determining whether or not the arbitral award's recognition and enforcement would violate the public policy of this country.' The SPC also disproved a lower court's opinion on the recognition and enforcement of an English arbitral award involving Western Bulk Pte. Ltd. (the *Western Bulk* case)[17] and held 'it is improper for your court to refuse the award's recognition and enforcement on the grounds of violating social and public interest because the arbitration results manifestly lack fairness'.

4.2.2.2 *Violation of Mandatory Laws for Registering Foreign Debt Guarantees*

In cases relating to registration of foreign debt guarantees, it can also be clearly observed that the SPC applies different standards for the recognition and enforcement of foreign arbitral awards as opposed to domestic arbitral awards. The PRC courts have always considered that the foreign exchange controls are implemented and that the provisions for approval and registration relating to foreign debt assumption are mandatory in Mainland China. Any agreement between the parties for assuming

---

15. Hainan Haikou Intermediate People's Court Enforcement Ruling (2011) Hai-Zhong-Fa-Zhi-Zi No. 121, September 2011.
16. Reply of the Supreme People's Court on Request for Instructions Re Application of GRD Minproc Limited for Recognition and Enforcement of the Arbitration Award of Arbitration Institute of the Stockholm Chamber of Commerce, Supreme People's Court (2008) Min-Si-Ta-Zi No. 48, 13 March 2009. *See* s. 4.4.2 of this Chapter for the details of this case.
17. Supreme People's Court (2012) Min-Si-Ta-Zi No. 12, 21 May 2012. *See* s. 4.7 of this chapter for the details of this case.

foreign debts without complying with the approval and registration formalities would be invalid. If the parties purport to evade such mandatory provisions of the PRC by agreeing on a foreign governing law in their foreign guarantee contract instead of complying with the PRC's approval and registration formalities, then such choice of foreign governing law would not be effective. This is clear from the answer to the Question No. 51 'if in their foreign guarantee contract the parties agree on a foreign governing law and such contract has not complied with the approval and registration formalities, how effective would this foreign law clause be?' in the *Answers to Practical Questions on Foreign-Related Commercial and Maritime Trials (I)*, edited by the SPC's Fourth Civil Tribunal in 2004:[18]

> According to Article 194 of the SPC's Opinions on Several Issues concerning the Implementation of the General Principles of the Civil Law of the People's Republic of China (For Trial Implementation), the parties' conduct in evading the mandatory or prohibitory provisions of the People's Republic of China does not have the effect of applying foreign law. The People's Republic of China is a country which implements foreign exchange controls. Its provisions concerning approval and registration formalities for foreign debt assumption are mandatory. The parties' non-compliance with these approval and registration formalities evades Chinese laws: it does not have the effect of applying foreign law and Chinese law should apply instead.

Although the above answer to the Question No. 51 in the *Answers to Practical Questions on Foreign-Related Commercial and Maritime Trials (I)* does not express its reasoning in relation to public policy considerations, in practice, many PRC courts have used violation of PRC public policy or evasion of PRC law by such type of choice of foreign law clauses as a reason for applying PRC law. In view of many scholars' criticisms of such use of 'violation of PRC public policy or evasion of PRC law', after the PRC Law on the Applicable Laws for Foreign-Related Civil Relations became effective on 1 April 2011,[19] subsequently in August 2011 at a national symposium on foreign-related commercial trials, the SPC's Fourth Civil Tribunal Chair, Justice Guixiang Liu, indicated in his concluding that the direct application of Article 4 of the Law of the PRC on Choice of Law for Foreign-related Civil Relationships to such foreign law clauses would suffice: 'mandatory laws of the People's Republic of China concerning foreign-related civil relations apply directly'. This avoids the potential criticisms and problems arising from the use of public policy or evasion of law or other reasons in such types of domestic cases. According to Guixiang Liu's detailed discussions:[20]

> The management system of requiring approval of foreign debts assumption by the state administration of foreign exchange has not changed, so the judicial stance

---

18. Exiang Wan (editor in chief), the Civil Fourth Tribunal of the Supreme People's Court (ed.), *Answers to Practical Questions on Foreign-Related Commercial and Maritime Trials (I)*, in 7 *Guide on Foreign-Related Commercial and Maritime Trial*, 56–57 (People's Court Press 2004).
19. Order of the President No. 36, promulgated on 28 October 2010 and implemented on 1 April 2011.
20. Guixiang Liu, *Some Questions Concerning Foreign-Related Commercial Trial System and Applicable Law*, cited from the website of PRC's Foreign-Related Commercial Maritime Trial, http://www.ccmt.org.cn/showexplore.php?id=4146 (accessed 4 May 2017).

that foreign debts assumption is invalid without approval also has not changed. It should be noted that, where the parties agree on the application of foreign law or the law of other PRC law jurisdictions to their foreign debt assumption, the courts in the past have always applied PRC law on the basis that the parties' agreement violated the PRC public policy or evaded PRC law, and have always determined such foreign debt assumption as invalid. Many scholars have criticized such judicial reasoning. The implementation of the Law of the People's Republic of China on Choice of Law for Foreign-related Civil Relationships has provided a direct legal basis for addressing similar situations, as Article 4 stipulates that 'mandatory laws of the People's Republic of China concerning foreign-related civil relations apply directly'. Pursuant to this provision, the PRC's foreign exchange control provisions can apply directly to determine the guarantee as invalid regardless of the applicability of the parties' agreement on choice of governing law.

However, as early as 2005, the SPC already adopted a different approach with respect to the recognition and enforcement of foreign arbitral awards in its Reply on the Request for Instructions on the Non-recognition and Non-enforcement of an Arbitral Award of the Arbitration Institute of the Stockholm Chamber of Commerce ('*Mitsui* case').[21] In the *Mitsui* case, the state-owned enterprise Hainan Textile Industry General Corporation entered into an agreement for repayment in Japanese currency with direct undertaking to assume Mitsui & Co Ltd.'s debts in Japanese currency and proceeded with registration procedures for foreign debts without approval by the state administration of foreign exchange. Although this is obviously contrary to the PRC's mandatory provisions for the approval and registration of foreign debts, the SPC nevertheless replied to the Haikou Intermediate People's Court's reported opinion on refusing recognition and enforcement of the arbitral award made by the SCC as follows:[22]

> As a State-owned enterprise, Hainan Textile Industry General Corporation directly assumed the debts of Mitsui (Mitsui & Co. Ltd) and carried out registration procedures without approval by the state administration of foreign exchange, thereby violating laws relating to approval and registration of foreign debts and the foreign control policies of the People's Republic of China. However, *violation of mandatory administrative regulations and departmental rules does not necessarily constitute violation of the public policy of the People's Republic of China*. The reasons for refusing recognition and enforcement of the arbitral award stated in your court's report are not established, and the arbitral award should not be refused recognition and enforcement on the ground of public policy violation (emphasis added).

Thus it can be seen that, with respect to the legal effect of violating mandatory laws for the approval and registration of foreign debts, the PRC courts differentiate between foreign arbitral awards and domestic arbitral awards by applying different standards to their recognition and enforcement.

---

21. Supreme People's Court (2001) Min-Si-Ta-Zi No. 12, 13 July 2005.
22. *Ibid.*

4.2.2.3 Award's Violation of Other Mandatory Laws

Apart from mandatory laws for registration of foreign debts assumption, in practice there are other cases where the PRC courts have refused to enforce domestic arbitral awards or mediated settlement agreements made by arbitration institutions on the basis of contravention of mandatory legal provisions. There are at least three examples, as discussed below.

In the case concerning contract for sale of housing between an individual with the surname Li and a certain residential construction company,[23] the Hunan Xiangtan Intermediate People's Court considered that the relevant housing did not have lawful conditions for sale as it was yet to conduct legal sale procedures with various government authorities of planning, land, housing management and administration. Xiangtan Arbitration Commission's finding that the sale of housing between relevant parties was valid contravenes mandatory legal provisions and violates social and public interest, and therefore its mediated settlement agreement was refused enforcement under Article 213 paragraph 3 of the PRC Civil Procedure Law, which states: 'The people's court shall refuse enforcement if it finds that the award's enforcement would violate social and public interest.'

In the dispute between Da Huang and Wei Huang concerning the confirmation of rights to homestead land use, Hainan Arbitration Commission made an arbitral award confirming Da Huang's homestead land use rights and requiring the respondent (Wei Huang) to assist the applicant (Da Huang) with transferring such land use right to the applicant (Da Huang). In response to Da Huang's application to enforce this arbitral award, the Hainan First Intermediate People's Court[24] found that Da Huang was an urban resident, and 'the Ministry of Land and Resource of the People's Republic of China's "Opinions on Strengthening the Administration of Rural homestead" stipulates that "purchasing rural homestead land by urban residents is strictly prohibited, issuing land use permits to urban residents who have purchased and illegally constructed housing in rural areas is strictly prohibited". Here Da Huang was an urban resident who did not qualify as a villager of Longlou Economic Cooperation. His conduct in purchasing homestead land violated national policy and infringed the public interest of the collective economic organisation. Hence the award's enforcement was refused under Article 213 paragraph 3 of the PRC Civil Procedure Law, which states: 'The people's court shall refuse enforcement if it finds that the award's enforcement would violate social and public interest.'

In the case concerning the confirmation of rights to land between Hainan Haocheng Real Estate Co., Ltd. (Haocheng) and Junpeng Ma,[25] the Hainan First Intermediate People's Court has previously in its ruling transferred the right to use the relevant land to a third party, but the land remained registered under the name of

---

23. Hunan Xiangtan Intermediate People's Court Enforcement Ruling (2011) Tan-Zhong-Zhi-Zi No. 58, 12 October 2011.
24. Hainan First Intermediate People's Court Enforcement Ruling (2011) Hai-Nan-Yi-Zhong-Zhi-Zi No. 54, 8 August 2011.
25. Hainan First Intermediate People's Court Enforcement Ruling (2009) Hai-Nan-Yi-Zhong-Zhi-Zi No. 26-4, 30 May 2011.

Chapter 4: PRC's Convergence with International Consensus

Hainan Saili'an Real Estate Development Co., Ltd., and the third party had never obtained the land use certificate because the third party had not applied to the Wanning Municipal Bureau of Land, Environment and Resources for change in registration of land use rights. Notwithstanding these circumstances, the third party without the land use certificate transferred the land to Junpeng Ma by contract as settlement of debts. Junpeng Ma (also without the land use certificate) further used the land as settlement of his debts with Haocheng by virtue of contract. After Haocheng applied to Hainan Arbitration Commission for arbitration, Hainan Arbitration Commission confirmed that the land use right belonged to Haocheng according to the agreement between Haocheng and Junpeng Ma, and required Junpeng Ma to directly change the land registration name from Saili'an to Haocheng. Upon the subsequent application by Haocheng to enforce the arbitral award, (2008) Hai-Zhong-Zi No. 245, the Hainan First Intermediate People's Court held that the award 'violated Article 38 item 6 of the PRC Law on Urban Real Estate Administration and contravened social and public interest' and therefore refused the award's enforcement under Article 213 paragraph 3 of the PRC Civil Procedure Law, which states: 'The people's court shall refuse enforcement if it finds that the award's enforcement would violate social and public interest.'

Yuxi Tian (Justice and President of the Executive Tribunal of the Beijing Higher People's Court) had clearly indicated in 2004 that, 'if an arbitral award violates the prohibitory provisions of the law, then judges can order that award's revocation or non-enforcement pursuant to the public interest provision'.[26]

By contrast, in cases concerning the recognition and enforcement of foreign arbitral awards, apart from the previously mentioned *Mitsui* case[27] (in which the SPC replied that violation of mandatory provisions for registering foreign debt assumption does not necessarily constitute violation of PRC public policy), the SPC again stated that 'a violation of mandatory provisions of the law of the PRC does not necessarily equate to a violation of the public policy of this country' in its Reply on Request for Instructions Re Application by ED&F Man (Hong Kong) Co., Ltd. for Recognition and Enforcement of the Arbitral Award of the Sugar Association of London (SAL).[28] Please *see* section 4.7 of this chapter for the detailed commentary on the *ED&F Man* case.

Scholars of the PRC also believe that public policy as stipulated in Article V(2)(b) of the New York Convention should be 'international public policy' and not domestic public policy.[29]

---

26. Yuxi Tian, *Comment on Domestic Judicial Review on Arbitration*, 51 Beijing Arbitration 6, 11 (2004).
27. Reply of the Supreme People's Court on the Request for Instructions on the Non-recognition and Non-enforcement of an Arbitral Award of the Arbitration Institute of the Stockholm Chamber of Commerce: *see* s. 4.2.2.2 of this Chapter for the details of this case.
28. Supreme People's Court (2003) Min-Si-Ta-Zi No. 3, 1 July 2003.
29. Decai Ma, *Analysis About the Character of the Public Policy in New York Convention*, 2010(4) Law Science Magazine 69, 70–71 (2010). Yaying Huang further states: 'Violation of public policy is the most commonly invoked ground for resisting the recognition and enforcement of arbitral awards, yet such invocation rarely succeeds. To a large extent this is because most national courts distinguish between the public policy of purely domestic affairs and the public policy applicable under international conventions.' *See* Yaying Huang, *Analysis About the International Standard of Paraphrase and Application of New York Convention*, 2010(10) Law Science Magazine 6, 11 (2010).

4.3 JOINT CONSIDERATION OF MERITS AND ARBITRAL DECISIONS

4.3.1 International Consensus

One very important question is whether the enforcement court should only consider the content of remedies granted by the arbitral tribunal or whether the enforcement court can also consider the substance of the parties' claims and the arbitral tribunal's decisions when determining whether to recognise and enforce a foreign arbitral award. The latter view seems to prevail internationally, because an arbitral award should be refused recognition or enforcement if the parties' substantive claims, the arbitral tribunal's decisions or procedures have violated the enforcement court's fundamental and mandatory principles of law. To interpret otherwise would require the recognition and enforcement of awards based on abhorrent laws (e.g., permitting slavery, drug trafficking or bribery), which is unacceptable.[30] For instance, in some cases involving slavery, drug trafficking or bribery, the remedies granted by the arbitral tribunal may be monetary payment only, such 'monetary payment' itself does not violate public policy and requires consideration of the parties' substantive claims, etc. in order to find that such monetary payment may involve slavery, drug trafficking, bribery or other violations of the enforcement State's public policy.

4.3.2 PRC Judicial Practice

In all the SPC's cases ascertained by the author in relation to the applicability of public policy in Article V(2)(b) of the New York Convention (please *see* Table 4.1 at the end of this chapter), the SPC's consideration was not limited to the remedies granted by the arbitral tribunals, but also included the parties' substantive claims, the arbitral tribunals' decisions and procedures, etc. Furthermore, as can be seen from the lower court's requests for instructions submitted to the SPC through the Reporting System, the lower courts also adopt the same manner of hearing in jointly considering the parties' substantive claims, the arbitral tribunals' decisions and procedures, etc. in specific cases.

4.4 PUBLIC POLICY IS APPLICABLE IN 'EXCEPTIONAL' CIRCUMSTANCES ONLY

4.4.1 International Consensus

In spite of the restriction about international public policy, the interpretation of public policy in New York Convention's Article V(2)(b) may still be unpredictable and even excessively broad. Recalling the vivid analogy of Justice Burrough of England (cited in Chapter 1),[31] public policy is an unruly horse which you never know where it will carry

---

30. Born, *supra* n. 2, at 3689–3690.
31. *Richardson v. Mellish*, All ER 258, 266 [1824-24].

Chapter 4: PRC's Convergence with International Consensus

you once you get astride it. Partially in reaction to this, the courts of most developed countries have taken very restrictive views of 'public policy' when determining whether or not to recognise and enforce foreign arbitral awards, or in other circumstances (such as deciding whether or not to set aside arbitral awards on the basis of public policy violation, etc.), as they do not wish to hastily refuse recognition and enforcement of foreign arbitral awards.[32] Many courts have explicitly stated the narrow and exceptional features of public policy in proceedings concerning the recognition and enforcement of foreign arbitral awards, repeatedly emphasising the fact that 'a tribunal applies a law that is different from that of the recognition forum's law, or wrongly applies the recognition forum's laws, or reaches a result that is contrary to that which the recognition forum's courts would reach, is not a basis for a violation of public policy' under New York Convention's Article V(2)(b).[33] As exemplified by the Swiss Court's concise statement in *Inter Maritime Mgt SA v Russin & Vecchi*:[34]

> The appellant forgets that the enforcement does not decide on the arbitral award as an appellate instance; the merits of an award cannot be reviewed under the cover of public policy.

The courts of other countries have also repeatedly expressed that errors in legal reasoning or the applicable law do not constitute violation of 'public policy' in New York Convention's Article V(2)(b). For the same reason, errors in fact-finding do not constitute violation of 'public policy' in New York Convention's Article V(2)(b).

Furthermore, many national courts have expressed their support for the New York Convention's 'pro-enforcement policy', opining that 'public policy' in New York Convention's Article V(2)(b) is exceptional and exceedingly narrow.[35]

4.4.2 PRC Judicial Practice

During his term as the SPC's Vice President, Exiang Wan co-authored an article 'Reason for the refusals of the recognition and enforcement of foreign arbitral awards in Chinese Courts – New York Convention case studies' with the SPC's Justice Xiaohong Xia. This article clearly states that 'violation of the enforcement State's public policy should be viewed as an "exceptional" rather than "definite" ground of refusal, which should be considered as a last resort to perform its function as a "safety valve"'.[36] In practice the SPC has indeed considered the 'public policy' in New York Convention's Article V(2)(b) in exceptional circumstances only.

---

32. Born, *supra* n. 2, at 3666.
33. Please *see* Gary B. Born, *International Arbitration: Law and Practice* 403–404 (Kluwer Law International 2012).
34. *Inter Maritime Mgt SA v. Russin & Vecchi*, 9 January 1995, XXII Yearbook Comm. Arb. 789, 796.
35. Born, *supra* n. 2, at 3670.
36. Exiang Wan & Xiaohong Xia, *Reason for the Refusals of the Recognition and Enforcement of Foreign Arbitral Awards in Chinese Courts – New York Convention Case Studies*, 13(2) International Law Review of Wuhan University 1, 43 (2010).

An example is the *GRD Minrpoc* case,[37] in which the SPC was of the opinion that the parties who chose to resolve their disputes by arbitration should bear the consequences of their choice and accept the arbitral tribunal's decision about the quality of the disputed equipment; 'whether or not the substantive results of arbitration are fair and reasonable should not be the criterion for determining whether or not the arbitral award's recognition and enforcement would violate the public policy of the People's Republic of China'. The specific facts of this case are as follows.

On 24 July 1994 Shanghai Foreign Trade Co., Ltd. ('Trade Co.') as the buyer, Werman International Co., Ltd. ('Werman Co.') as the seller and Shanghai Flyingwheel Industry Co., Ltd. ('Flyingwheel Co.') as the end user executed a contract, under which Werman Co. agreed to provide and Trade Co. agreed to purchase the equipment and materials for the recycling of used batteries while Flyingwheel Co. would be the end user of such equipment.

On 30 April 1995 GRD Minproc Ltd. ('GRD'), Trade Co. and Flyingwheel Co. executed the 'Amendment to Contract 94YN150-MS7109Au' to change the seller from Werman Co. to GRD.

Between July and December of 1997, the equipment specified in the contract was successively imported from Australia to Shanghai via Trade Co. and received by Flyingwheel Co. Subsequently disputes arose between Flyingwheel Co. and GRD about the efficacy of the equipment. Flyingwheel Co. claimed that GRD was in fundamental breach of the contract by providing equipment which did not conform to the more specific industrial design criteria, which not only failed to produce the quantity of lead specified for the same design criteria (16,650 tons per year) but 'simply failed to produce any lead'. Flyingwheel Co. filed a request for arbitration with the SCC claiming termination of contract together with restitution of purchase price and compensation for damages against GRD.

The arbitral tribunal made the following findings: (1) The specifications and industrial design criteria merely aimed at describing the equipment and did not constitute any legal obligations binding on GRD. (2) The original Annex H to the contract about guaranteeing specified production capacity and recycling performance was deleted due to amendment to the contract; Flyingwheel Co.'s belief that there is no evidence in support of the production information being 'performance guarantee' is merely an estimate based on some assumptions. (3) There was no evidence to support Flyingwheel Co.'s main claim that the equipment 'simply failed to produce any lead' and, on the contrary, there was convincing evidence that the equipment had in fact produced lead under certain circumstances. (4) Designing and building the ventilation shaft was the obligation of Flyingwheel Co., so any claims about the ventilation shaft cannot constitute a legal basis of GRD's fundamental breach.

After finding that there was no evidence about the equipment provided by GRD being unable to operate and meet the envisaged standard, the arbitral tribunal rejected

---

37. Reply of the Supreme People's Court on Request for Instructions Re Application of GRD Minproc Limited for Recognition and Enforcement of the Arbitration Award of Arbitration Institute of the Stockholm Chamber of Commerce, Supreme People's Court (2008) Min-Si-Ta-Zi No. 48, 13 March 2009.

Chapter 4: PRC's Convergence with International Consensus

Flyingwheel Co.'s substantive claims and ordered Flyingwheel Co. to pay AUD 1.68 million to GRD as compensation for arbitration expenses.

In response to GRD's application for this arbitral award's recognition and enforcement, the Shanghai First Intermediate People's Court held that the SCC Award No. 024/2003 should be refused recognition as its recognition would 'violate the basic principles of the laws of the People's Republic of China and conflict with the social and public interest of the People's Republic of China in accordance with Article V(2)(b) of the New York Convention'.[38] In support of the Shanghai First Intermediate People's Court's opinion, the Shanghai Higher People's Court stated:[39]

> Although the applicant in this case applied to enforce only the compensation for arbitration costs in the arbitral award, however such arbitration costs precisely reflect the final outcome of the arbitral dispute. After a preliminary examination of the arbitral proceedings and thorough understanding of the whole case background, this Court is of the view that the parties' dispute originated from the special production equipment's inability to meet industry safety standards, resulting in severe pollution and damage to the applicant's factory environment and workers' health followed by damage to public interest due to prolonged closure and non-use, thereby causing substantive frustration of the contractual purpose and the applicant's substantial loss of economic interests. Unexpectedly the arbitral tribunal did not pay due attention to these very important circumstances, but merely and simply decided that the equipment provided by the seller did not constitute breach of contract according to the formal terms of the contract. Clearly this approach is contrary to the arbitration spirits of fairness and justice, and has objectively caused consequences that are harmful to the social and public interest of the People's Republic of China. All of these precisely correspond with the conditions in Article V(2)(b) of the New York Convention, and accordingly the arbitral award's recognition and enforcement should be refused.

Nonetheless the SPC adopted a different view in its reply to the case reporting:[40]

> The equipment's importation was not prohibited in the People's Republic of China as its purchase overseas by Flyingwheel Co. was approved by the relevant administrative departments. The environmental pollution caused during the equipment's installation, testing and operation could be attributed to various causes. In circumstances where Flyingwheel Co. requested arbitration of equipment quality disputes pursuant to a valid arbitration clause, the arbitral tribunal's judgment on equipment quality was within the arbitral tribunal's authority as well as an outcome that should be borne by the parties using arbitration to resolve their disputes. Whether or not the substantive results of arbitration are fair and reasonable should not be the criterion for determining whether or not the arbitral award's recognition and enforcement would violate the public policy of the People's Republic of China. This arbitral award's recognition and enforcement would not constitute violation of fundamental societal interest, basic principles of

---

38. Cited from Shanghai Higher People's Court's Request for Instructions Re Application of GRD Minproc Limited for Recognition and Enforcement of the Arbitration Award of Arbitration Institute of the Stockholm Chamber of Commerce, Shanghai Higher People's Court (2008) Hu-Gao-Min-Si(Shang)-Ta-Zi No. 2, 18 August 2008.
39. Ibid.
40. Supreme People's Court (2008) Min-Si-Ta-Zi No. 48, 13 March 2009.

law or good morals of the People's Republic of China, consequently the circumstance prescribed in Article V(2)(b) of the New York Convention does not exist in this case.

Subsequently the SPC reiterated this position in its Reply on Request for Instructions Re Application by Western Bulk Pte., Ltd. for the Recognition and Enforcement of an English Arbitral Award on 21 May 2012. In that case the Tianjin Higher People's Court agreed with the respondent's submission and stated that 'the result of the arbitral award lacked factual and legal basis, significantly lacked fairness, severely jeopardized the Chinese parties' interests in contravention of the social and public interest of the People's Republic of China'; this pertains to the circumstance prescribed in New York Convention's Article V(2)(b) and the arbitral award should be refused recognition and enforcement.[41] The SPC nevertheless replied as follows:[42]

> Public policy in New York Convention's Article V(2)(b) should be interpreted and applied strictly. The public policy ground can only be invoked to refuse recognition and enforcement if recognition and enforcement of foreign commercial arbitral awards would violate the basic principles of law, infringe national sovereignty, jeopardize national and societal safety, violate good morals, jeopardize fundamental societal interest etc. of the People's Republic of China. It is inappropriate for your court to refuse the award's recognition and enforcement on the ground of violating social and public interest because the arbitration results manifestly lack fairness.

Additionally, in the *Louis Dreyfus* case (*see* Reply of the Supreme People's Court on Request for Instructions Re Application of Louis Dreyfus Commodities Asian Co., Ltd. for Recognition and Enforcement of Arbitration Award No. 3980 of International Federation of Oils, Seeds & Fats Associations),[43] the SPC and the arbitral tribunal held different views and the SPC considered the arbitral tribunal's statement that '[t]here is a very significant gap between the stipulation of PRC laws and their application in practice' as a 'misconception'. Yet the SPC still decided that such 'misconception' of the arbitral tribunal would not cause the arbitral award's recognition and enforcement to violate the PRC public policy and therefore the arbitral award should be recognised and enforced. Section 5.2.2 of Chapter 5 discusses the details of this case.

An example of a lower court decision is the application to Sichuan Chengdu Intermediate People's Court by Pepsi-Cola for recognition and enforcement of the SCC Award No. 076/2002.[44] In that case the respondent Sichuan Pepsi-Cola Beverage Co., Ltd. submitted that 'the arbitral award's contravention of Chinese public policy manifests in its serious contravention of the principles of fairness and justice in Chinese law, which includes finding no breach or minor breach as fundamental breach and thereby terminating the contract; violation of procedural principles prescribed by

---

41. Tianjin Higher People's Court's Request for Instructions Re Application of Western Bulk Pte., Ltd. for the Recognition and Enforcement of an English Arbitral Award, Tianjin Higher People's Court (2011) Jin-Gao-Min-Si-Ta-Zi No. 4, 19 March 2012.
42. Supreme People's Court (2012) Min-Si-Ta-Zi No. 12, 21 May 2012.
43. Supreme People's Court (2010) Min-Si-Ta-Zi No. 48, 10 October 2010.
44. Sichuan Chengdu Intermediate People's Court Civil Ruling (2005) Cheng-Min-Chu-Zi No. 912, 30 April 2008.

Chapter 4: PRC's Convergence with International Consensus

Chinese law; severe damage to major economic interests and social order and stability of the PRC.[45] Yet the Sichuan Chengdu Intermediate People's Court did not accept this submission, stating that 'whether or not an arbitral award would violate a nation's public policy should be considered from the perspective of the fundamental legal order, fundamental morality and justice of the entire nation and entire society'.[46] Here the arbitral award does not have any contents which are in violation of the PRC's social public policy rendering the award unacceptable to the PRC's legal order. Consequently the Sichuan Chengdu Intermediate People's Court did not support Sichuan Pepsi-Cola Beverage Co., Ltd.'s submission that the award's violation of PRC public policy fell within Article V(2)(b) of the New York Convention requiring the people court's non-recognition and non-enforcement.

4.5 PROCEDURAL PUBLIC POLICY IN NON-RECOGNITION AND NON-ENFORCEMENT OF FOREIGN ARBITRAL AWARDS

4.5.1 International Consensus

Recommendation 1(e) and paragraph 29 of the Final Report of the ILA illustrate 'procedural public policy' with examples. Procedural public policy requires arbitral tribunals to be impartial. Examples of violation of procedural public policy include: the making of arbitral award is induced or affected by fraud or corruption; violation of the rules of natural justice; the parties' unequal footing in the appointment of arbitrators. In addition, enforcing an arbitral award that is inconsistent with a court decision or arbitral award that has res judicata effect in the enforcement forum may also be regarded as violation of procedural public policy. According to the Final Report, manifest disregard of the law and manifest disregard of the facts should not be considered as violation of procedural public policy.[47]

The content of procedural public policy overlaps with the requirements of due process stipulated in Article V(1)(b).[48] Despite this, 'public policy' in New York Convention's Article V(2)(b) still co-exists with Article V(1)(b) in Albert Jan van den Berg's view.[49] Article V(1)(b) of the New York Convention requires one of the parties to furnish to the competent authority proof about the specified circumstance, whereas

---

45. Ibid.
46. Ibid.
47. *Final Report on Public Policy as a Bar to Enforcement of International Arbitration Awards*, 19 Arbitration International 249 (ILA's Final Report), Recommendation 1(e), para. 29. For other examples, *see* Loukas A. Mistelis (ed.), *Concise International Arbitration* 22 (Kluwer Law International 2010). In this book, 'manifest disregard of the law' and 'manifest disregard of the facts' are also listed as examples of 'violation of procedural public policy'.
48. ILA's Final Report, Recommendation 1(e), para. 29 last sentence.
49. Albert Jan van den Berg, *The New York Convention of 1958 – Towards a Uniform Judicial Interpretation* 376, 382 (Kluwer Law International 1981). For specific cases refusing enforcement of arbitral awards because of violation of due process pursuant the public policy ground in Art. V(2)(b) of the New York Convention, *see* Herbert Kronke, Patricia Nacimiento et al., *The New York Convention: Recognition and Enforcement of Foreign Arbitral Awards* 387-389 (Kluwer Law International 2010).

Article V(2)(b) provides for ex officio consideration by the competent authority about any violation of public policy. The need for the enforcement court to invoke Article V(2)(b) ex officio (i.e., on the court's own motion) may arise especially when the opposing party refuses to participate in the court proceedings concerning whether to recognise and enforce the arbitral award.

Yet Gary B. Born opines that the more appropriate view is not to extend the interpretation of 'public policy' in New York Convention's Article V(2)(b) to the so-called 'procedural public policy', so that 'public policy' in New York Convention's Article V(2)(b) is confined to 'substantive public policy'.[50] According to his main reason, New York Convention's Article V(1)(b) already provides for '[t]he party against whom the award is invoked was not given proper notice of the appointment of the arbitrator or of the arbitration proceedings or was otherwise unable to present his case' as one of the grounds that the party can request the enforcement court to refuse the recognition and enforcement of foreign arbitral awards, with the purpose of establishing unified international standards for arbitral procedures. At the same time, the latter part of New York Convention's Article V(1)(d) also provides another ground for the enforcement court's refusal to enforce and recognise foreign arbitral award at the party's request, namely 'the arbitral procedure was not in accordance with the agreement of the parties, or, failing such agreement, was not in accordance with the law of the country where the arbitration took place'.[51] Under these circumstances, the application of procedural public policy in New York Convention's Article V(2)(b) to refuse recognition and enforcement of foreign arbitral awards merely allows the enforcement court to apply the enforcement State's public policy within a limited range to international arbitration which was conducted outside the enforcement State and which already complied with international procedural standards (this is because New York Convention's Article V(1)(b) already stipulates the international procedural standard). Put simply, Article V(1)(b) and (d) of the New York Convention already expressly provide for procedural defects, it should not be necessary to interpret Article V(2)(b) of the New York Convention as including 'procedural public policy' in light of its purpose of specification.

4.5.2 PRC Judicial Practice

It can be seen from some cases that the PRC courts would not apply 'public policy' in New York Convention's Article V(2)(b) if the other grounds for refusing recognition and enforcement of foreign arbitral awards in New York Convention's Article V(1)(b) or (d) were applicable. Examples are as follows.

In its Reply on Application of First Investment Corp. of the Marshall Islands for Recognition and Enforcement of Arbitration Award of an Ad Hoc Arbitration Tribunal

---

50. Born, *supra* n. 2, at 3687.
51. Article V(1)(d) of the New York Convention stipulates: 'The composition of the arbitral authority or the arbitral procedure was not in accordance with the agreement of the parties, or, failing such agreement, was not in accordance with the law of the country where the arbitration took place'.

in London, the SPC found that:[52] although the arbitral tribunal in this case was constituted by three arbitrators, arbitrator Shengchang Wang did not participate in the entire arbitration proceedings and did not participate in the entire delivery of the final arbitral award. Consequently, the composition of the arbitral tribunal or the arbitral procedure was not in accordance with the parties' arbitration agreement, and was also contrary to English law (as the law of the arbitral seat). Thus the arbitral award's recognition and enforcement should be refused under Article V(1)(d) of the New York Convention. During the hearing of this case by the Xiamen Maritime Court, the respondents Fujian Mawei Shipbuilding Ltd. and Fujian Shipbuilding Industry Group Company Limited had alleged that the arbitral tribunal violated the principle of impartiality and the arbitral award violated the public policy of this country by admitting forged evidence,[53] nevertheless the people's court did not accept this submission, nor did the court consider, on its own motion (ex officio), the potential violation of public policy as stipulated in Article V(2)(b) of the New York Convention due to the defects in arbitral procedure (namely, one of the arbitrators did not participate in the entire arbitration process as well as in the entire hearing of the final award). Instead, the court decided on the basis of Article V(1)(d) of the New York Convention.

Similar decisions arose with respect to the enforcement of arbitral awards made in Hong Kong. An example is the application by Amlon Metals Ltd for enforcement of an award made in Hong Kong,[54] in which Kunming Railway Bureau Import and Export Corporation (one of the parties subject to enforcement) submitted that: 'the legal consequences incurred by the conducts of Kunming Railway Bureau Import and Export Corporation as an agent shall be directly attributed to its principal and its principal should assume all liabilities. Therefore, the decision made in the arbitral award that Kunming Railway Bureau shall assume joint and several liabilities violates the basic system and principle of the country regarding agency.' Yet the Yunnan Kunming Intermediate People's Court did not refuse the award's enforcement on the grounds of violation of PRC social and public interest. It is agreed under Article 19 of the Contract that all disputes arising under the Contract shall be determined under the Rules of the London Court of International Arbitration by two arbitrators and an umpire to be appointed pursuant to the English Arbitration Act 1996.[55] Article 20 then stipulates that all disputes shall be exclusively determined by Hong Kong International Arbitration

---

52. Reply of the Supreme People's Court on Application of First Investment Corp. of the Marshall Islands for Recognition and Enforcement of Arbitration Award of an Ad Hoc Arbitration Tribunal in London, Supreme People's Court (2007) Min-Si-Ta-Zi No. 35, 27 February 2008.
53. Cited from Xiamen Maritime Court Civil Ruling (2006) Xia-Hai-Fa-Ren-Zi No. 1, 11 May 2008.
54. Yunnan Kunming Intermediate People's Court (2008) Kun-Fei-Zhi-Zi No. 48-1, 10 November 2009, cited from National Judges College & Renmin University of China Law School (ed.), *An Overview of Chinese Court Cases (Volume of Commercial Judgments 2010), Case No. 71: Amlon Metals Ltd.'s Application for Enforcement of an Arbitral Award against Yunnan Nickel and Cobalt Co., Ltd. (Non-recognition of an Arbitral Award made in Hong Kong)* 450–455 (China Renmin University Press 2012).
55. The content of Articles 19 & 20 of the Contract is cited from: Xianming Shi, *Amlon Dilemma: Another Hilmarton Nightmare in International Commercial Arbitration*, 10 (3) Canadian Social Science 29, 29-30 (2014); See also: Yunnan Kunming Intermediate People's Court (2008) Kun-Fei-Zhi-Zi No. 48-1, 10 November 2009.

Centre (HKIAC) in Hong Kong in accordance with English laws. Nevertheless the HKIAC appointed a sole arbitrator instead of following the parties' agreement about the arbitral tribunal's composition. Such alternation was neither in accordance with English arbitration law nor in accordance with the parties' agreement. Consequently the arbitral award's enforcement was refused pursuant to Article 7 paragraph 1 item 4 of the Arrangement Concerning Mutual Enforcement of Arbitral Awards Between the Mainland and the Hong Kong Special Administrative Region, which states: 'the composition of the arbitral tribunal or the arbitral procedure was not in accordance with the agreement of the parties'.

4.6 SUBSTANTIVE PUBLIC POLICY IN NON-RECOGNITION AND NON-ENFORCEMENT OF FOREIGN ARBITRAL AWARDS

4.6.1 International Consensus

Examples of 'substantive public policy' cited by scholars include the 'fundamental principles of law; actions contrary to good morals; and national interests/foreign relations', etc.[56] According to the ILA's Final Report,[57] 'substantive fundamental principles' include the principle of good faith and prohibition of abuse of rights. A court in the US held that the interest rate in an arbitral award which was 5% higher than the market interest rate under the applicable foreign law was contrary to the US public policy against contractual punishment,[58] and therefore refused to enforce the parts of the arbitral award concerning interest rate. In addition, it is commonly considered that the enforcement of arbitral awards requiring payments of proceeds of corruption would be contrary to public policy.[59]

4.6.2 PRC Judicial Practice

The author is yet to *see* any PRC judicial cases in this regard.

4.7 VIOLATION OF ENFORCEMENT STATE'S MANDATORY LAWS IS NOT NECESSARILY VIOLATION OF ENFORCEMENT STATE'S PUBLIC POLICY

4.7.1 International Consensus

In many developed countries, claims relating to anti-trust law, competition law, securities law and other 'public law' are arbitrable (i.e., capable of settlement by arbitration). The courts may review the merits of these cases when determining

---

56. Loukas A. Mistelis (ed.), *Concise International Arbitration* 22 (Kluwer Law International 2010).
57. ILA's Final Report, Recommendation 1(e), para. 28.
58. *Laminoris-Trefileries-Cableries de Lens, S.A. v. Southwire Co.*, 484 F. Supp. 1063 (N.D. Ga. 1980).
59. Born, *supra* n. 2, at 3672.

whether to revoke, recognise or enforce the arbitral awards in these cases. (This differs from cases concerning contractual interpretation or private law disputes, in which the enforcement court commonly should not engage in merits review.) This prompts the view that the court should be able to reconsider whether the arbitral tribunal's decisions concerning public law claims are appropriate when deciding whether to enforce the arbitral awards in this type of cases. Although such type of cases is rare, limited case law reveals that the US courts 'appear to have subjected arbitral determinations of public policy to relatively deferential review'.[60]

4.7.2 PRC Judicial Practice

According to Article 2 of PRC Arbitration Law, 'contractual disputes and other disputes over rights and interest in property between equal citizens, legal persons and other organizations may be arbitrated'. From the cases currently ascertained by the author, there appears to be no cases in which the arbitral tribunal directly determined public law claims. Yet in other cases concerning violation of mandatory laws, it is evident that the PRC courts have synchronised with international consensus that violation of PRC's mandatory laws does not necessarily equate with violation of PRC's public policy. Specific case illustrations are as follows.

In *Mitsui* case (concerning the SPC's Reply to Haikou Intermediate People's Court's), the arbitral award was premised on legal facts concerning violation of PRC mandatory laws. Hainan Textile Industry General Corporation, a state-owned enterprise, directly assumed the debts of Mitsui & Co., Ltd. by executing the agreement for repayment in Japanese currency without following the approval and registration procedures of the state administration of foreign exchange, thereby violating the PRC laws relating to approval and registration of foreign debts as well as other mandatory foreign control regulations. Yet the arbitral tribunal did not find such agreement for repayment in Japanese currency to be invalid and made an award according to this agreement. Nor did the SPC consider the enforcement of this arbitral award contrary to PRC public policy, instead stating in its reply that 'violation of mandatory administrative regulations and departmental rules does not necessarily constitute violation of the public policy of the People's Republic of China'.[61]

Furthermore, in the *ED&F Man* case (concerning its Reply on Request for Instructions Re Application of ED&F Man (Hong Kong) Co., Ltd. for Recognition and Enforcement of the Arbitral Award of the SAL), the SPC also pointed out that 'violation of mandatory laws of this country cannot completely equate with violation of public policy of this country'. The details of this case are as follows.[62]

---

60. Born, *supra* n. 2, at 3688.
61. Reply of the Supreme People's Court on the Request for Instructions on the Non-recognition and Non-enforcement of an Arbitral Award of the Arbitration Institute of the Stockholm Chamber of Commerce, Supreme People's Court (2001) Min-Si-Ta-Zi No. 12, 13 July 2005. *See* s. 4.2.2.2 of this Chapter for the details of this case.
62. Supreme People's Court (2003) Min-Si-Ta-Zi No. 3, 1 July 2003.

On 14 December 1994, China National Sugar & Alcohol Group Corp ('China Sugar Group') and ED&F Man (Hong Kong) Co., Ltd. ('ED&F Man') executed a contract for raw sugar option ('8008 Contract'). China Sugar Group did not establish the letter of credit in accordance with Annex 19 of the Contract, nor did ED&F Man make the actual delivery. On 26 January 1999, ED&F Man sent a facsimile to China Sugar Group terminating the 8008 Contract and submitted request for arbitration to SAL, claiming compensation for the difference between the contract price and market price.

On 6 August 2001, SAL rendered Award No. 158, ordering China Sugar Group to pay to ED&F Man USD 14,162,505 as compensation for breaching the 8008 Contract together with interest and arbitration costs, etc.

ED&F Man applied to the Beijing First Intermediate People's Court for the recognition and enforcement of the SAL's Award No. 158 on 22 January 2002. The Beijing First Intermediate People's Court was inclined to refuse the award's recognition and reported to the Beijing Higher People's Court. According to the Beijing Higher People's Court's opinion:[63] 'The operation process of 8008 Contract and its annexes utilize futures trading to seek speculative profits, such futures trading activities violate the prohibitive provisions of the laws of this country. Award No. 158 approved the parties' illegal benefits obtained from illegal overseas future transactions through the evasion of the PRC laws governing futures trading. This violation of the PRC mandatory laws constitutes violation of the PRC public policy. Based on article V(2)(b) of the "Convention on the Recognition and Enforcement of Foreign Arbitral Awards," we intend to reject the application of ED&F Man, and refuse recognition and enforcement of Award No.158 of the Sugar Association of London.' Yet the SPC stated in its reply to Beijing Higher People's Court:[64]

> Pursuant to the laws and regulations of this country, domestic enterprises are not allowed to conduct overseas futures trading without obtaining prior approval from the competent authority. China National Sugar & Alcohol Group's conduct in overseas future trading without approval should undoubtedly be considered as invalid. However, a violation of mandatory laws of this country cannot completely equate with violation of public policy of this country. Therefore, this case did not involve the circumstances prescribed in Article V(2) of the New York Convention concerning inarbitrability and the violation of PRC public policy by recognizing and enforcing the arbitral award. The arbitral award should be recognized and enforced in accordance with Article 269 of the PRC Civil Procedure Law and Article V of the New York Convention.

The SPC has established the concept that 'violation of the PRC's individual mandatory laws may not necessarily constitute violation of the PRC's public policy' through its Replies in cases such as Haikou Intermediate People's Court's request for instructions on non-recognition and non-enforcement of an arbitral award made by the SCC, as well as the *ED&F Man* case (concerning application by ED&F Man (Hong Kong) Co. Ltd for recognition and enforcement of arbitral award made by the SAL, etc. Another case can be found in the SPC's Reply on Request for Instructions Re

---
63. *Ibid.*
64. *Ibid.*

Chapter 4: PRC's Convergence with International Consensus

Recognition of the Arbitral Award in the case of *Tianrui Hotel Investment Co., Ltd. (Petitioner) v. Hangzhou Yiju Hotel Management Co., Ltd. (Respondent)*. Tianrui Hotel Investment Co., Ltd. ('Tianrui', a company constituted under the laws of the Samoa Islands) and Hangzhou Yiju Hotel Management Co., Ltd. ('Yiju'),[65] in which the applicant Tianrui Co. (Tianrui Hotel Investment Co. Ltd.) and the respondent Yiju Co. (Hangzhou Yiju Hotel Management Co. Ltd) executed a 'Unit System Agreement' of the 'Super 8 Hotels' franchise system in October 2004. Pursuant to the Unit System Agreement, Tianrui Co. permitted Yiju Co. to use the trademark and other symbols of the Super 8 Hotels as well as to provide hotel services in specified locations. Tianrui Co. also agreed to provide other various services relating to hotel management, specifically the reservation system services, while Yiju Co. agreed to pay various fees including consultancy fees, annual royalties, fees for using the reservation system and other related fees. At the same time, Yiju Co. also executed a 'Unit Service Agreement' with SuBoAiTe (Beijing) International Hotel Management Co., Ltd., ('SuBoAiTe', a company registered in the PRC and affiliated to Tianrui Co.).

Yiju Co. began operating the Super 8 Hotels after executing the Unit System Agreement, and subsequently dispute arose between the parties over payment of fees. On 21 November 2007 Tianrui Co. filed a request for arbitration with the London Court of International Arbitration pursuant to clause 14.7 of the Unit System Agreement, which stipulated:[66] 'Any dispute or claim arising from the parties' relationship or relating to this Agreement shall be submitted to arbitration by the London Court of International Arbitration, whose Arbitration Rules are deemed to be part of this clause. A sole arbitrator should be appointed.' After the LCIA made a final award (No. 7983) on 5 December 2008, Tianrui Co. applied to the Hangzhou Intermediate People's Court for the recognition of this LCIA award. According to the Hangzhou Intermediate People's Court's ruling:[67]

> The Unit System Agreement between Tianrui Co. and Yiju Co was a franchise agreement, and franchising belongs to the restricted business sector in the PRC. Article 3 of the Measures for the Administration of Foreign Investment in Commercial Fields provides: 'Foreign-invested commercial enterprises means foreign-invested enterprises engaging in the following management activities:.. (4) Franchising: entitling someone to use its trademark, trade name and business model etc. through contractual means in order to receive remuneration or franchising fees. Foreign companies, enterprises and other economic organizations or individuals must engage in business activities stipulated in items 1 to 4 through foreign-invested companies established within China'. Article 33 of the Measures for Administration of Commercial Franchise stipulates that foreign-invested enterprises engaging in commercial activities by franchising must apply to the original approval authority to add 'engaging in commercial activities by franchising' to its business scope. Franchising is listed as a restricted industry in the Catalogue of

---

65. Reply of the Supreme People's Court on Request for Instructions Re Application by ED&F Man (Hong Kong) Co., Ltd. for Recognition and Enforcement of the Arbitral Award of the Sugar Association of London, Supreme People's Court (2003) Min-Si-Ta-Zi No. 3, 1 July 2003.
66. Cited from Zhejiang Higher People's Court's Request for Instructions Re Recognition of the Arbitral Award in the Case of Tianrui Hotel Investment Co., Ltd, Zhejiang Higher People's Court (2010) Zhe-Shang-Wai-Ta-Zi No. 3, 15 March 2010.
67. *Ibid.*

Industries for Guiding Foreign Investment and belongs to the restricted business sector of the PRC. As a company registered and existing under the laws of the Samoan Islands, Tianrui Co. could not directly engage in franchise business in China pursuant to the Chinese administrative regulations relating to franchising. According to Article 10 of the 'Interpretation I of the Supreme People's Court of Several Issues Concerning the Application of the Contract Law of the People's Republic of China': 'where a party enters into a contract that exceeds its business scope, the people's court shall accordingly find such contract to be null and void, unless such a contract violates the provisions of the state on restricted business operations or franchise operations or the provisions of laws and administrative regulations on prohibited business operation'. This shows that the launch of the franchise business activities through executing the Unit System Agreement between Tianrui Co. and Yiju Co. violated the PRC's mandatory provisions. The purpose of the PRC's franchising provisions was to strictly limit foreign capital's access in order to maintain the PRC's economic order and social order. Yet Tianrui Co.'s conduct violated the PRC's basic system for introducing foreign capital and infringed the PRC's public interest. Consequently the arbitral award should be refused recognition pursuant to Article V(2)(b) of the New York Convention.

Upon reporting by the Hangzhou Intermediate People's Court, the Zhejiang Higher People's Court, despite being cognizant that 'violation of the PRC's mandatory laws does not necessarily constitute infringement of PRC's social and public interest', still found that:[68] 'In this case, SuBoAiTe Co. and Tianrui Co. were actually related companies that deliberately divided the franchising contract into two agreements with an attempt to evade the PRC's system for restricting foreign companies' access to franchise businesses, and can be considered as violating the PRC's social and public interest.' Nevertheless the SPC held a different opinion:[69]

> The Unit System Agreement between Tianrui Co. and Yiju Co. executed on 28 October 2004 was by nature a commercial franchise agreement. According to this country's commercial franchise management system in force at the time, foreign companies carrying out commercial franchise management business must do so through the establishment of foreign-invested enterprises, and must obtain approval from administrative authorities. However, after the implementation of the State Council's Regulation on Administration of Commercial Franchise on 1 May 2007, prior approval is no longer required and instead, there is merely a requirement of registration with the regulatory authority after the entering of a franchise agreement. It no longer requires approval. Such registration requirement is a part of mandatory norms within administrative regulations, and does not affect validity of civil agreements between the parties. The decision of the arbitral award regarding the Unit System Agreement was not contrary to the PRC's mandatory legal provisions, let alone contrary to the PRC's public policy. Thus Article V(2)(b) of the New York Convention was inapplicable.

It can be seen from the above statement that, on the one hand, the SPC acknowledged that the Unit System Agreement between Tianrui Co. and Yiju Co. indeed required approval by the administrative authorities under the legal provisions at

---

68. Zhejiang Higher People's Court's Request for Instructions Re Recognition of the Arbitral Award in the Case of Tianrui Hotel Investment Co., Ltd, Zhejiang Higher People's Court (2010) Zhe-Shang-Wai-Ta-Zi No. 3, 15 March 2010.
69. Supreme People's Court (2010) Min-Si-Ta-Zi No. 18, 18 May 2010.

the time (i.e., Measures for the Administration of Commercial Franchises). Yet on the other hand the SPC also found that the arbitral award on the Unit System Agreement did not violate the PRC's mandatory legal provisions as the change in law two years after the execution of the Unit System Agreement (i.e., Regulation on the Administration of Commercial Franchises, as implemented from 1 May 2007) merely required the subsequent registration of commercial franchising agreements without requiring prior approval. The SPC did not explain why it determined the case on the basis of the change in law two years after the parties executed the Unit System Agreement. However, this case provides a glimpse of the SPC's inclination to avoid, as much as possible, refusing the recognition and enforcement of arbitral awards on the ground of 'violation of the PRC's mandatory legal provisions'.

It is also noteworthy that judges from the lower courts have adopted the same view. An example is the *Leaf Confectionary* case in which the Shanghai Second Intermediate Court granted recognition and enforcement of an arbitral award made by SIAC.[70] The parties in this case executed an asset purchase contract on 20 December 2001 under which Leaf Confectionary (Shanghai) Co., Ltd. (foreign wholly owned enterprise) would sell its assets and confectionary business to agreements executed by Shanghai Lainfu Food Co., Ltd. However, Article 23 of the Implementing Rules for the Implementation of the Law of the PRC on Wholly Foreign-Owned Enterprises stipulates that 'Where any foreign-invested enterprise intends to mortgage or transfer of assets or rights and interests, it must obtain approvals from approving authority and register with the administration of industry and commerce.'[71] Here the assets purchase agreement was not approved by the relevant approving authority (i.e., Shanghai Foreign Investment Commission) in contravention of the PRC's mandatory laws. On this issue, Justice Xuejie Cui, one of the three judges of the Shanghai Second Intermediate People's Court in this case,[72] specifically expressed in writing that,[73] 'even if the assets purchase agreement were invalid by virtue of violation of the mandatory laws of this country, the debtor-creditor relationship arising from this agreement was confined to the parties, which does not suffice to constitute damage to this country's basic legal system or principles, and therefore this case cannot invoke public policy to refuse the arbitral award's recognition and enforcement'.

In another case, the applicant, Jacobson Golf Course Design, Inc. applied with the Guangdong Zhaoqing Intermediate People's Court for the recognition and enforcement

---

70. Case concerning the application for recognition of the foreign arbitral award in the case of *Wuxi Leaf Confectionery Co., Ltd. (Petitioner) v. Shanghai Lianfu Food Co., Ltd. (Respondent)*, Shanghai Second Intermediate People's Court Civil Ruling (2008) Hu-Er-Zhong-Min-Wu-(Shang)-Chu-Zi No. 19, 24 June 2009.
71. Implementing Rules for the Implementation of the Law of the People's Republic of China on Wholly Foreign-Owned Enterprises (2001 Revision), State Council Order No. 301, promulgated and implemented on 12 April 2001.
72. This civil ruling was made by Presiding Judge Weimin Lu, acting Judge Yimin Wang and acting Judge Xuejie Cui.
73. Xuejie Cui & Yun He, *On Recognition and Enforcement of Foreign Arbitral Awards Reached from Contracts Violating Management and Compulsory Regulations – Comment on the case of Leaf Candy Limited Corporation of Shanghai's Application of Recognition and Enforcement of the Arbitral Award given by SIAC*, 72 Beijing Arbitration 152, 159 (2010).

of an arbitral award by the International Centre for Dispute Resolution of the American Arbitration Association. The respondents argued that the applicant violated the Chinese mandatory laws, regulations and departmental rules by failing to cooperate with a Chinese design company as required by the Chinese mandatory laws and regulations; therefore, the recognition and enforcement of the American arbitral award should be refused on the grounds of violation of the public interest. However, Zhaoqing Intermediate People's Court held that:[74] 'violation of mandatory laws does not necessarily equal to violation of the public policy of this country; recognition and enforcement of the arbitral award would not violate the fundamental social interest and basic principles of law of this country'.

Furthermore, there is a recent application by Fujian Across Express Information Technology Co., Ltd., Fujian Fenzhong Media Co., Ltd. and Zheng Cheng to Fujian Fuzhou Intermediate People's Court for non-enforcement of two arbitral awards made by HKIAC under Article 7 of the SPC's Arrangement Concerning Mutual Enforcement of Arbitral Awards Between the Mainland and the Hong Kong Special Administrative Region, namely, 'the enforcement of the award may be refused if the Mainland court holds that the enforcement of Hong Kong arbitral award in the Mainland would be contrary to the social and public interest of the Mainland'. The applicants submitted that this case's involvement of Variable Interest Entity (VIE) structural arrangements and Value Adjustment Mechanism (VAM)[75] violated the 'Provisions on the Administration of Foreign-Funded Telecommunications Enterprises' of the State Council, 'Circular of the Ministry of Information Industry on Intensifying the Administration of Foreign Investment in Value-added Telecommunications Services' of and 'Provisions of the Ministry of Commerce on the Implementation of the Security Review System for Mergers and Acquisitions of Domestic Enterprises by Foreign Investors' of the Ministry of Commerce which fall within the violation of 'the social and public interest of the Mainland' as stipulated in Article 7 and should be refused enforcement. After directly citing the SPC's statement in its Reply to Haikou Intermediate People's Court's request for instructions on the Non-recognition and Non-enforcement of an Arbitral Award of the Arbitration Institute of the Stockholm Chamber of Commerce where it stated 'violation of mandatory administrative regulations and departmental rules does not necessarily constitute violation of the public policy of the People's Republic of China', the Fujian Fuzhou Intermediate People's Court found that whether this case involved 'VIE' structural arrangements and 'VAM' or whether it violated the regulations and

---

74. Guangdong Zhaoqing Intermediate People's Court Civil Ruling (2015) Zhao-Zhong-Fa-Min-Yi-Zhong-Zi No. 26, 19 October 2015.
75. 'VAM' (Valuation Adjustment Mechanism) is a commonly used tool of private equity. By its nature, VAM is the mechanism for adjusting the valuation of the invested equity. Put simply, the basic concept of VAM is that, when the investor and financier of private equity disagree on the existing value of the company to be invested, and in order to prevent endless disputes from affecting the carrying out of transactions, the parties agree to temporarily cast aside this point of contention, to jointly set the future performance targets of the company to be invested, and to use the actual performance of the company to be invested to adjust the valuation of the company to be invested as well as the equity ratio of both parties. For VAM's definition and validity under Chinese law, see Helena Hsi-Chia Chen & Alison Shih-Yun Chang, A Nutshell on VAM Agreements, 196 Master Chang Monthly 7 (2015).

rules of the State Council, Ministry of Information Industry and Ministry of Commerce, etc. do not necessarily amount to violation of PRC's social and public interest, and accordingly rejected the applicants' request for non-enforcement on 5 November 2014.[76]

Some scholars have also clearly stated that 'violation of PRC laws does not necessarily violate PRC public policy'.[77]

Table 4.1   Cases Concerning Non-recognition and Non-enforcement of Foreign Arbitral Awards

Opinions of the Supreme People's Court (Replies of the Supreme People's Court Are Listed in Reverse Chronological Order)	Opinions of the Lower Courts
1. Reply of the Supreme People's Court to the Request for Instructions on Application for Recognition and Enforcement of an Foreign Arbitral Award (the *Castel* case) 10 October 2013, Supreme People's Court (2013) Min-Si-Ta-Zi No. 46 'The arbitral awards were made on 23 December 2010 and 27 January 2011; while the PRC court's ruling that the arbitration agreement in dispute was invalid was rendered on 20 December 2011. It is obvious that the arbitral awards were made before the PRC's court ruling became effective. Moreover, TCL company did not raise any jurisdictional objection during the arbitral proceedings on the grounds that the underlying arbitration agreement was invalid. Instead, TCL company submitted counterclaims to the arbitral tribunal, which accordingly confirmed the validity of the arbitration agreement and its jurisdiction. This is in compliance with the arbitration law and arbitration rules of the seat of arbitration and does not violate the	Guangdong Higher People's Court's Request for Instructions on Application for Recognition and Enforcement of an Foreign Arbitral Award 10 July 2013, Guangdong Higher People's Court (2012) Yue-Gao-Fa-Zhong-Fu-Zi No. 7 'The arbitration clause in the "Master Distribution Agreement" was confirmed by the Supreme People's Court as invalid through the reporting system in another case, and the Zhongshan Intermediate People's Court, through its ruling (2009) Zhong-Zhong-Fa-Ming-Si-Chu-Zi No. 3, determined it to be invalid. The civil ruling has entered into force. The Australian ad hoc arbitral tribunal accepted the application of Castel based on article 12(1) of the "Master Distribution Agreement," and made two arbitral awards, which conflicted with the res judicata of the decision of a court of this country. Based

---

76. Fujian Fuzhou Intermediate People's Court Civil Ruling (2014) Rong-Zhi-Jian-Zi No. 51, 5 November 2015.
77. Xiangquan Qi, *On the Legal Issues Concerning Application for Recognition and Enforcement of London Metal Exchange Arbitral Award by Glencore International AG - Concurrently on the Supreme Court's Official Reply for this Case*, 20 Arbitration Study 85, 97 (2009), as referred to in Xiaojian Zhang & Hui Han, *A Review on Articles Concerning Arbitration Study from Chinese Legal Journals in 2009*, 72 Beijing Arbitration 27, 43 (2010).

Opinions of the Supreme People's Court (Replies of the Supreme People's Court Are Listed in Reverse Chronological Order)	Opinions of the Lower Courts
PRC's judicial sovereignty. The violation of public policy in New York Convention's Article V(2)(b) should be interpreted as in situations where the recognition and enforcement of a foreign award would lead to the violation of the basic principles of law, infringe national sovereignty, jeopardize societal and public safety, violate good morals, etc., which would jeopardize fundamental societal interest of this country. In this case, the inconsistency/conflict existing between the foreign arbitral award and effective PRC court ruling about the validity of the same arbitration clause nevertheless did not suffice to constitute violation of the public policy of this country.'	on the above circumstances, and from the stand point of protecting this country's judicial sovereignty and the jurisdictions of Chinese courts, the two arbitral awards should be refused recognition and enforcement.'
2. Reply of the Supreme People's Court on Request for Instructions Re Application by Western Bulk Pte., Ltd. for the Recognition and Enforcement of an English Arbitral Award (the *Western Bulk* case) 21 May 2012, Supreme People's Court (2012) Min-Si-Ta-Zi No. 12 'In relation to the principle of public policy, Public policy in New York Convention's Article V(2)(b) should be interpreted and applied strictly. The public policy ground can only be invoked to refuse recognition and enforcement if recognition and enforcement of foreign commercial arbitral awards would violate the basic principles of law, infringe national sovereignty, jeopardize national and societal safety, violate good morals, jeopardize fundamental societal interest, etc. of the People's Republic of China. It is inappropriate for your court to refuse the award's recognition and enforcement on the ground of violating social and public interest because the arbitration results manifestly lack fairness.'	Tianjin Higher People's Court's Request for Instructions Re Application by Western Bulk Pte., Ltd. for the Recognition and Enforcement of an English Arbitral Award 19 March 2012, Tianjin Higher People's Court (2011) Jin-Gao-Min-Si-Ta-Zi No. 4 – Tianjin Higher People's Court found that: 'Under these circumstances, the arbitral tribunal still ascribed expected profits of the applicant as its damages, and furthermore when calculating expected profits, calculated costs of freight and expected profits under the assumption that the ships were fully loaded, and demanded the respondent to pay compensation for the above costs that were not actually incurred. "the result of the arbitral award lacked factual and legal basis, significantly lacked fairness, severely jeopardized the Chinese parties' interests in contravention of the social and public interest of the People's Republic of China;" this pertains to the circumstance prescribed in New York Convention's Article V(2)(b) and the arbitral award should be refused recognition and enforcement.'

Chapter 4: PRC's Convergence with International Consensus

Opinions of the Supreme People's Court (Replies of the Supreme People's Court Are Listed in Reverse Chronological Order)	*Opinions of the Lower Courts*
	– Tianjin Maritime Court considered that: (cited from Tianjin Higher People's Court's Request for Instructions Re Application by Western Bulk Pte., Ltd. for the Recognition and Enforcement of an English Arbitral Award) 'The constitution of the arbitral tribunal was not in accordance with the arbitration agreement and English Arbitration Act 1996, and circumstances existed where a party was otherwise unable to present his case, based on the "Convention on the Recognition and Enforcement of Foreign Arbitral Awards" (New York Convention), Article V(1)(b) and (d), the award should not be recognized and enforced.' Tianjin Maritime Court did not consider the existence of the grounds under Article V(2)(b).
3. Reply of the Supreme People's Court on Request for Instructions Re Application by Louis Dreyfus Commodities Asian Co., Ltd. for Recognition and Enforcement of Arbitration Award No. 3980 of International Federation of Oils, Seeds & Fats Associations (the *Louis Dreyfus* case) 10 October 2010, Supreme People's Court (2010) Min-Si-Ta-Zi No. 48 'Even though the cargo in this case contained toxic soybeans treated with coating agent, the selection process had been carried out before unloading. There was no evidence suggesting that the cargo caused serious hygiene and safety issues and damaged public health. The arbitrator in this case mistakenly considered that there is a very significant gap between the stipulation of PRC laws and their application in practice, but such	Guangdong Higher People's Court's Request for Instructions Re Application for Recognition and Enforcement of a Foreign Arbitration Award Concerning Louis Dreyfus Commodities Asian Co., Ltd. and Guangdong Fuhong Edible Oil Co. Ltd. 20 June 2010, Guangdong Higher People's Court (2009) Yue-Gao-Fa-Min-Si-Ta-Zi No. 10 – Guangdong Higher People's Court found that: 'Majority opinion of the collegiate bench: Agreed with the opinions of the Guangdong Zhanjiang Intermediate People's Court. The arbitral award's negative assessment and misinterpretation of the law of this country infringe upon the authoritativeness of the laws and regulations of this country and violate the public policy of this country, consequently falling within the grounds for non-recognition and non-enforcement in Article V(2)(b) of the New York Convention.'

Opinions of the Supreme People's Court (Replies of the Supreme People's Court Are Listed in Reverse Chronological Order)	Opinions of the Lower Courts
misconception will not result in the violation of the public policy of this country by recognizing and enforcing the arbitral award. As a result, the refusal to recognize and enforce the arbitral award lacks sufficient grounds.'	'Minority opinion of the collegiate bench: ...' although the arbitrator made improper assessment of the law of this country, however the consequences of recognising and enforcing this award would not lead to a violation of this country's public policy, thus the award does not violate the public policy of this country. – Zhanjiang Intermediate People's Court found that: (cited from Guangdong Higher People's Court's Request for Instructions Re Application by Louis Dreyfus Commodities Asian Co., Ltd. for Recognition and Enforcement of Arbitration Award) 'But the award considered that there is a very significant gap between the stipulation of PRC laws and their application in practice. The details relating to PRC law provisions are ultimately not very important. Chinese laws and regulations are complex regardless of viewing them from which angle. Just as any supervisory system can influence certain international sale and purchase contract, what matters to the parties is not how the local laws should be interpreted, but how these laws are applied in practice. The award concluded that in relation to the damages to the cargo – LDA was not responsible for damages due to the mildew and high temperature, as well as the inclusion of red soybeans, irrespective of when such damages or the inclusion of red soybeans occurred. The reasons in that award severely challenge the authoritativeness of the laws and regulations of this country and violate the public policy of this country. Therefore we support the claim of the respondent Guangdong Fuhong Edible Oil Co., Ltd.'

Chapter 4: PRC's Convergence with International Consensus

Opinions of the Supreme People's Court (Replies of the Supreme People's Court Are Listed in Reverse Chronological Order)	Opinions of the Lower Courts
4. Reply of the Supreme People's Court on Request for Instructions Re Recognition of the Arbitral Award in the Case of *Tianrui Hotel Investment Co., Ltd. (Petitioner) v. Hangzhou Yiju Hotel Management Co., Ltd. (Respondent)* 18 May 2010, Supreme People's Court (2010) Min-Si-Ta-Zi No. 18 'The Unit System Agreement between Tianrui Co. and Yiju Co. executed on 28 October 2004 was by nature a commercial franchise agreement. According to this country's commercial franchise management system in force at the time, foreign companies carrying out commercial franchise management business must do so through the establishment of foreign-invested enterprises, and must obtain approval from administrative authorities. However, after the implementation of the State Council's Regulation on Administration of Commercial Franchise on 1 May 2007, prior approval is no longer required and instead, there is merely a requirement of registration with the regulatory authority after the entering of a franchise agreement. It no longer requires approval. Such registration requirement is a part of mandatory norms within administrative regulations, and does not affect validity of civil agreements between the parties. The decision of the arbitral award regarding the Unit System Agreement was not contrary to the PRC's mandatory legal provisions, let alone contrary to the PRC's public policy.'	Zhejiang Higher People's Court's Request for Instructions Re Recognition of the Arbitral Award in the Case of *Tianrui Hotel Investment Co., Ltd. (Petitioner) v. Hangzhou Yiju Hotel Management Co., Ltd. (Respondent)* 15 March 2010, Zhejiang Higher People's Court (2010) Zhe-Shang-Wai-Ta-Zi No. 3 – Zhejiang Higher People's Court found that: 'As to whether the arbitral award violates the social and public interests of this country, although violation of the PRC's mandatory laws does not necessarily constitute infringement of PRC's social and public interest, however, in this case, SuBoAiTe Co. and Tianrui Co. were actually related companies that deliberately divided the franchising contract into two agreements with an attempt to evade the PRC's system for restricting foreign companies' access to franchise businesses, and can be considered as violating the PRC's social and public interest.Based on the above, this court considers that Arbitral Award No. 7983 of the London Court of International Arbitration violates the public interests of this country. Based on Article V(2)(b) of the "Convention on the Recognition and Enforcement of Foreign Arbitral Awards," recognition of the arbitral award should be refused.' – Hangzhou Intermediate People's Court found that: (cited from Zhejiang Higher People's Court's Request for Instructions Re Recognition of the Arbitral Award in the Case of *Tianrui Hotel Investment Co., Ltd. (Petitioner) v. Hangzhou Yiju Hotel Management Co., Ltd. (Respondent)*) '(1) The Unit System Agreement between Tianrui Co. and Yiju Co was a franchise agreement, and franchising belongs to the restricted business sector in the PRC.

Opinions of the Supreme People's Court (Replies of the Supreme People's Court Are Listed in Reverse Chronological Order)	Opinions of the Lower Courts
	Article 3 of the Measures for the Administration of Foreign Investment in Commercial Fields provides: "Foreign-invested commercial enterprises means foreign-invested enterprises engaging in the following management activities:.. (4) Franchising: entitling someone to use its trademark, trade name and business model etc. through contractual means in order to receive remuneration or franchising fees. Foreign companies, enterprises and other economic organizations or individuals must engage in business activities stipulated in items 1 to 4 through foreign-invested companies established within China." Article 33 of the Measures for Administration of Commercial Franchise stipulates that foreign-invested enterprises engaging in commercial activities by franchising must apply to the original approval authority to add "engaging in commercial activities by franchising" to its business scope. Franchising is listed as a restricted industry in the Catalogue of Industries for Guiding Foreign Investment and belongs to the restricted business sector of the PRC. As a company registered and existing under the laws of the Samoan Islands, Tianrui Co. could not directly engage in franchise business in China pursuant to the Chinese administrative regulations relating to franchising. According to Article 10 of the "Interpretation I of the Supreme People's Court of Several Issues Concerning the Application of the Contract Law of the People's Republic of China": "where a party enters into a contract that exceeds its business scope, the people's court shall accordingly find such contract to be null and void, unless such a contract violates

Chapter 4: PRC's Convergence with International Consensus

Opinions of the Supreme People's Court (Replies of the Supreme People's Court Are Listed in Reverse Chronological Order)	Opinions of the Lower Courts
	the provisions of the state on restricted business operations or franchise operations or the provisions of laws and administrative regulations on prohibited business operation." This shows that the launch of the franchise business activities through executing the Unit System Agreement between Tianrui Co. and Yiju Co. violated the PRC's mandatory provisions. The purpose of the PRC's franchising provisions was to strictly limit foreign capital's access in order to maintain the PRC's economic order and social order. Yet Tianrui Co.'s conduct violated the PRC's basic system for introducing foreign capital and infringed the PRC's public interest. Consequently the arbitral award should be refused recognition pursuant to Article V(2)(b) of the New York Convention. (2) Even though the arbitration before the London Court of International Arbitration relates to the "Unit System Agreement" between Tianrui and Yiju, the "Unit Service Agreement" between Yiju and Super 8 is closely related thereto. Yiju has brought a proceeding in relation to this before the London Court of International Arbitration. Tianrui Co. and SuBoAiTe Co. intentionally separated them into two agreements in order to evade this country's system in relation to restricting foreign companies' access to franchise businesses. If the arbitral award of the London Court of International Arbitration in favor of Yiju Co. is recognized, it will lead to contradictions and conflicts.'
5. Reply of the Supreme People's Court on Request for Instructions Re Application by GRD Minproc Limited for Recognition and Enforcement of the Arbitration Award of Arbitration Institute of the Stockholm Chamber of Commerce (the *GRD Minproc* case)	Shanghai Higher People's Court's Request for Instructions Re Application by GRD Minproc Limited for Recognition and Enforcement of the Arbitral Award of Arbitration Institute of the Stockholm Chamber of Commerce

Opinions of the Supreme People's Court (Replies of the Supreme People's Court Are Listed in Reverse Chronological Order)	Opinions of the Lower Courts
13 March 2009, Supreme People's Court (2008) Min-Si-Ta-Zi No. 48 'Equipment purchased from abroad by Shanghai Flyingwheel Industry Co., Ltd. was examined and approved by the relevant authority. It is not equipment prohibited from importation into this country. There may be various reasons for environmental pollution caused during installation, commissioning and operation of the equipment. In circumstances where Shanghai Flyingwheel Industry Co. Ltd requested arbitration of equipment quality disputes pursuant to a valid arbitration clause, the arbitral tribunal's judgment on equipment quality was within the arbitral tribunal's authority. Parties resolving their disputes through arbitration should bear the results. Whether or not the substantive results of arbitration are fair and reasonable should not be the criterion for determining whether or not the arbitral award's recognition and enforcement would violate the public policy of this country. Recognition and enforcement of the arbitral award in this case does not constitute a violation of the fundamental interests of the society, basic principles of the laws, or good morals of this country. Therefore circumstances under article V(2)(b) of the New York Convention do not exist.'	18 August 2008, Shanghai Higher People's Court (2008) Hu-Gao-Min-Si-(Shang)-Ta-Zi No. 2 – Shanghai Higher People's Court found that: 'In this case, although the applicant only sought to enforce part of the award that relates to the costs of the arbitration, the costs of the arbitration precisely reflected the ultimate outcome of the substantive disputes of the arbitration. After preliminary examination of the arbitral proceedings and detailed understanding of the background of the whole case, this court considers that the dispute originated from the fact that the special equipment being traded did not achieve industry production safety standards, which caused serious pollution and damages to the respondent's factory environment and workers' health, damaged public interests and led to shut down and long term suspension of use, and then caused loss of the substantive purpose of the contract and substantial economic loss to the respondent. The arbitral tribunal failed to give due attention to such an important situation, and simply determined that the equipment supplied by the seller did not violate the contract based on the terms of the contract. Such practice is contrary to the fairness and justness of arbitral spirit, and objectively led to a result unfavorable to the social and public interests of this country. All of these are consistent with the conditions set out under Article V(2)(b) of the New York Convention, and as such, the arbitral award shall not be recognized and enforced.' – Shanghai First Intermediate People's Court found: (cited from Shanghai Higher People's Court's Request for Instructions Re Application by GRD Minproc Limited for Recognition and Enforcement of the Arbitral Award of

Chapter 4: PRC's Convergence with International Consensus

Opinions of the Supreme People's Court (Replies of the Supreme People's Court Are Listed in Reverse Chronological Order)	*Opinions of the Lower Courts*
	Arbitration Institute of the Stockholm Chamber of Commerce) 'The result of the arbitration indicated that GRD already delivered equipment in compliance with the terms of the contract and the equipment can operate normally. The three inspection reports of Flyingwheel all indicated that the equipment in dispute produced large amount of lead powders when operating, and the lead powder concentration in the workshop far exceeds the standards. The Ministry of Health of this country drafted and implemented "Industrial Enterprises Design Health Standards TJ36-79," and Chapter 3 Article 32 provided that lead powders constitute toxic substance, and the maximum concentration in workshops shall be 0.05mg/cubic meter. The Health Standards were subsequently amended by the Ministry of Health on 1 June 2002 to "National Occupational Health Standards of the People's Republic of China GBZ2-2002," in which Article 4.1 of the "Workplace Hazardous Materials Occupational Exposure Limits" contains the same requirement. That is, lead powder is a toxic substance, and the maximum concentration in the workplace is 0.05mg/cubic meter. Based on the result of the three inspections, the lead concentration produced by the equipment in dispute substantially exceeded these standards. The court considered that Article 3(1) of the Labour Law of the People's Republic of China provides that workers have the right to receive labour safety and sanitation protection. Article 52 provides that, the employer shall establish and perfect its system for labour safety and sanitation, strictly abide by State rules and standards

Opinions of the Supreme People's Court (Replies of the Supreme People's Court Are Listed in Reverse Chronological Order)	Opinions of the Lower Courts
	on labour safety and sanitation, educate labourers in labour safety and sanitation, prevent accidents in the process of labour, and reduce occupational hazards. Article 54 provides that the employer shall provide labourers with labour safety and sanitation conditions meeting State stipulations and necessary articles of labour protection, and carry out regular health examination for labourers engaged in work with occupational hazards. Accordingly, recognition and enforcement of the arbitral award of the Stockholm Chamber of Commerce means that the equipment can operate and be used normally. However, as the concentration of the lead powders far exceeds the standard established by the Ministry of Health, Flyingwheel will not be able to comply with the workplace health and safety standards of this country. It cannot provide effective protection measures to the workers, resulting in endangerment of the health and well-being of the workers, and damage to the rights of the workers for protection under workplace health and safety. If Flyingwheel chooses not to use the equipment in dispute, although it will not violate of the legal requirements on workplace safety, it cannot use the equipment which it has already made substantial payments for. This will lead to substantial imbalance regarding its rights and obligations, and do not comply with the principles of fairness under Article 4 of the "General Principles of the Civil Law of the People's Republic of China." Accordingly, recognition and enforcement of the award of the Arbitration Institute of the Stockholm Chamber of Commerce violates the basic principles of this country's laws, and is contrary to the social and public interests of this country.

Chapter 4: PRC's Convergence with International Consensus

Opinions of the Supreme People's Court (Replies of the Supreme People's Court Are Listed in Reverse Chronological Order)	*Opinions of the Lower Courts*
	This fulfills the conditions under Article V(2)(b) of the New York Convention, therefore Award No. 024/2003 of the Arbitration Institute of the Stockholm Chamber of Commerce shall not be recognized and enforced.'
6. Reply of the Supreme People's Court to a Request for Instructions on the Non-recognition and Non-enforcement of an Arbitral Award of the ICC International Court of Arbitration (the *Hemofarm* case) 2 June 2008 Supreme People's Court (2008) Min-Si-Ta-Zi No. 11 'The relevant Chinese courts had previously issued property preservation orders and entered judgments regarding the lease disputes between Jinan Yongning Pharmaceutical Co., Ltd. and the joint venture company, Jinan-Hemofarm Pharmaceutical Co., Ltd. Given this, the ICC International Court of Arbitration's hearing and ruling on the same lease disputes between Yongning and the joint venture company, Jinan-Hemofarm Pharmaceutical Co., Ltd., *infringed the judicial sovereignty of the PRC and the jurisdiction of the PRC courts*. The recognition and enforcement of the ICC award No. 13464/MS/JB/JEM should be refused under Articles V(1)(c) and (2)(b) of the New York Convention.'	Shandong Higher People's Court's Request for Instructions on the Non-recognition and Non-enforcement of an Arbitral Award of the ICC International Court of Arbitration 30 January 2008, Shandong Higher People's Court (2007) Lu-Min-Si-Ta-Zi No. 12 – Shandong Higher People's Court found that: 'The arbitral award in this case infringed the legal jurisdiction of the people's courts, and undermined the judicial sovereignty of this country. Specifically this includes the following aspects: firstly, the arbitral award examined and made a determination on the legality of Yongning's application to the people's court for the preservation of the property, which interfered with the rights of the people's court to review the parties' application to the people's court for preservation of property; secondly, the ICC award ruled that Yongning's Land Lease Litigation against the joint venture company for lease disputes contravened the arbitration clause. This not only denied the PRC courts' right to hear jurisdictional objection and determine their jurisdiction, but also directly denied the PRC court's jurisdiction over the Land Lease Litigation; thirdly, the arbitral award carried out an independent review of the lease agreement between Yongning and the joint venture company. However according to the laws of this country and the ruling of the people's court on jurisdictions, jurisdiction to the lease disputes between Yongning

Opinions of the Supreme People's Court (Replies of the Supreme People's Court Are Listed in Reverse Chronological Order)	Opinions of the Lower Courts
	and the joint venture company belongs to the courts of this country. Jinan Intermediate People's Court has already heard the matter and rendered its decisions; fourthly, the arbitral award ordered that Yongning compensate the three applicants for the costs of litigation in China, thereby infringing the people's court's rights to determine who bear the burden over the costs of litigation.' – Jinan Intermediate People's Court found that (cited from Shandong Higher People's Court's Request for Instructions on the Non-recognition and Non-enforcement of an Arbitral Award of the ICC International Court of Arbitration): 'Yongning's application for litigation and property preservation had the support from the people's court, which demonstrated that its application was legitimate. But the arbitral tribunal ignored the effective judgment of the court of this country, and rendered an award on the grounds of regarding Yongning's proper conduct of the litigation proceedings as a breach of contract. This equates to a rejection of the force of a judgment of the court of this country. The arbitral award determined that proceedings in relation to the land lease should have been submitted to arbitration by the International Chamber of Commerce, which obviously conflicted with the judgment of the court of this country, constituted a rejection of the force of a judgment of the people's court, and seriously challenged the judicial authority of the courts of this country. It violates social and public interest of this country.'
7. Reply of the Supreme People's Court on the Report of Non-recognition of No. 04-05 (Tokyo) Arbitration Award of Japan Commercial Arbitration Association (the *Shin-Etsu* case)	Jiangsu Higher People's Court's Report of Non-recognition of No. 04-05 (Tokyo) Arbitration Award of Japan Commercial Arbitration

Chapter 4: PRC's Convergence with International Consensus

Opinions of the Supreme People's Court (Replies of the Supreme People's Court Are Listed in Reverse Chronological Order)	*Opinions of the Lower Courts*
3 March 2008, Supreme People's Court (2007) Min-Si-Ta-Zi No. 26 The Supreme People's Court agrees with the Jiangsu Higher People's Court that this arbitral award's recognition should be refused under Article V(1)(b) and (d) of the New York Convention. It did not find that the arbitral award breached 'public policy'.	25 May 2007, Jiangsu Higher People's Court (2007) Su-Min-San-Ta-Zi No. 0002 – Jiangsu Higher People's Court found that: '(2) The arbitral award falls under the circumstances of Article V(2)(b) of the New York Convention. Based on that provision, if the competent authority in the country where recognition and enforcement is sought finds that the recognition and enforcement of the award would be contrary to the public policy of that country, recognition and enforcement of the award may be refused. Since 2002, companies from Japan, the US and Korea had been dumping conventional single-mode optical fibre and thereby significantly harming the PRC domestic conventional single-mode optical fibre industry. After its investigation and verification, the Ministry of Commerce decided to impose anti-dumping levies ranging from 7% to 46% on conventional single-mode optical fibre imported from these three countries starting on 1 January 2005, specifically charging 46% for all conventional single-mode optical fibre imported from Japan. The subjects of the long term sale and purchase agreement in this case were the raw materials of the above mentioned imported goods. The average price of optical fibre in the domestic market dropped from CNY 119 per kilometre in 2003 to CNY 100 per kilometre in 2004. Zhongtian's total production costs would be CNY 175.46 per kilometre in 2003 and CNY 167.47 per kilometre in 2004 if it had continued to perform the sales contract. Obviously, Shin-Etsu is using its international monopoly in the production and sale of pattern-matching single-film (note, should be "mode") optical fibre preforms to sell raw materials to Zhongtian, the main manufacturer of optical

Opinions of the Supreme People's Court (Replies of the Supreme People's Court Are Listed in Reverse Chronological Order)	Opinions of the Lower Courts
	fibre products in China, at high prices only a monopolist could manage. Inevitably this would severely increase production costs and significantly reduce Zhongtian's market competitiveness. In addition to Zhongtian, other Chinese optical fibre product manufacturers, Tianjin Xinmao Science & Technology Co., Ltd. and Jiangsu Fasten Group Co., Ltd. are also victims of Shin-Etsu's monopoly high prices. Consequently, Shin-Etsu's exploitation of its international monopoly in the production and sale of pattern-matching single-film (note, should be "mode") optical fibre preforms to monopolise its high prices for selling the relevant products has the same effect as dumping finished products, thereby seriously jeopardising the subsistence of the optical fibre industry in this country. In light of our government's decision to impose the highest anti-dumping levy on conventional single-mode optical fibre imported from Japan, enforcing the arbitral award would undoubtedly counteract the effects of imposing anti-dumping levies, as well as support Japanese enterprises in damaging the interests of optic fibre industry of this country. The recognition of the arbitral award will therefore contravene the public policy of this country.' – Nantong Intermediate People's Court found that: (cited from Jiangsu Higher People's Court's Report of Non-recognition of No. 04-05 (Tokyo) Arbitration Award of Japan Commercial Arbitration) 'In relation to whether the recognition and enforcement of the arbitral award in this case will violate the public policy of this country, Nantong Intermediate People's Court has two different opinions: one considers that it is in violation of public policy. The arbitration concerned was carried out under the

Chapter 4: PRC's Convergence with International Consensus

Opinions of the Supreme People's Court (Replies of the Supreme People's Court Are Listed in Reverse Chronological Order)	*Opinions of the Lower Courts*
	context that fiber companies, including those from Japan, carried out dumping in China, which has been confirmed by the Chinese government. Shin-Etsu used its technological superiority in optic fiber preforms, selling at a high price to Zhongtian and two other companies in China. They also refused requests for contract amendments due to change of circumstances. If the arbitral award in this case is recognized, it would cause substantial damages to Zhongtian. Shin-Etsu exported to several companies in China at the same time during the same period, and the same arbitration institution has already delivered two similar awards. Zhongtian is a main optic fiber manufacturing company of this country; damages to the company will certainly damage the optic fiber industry in this country. Thus, this would inevitably increase the damages caused by the sanctioned companies from Japan, the United States and Korea to Chinese optic fiber industry. From this perspective, the recognition and enforcement of the arbitral award in this case will damage the public interests of this country. The other opinion is that, public interests should be applied strictly, and the arbitral award only involves individual entities. It relates to optic fiber preforms not the finished products. There was no evidence that Shin-Etsu was involved in dumping. Accordingly it is inappropriate to refuse recognition and enforcement based on damages to public interest.'
8. Reply of the Supreme People's Court on Application of First Investment Corp. of the Marshall Islands for Recognition and Enforcement of Arbitration Award of an Ad Hoc Arbitration Tribunal in London 27 February 2008, Supreme People's Court (2007) Min-Si-Ta-Zi No. 35	The applicant First Investment Corp (Marshall Island) requested that the Xiamen Maritime Court recognized the arbitral award made by an ad hoc arbitration tribunal in London, UK on 19 June 2006.

Opinions of the Supreme People's Court (Replies of the Supreme People's Court Are Listed in Reverse Chronological Order)	Opinions of the Lower Courts
'Although the arbitral tribunal in this case was constituted by three arbitrators, however arbitrator Shengchang Wang did not participate in the entire arbitration proceedings and did not participate in the entire delivery of the final arbitral award. Consequently the composition of the arbitral tribunal or the arbitral procedure was not in accordance with the parties' arbitration agreement, and was also contrary to English law (as the law of the arbitral seat). Thus the arbitral award's recognition and enforcement should be refused under Article V(1)(d) of the New York Convention.'	The respondents, FuJian Mawei Shipbuilding Ltd. and Fujian Shipbuilding Industry Group Company Limited, objected to the application of First Investment Corp., one of the reasons was that: 'the arbitral tribunal violated the principle of impartiality and the arbitral award violated the public policy of this country by admitting forged evidence.' (cited from 11 May 2008, Xiamen Maritimes Court Civil Ruling (2006) Xia-Hai-Fa-Ren-Zi No. 1). But the people's courts at all levels did not adopt this reason.
9. Reply of the Supreme People's Court on the Request for Instructions on the Non-recognition and Non-enforcement of an Arbitral Award of the Arbitration Institute of the Stockholm Chamber of Commerce (the *Mitsui* case) 13 July 2005, Supreme People's Court (2001) Min-Si-Ta-Zi No. 12 'Hainan Textile Industry General Corporation, a State-owned enterprise, directly assumed the debts of Mitsui & Co., Ltd. by executing the agreement for repayment in Japanese currency without following the approval and registration procedures of the state administration of foreign exchange, thereby violating the PRC laws relating to approval and registration of foreign debts as well as other mandatory foreign control regulations. However, a violation of mandatory administrative regulations and departmental rules does not necessarily constitute violation of the public policy of the People's Republic of China. The grounds for refusing recognition and	Hainan Higher People's Court's Request for Instructions on the Hainan Haikou Intermediate People's Court's Non-recognition and Non-enforcement of No. 060/1999 Arbitral Award of the Arbitration Institute of the Stockholm Chamber of Commerce 5 April 2001, No. 1 [2001] of the Economic Division of the Hainan Higher People's Court 'On 9 March 2001, this court has already rendered a judgment in Hainan Higher People's Court (2000) Qiong-Jing-Fu-Zi No. 7 concerning the contract dispute between Hainan Textile Industry General Corporation and Hainan Qionghai Polyester Factory. The content of the judgment was that Article 9 of the Contract was partially invalid. The relevant parts held invalid were: "the contract price as JPY 2,436,974,490 plus specified interest and HKD 440,480 plus specified interest and the price should be paid in Japanese currency and Hong Kong currency respectively." The contract also provided that: "the above enforcement of the arbitral

Chapter 4: PRC's Convergence with International Consensus

Opinions of the Supreme People's Court (Replies of the Supreme People's Court Are Listed in Reverse Chronological Order)	*Opinions of the Lower Courts*
enforcement of the arbitral award in this case in your court's request for instructions were not established. Recognition and enforcement of the arbitral award in this case should not be refused based on violation of public policy.'	award in this contracted principal and interest in Japanese Yen, as authorized by Party A (Polyester Factory), should be paid to Japanese Mitsui Co., Ltd. by Party B (Hainan Textile). The principal and interest in Hong Kong Dollar, as authorized by Party A (Polyester Factory), should be paid to Nelson Enterprises (Timber) Company Limited, a HK company within their respective agreed periods. Although the court's judgment and the arbitral award dealt with two different issues, the Japanese Yen repayment agreement is an annexure to the Contract. Considering the cause and source of the debt, Article 9 of the Contract was the precondition and basis to confirm the Japanese Yen debt owed by Hainan Textile Industry General Corporation to Mitsui. Now that Article 9 of the Contract has been held invalid by the court, the court of enforcement held that the debt owed by Hainan Textile Industry General Corporation under the Japanese Yen repayment agreement no longer has legitimacy and justification; thus Hainan Textile Industry General Corporation does not owe any legal obligations for payment for the debt promised under Article 9 of the Contract. From the above, although we should not deny a foreign arbitral award due to a court judgment, what we have to consider is the legitimacy and justification ground for a court to recognize and enforce a debt, if such debt confirmed by a foreign arbitral award was also already recognized as invalid in an effective judgment issued by the court of the place of enforcement. Clearly, if we do so, wouldn't it conflict with the judicial sovereignty, judicial authority and res judicata effect of a court judgment? Wouldn't it conflict with the

Opinions of the Supreme People's Court (Replies of the Supreme People's Court Are Listed in Reverse Chronological Order)	Opinions of the Lower Courts
	legal principles reflected in the civil relations protected by the effective judgment? Wouldn't it also damage the legal orders confirmed through the effective judgment? As a result, *recognising and enforcing a debt that was already determined to be invalid or nonexistent in the court of the enforcement State and the resulting legal and social consequences should be seen as violating that enforcement State's public policy.* Thus it constitutes the legal ground for refusing recognition and enforcement of foreign arbitral awards under Article V(2) of the New York Convention.'
10. Reply of the Supreme People's Court on Request for Instructions Re Application by ED&F Man (Hong Kong) Co., Ltd. for Recognition and Enforcement of the Arbitral Award of the Sugar Association of London (the *ED&F Man* case) 1 July 2003, Supreme People's Court (2003) Min-Si-Ta-Zi No. 3 'Pursuant to the laws and regulations of this country, domestic enterprises are not allowed to conduct overseas futures trading without obtaining prior approval from the competent authority. China National Sugar & Alcohol Group's conduct in overseas future trading without approval should undoubtedly be considered as invalid. However, a violation of mandatory laws of this country cannot completely equate with violation of public policy of this country. Therefore, this case did not involve the circumstances prescribed in Article V(2) of the New York Convention concerning inarbitrability and the violation of PRC public policy by recognizing and enforcing the arbitral award.'	Beijing Higher People's Court's Request for Instructions Re Application by ED&F Man (Hong Kong) Co., Ltd. for Recognition and Enforcement of the No. 158 Arbitral Award of the SAL 15 January 2003, Beijing Higher People's Court (2003) Jing-Gao-Fa No. 7 'The operation process of 8008 Contract and its annexes utilize futures trading to seek speculative profits, such futures trading activities violate the prohibitive provisions of the laws of this country. Award No. 158 approved the parties' illegal benefits obtained from illegal overseas future transactions through the evasion of the PRC laws governing futures trading. This violation of the PRC mandatory laws constitutes violation of the PRC public policy. Based on article V(2)(b) of the "Convention on the Recognition and Enforcement of Foreign Arbitral Awards," we intend to reject the application of ED&F Man, and refuse recognition and enforcement of Award No. 158 of the Sugar Association of London.'

Table 4.2 Cases Concerning Non-enforcement of Arbitral Awards Made in Hong Kong[78]

Opinions of the Supreme People's Court (Replies of the Supreme People's Court Are Listed in Reverse Chronological Order)	Opinions of the Lower Courts
1. Upon examination, the Supreme People's Court agreed to the opinions of the lower court (as shown at the right column).	2 June 2016, Jiangsu Taizhou Intermediate People's Court Civil Ruling (2015) Tai-Zhong-Shang-Zhong-Shen-Zi No. 00004 (the *Wicor* case) 'When Jiangsu Higher People's Court had heard another dispute between Wicor Holding AG and Taizhou Hope Investment Co., Ltd. arising from the "Sino-foreign Taizhou Huawei Insulation Materials Co. Ltd. Joint Venture Contract," it held on 11 December 2012 in its Civil Ruling (2012) Su-Shang-Wai-Xia-Zhong-Zi No 0012 that the arbitration agreement in dispute was invalid. This Civil Ruling has come into force. However, the arbitrator rendered the arbitral award under the condition precedent that the arbitral agreement was valid. Enforcing the arbitral award in Mainland China would contravene with the above effective Court Ruling and thus, violate the social and public interest. Therefore, this court held that the arbitral award should not be enforced; pursuant to Article 7.3 of the "SPC's Arrangement Concerning Mutual Enforcement of Arbitral Awards Between the Mainland and the Hong Kong Special Administrative Region" and Article 154 paragraph 1 item (11) of the SPC's Civil Procedure Law, the court has decided not to enforce the 18295/CKY arbitral awards respectively rendered on 18 July 2014 and 27 November 2014 by the ICC International Court of Arbitration.'
2. Amlon Metals Ltd.'s Application for Enforcement of the arbitral award concerning Yunnan Nickel and Cobalt Co., Ltd. and others (Non-enforcement of the arbitral award made in HKSAR)	Yunnan Kunming Intermediate People's Court The Enforcement Proceedings closed on 10 November 2009

---

78. Please *see* section 3.2.1 of Chapter 3.

Opinions of the Supreme People's Court (Replies of the Supreme People's Court Are Listed in Reverse Chronological Order)	Opinions of the Lower Courts
Upon examination, the Supreme People's Court agreed to the opinions of the lower court (as shown at the right column).	Yunnan Kunming Intermediate People's Court (2008) Kun-Fei-Zhi-Zi No. 48-1 Amlon Metals Ltd., as the enforcement applicant, applied to people's court for recognition and enforcement of the arbitral award made in HKSAR Kunming Railway Bureau Import and Export Corporation, as the party subject to enforcement, claimed that: 'the recognition and enforcement of the arbitral award will be against the country's social and public interest' on the grounds that the subject goods were deemed by PRC Hekou Customs as hazardous substance forbidden to be imported into China (please refer to Notice of Goods Rejection by PRC Hekou Customs'). This not only failed to comply with the parties' agreement on the quality of the goods under the contract, but was also against the country's environment-related public interests. Therefore, if such arbitral award is recognized and enforced, the country's environment-related public interests would be infringed. Moreover, the legal consequences incurred by the conducts of Kunming Railway Bureau Import and Export Corporation as an agent shall be directly attributed to its principal and its principal should assume all liabilities. Therefore, the decision made in the arbitral award that Kunming Railway Bureau shall assume joint and several liabilities violates the basic system and principle of the country regarding agency.' Yunnan Kunming Intermediate People's Court held that, Amlon entered into 'Copper Mine Sales Contract' ('Contract') with Yunnan Nickel and Cobalt Co., Ltd. and Kunming Railway Bureau Import and

Chapter 4: PRC's Convergence with International Consensus

Opinions of the Supreme People's Court (Replies of the Supreme People's Court Are Listed in Reverse Chronological Order)	*Opinions of the Lower Courts*
	Export Corporation on 7 November 2005. It is agreed under Clause 19 of the Contract that the arbitration proceedings shall be conducted by an arbitration tribunal consisting of two arbitrators and one umpire in accordance with the law the England. It is also agreed under Clause 20 of the Contract that the arbitration shall be conducted in Hong Kong and the applicable law shall be the law of the England. During the performance of the Contract, the enforcement applicant submitted a request for arbitration to Hong Kong International Arbitration Centre ('HKIAC') due to Nickel and Cobalt's failure to make payment for the goods above. On 27 March 2007, HKIAC issued a letter to both parties subject to the enforcement, specifying its intent of appointing Russell Coleman SC as arbitrator and noting that the objection thereto (if any) shall be raised before 10 April. On 2 May 2007, HKIAC issued a letter to both parties subject to the enforcement, duly notifying them in writing of appointing Russell Coleman SC as arbitrator in accordance with Article 20 on arbitration of the Contract. The two parties subject to the enforcement were not present at the arbitration hearing. In the course of the hearing, there was no evidence showing that HKIAC would notify in due course the two parties subject to the enforcement to appoint an arbitrator respectively. In conclusion, in this case, HKIAC didn't form an arbitration tribunal consisting of two arbitrators and one umpire as agreed by the parties, but appointed only one arbitrator as the sole arbitrator. Such change complied with neither the relevant provisions of the UK arbitration law, nor the agreements between the parties. Since the composition of the arbitration tribunal failed to comply with the agreements between the parties,

Opinions of the Supreme People's Court (Replies of the Supreme People's Court Are Listed in Reverse Chronological Order)	Opinions of the Lower Courts
	the People's Court may determine not to enforce the arbitral award. It is justified not to enforce the arbitral award against Kunming Railway Bureau Import and Export Corporation. Meanwhile the case was reported to Yunnan Higher People's Court and then to the Supreme People's Court for review according to Article 2 of the 'Notice of the Supreme People's Court on the Disposal of the Relevant Issues concerning the Foreign-Related Arbitration and Foreign Arbitral Matters by People's Courts' (28 August 1995, (1995) Fa-Fa No. 18) and Article 28 of the 'Minutes of the Symposium on the Trial of Commercial Cases involving Hong Kong or Macao by Courts Nationwide.' The Supreme People's Court concurs with the above court opinions after review. Therefore, *in accordance with* Article 7.1 (4) of the 'SPC's Arrangement Concerning Mutual Enforcement of Arbitral Awards Between the Mainland and the Hong Kong Special Administrative Region', the court decided not to enforce the HKIAC arbitral award made by Russell Coleman SC.
3. Reply of the Supreme People's Court on Request for Instructions Re Application by Zhoushan Zhonghai Cereals & Oils Industry Co., Ltd. for Non-enforcement of Arbitration Award of HKIAC 18 March 2009, Supreme People's Court (2009) Min-Si-Ta-Zi No. 2 'However the "Extra Urgent Warning Notification" explicitly specifies that soybeans in transit are allowed for entry into China so long as the entry inspection and quarantine requirements are met. In this case, the subject goods had been loaded and become the goods in transit before the Notification was issued. On 23 June of the same year, General	Zhejiang Higher People's Court's Request for Instructions Re Application by Zhoushan Zhonghai Cereals & Oils Industry Co., Ltd. for Non- Enforcement of the Arbitral Award of Hong Kong International Arbitration Centre 15 December 2008, Zhejiang Higher People's Court (2007) Zhe-Zhi-Ta-Zi No. 4 – Opinions of Zhejiang Higher People's Court: 'Upon discussion, the Judicial Committee of the Court has two opinions: The majority opinion is that the arbitral award shall not be enforced in this case.

Chapter 4: PRC's Convergence with International Consensus

Opinions of the Supreme People's Court (Replies of the Supreme People's Court Are Listed in Reverse Chronological Order)	*Opinions of the Lower Courts*
Administration of Quality Supervision Inspection and Quarantine of the People's Republic of China ("AQSIQ") terminated such import ban and re-qualify the relevant suppliers, including Noble Resources Pte., Ltd. ("Noble"), for export to China. Noble received Soybeans Genetically Modified Organisms Safety Certificate in July that year and Zhoushan Zhonghai Cereals & Oils Industry Co., Ltd. received Soybeans Import Certificate as well. Therefore, the subject goods complied with the entry inspection and quarantine requirements and couldn't be classified as those banned for import. Moreover, there is no evidence that the subject goods will cause significant problems with safety and health, nor any fact that the subject goods will be harmful to the public health. Therefore, enforcement of the arbitral award of HKIAC will not breach social and public interests.'	The reason is that Xiamen Entry-Exit Inspection and Quarantine Bureau found that the toxic soybeans dyed with red alert agent imported to Xiamen by Noble might cause significant safety and hygiene problems in cooking oil and bean pulp. Chinese government issued a ban in order to protect national food sanitation and safety and consumers' lives and health. This complied with national practices and Chinese laws. Compliance with governments' legitimate administrative orders is not only an obligation that Zhoushan Zhonghai Cereals & Oils Industry Co., Ltd should fulfill as a company under Chinese law, but also a basic requirement for Zhoushan Zhonghai Cereals & Oils Industry Co., Ltd to perform its social responsibilities. Zhoushan Zhonghai Cereals & Oils Industry Co., Ltd had no fault throughout the process, while the arbitration tribunal passively evaded the basic principle that a government's ban constitutes a force majeure event and let the Chinese company bear all liabilities and losses, which is unfair. Should the arbitral award be recognized and enforced, it would not only violate social and public interests of the country, but also result in the administrative orders issued by Chinese governments losing credibility globally and not being respected by foreign parties in the future, which would result in disadvantageous and harmful impacts on the Chinese law, the Chinese government and the Chinese national interests. The minority opinion is that soybeans made in Brazil and purchased by Zhoushan Zhonghai Cereals & Oils Industry Co., Ltd from Noble had already been in transit after General Administration of Quality

Opinions of the Supreme People's Court (Replies of the Supreme People's Court Are Listed in Reverse Chronological Order)	Opinions of the Lower Courts
	Supervision Inspection and Quarantine of the People's Republic of China issued the ban. Therefore, Zhoushan Zhonghai Cereals & Oils Industry Co., Ltd's failure in issuing a letter of credit ("L/C") constitutes a default. Zhoushan Zhonghai Cereals & Oils Industry Co., Ltd shall bear the relevant liabilities for such default as agreed. Recognition and enforcement of this arbitral award will not prejudice the authority of the administrative orders of the country.' – Upon examination, Ningbo Intermediate People's Court held the following opinions: (cited from Zhejiang Higher People's Court's Request for Instructions Re Application by Zhoushan Zhonghai Cereals & Oils Industry Co., Ltd. for Non-Enforcement of the Arbitral Award of HKIAC) 'Zhoushan Zhonghai Cereals & Oils Industry Co., Ltd failed to issue the L/C on time because AQSIQ found significant problems in the quality of the soybeans made in Brazil and purchased by Zhoushan Zhonghai Cereals & Oils Industry Co., Ltd from Noble, and issued an import ban in order to protect national food safety and consumers' lives and health. What Zhoushan Zhonghai Cereals & Oils Industry Co., Ltd did was to comply with the government's ban with no intention of default. Recognition and enforcement of this arbitral award will prejudice the authority of the administrative orders of the country and therefore will be contrary to social and public interests. Based on the above, this court decides not to enforce both the final HKIAC award of 25 August 2006 and the revised award of 16 October 2006.'

Chapter 4: PRC's Convergence with International Consensus

Opinions of the Supreme People's Court (Replies of the Supreme People's Court Are Listed in Reverse Chronological Order)	*Opinions of the Lower Courts*
4. Reply of the Supreme People's Court Re Application by Head Choice Cereals, Oils & Foodstuffs Limited for Enforcement of the Arbitral Award of HKIAC 14 November 2003, Supreme People's Court (2003) Min-Si-Ta-Zi No. 9 'Based on the facts stated by your court, Anhui Cereals Oils & Foodstuffs I/E (Group) Corp. is a shareholder of Hainan Gao Fu Rui Industry and Trade Co., Ltd. ("Hainan Gao Fu Rui"). The subject contract was entered into by Genjie Zhang, General Manager of Hainan Gao Fu Rui, in the name of Anhui Cereals Oils & Foodstuffs with Head Choice Cereals, Oils & Foodstuffs Limited ("Head Choice") in such a way that he utilized illegally (such as clipping, pasting, copying, faxing, etc.) documents he possessed in relation to staff seconded from Anhui Cereals Oils & Foodstuffs to Hainan Gao Fu Rui and stole Anhui Cereals Oils & Foodstuffs' round-shape special seal for administrative purpose. Genjie Zhang entered into the contract without the explicit authorization from Anhui Cereals Oils & Foodstuffs, but through fraudulent use of its seal, and didn't inform Anhui Cereals Oils & Foodstuffs of this fact thereafter. The act was not recognized retroactively by Anhui Cereals Oils & Foodstuffs. In accordance with the personal jurisdiction over the concerned parties, namely the relevant Mainland China provisions, Genjie Zhang had no power of agency to enter into the contract on behalf of Anhui Cereals Oils & Foodstuffs, i.e., he had no legal capacity to enter into the contract on behalf of Anhui Cereals Oils & Foodstuffs. Accordingly he	Anhui Higher People's Court's Request for Instructions Re the Non-enforcement of the Arbitral Award of HKIAC On Dispute Over Sales Contract Between Head Choice Cereals, Oils & Foodstuffs Limited and Anhui Cereals Oils & Foodstuffs I/E (Group) Corp. Date unknown Anhui Higher People's Court (2003) Wan-Zhi-Ta-Zi No. 01 – Opinions of Anhui Higher People's Court: 'In accordance with Article VII Section 3 of the "Arrangements of the Supreme People's Court on the Mutual Enforcement of Arbitral Awards between the Mainland and the Hong Kong Special Administrative Region" that "where the court in the Mainland finds that the enforcement of the arbitral award would be contrary to the public interest of the Mainland,… the enforcement of the award may be refused," and also other relevant laws such as the "Economic Contract Law of the People's Republic of China" and the "General Principles of the Civil Law of the People's Republic of China," the liabilities for any fault awarded by HKIAC ought to have been undertaken by Hainan Gao Fu Rui and Head Choice. It is against the country's legislative spirit of civil and commercial laws, as well as the basic principles of free will, fairness, making compensation for equal value, honesty and credibility in civil and commercial activities if Anhui Cereals Oils & Foodstuffs is to bear such liabilities. Compulsory enforcement will not only infringe legitimate rights and interests of Anhui Cereals Oils & Foodstuffs, but also

Opinions of the Supreme People's Court (Replies of the Supreme People's Court Are Listed in Reverse Chronological Order)	Opinions of the Lower Courts
had no legal capacity for signing the arbitration clauses under the contract on behalf of Anhui Cereals Oils & Foodstuffs. Since the subject arbitration agreement was entered into by Genjie Zhang as a result of fraud, it shall be deemed void according to the law of the seat of the arbitration, namely the law of Hong Kong SAR. Therefore, the arbitral award shall not be enforced in accordance with Article VII Section 1(1) of the "Arrangements of the Supreme People's Court on the Mutual Enforcement of Arbitral Awards between the Mainland and the Hong Kong Special Administrative Region." We agree with the opinions of your court in handling this case, but Article VII Section 3 of the "Arrangements of the Supreme People's Court on the Mutual Enforcement of Arbitral Awards between the Mainland and the Hong Kong Special Administrative Region" should not be taken as the legal basis for non-enforcement of the arbitral award.'	disturb social economic order and harm social and public interests. Anhui Cereals Oils & Foodstuffs' application for non-enforcement complies with the inherent spirit of Article VII Section 3 of the above judicial interpretation. In light of this, this court intends not to enforce the arbitral award upon discussion of the judicial committee of this court.' – Hefei Intermediate People's Court holds the following opinions: (cited from the 'Request for Instructions of Anhui Higher People's Court Re Non-Enforcement of HKIAC Arbitral Award On Dispute Over Sales Contract Between Choice Cereals, Oils & Foodstuffs Limited and Anhui Cereals Oils & Foodstuffs I/E (Group) Corp.') 'The contract upon which the arbitral award was made was entered into by Genjie Zhang, General Manager of Hainan Gao Fu Rui, in the name of Anhui Cereals Oils & Foodstuffs. Genjie Zhang was neither a staff nor the authorised representative of Anhui Cereals Oils & Foodstuffs. The stated "The address of Anhui Cereals Oils & Foodstuffs: Room 305 Anhui Mansion, 18 Cuizhu Road, Shenzhen; Legal Representative: Genjie Zhang" specified in the contract was obviously not true. The actual address of Anhui Cereals Oils & Foodstuffs at the time was Financial Tower, 256 Jinzhai Road, Hefei, Anhui Province, and its legal representative was Zhang Weigen. Documents for foreign trade between Hainan Gao Fu Rui and Head Choice for customs clearance, inspection, shipping, etc. were all handled by Hainan Gao Fu Rui, with no involvement by Anhui Cereals Oils & Foodstuffs at all. The No. 493

Chapter 4: PRC's Convergence with International Consensus

Opinions of the Supreme People's Court (Replies of the Supreme People's Court Are Listed in Reverse Chronological Order)	Opinions of the Lower Courts
	contract is not legally binding on Anhui Cereals Oils & Foodstuffs which is not a party to the contract. The liabilities for any fault awarded by HKIAC ought to have been undertaken by Hainan Gao Fu Rui and Head Choice. It is against the country's legislative spirit of civil and commercial laws and basic principles of free will, fairness, making compensation for equal value, honesty and credibility in civil and commercial activities in the country to have Anhui Cereals Oils & Foodstuffs bear such liabilities for default. Compulsory enforcement will not only infringe legitimate rights and interests of Anhui Cereals Oils & Foodstuffs, but also disturb social economic order and harm social and public interests. In light of this, this court intends to rule not to enforce the arbitral award.'

Table 4.3 Cases Concerning Non-enforcement of Foreign-Related Arbitral Awards[79]

Opinions of the Supreme People's Court (Replies of the Supreme People's Court Are Listed in Reverse Chronological Order)	Opinions of the Lower Courts
1. Reply of the Supreme People's Court on the Non-enforcement of an Arbitral Award concerning Shenzhen Guangxia Culture Industry Company, Ningxia Islamic International Trust and Investment Company, Shenzhen Xingqing Electronics Company and Misuer Co., Ltd. (the *Guangxia Culture* case) 20 April 2002, Supreme People's Court (2000) Zhi-Jian-Zi No. 96-2 'This court finds, after examination, that: Page 26 of the original text of the arbitral award No. 0271 [1996] of CIETAC stated that "In the opinion of this arbitral tribunal, the applicants obtained a capital	

---

79. Please *see* section 3.2.1 of Chapter 3.

Opinions of the Supreme People's Court (Replies of the Supreme People's Court Are Listed in Reverse Chronological Order)	Opinions of the Lower Courts
verification report inconsistent with the facts through improper means, and filed a request with the relevant government department for change of shareholders based thereon. The aforesaid administrative decision made by the relevant government department was the result of tortious acts of the applicants and in no way of an isolated administrative act, so the applicants cannot escape the tortious liability they should assume on the excuse of an administrative act of an administrative organization." This opinion violated the relevant provisions of the Civil Procedure Law and the Arbitration Rules on the scope of arbitration and jurisdiction of the arbitral tribunal.' The SPC pointed out the following two procedural defects in the award: 'Firstly, the arbitrated matter in the arbitral award was beyond the scope of arbitration. The arbitral award (1996) Mao-Zhong-Cai-Zi No. 0271 of CIETAC confirmed that Misuer Company had fulfilled its obligation of contribution to the joint venture company, which factually denied the conclusion of the Shenzhen Administration for Industry and Commerce that Misuer Company failed to make contribution as per the time limit and amount under the Joint Venture Contract and therefore breached the contract; and at the same time, violated the decision of the Shenzhen Municipal People's Government on cancellation of the shareholder eligibility of Misuer Company. If a joint venture company deems that a shareholder fails to make contribution in full, it may, according to its by-laws and other relevant provisions, apply to the relevant administrative department for the	

Chapter 4: PRC's Convergence with International Consensus

Opinions of the Supreme People's Court (Replies of the Supreme People's Court Are Listed in Reverse Chronological Order)	Opinions of the Lower Courts
replacement or cancellation of eligibility of the shareholder, and the administrative organ may make an administrative decision according to law after examination. *An arbitral tribunal shall not be entitled to rule on the legality of an administrative decision legally made by an administrative organ. In accordance with Article 260 [currently Article 274] paragraph 1 item (4) of the Civil Procedure Law, the matter arbitrated by the said arbitral tribunal was beyond the scope of arbitration, and the arbitral tribunal had no authority to arbitrate the matter at issue.* Secondly, the contents of the arbitral award violated the arbitration rules. Article 2 of the Arbitration Rules of the China International Economic and Trade Arbitration Commission provides that "The China International Economic and Trade Arbitration Commission independently and impartially resolves, by means of arbitration, disputes arising from international or foreign-related economic and trade transactions of a contractual or non-contractual nature." As one may see, the cases arbitrated by arbitral tribunals are limited to civil and commercial disputes of a contractual or non-contractual nature, and arbitral tribunals do not have the authority to arbitrate cases involving tort disputes. The arbitral tribunal in this case held in the award that the specific administrative acts of the government departments were results of tortious acts of the three applicants; that is to say, it deemed that the replacement of shareholders by the joint venture company with the approval of the governmental departments was a tort. Accordingly, it made an award that the three applicants	

Opinions of the Supreme People's Court (Replies of the Supreme People's Court Are Listed in Reverse Chronological Order)	Opinions of the Lower Courts
should assume tort liability. The aforesaid award of the arbitration tribunal clearly violated the relevant provisions of the Arbitration Rules of the China International Economic and Trade Arbitration Commission on jurisdiction.'	
2. Reply of the Supreme People's Court on the Non-enforcement of an Arbitral Award in Dispute Over Performance Contract Concerning USA Productions, Tom Hulett & Associates and China Women Travel Service (the *Tom Hulett* case) 26 December 1997, Supreme People's Court (1997) Ta No. 35 'On 28 August 1992 USA Productions and Tom Hulett & Associates signed a performance agreement on inviting American artists to perform in Mainland China. Clause 2(B) of the performance agreement stated that "the performers shall make every effort to observe PRC laws, regulations and policies and shall ensure the entertaining character of their performances." Clause 7(2) of the supplemental agreement signed on 9 September 1992 by the same US companies further provided that "China has the power to censor and approve every details of the performers' performances." Based on the aforementioned performance agreement, on 23 December 1992, the two US companies signed a performance contract with China Women Travel Service concerning US Southern Bands' twenty to twenty-three performances in China from 25 January until 28 February 1993. However, during the performance, the US performers breached the performance contract by failing to perform in	Beijing Higher People's Court's Request for Instructions on the Non-enforcement of an Arbitral Award in Dispute Over Performance Contract Concerning USA Productions, Tom Hulett & Associates and China Women Travel Service Date unknown Beijing Higher People's Court (1996) Jing-Gao-Fa No. 239

Opinions of the Supreme People's Court (Replies of the Supreme People's Court Are Listed in Reverse Chronological Order)	Opinions of the Lower Courts
accordance with the Ministry of Culture's scope of approval, performing heavy metal rock songs which were inappropriate for the PRC's public sentiments (*guo-qing*) and contrary to the PRC's social and public interest, causing very bad influences which led to the Ministry of Culture's cancellation of the remaining performances. Accordingly, the cancellation of performances and reduction in revenue resulted from the serious breach of the performance contract by the Claimants (i.e., the two US companies). These facts were overlooked in the CIETAC Award ((1994) CIETAC Award Mao-Zhong-Zi No. 0015) and such arbitral award was completely wrong. If the people's court were to enforce the award, the PRC's social and public interest would thus be damaged.'	
3. [The author has not located the Reply of the Supreme People's Court on this matter.]	Guangdong Zhanjiang Intermediate People's Court Civil Ruling 30 December 1998, Guangdong Zhanjiang Intermediate People's Court (1996) Zhan-Zhong-Fa-Zhi-Zi No. 1 'The main evidence for the factual findings in the arbitral award did not conform to the facts and the award's enforcement would be contrary to social and public interest.'
4. Reply of the Supreme People's Court 16 November 1992 [Letter number unknown] This court finds, after examinations, that the decision by the Zhengzhou Intermediate People's Court not to enforce the arbitral award based on the ground that doing so would seriously damage the national economic interest and social and public interest and negatively impacted on the order of national foreign trade is incorrect.	Dongfeng Clothing Factory of Kaifeng Case (the *Dongfeng* case) Henan Zhengzhou Intermediate People's Court Civil Ruling 28 September 1992, [Docket number unknown] 'According to existing national policies and regulations, if the award was to be enforced, it would severely damage national economic interest and social and public interest and negatively impacted on the order of national foreign trade.

Helena Hsi-Chia Chen

Opinions of the Supreme People's Court (Replies of the Supreme People's Court Are Listed in Reverse Chronological Order)	Opinions of the Lower Courts
	Therefore, in accordance with Article 260 clause 2 of the "Civil Procedure of the People's Republic of China," enforcement of the award is refused.' (The original text of this arbitral award cannot be found and we have only seen reporting of this case in various articles.)

Table 4.4 Cases Concerning the Validity of Foreign-Related Arbitration Agreements[80]

Opinions of the Supreme People's Court	Opinions of The lower Courts
Determination on the validity of an agreement of the parties to a case without a foreign element to submit the dispute to the jurisdiction of a foreign arbitration institution – Objection to the jurisdiction over a mining right transfer contract concerning Liupanshui Hidili Industry Co., Ltd. and Zhang Hongxing (the *Liupanshui* case) Civil Ruling of the Supreme People's Court 26 August 2010, Supreme People's Court (2010) Min-Er-Zhong-Zi No. 86 'Upon examination of the case, we are of the view that it is apparent from the basic facts of the case that both parties thereto are either a Chinese legal person or a Chinese natural person, and the legal facts concerning the formation, change and termination of the civil legal relationship between the parties as well as the subject matter of the litigation all took place or are situated within the territory of Mainland China. Therefore the case does not fall within the category of cases involving a foreign element in accordance with the stipulations of the Civil Procedure Law of the People's Republic of China. The issue of contention under this case is about whether it is valid for the parties to a civil	

---

80. Please *see* section 3.2.1 of Chapter 3.

Chapter 4: PRC's Convergence with International Consensus

Opinions of the Supreme People's Court	Opinions of The lower Courts
case with no foreign element to agree to submit a dispute between them to the jurisdiction of an arbitration institution outside Mainland China. The mechanisms for resolving civil and commercial disputes which occurred within the territory of a country is a matter of that country's judicial sovereignty and is also part of that country's public policy. The contracting parties shall only be allowed to agree upon mechanisms to the extent permitted by the prevailing laws of that country. Any agreement made arbitrarily which deviates from or goes beyond the scope permitted by the laws of that country shall be deemed invalid due to a violation of the public policies of that country. Even in a sovereign state, there are public policy considerations among its different legal jurisdictions. Article 255 of the Civil Procedure Law of the People's Republic of China provides that "Where, for disputes involving foreign economic and trade activities or international transportation or maritime activities, the parties have included an arbitration clause in the contracts or have reached a written arbitration agreement after a dispute arose to refer such disputes to an international arbitration institution of the People's Republic of China or any other arbitral institution for arbitration, the parties shall not institute an action in a people's court." Its reference to "any other arbitral institution" can be understood as arbitration institutions situated outside Mainland China, and its legislative purpose is to confirm that parties to foreign-related civil disputes and with arbitration agreement cannot litigate in the PRC people's courts. Meanwhile, Article 255 of the PRC Civil Procedure Law has also made it clear that only for disputes arising from foreign-related economic, trade, transportation or maritime activities which	

Opinions of the Supreme People's Court	Opinions of The lower Courts
involve foreign elements, may the parties concerned enter into an arbitration agreement or arbitration clause to submit the dispute for arbitration to an foreign-related arbitration institution of the People's Republic of China or to other arbitration institution. Article 128 (2) of the PRC Contract Law also provides that "[p]arties to a foreign-related contract may apply to a Chinese arbitration institution or other arbitration institution for arbitration." Again this confirms the principle that only parties to civil cases involving foreign elements may select arbitration institutions outside the territory of Mainland China. In line with these legislative provisions, *if the parties to non-foreign-related disputes have agreed to submit their disputes to arbitration institutions outside the territory of Mainland China, then such an agreement would exceed beyond the permitted legal parameters and would not be valid.* Although the parties' arbitration agreement in this case specified a dispute resolution mechanism and agreed to arbitration by an arbitration institution outside the territory of Mainland China, such agreement is nevertheless invalid because this case is not a foreign-related civil case.'	

CHAPTER 5
Mainland China's Departure from International Consensus

Chapter 4 illustrates that the PRC courts' interpretation and application of public policy have been rather consistent with international consensus. This chapter explains the distinctive Chinese characteristics or flavours in the judicial interpretation and application of public policy. In the early days, especially before the implementation of the Reporting System, such Chinese characteristics or flavours were primarily rooted in the protection of departmental or local interests in the early Chinese judicial practice, namely influenced by local protectionism. These improved significantly after the Reporting System's implementation.

This chapter then illustrates how the SPC protects the PRC's judicial sovereignty through its interpretation and application of public policy. It will give a thorough and critical analysis of the *Hemofarm* case, the first case which refused enforcement of foreign arbitral award on the basis of public policy violation (*see* section 5.2.1) and compare it with the SPC's approaches in other similar cases. It can be observed from the *Hemofarm* case that the SPC highly values 'the judicial sovereignty of the PRC' and 'the jurisdiction of the PRC courts'. In the same consideration of national judicial sovereignty, the SPC in the *Liupanshui* case, the Beijing Second Intermediate People's Court in the *Chao Lai Xin Sheng* case and the Shanghai Second Intermediate People's Court in the *Leaf Confectionery* case held that arbitration agreements between parties in non-foreign-related civil cases submitting disputes to arbitration institutions outside the PRC's territory would be invalid on the basis of public policy violation.

It is within the PRC's special legal framework of distinguishing domestic arbitration from foreign-related arbitration that the PRC courts' interpretation and application of public policy under Article V(2)(b) of the New York Convention are flavoured with Chinese characteristics.

5.1 PROTECTION OF DEPARTMENTAL OR LOCAL INTERESTS

5.1.1 Before the Reporting System's Implementation: *Dongfeng* Case

The author was unable to find any PRC cases concerning the recognition and enforcement of *foreign* arbitral awards before the Reporting System's implementation. However, the *Dongfeng* case of 1992 refused enforcement of a *foreign-related* arbitral awards and is commonly 'believed to be the first case dealing with the issue of public policy',[1] specifically the application of 'social and public interest' by the PRC courts in cases concerning arbitration.[2] In that case, three companies, Henan (Henan Clothing Import & Export (Group) Company), Dongfeng (Dongfeng Clothing Factory of Kaifeng) and Advancetex (Advancetex International Trading (H.K.) Co. Ltd.), in the proportion of 4:3:3 respectively, funded and established Henan Kaida Garments Co., a joint venture company for manufacturing and exporting clothing. According to the joint venture agreement, Henan was primarily responsible for handling the joint venture's approval and registration procedures while providing the quota for exporting to the US in the first ten years. All of the joint venture company's qualified products were to be sold abroad, with Henan acting as the export agent. Disputes arose within two years after the joint venture agreement became effective.

The main dispute arose as Henan discontinued its provision of the US export quota on the basis of the PRC's restrictions on the use of export quota by tripartite joint ventures, while withholding the joint venture company's export revenue for 1989 and 1990 of more than USD 700,000. In April 1991, Dongfeng submitted the dispute to CIETAC in accordance with the arbitration clause in the joint venture agreement, naming Henan and Advancetex as the respondents. The arbitral tribunal rendered a partial award on 25 January 1992 and a final award on 20 April 1992. According to both

---

1. *Dongfeng Clothing Factory of Kaifeng v. Henan Clothing Import & Export (Group) Company.* (1992), Reply of the Supreme People's Court, 6 November 1992.

    For commentaries on this case, please *see* Shengchang Wang, *Enforcement of Foreign Arbitral Awards in the People's Republic of China*, in *Improving the Efficiency of Arbitration Agreements and Awards: 40 Years of Application of the New York Convention* 461, 491 (Albert Jan van den Berg ed., Kluwer Law International 1999) ('was believed to be the first case dealing with the issue of public policy'); Xiuwen Zhao (ed.), *International Commercial Arbitration Law* 381 (3rd ed., China Renmin University Press 2012); Shengchang Wang, *Recognition and Enforcement of Forward Arbitral Awards in China*, in An Chen, 2 Journal of International Economic Law 509–510 (1980); Dejun Cheng, Shengchang Wang & Ming Kang, *International Practice and Foreign-Related Arbitration* 258–260 (China Youth Press 1993); Weidong Zhao, *See the Public Policy of International Trading Arbitration – From 'New York Convention' in Asian Countries' Implementation*, 27 Arbitration Study 58 (2011); Xinli Du, *International Commercial Arbitration Theory and Practice* 395–396 (China University of Political Science and Law Press 2009); Yifei Lin, *Law and Practice of Challenges to Arbitral Awards* 267–268 (Wuhan University Press 2008); Lianbin Song & Jian Zhao, *Analysis on Amendments to Arbitration Act 1994*, 4 Journal of International Economic Law 604 (2001); Hang Song, *Recognition and Enforcement of International Commercial Arbitral Awards* 231 (Law Press 2000); Jian Zhao, *On the Public Order and the Recognition and Enforcement of International Commercial Arbitral Awards*, 6 Arbitration and Law Communication 23 (1998).
2. Shengchang Wang & Xiuwen Zhao, etc. all believe the *Dongfeng* case to be the first case on the PRC courts' application of 'social and public interest' to arbitration. Please *see* Shengchang Wang, *ibid.* and Xiuwen Zhao, *ibid.*

awards, the joint venture company appointed Henan as the exclusive export agent pursuant to the joint venture agreement. The joint venture agreement's provisions about quota are essentially provisions about quota-related business arrangement between the respondents (i.e., Henan and Advancetex) and the joint venture company, which neither required the joint venture company to directly apply for national quota nor required the respondents to apply for national quota on the joint venture company's behalf, and therefore neither required nor affected the balance of national quotas. The arbitral tribunal ruled that the joint venture agreement was valid, and that the respondents were liable for compensation of economic loss due to their breach of the joint venture agreement by failing to provide sufficient quota and failing to export all of the joint venture company's products. Henan's non-compliance with the arbitral award led to Dongfeng's application for enforcement proceedings before the Henan Zhengzhou Intermediate People's Court on 28 May 1992. Henan pleaded against enforcement. On 28 September 1992 the Zhengzhou Intermediate People's Court held: 'Pursuant to current national policies, laws and regulations, enforcing this arbitral award would seriously harm national economic interest and social and public interest, or adversely affect the nation's foreign trade order; therefore, the court has decided to refuse enforcement of this arbitral award under Article 260(2) of the PRC Civil Procedure Law.'[3]

The *Dongfeng* case has been widely criticised. Some stated that the Zhengzhou Intermediate People's Court simply rejected enforcement of the award '[w]ithout much logical or reasoned analysis',[4] while many scholars regarded this case as representing the improperly wide interpretation of 'social and public interest' motivated by local protectionism.[5] Although the Reporting System was not yet implemented at the time, on 6 November 1992 the SPC specifically issued a Reply to the Henan Higher People's Court of its finding that the Zhengzhou Intermediate People's Court's refusal against enforcement and reasons were incorrect.[6] The SPC's intervention ultimately led to the arbitral award's enforcement.

---

3. The content of the Zhengzhou Intermediate People's Court's judgment in this case was quoted from Weidong Zhao, *supra* n. 1, at 58; Jian Zhao, *supra* n. 1, at 23; Hang Song, *supra* n. 1, at 231.
4. Shengchang Wang, *Enforcement of Foreign Arbitral Awards in the People's Republic of China*, in *Improving The Efficiency of Arbitration Agreements and Awards: 40 Years of Application of the New York Convention* 461, 491 (Albert Jan van den Berg ed., Kluwer Law International 1999) ('Without much logical or reasoned analysis, the Zhengzhou Intermediate People's Court simply rejected enforcement of the award, by stating...').
5. Justice Hang Song stated: 'This is a typical case of local protectionism under the guise of refusing an arbitral award's recognition and enforcement on the basis of violation of social and public interest'. Cited from Hang Song, *Enforcement of Foreign-Related Arbitral Awards in China – Issues in Practice*, 4 Arbitration and Law Communication 13 (1998); Xinli Du stated: 'Zhengzhou Intermediate People's Court's approach to social and public interest is debatable, as such practice has turned social and public interest into a safety valve and the last line of defence for local protectionism'. Cited from Xinli Du, *supra* n. 1, at 396.
6. The content of the SPC's Reply in this case was quoted from Jian Zhao, *supra* n. 1, at 23; Hang Song, *supra* n. 1, at 231; *See also*: Xiuwen Zhao (ed.), *International Commercial Arbitration Law* 381 (3rd ed., China Renmin University Press 2012); Yifei Lin, *Law and Practice of Challenges to Arbitral Awards* 267–268 (Wuhan University Press 2008).

5.1.2 After the Reporting System's Implementation: *Tom Hulett* Case, *Shin-Etsu* Case and *Baosheng* Case

5.1.2.1 Tom Hulett *Case*

The Reporting System for applications for enforcement of foreign-related arbitral awards as well as recognition and enforcement of foreign arbitral awards began its implementation on 28 August 1995.[7] Since then the first SPC case in which the court refused enforcement of a *foreign-related* arbitral award on the basis of violation of 'social and public interest' is found in the Reply of the Supreme People's Court on the Non-enforcement of an Arbitral Award on Dispute over the Performance Contract among USA Productions, Tom Hulett & Associates and China Women Travel Service dated December 1997.[8] On 28 August 1992, USA Productions and Tom Hulett & Associates signed a performance agreement on inviting American artists to perform in Mainland China. Clause 2(B) of the performance agreement stated that 'the performers shall make every effort to observe PRC laws, regulations and policies and shall ensure the entertaining character of their performances'. Clause 7(2) of the supplemental agreement signed on 9 September 1992 by the same US companies further provided that 'China has the power to censor and approve every details of the performers' performances.' Based on the aforementioned performance agreement, on 23 December 1992, the two US companies signed a performance contract with China Women Travel Service concerning US Southern Bands' twenty to twenty-three performances in China from 25 January until 28 February 1993.

The US performers did not conform to the demo tape. They performed 'heavy metal rock songs'. That is the performers acted crazily, smoking, drinking, splashing water, lying on the floor while singing, doing cartwheels, jumping off the platform and discontinuing performances at will, etc. After eleven performances, the PRC Ministry of Culture decided to cancel the remaining performances. USA Productions and Tom Hulett & Associates filed a request for arbitration with CIETAC, claiming compensation for the outstanding payment and damages against China Women Travel Service. China Women Travel Service requested dismissal of the claims and counterclaimed against the two US companies for compensation of economic loss as the performances were not in conformity with the demo tape and therefore breached the performance contract. The arbitral tribunal dismissed the counterclaims and rendered an award ((1994) CIETAC Award Mao-Zhong-Zi No. 0015) ordering China Women Travel Service to pay 70% of the outstanding payment as claimed by the two US companies approximately USD 89,950. In the enforcement proceedings before Beijing First Intermediate People's

---

7. Article 2 of the Supreme People's Court's Notification of Certain Issues Relating to the People's Courts' Dealing with Foreign-Related and Foreign Arbitration, Fa-Fa (1995) No. 18, issued and implemented on 28 August 1995.
8. Reply of the Supreme People's Court on the Non-enforcement of an Arbitral Award on Dispute over the Performance Contract among USA Productions, Tom Hulett & Associates and China Women Travel Service (1997) Ta No. 35, 26 December 1997.

Chapter 5: Mainland China's Departure from International Consensus

Court, China Women Travel Service applied for non-enforcement of the arbitral award on the basis of violation of the PRC's social and public interest.[9]

In its Reply to the Beijing court, the SPC stated that, during the performance, the US performers breached the performance contract by failing to perform in accordance with the Ministry of Culture's scope of approval, performing heavy metal rock songs which were inappropriate for the PRC's public sentiments (*guo-qing*) and contrary to the PRC's social and public interest, causing very bad influences which led to the Ministry of Culture's cancellation of the remaining performances. Accordingly, the cancellation of performances and reduction in revenue resulted from the serious breach of the performance contract by the Claimants (i.e., the two US companies). These facts were overlooked in the CIETAC Award ((1994) CIETAC Award Mao-Zhong-Zi No. 0015) and such arbitral award was completely wrong. If the people's court were to enforce the award, the PRC's social and public interest would thus be damaged. The SPC's decision is subject to strong criticisms by scholars outside Mainland China. For instance, some scholars opined that '[w]hatever one may think of heavy metal music, it is difficult not to reach the conclusion that this amounted to a troublingly broad interpretation of the public policy exception to the enforcement of arbitral awards'.[10] Furthermore, Professor Lanfang Fei thinks that: '[t]he real reason for the application of social and public interest in this case was that the contents of the performance advocated democracy and freedom, which might damage the Chinese government's hold on power and so was regarded as having a negative impact on China's cultural atmosphere and culture orientation'.[11]

In addition, on 30 December 1998, the Guangdong Zhanjiang Intermediate People's Court refused to enforce an arbitral award made by the CIETAC Shengzhen Sub-Commission because 'the main evidence for the factual findings in the arbitral award did not conform to the facts and the award's enforcement would be contrary to social and public interest'.[12] It cannot be ascertained from the judgment of the Zhanjiang Intermediate People's Court's unusual opinion as to whether the Zhanjiang Intermediate People's Court has followed the Reporting System and reported the case to the SPC,[13] nor has the author ascertained any reply by the SPC regarding this case. Thus it is uncertain as to whether the Zhanjiang Intermediate People's Court arbitrarily

---

9. Honglei Yang, *A Study on New York Convention – From the Perspective of Judicial Practice in Mainland China* 363 (Law Press 2006).
10. 'Whatever one may think of heavy metal music, it is difficult not reach the conclusion that this amounted to a troublingly broad interpretation of the public policy exception to the enforcement of arbitral awards.' Please *see* Nigel Blackby, Constantine Partasides et al., *Redfern and Hunter on International Arbitration* 660 (5th ed., Oxford University Press 2009).
11. 'The real reason for the application of social and public interest in this case was that the contents of the performance advocated democracy and freedom, which might damage the Chinese government's hold on power and so was regarded as "having a negative impact on China's cultural atmosphere and culture orientation".' Please *see* Lanfang Fei, *Public Policy as a Bar to Enforcement of International Arbitral Awards: A Review of the Chinese Approach*, 26(2) Journal of Arbitration International 301, 311 (2010).
12. Guangdong Zhanjiang Intermediate People's Court Civil Ruling (1996) Zhan-Zhong-Fa-Zhi-Zi No. 1, 30 December 1998.
13. Lianbin Song & Jian Zhao, *supra* n. 1 at 604 (n. 15).

made this ruling without following the Reporting System, or whether the SPC adopted a wider approach to 'social and public interest' in the early days of implementing the Reporting System.

5.1.2.2 Shin-Etsu *Case*

With respect to the Reporting System for the recognition and enforcement of foreign arbitral awards, the *Shin-Etsu* case seemingly demonstrates the SPC's involvement in protecting the interests of specific industries: please *see* Reply of the Supreme People's Court on the Report of Non-recognition of No. 04-05 (Tokyo) Arbitration Award of JCAA.[14] In that case, the Jiangsu Higher People's Court reported to the SPC that: 'enforcing the arbitral award would undoubtedly counteract the effects of imposing anti-dumping levies, as well as support Japanese enterprises in damaging the interests of optic fiber industry of this country. The recognition of the arbitral award will therefore contravene the public policy of this country.' Nonetheless the SPC did not adopt this view in its Letter of Reply.

In the *Shin-Etsu* case, Zhongtian (Jiangsu Zhongtian Technology Co., Ltd.) and Shin-Etsu (Shin-Etsu Chemical Co., Ltd.) signed a sales contract on 27 November 2001 under which Zhongtian was to purchase pattern-matching single-mode optical fibre preforms from Shin-Etsu for five years commencing on 1 January 2003 at a price no higher than JPY 70 per gram. In Public Announcement No. 28 of 2004, the PRC Ministry of Commerce initially decided to collect security deposits on conventional single-mode optical fibre imported from the US, Japan and Korea. On 1 January 2005, the Ministry of Commerce finally decided to impose anti-dumping levies ranging from 7% to 46% on conventional single-mode optical fibre imported from these three countries, causing enormous changes to the pricing of optical fibre. Zhongtian requested Shin-Etsu to adjust the price. But Zhongtian and Shin-Etsu failed to reach any agreement on price adjustment. The sales contract was not executed in full. On 12 April 2004, Shin-Etsu filed a request for arbitration with JCAA pursuant to the parties' arbitration agreement.

The arbitral tribunal rendered its award ordering Zhongtian to pay JPY 1.52 billion to Shin-Etsu plus interest accruing at the annual rate of 6% starting from 12 April 2004 to the day when the payment is made in full and arbitration costs in the amount of JPY 3,173,283.

On 26 May 2006, Shin-Etsu applied to the Nantong Intermediate People's Court for recognition of the arbitral award. The Nantong Intermediate People's Court considered that the award should not be recognised under several grounds in Article V of the New York Convention, and reported the case to the Jiangsu Higher People's Court. The Jiangsu Higher People's Court concurred with the Nantong Intermediate People's Court in refusing recognition under Article V(1)(d) and (2)(b) of the New York

---

14. (2(2007) Min-Si-Ta-Zi No. 26, 3 March 2008.

Chapter 5: Mainland China's Departure from International Consensus

Convention. The Jiangsu Higher People's Court made the following comments on the award's contravention of PRC public policy:[15]

> Since 2002, companies from Japan, the US and Korea had been dumping conventional single-mode optical fibre and thereby significantly harming the PRC domestic conventional single-mode optical fibre industry. After its investigation and verification, the Ministry of Commerce decided to impose anti-dumping levies ranging from 7% to 46% on conventional single-mode optical fibre imported from these three countries starting on 1 January 2005, specifically charging 46% for all conventional single-mode optical fibre imported from Japan. The subjects of the long term sale and purchase agreement in this case were the raw materials of the above mentioned imported goods. The average price of optical fibre in the domestic market dropped from CNY 119 per kilometre in 2003 to CNY 100 per kilometre in 2004. Zhongtian's total production costs would be CNY 175.46 per kilometre in 2003 and CNY 167.47 per kilometre in 2004 if it had continued to perform the sales contract. Obviously, Shin-Etsu is using its international monopoly in the production and sale of pattern-matching single-film (note, should be 'mode') optical fibre preforms to sell raw materials to Zhongtian, the main manufacturer of optical fibre products in China, at high prices only a monopolist could manage. Inevitably this would severely increase production costs and significantly reduce Zhongtian's market competitiveness. In addition to Zhongtian, other Chinese optical fibre product manufacturers, Tianjin Xinmao Science & Technology Co., Ltd. and Jiangsu Fasten Group Co., Ltd. are also victims of Shin-Etsu's monopoly high prices. Consequently, Shin-Etsu's exploitation of its international monopoly in the production and sale of pattern-matching single-film (note, should be 'mode') optical fibre preforms to monopolise its high prices for selling the relevant products has the same effect as dumping finished products, thereby seriously jeopardising the subsistence of the optical fibre industry in this country. In light of our government's decision to impose the highest anti-dumping levy on conventional single-mode optical fibre imported from Japan, enforcing the arbitral award would undoubtedly counteract the effects of imposing anti-dumping levies, as well as support Japanese enterprises in damaging the interests of optic fiber industry of this country. The recognition of the arbitral award will therefore contravene the public policy of this country.

Instead of refusing recognition and enforcement under Article V(2)(b) of the New York Convention, the SPC in its Letter of Reply invoked Article V(1)(b) and (d) to refuse recognition and enforcement of the arbitral award and stated as follows:

> Firstly, the arbitral tribunal did not conform to the time limit prescribed in the JCAA Commercial Arbitration Rules for rendering an award. According to Article 53.1 of the Arbitration Rules, '[o]nce the arbitral tribunal has determined that the proceedings have matured enough for it to render an arbitral award and the examination has been concluded, the arbitral tribunal shall make an arbitral award within five (5) weeks from the date of such conclusion; provided that the arbitral tribunal may, if it deems it necessary in view of the complexities of the case or for any other reason, extend such period of time to an appropriate period of not more than eight (8) weeks'. On 7 July 2005 the arbitral tribunal accepted Shin-Etsu's request for modifying the claims and closed/concluded the arbitral proceedings.

---

15. Cited from Jiangsu Higher People's Court's Report of Non-recognition of No. 04-05 (Tokyo) Arbitration Award of Japan Commercial Arbitration Association, (2(2007) Su-Min-San-Ta-Zi No. 0002, 25 May 2007.

On 31 August 2005 the arbitral tribunal announced that it would postpone twenty days and render the award by 20 September 2005. Yet the arbitral tribunal did not actually render its award until 23 February 2006. The arbitral tribunal did not comply with the time-limit for award-making provided in the JCAA Commercial Arbitration Rules after its closing/concluding of the arbitral proceedings. The parties agreed in the sales contract that if the parties fail to settle amicably, any disputes arising from or in connection with this contract shall be submitted to arbitration in accordance with the JCAA Commercial Arbitration Rules in Tokyo, Japan. When the parties choose arbitration to resolve their disputes and clearly agree to apply the JCAA Commercial Arbitration Rules, the relevant content of such arbitration rules becomes part of the parties' agreement. The arbitral tribunal's contraventions of the JCAA Commercial Arbitration Rules and Japan's Arbitration Law fall within Article V(1)(d) of the New York Convention, namely '[t]he composition of the arbitral authority or the arbitral procedure was not in accordance with the agreement of the parties, or, failing such agreement, was not in accordance with the law of the country where the arbitration took place'.

Secondly, Article 53.2 of the JCAA Commercial Arbitration Rules provides that, '[u]pon the conclusion of the examination pursuant to the preceding paragraph, notify the parties of the period of time during which it shall make a arbitral award'. Between its announcement about rendering an award on 20 September 2005 and its actual rendering of the award on 23 February 2006, the arbitral tribunal did not extend the time period again and notify the parties in accordance with the arbitration rules. This falls within Article V(1)(b) of the New York Convention: '[t]he party against whom the award is invoked was not given proper notice of the appointment of the arbitrator or of the arbitration proceedings or was otherwise unable to present his case'.

Thus, this Court agrees with the Jiangsu Higher People's Court that this arbitral award's recognition should be refused under Article V(1)(b) and (d) of the New York Convention.

As can be seen from the SPC's Letter of Reply above, public policy in Article V(2)(b) of the New York Convention was not the reason for refusing the arbitral award's enforcement, nor can we conclude from the content of the SPC's Letter of Reply that enabling Japanese industries to harm the interests of the PRC's optical fibre industry would be contrary to PRC public policy. Some Japanese scholars nevertheless regard the SPC's conclusion on Article V(1)(b) and (d) as both controversial and state that 'this case may also be criticized as an improper judgment in order to protect the interests of the PRC industries from being harmed by losses resulting from rapid market price changes'.[16]

Apart from the statements of the Jiangsu Higher People's Court in the *Shin-Etsu* case on refusing enforcement of arbitral awards on the basis of PRC public policy violation in order to avoid damage to the interests of specific PRC industries (such as optical fibre), the author is yet to see similar comments after the Reporting System's implementation.

---

16. Tatsuya Nakamura, *Couple Questions Concerning PRC Court's Decision to Refuse Recognition and Enforcement of JCAA's Arbitral Award*, 38(5) International Business Law and Practice (Kokusai - Shoji - Homu) 628–634 (2010). He concluded that: 'Such ruling might be criticized as an improper ruling in order to protect the interest of Chinese enterprises and to prevent them from suffering loss caused by rapid change in prices on the market.'

5.1.2.3 Baosheng *Case*

In cases concerning non-enforcement of *foreign-related* arbitral awards, lower courts of the PRC also have reasoning based upon protection of local interests.

In the *Baosheng* case, the lower courts held that enforcing the relevant award would be manifestly contrary to social and public interest, as the PRC government (through Hefei City Bureau of Environmental Protection and Hygiene and Hefei Import and Export Co. Ltd.) had invested CNY 105 million in a waste treatment plant, which was left unused due to equipment and technical problems. Yet the SPC disagreed and held that the foreign-related arbitral award should be enforced. In this case concerning the sale and purchase of waste treatment equipment, Baosheng (Shenzhen Baosheng Jinggao Environment Protection Development Co. Ltd.), Hopsing International Limited, Hefei City Environmental Protection and Hygiene Administration Commission (later converted to 'Hefei City Bureau of Environmental Protection and Hygiene', hereinafter referred to as 'Hefei Bureau'), Hefei Import and Export Co. (later converted to 'Hefei Import and Export Co. Ltd.') and US Wildcat (Wildcat Mfg. Co., Inc.) entered into a contract on 22 November 1998 about Hefei City Environmental Protection and Hygiene Administration Commission importing US Wildcat's waste treatment equipment and technology. Disputes arose during the performance of the contract, both Baosheng and Hopsing initiated arbitration with CIETAC pursuant to the arbitration clause in the contract. On 2 June 2003, the arbitral tribunal made an award ordering the respondents, Hefei Bureau and Hefei Import and Export Co. Ltd., to pay Baosheng USD 272,120.20 as reimbursement for the quality deposit plus interest (accruing at the annual rate of 5% from 1 January 2001 to the actual payment date) and costs of arbitration at CNY 101,172. In the enforcement proceedings initiated by Baosheng, the judicial committee of the Hefei Intermediate People's Court unanimously held that the arbitral award's enforcement should be refused under Article 260(2) of the PRC Civil Procedure Law (currently Article 274(2)), and reported the case to the Anhui Higher People's Court. The majority of the judicial committee in the Anhui Higher People's Court agreed with the Hefei Intermediate People's Court, stating: 'While this is a foreign-related arbitral award, the waste treatment plant with governmental investment of CNY 105 million remains unused due to equipment and technical problems, accordingly this award's enforcement would be manifestly contrary to social and public interest. Thus its enforcement should be refused under Article 260(2) of the PRC Civil Procedure Law.'[17]

The *Baosheng* case was reported to the SPC, which took a different view: 'Article 274 (previously Article 260) of the PRC Civil Procedure Law concerning social and public interest was meant to safeguard the fairness of arbitral proceedings, as well as to protect the fundamental legal order of the country. Here the execution and performance of the contract do not seem to violate social and public interest to the extent which would be intolerable by this country's fundamental legal order. At the

---

17. Anhui Higher People's Court's Request for Instruction Concerning Whether or Not to Revoke the Arbitral Award (2003) Mao-Zhong-Cai-Zi No. 0138 of China International Economic and Trade Arbitration Commission (2005) Wan-Zhi-Ta-Zi No. 11, 29 August 2005.

same time, the non-use of equipment did not result from this award's enforcement. Accordingly, the refusal to enforce the arbitral award for reason of violating social and public interest would be unfounded.'[18] As this case demonstrates, it may be difficult to change some lower court's thinking that damage to local interests (i.e., unused waste treatment plant in Hefei with CNY 105 million investment from Hefei Bureau and Hefei Import and Export Co. Ltd. due to equipment and technical problems) would make the award's enforcement in violation of the PRC's social and public interest. However, after the case was reported to the SPC through the Reporting System, the SPC adopted a narrower approach and confirmed that 'under the circumstances of this case, the contract's execution and performance would not violate social and public interest'.

In addition, the former Deputy President of the SPC (Professor Exiang Wan[19]) and SPC Justice Honglei Yang[20] have both expressed that 'mere involvement of departmental or local interests does not necessarily constitute contravention of the PRC's social and public interest'. It is reasonably foreseeable that departmental or local interests are unlikely to directly justify non-enforcement of foreign arbitral awards because of public policy violation, or non-enforcement of foreign-related arbitral awards because of social and public interest violation. On the other hand, Japanese scholars have criticised the SPC's approach in the previously mentioned Reply of the Supreme People's Court on the Report of Non-recognition of No. 04-05 (Tokyo) Arbitration Award of JCAA (the *Shin-Etsu* case) – namely, the apparent use of other grounds such as Article V(1) of the New York Convention (which were arguably not established in fact) to refuse recognition and enforcement of foreign arbitral awards in disguise of its excessively wide application of public policy. It remains to be seen whether such a wide approach will arise again.

5.2 PROTECTION OF PRC'S JUDICIAL SOVEREIGNTY AND JURISDICTION: ARBITRAL TRIBUNAL CANNOT VIOLATE PRC COURTS' JURISDICTION

5.2.1 *Hemofarm* Case: Arbitral Tribunal's Violation of PRC's Judicial Sovereignty and PRC Courts' Jurisdiction

5.2.1.1 *Case Summary*

Being the first PRC case refusing recognition of foreign arbitral award on the basis of public policy, the Reply of the Supreme People's Court to a Request for Instructions on the Non-recognition and Non-enforcement of an Arbitral Award of the ICC

---

18. (2005) Min-Si-Ta-Zi No. 45, 23 January 2006.
19. Professor Exiang Wan was elected as the Vice-Chairperson of the Standing Committee of the National People's Congress in March 2013.
20. Exiang Wan, *Judicial Practice with Regards to the New York Convention in China*, 276 Journal of Law Application 6 (2009); Honglei Yang, *Report on the Judicial Review of International Arbitration in Chinese Courts*, 9 International Law Review of Wuhan University 319 (2009).

Chapter 5: Mainland China's Departure from International Consensus

International Court of Arbitration (the *Hemofarm* case)[21] has attracted special media attention[22] and numerous discussions. In that case, Hemofarm (Hemofarm DD), MAG (MAG Intertrade Holding DD) and Yongning (Jinan Yongning Pharmaceutical Co., Ltd.) entered into a JVC on 22 December 1995 to establish a joint venture company named Jinan-Hemofarm Pharmaceutical Co., Ltd.

On 6 August 2002, Yongning commenced proceedings against the joint venture company in the Jinan Intermediate People's Court ('Jinan Court') for rent payment and return of certain leased property. The joint venture company challenged the Jinan Court's jurisdiction on the basis that Article 58 of the JVC requires leasing disputes to be submitted to arbitration by the ICC in Paris. The Jinan Court dismissed this jurisdictional objection on the basis that the arbitration clause in the JVC was only applicable to disputes regarding the joint venture between the parties to the JVC and the joint venture company was not one of these parties; however, here the disputes arose between the joint venture company and Yongning in respect of land and property leases. During the court proceedings, Yongning provided security and successfully applied for property preservation orders from the Jinan Court to seize certain bank deposits and products of the joint venture company. On 9 April 2003, the Jinan Court gave its judgment in Yongning's favour, and Shandong Higher People's Court upheld this decision on 23 July 2003 (the First Litigation).

Subsequently Yongning commenced further court proceedings against the joint venture company for rent payment and return of certain leased property (i.e., the Second Litigation, the Third Litigation and the Land Lease Litigation). In the First, Second and Third Litigations, Yongning asserted its de facto lease relationship with the joint venture company with respect to certain rental property. In the Land Lease Litigation, Yongning sought to establish its lease agreement with the joint venture company granting the right to the joint venture company to use its land with a surface area of 46,666 square metres. The Jinan Intermediate People's Court and Shandong Higher People's Court both ruled in favour of Yongning in the First and Third Litigations, while Yongning withdrew its claim from the Second Litigation.

On 3 September 2004, Hemofarm, MAG and Suram Media (Suram Media Ltd. (Liechtenstein)) filed a request for ICC arbitration as co-claimants demanding the following against Yongning: (1) loss of profit; (2) compensation for investment in the joint venture company; (3) litigation costs incurred by the co-claimants in the litigation proceedings; and (4) arbitration costs incurred by the co-claimants in the arbitration proceedings.

Consisting of Custodio O. Parlade, Bai Yanchun and Zhang Yuejiao, the arbitral tribunal rendered the award on 7 March 2007 (ICC No. 13464/MS/JB/JEM) in Paris, France.

In September 2007, the co-claimants requested the Jinan Intermediate People's Court to recognise and enforce the ICC award. The Jinan Intermediate People's Court

---

21. (2008) Min-Si-Ta-Zi No. 11, 2 June 2008.
22. After the Shandong Jinan Intermediate People's Court issued its ruling on 11 July 2008, the website of the Supreme People's Court reported on this case on 18 July 2008: http://www.chinacourt.org/article/details/2008/07/id/313519.shtml (accessed 4 May 2017).

and the Shandong Higher People's Court both are of the opinion that the recognition of the arbitral award should be refused. Through the Reporting System, the SPC also held that the ICC award should not be recognised for the following reasons:[23]

> The arbitration clause in the Joint Venture Contract among Hemofarm, MAG, Suram Media and Yongning applies only to disputes regarding the joint venture among the joint venture investors, but does not govern disputes arising from the lease agreement between Yongning and the joint venture company. The ICC tribunal *went beyond the scope of the arbitration clause in the Joint Venture Contract* by hearing and adjudicating on disputes arising from the lease agreement between Yongning and the joint venture company. The relevant Chinese courts had previously issued property preservation orders and entered judgments regarding the lease disputes between Jinan Yongning Pharmaceutical Co., Ltd. and the joint venture company, Jinan-Hemofarm Pharmaceutical Co., Ltd. Given this, the ICC International Court of Arbitration's hearing and ruling on the same lease disputes between Yongning and the joint venture company, Jinan-Hemofarm Pharmaceutical Co., Ltd., *infringed the judicial sovereignty of the PRC and the jurisdiction of the PRC courts*. The recognition and enforcement of the ICC award No. 13464/MS/JB/JEM should be refused under Articles V(1)(c) and (2)(b) of the New York Convention. [emphasis added]

5.2.1.2 Comment

The SPC's simple and concise discussions on 'public policy' in its Reply Letter in the *Hemofarm* case do not adequately indicate exactly which specific parts of the ICC award infringed 'the judicial sovereignty of the PRC and the jurisdiction of the PRC courts'. By comparison, the Shandong Higher People's Court's Request for Instructions on the Non-recognition and Non-enforcement of an Arbitral Award of the ICC International Court of Arbitration[24] contains more detailed discussions. To ascertain which of the Shandong court's views were adopted by the SPC, the author recommends comparing the Shandong court's Request for Instructions to the SPC with 'Application of Public Policy in Judicial Review of Foreign Arbitration: Comment on the *Hemofarm* Case', a paper published in 2010 and written by Justice Xiaolong Lu (President of the SPC Fourth Civil Tribunal at that time) and Justice Xifu Yu (one of the judge hearing this case from the Shandong Higher People's Court). The following cites the specific examples in that paper regarding many aspects in which the arbitral tribunal in this ICC award 'challenged the res judicata effect and authority of the PRC court judgments and thereby infringed the PRC's judicial sovereignty and the PRC court's jurisdiction':[25]

---

23. Reply of the Supreme People's Court to a Request for Instructions on the Non-recognition and Non-enforcement of an Arbitral Award of the ICC International Court of Arbitration (2008) Min-Si-Ta-Zi No. 11, 2 June 2008.
24. (2007) Lu-Min-Si-Ta-Zi No. 12, 30 January 2008.
25. Xiaolong Lu & Xifu Yu, *The Application of Public Policy in the Judicial Review of Foreign Arbitration – Comments on Hemofarm, MAG and Suram Media's Application for Recognition and Enforcement of an ICC Award*, in *Judicial Practice of New York Convention and International Commercial Arbitration* 404–405 (CIETAC ed., Law Press 2010).

(1) Determining whether the PRC courts had jurisdiction to hear the lease disputes.
(2) Deciding that the PRC courts did not have jurisdiction over the lease disputes and that such disputes should be submitted to arbitration.
(3) Holding that Yongning's application for and acquisition of the property preservation orders from the PRC courts did not have any legal or commercial justifications.
(4) Holding that the PRC courts' property preservation orders led to the termination of the joint venture company's operation and other consequences, which practically negated the justiciability and legality of the PRC court decisions to seize and detain the joint venture company's assets.
(5) Ordering Yongning to compensate the litigation costs paid for the joint venture company by the co-claimants, which objectively negated the res judicata effect of the PRC court judgments on litigation costs concerning the lease disputes.

The above points of contention from Justice Xiaolong Lu and Justice Xifu Yu are rather complete and basically encompass the discussions of many other scholars.[26] This leads to the following analyses of each of the five points.

(1) The First and Second Points of Contention

The first two points of contention (namely, arbitral tribunal's decisions concerning whether the PRC courts had jurisdiction to hear the lease disputes, or whether such disputes should be submitted to arbitration) are reflected in the Shandong Higher People's Court's Request for Instructions to the SPC:[27] '[t]he ICC award ruled that Yongning's Land Lease Litigation against the joint venture company for lease disputes contravened the arbitration clause. This not only denied the PRC courts' right to hear jurisdictional objection and determine their jurisdiction, but also directly denied the PRC court's jurisdiction over the Land Lease Litigation.'

In this regard, the author believes that the key lies in the absence of arbitration clause in the Land Lease Agreement between Yongning and the joint venture company. Although the JVC contained an arbitration clause, its signatories were the joint venture investors and did not include the joint venture company. In the Land Lease Litigation, Yongning pursued court proceedings against the joint venture company pursuant to the Land Lease Agreement (and not the JVC); it was not improper for Yongning to litigate in the Jinan Intermediate People's Court (situated in the joint venture company's place of incorporation) as the Land Lease Agreement did not have any arbitration clause. Although the merits of the Land Lease Litigation may involve determining the performance of the JVC, nevertheless it does not follow that Yongning should submit

---

26. For other academic discussions, please *see* Exiang Wan & Xiaohong Xia, *Reason for the Refusals of the Recognition and Enforcement of Foreign Arbitral Awards in Chinese Courts*, 13(2) International Law Review of Wuhan University 22–23 (2010); Xiuwen Zhao, *Refusing Recognition and Enforcement of Foreign Arbitral Awards on the Ground of Public Policy from the Case of Yongning Corporation*, 4 The Jurist 98–105 (2009).
27. (2007) Lu-Min-Si-Ta-Zi No. 12, 30 January 2008.

its disputes with 'the joint venture company' to arbitration pursuant to Article 58 of the JVC, since the signatories to that JVC were the joint venture investors and did not include the joint venture company. Therefore, Yongning should not be able to request arbitration and claim rent against the 'joint venture company' under the JVC. In other words, although 'the questions whether the JVC's obligations to pay rent existed, and if so, whether such payment obligation had already begun' directly involved the JVC's interpretation; however, the lease disputes between Yongning and the joint venture company could not be submitted to arbitration pursuant to the JVC.

In practice, it is common for Sino-foreign JVCs to provide for arbitration in a foreign seat or by a foreign arbitration institution. Since the parties to the JVCs are the joint venture investors and do not include the joint venture company, the Chinese investor(s) wishing to circumvent the JVC's arbitration clause may seek to have the dispute resolved before the PRC courts, by including both the foreign investor(s) and the joint venture company which are not party to the arbitration agreement.[28] To avoid such a situation, experienced foreign investors often require contracts executed between each of the investors and the joint venture company to expressly stipulate an arbitration clause. Yet this may raise another problem: if the joint venture investor and the joint venture company are both Chinese legal entities, then in the absence of any foreign element,[29] the contracts between these parties cannot provide for arbitration in a foreign seat or by a foreign arbitration institution outside the PRC's territory (*see* the relevant explanations in sections 5.3.2.1 and 5.3.2.2). Consequently, a more comprehensive and concrete approach for foreign investors is to demand that the foreign investors become the signing parties to all the contracts between the Chinese investors and the joint venture company. This can be in the form of the foreign investor undertaking actions that are relevant and necessary for the joint venture company to fulfil its obligations under the relevant contract, which provide this contract with a foreign element (as the foreign joint investor is one of the parties). The relevant contract should also provide for arbitration in a foreign seat or by a foreign arbitration institution outside the PRC's territory. Using the *Hemofarm* case to illustrate, if the foreign investors were added as the parties to the Land Lease Agreement (such as the foreign investors' contractual undertaking to take actions that are relevant and necessary for the joint venture company to fulfil its obligations under the Land Lease Agreement), and if the Land Lease Agreement had provided for submitting disputes arising under or in connection with the Land Lease Agreement to ICC arbitration (akin to Article 58 of the JVC), then Yongning would have to pursue ICC arbitration in accordance with this arbitration clause and could not litigate in the PRC courts when claiming rent from the joint venture company. Since the parties in the *Hemofarm* case did not make these arrangements and did not provide for an arbitration clause, it was not improper for the PRC courts to assume jurisdiction over disputes arising from the Land Lease Agreement (i.e., Yongning's rent claim against the joint venture company).

---

28. Kun Fan, *Arbitration in China: A Legal and Cultural Analysis* 112 (Hart Publishing 2013).
29. Please *see* the discussions on 'foreign elements' in Ch. 3 s. 3.2.2.1.

Chapter 5: Mainland China's Departure from International Consensus

(2) The Third Point of Contention

The third point of contention arises from the arbitral tribunal's view that Yongning's *application for and acquisition of* the property preservation orders from the PRC courts did not have any legal or commercial justifications. According to similar discussions by Professor Xiuwen Zhao:[30]

> But in China, arbitral tribunals have no rights to grant preservation orders over property situated within our country, as such orders are exclusive to the PRC courts in accordance with the PRC law. This ICC award stated that Yongning's application for the issuance and enforcement of the preservation orders by the PRC courts according to the PRC law had 'no legal nor commercial justification for the application for the issuance and enforcement of the preservation orders'. This *clearly disregards the current law of this country, challenges the PRC courts' exclusive jurisdiction to issue and enforce preservation orders for property situated in this country*, and therefore violates the social and public interest of this country. Arbitral awards that are contrary to the social and public interest of this country should be refused recognition and enforcement by this country's courts pursuant to the law of this country. [emphasis added]

(3) The Fourth Point of Contention

The fourth point contends that the PRC courts' preservation orders led to the termination of the joint venture's operation and other consequences, which practically denied the justiciability and legality of the PRC court decisions to seize and detain the joint venture company's assets. This is reflected in the Shandong Higher People's Court's Request for Instructions to the SPC:[31] 'the Chinese court decided on Yongning's application for preservation orders, yet the arbitral tribunal believed that the enforcement of such preservation orders issued by the Chinese court in the litigations was the most direct and immediate cause of the failure and eventual termination of the operations of the joint venture company, thereby effectively denying the justiciability and legality of the PRC court's preservation orders'.

Whether the PRC courts' preservation orders caused the termination of the joint venture company's operations and whether the PRC orders for seizing and detaining the joint venture company's assets are justiciable and legal are two distinct issues in the author's view. The former is a question of fact: did the PRC court's preservation orders in fact lead to the termination of the joint venture company's operations, or were there other causes of termination? The latter is a question of law concerning justiciability and legality. Moreover, the information required to determine these two different matters is not the same. The former examines the relevant facts after the PRC court granted Yongning's application to seize and detain the joint venture company's assets to determine whether or not the enforcement of such preservation orders caused the termination of the joint venture company's operations. The latter examines the facts at the time of Yongning's application for preservation orders to determine whether or not

---

30. Xiuwen Zhao, *Research on Modernization of International Commercial Arbitration* 318–319 (Law Press 2010).
31. (2007) Lu-Min-Si-Ta-Zi No. 12, 30 January 2008.

the grounds for granting preservation orders were established in accordance with the PRC Civil Procedure Law.[32] Thus it is indeed difficult to see how one can conclude that the arbitral tribunal denied the justiciability and legality of the PRC court orders for seizing and detaining the joint venture company's assets merely from the arbitral tribunal's comment that the enforcement of the PRC court's preservation orders resulted in the termination of the joint venture company's operations.

(4) The Fifth Point of Contention

The fifth point contends that the arbitral tribunal's order against Yongning to compensate the litigation costs paid for the joint venture company by the three co-claimants objectively negated the res judicata effect of the PRC court judgments on litigation costs concerning the lease disputes. Again this correlates with the Shandong Higher People's Court's Request for Instructions to the SPC:[33] 'the arbitral tribunal's order against Yongning to compensate the three co-claimants' litigation costs in the PRC infringes the PRC court's jurisdiction to award costs. The PRC courts had already decided on costs allocation in the four litigations between Yongning and the joint venture company, but the arbitral tribunal still ordered Yongning to compensate the three co-claimants' related litigation costs, which also negated the res judicata effect of the PRC court judgments'. This point of contention seems justified at first glance; however, parts of it appear questionable after a closer scrutiny.

Although the co-claimants requested USD 182,951.13 with respect to litigation costs during the arbitration proceedings, after the hearings the arbitral tribunal held that this was the total amount charged by the law firm Chen & Co., which would be divided into two portions: one relevant to the litigations and the other irrelevant to the litigations. The portion relating to the litigations was calculated as USD 63,397.10. The tribunal then considered the co-claimants' conduct which provoked Yongning to initiate the litigations, and, pursuant to the theory of contributory negligence, ordered Yongning to reimburse the co-complaints 30% of half of USD 63,397.10 (or the amount of USD 9,509.55), 30% being Yongning's shareholding ratio in the joint venture company.

It can be seen from the arbitral tribunal's calculation and explanation that the amount awarded to the co-claimants was actually the legal fees paid to Chen & Co. by the co-claimants in defending the joint venture company in litigations initiated by Yongning, which was apportioned to 30% in accordance with Yongning's shareholding ratio in the joint venture company. The tribunal then further divided this 30% by half, in consideration of the co-claimants' conduct in provoking Yongning to commence the litigations pursuant to the theory of contributory negligence.

However, pursuant to Article 118 of the PRC Civil Procedure Law, 'litigation expenses' referred to in Article 152(3) means litigation costs paid by the parties to the PRC courts in accordance with Article 6 of the Measures on the Payment of Litigation

---

32. The 2007 version of the PRC Civil Procedure Law was in effect at the time of the case, in which Ch. 9 stipulated the preservation provisions.
33. (2007) Lu-Min-Si-Ta-Zi No. 12, 30 January 2008.

Costs, including:[34] '(1) case acceptance fee; (2) application fee; and (3) the traffic expenses, accommodation expenses, living expenses, and subsidies for missed work, as incurred by witnesses, authenticators, interpreters and adjustment makers for appearing in the people's court at designated dates'. These do not include lawyers' fees. It is thus evident that the reimbursement of lawyers' fees paid to Chen & Co. awarded by the arbitral tribunal against Yongning was different from the 'litigation costs' as provided in the PRC Civil Procedure Law, and therefore was also unrelated to the PRC court judgment on loading/sharing of litigation costs.

Since the arbitral tribunal believed that Yongning abused its right by initiating the PRC court proceedings, its non-compliance with the fairness principle and the legal duty to mitigate the loss to the joint venture company forced the co-claimants to advance the legal fees to Chen & Co. for defending the joint venture company in order to protect their interests in the joint venture company. According to the arbitral tribunal's logic, such legal fees paid by the co-complaints were caused by Yongning's initiation of court proceedings without any legal or commercial justifications. Regardless of whether the PRC courts ruled in favour of Yongning, the co-complaints would incur such legal fees by engaging lawyers to defend the joint venture company. Originally Yongning should bear 30% of such legal fees in accordance to its 30% shareholdings in the joint venture company, yet the arbitral tribunal only ordered Yongning to reimburse half (rather than 100%) of this amount, after considering the co-complaints' contributory negligence in their conducts which provoked Yongning to commence the litigations.

Hence the costs ordered by the arbitral award in this regard had no connection with the PRC court decisions on litigation costs with respect to the First, Second and Third Litigations and the Land Lease Litigation, and it would seem inappropriate to find that the arbitral award has 'interfered with the rights of the PRC courts in apportioning litigation costs'.[35] The fifth point of contention, namely, the arbitral tribunal's order against Yongning to compensate the litigation costs paid for the joint venture company by the three co-claimants objectively negated the res judicata effect of PRC court judgments on litigation costs concerning the lease disputes, is arguably illogical and questionable. Yet another noteworthy question is whether the co-claimants' claim against Yongning with respect to their payment of PRC litigation costs on the joint venture company's behalf was within the scope of the arbitration clause in the JVC. Neither the SPC's reply nor the Shandong Higher People's Court's reporting opinion appears to analyse from this point of view.

---

34. Article 118 of PRC Civil Procedure Law and Art. 6 of PRC Measure on the Payment of Litigation Costs, Order of the State Council No. 481, effective from 1 April 2007.
35. This was the view of the Shandong Higher People's Court as cited from Shandong Higher People's Court's Request for Instructions on the Non-recognition and Non-enforcement of an Arbitral Award of the ICC International Court of Arbitration (2007) Lu-Min-Si-Ta-Zi No. 12, 30 January 2008.

5.2.1.3 Reviewing the SPC's Reply Letter

It is worth reviewing the SPC's comments on 'public policy' in light of the above analyses:

> The PRC courts had previously issued property preservation orders and decided on the lease disputes between Yongning and the joint venture company. Given this, the ICC tribunal's hearing and ruling on the same lease disputes between Yongning and the joint venture infringed the judicial sovereignty of the PRC and the jurisdiction of the PRC courts.

There are three specifically noteworthy points from the SPC's decision that enforcing the ICC award would violate PRC public policy.

First, if the arbitral tribunal's decision differs from that of the PRC court on the same matter, the PRC court may regard the arbitral award's enforcement as contrary to PRC public policy. For instance, some scholars believe that the SPC in the *Hemofarm* case refused to enforce the ICC award on the basis of PRC public policy violation because the ICC tribunal 'made an award which was contrary to the court judgment':[36]

> The arbitral tribunal retried and re-determined the same disputes which were already tried and determined by the PRC courts, essentially allowing its arbitral jurisdiction to override the court jurisdiction, and supervising the PRC courts' jurisdiction through reopening decided cases. This is severe infringement of the PRC's judicial sovereignty and the PRC courts' jurisdiction; this is severe violation of the PRC public policy... Arbitration institutions cannot supervise the courts. They cannot accept and adjudicate on decided cases, and they cannot make awards that are contrary to the court decisions... The ICC disregarded the PRC's judicial sovereignty and the PRC courts' jurisdiction by accepting and hearing disputes which the parties did not submit to arbitration and which the PRC courts already decided. Its arbitral award severely violated the PRC public policy and should be refused recognition and enforcement.

Similar views were adopted by some foreign scholars, who classified this case as an example of violating the res judicata principle and therefore violating public policy under Article V(2)(b) of the New York Convention.[37]

Yet there are cases with contrary opinion in the PRC judicial practice. An example is the *Mitsui* case,[38] in which the Hainan Higher People's Court decided on 9 March 2001 the dispute arising under the contract between Hainan Textile (Hainan Textile Industry General Corporation) and the Hainan Qionghai Polyester Factory (Polyester Factory).[39] The Court held that Article 9 of the Contract was partially invalid. The

---

36. Xiangquan Qi, *Study on the Recognition and Enforcement of Foreign Arbitral Awards* 328 (Law Press 2010); *see also*: Wei Gao, Res Judicata in Relationship Between State Courts and Arbitral Tribunals, 6 The Jurist 162–163 (2010).
37. Herbert Kronke & Patricia Nacimiento et al., *The New York Convention: Recognition and Enforcement of Foreign Arbitral Awards* 393 (Kluwer Law International 2010).
38. For the details of the *Mitsui* case, please *see* Ch. 4 s. 4.2.2.2.
39. Cited from Hainan Higher People's Court's Request for Instructions on the Hainan Haikou Intermediate People's Court's Non-recognition and Non-enforcement of No. 060/1999 Arbitral Award of the Arbitration Institute of the Stockholm Chamber of Commerce (2001) Qiong-Jing-Fu-Zi No. 1, 5 April 2001.

Chapter 5: Mainland China's Departure from International Consensus

relevant parts held invalid were: 'the contract price as JPY 2,436,974,490 plus specified interest and HKD 440,480 plus specified interest and the price should be paid in Japanese currency and Hong Kong currency respectively'. The contract also provided that: 'the above contracted principal and interest in Japanese Yen, as authorized by Party A (Polyester Factory), should be paid to Japanese Mitsui Co., Ltd. by Party B (Hainan Textile). The principal and interest in Hong Kong Dollar, as authorized by Party A (Polyester Factory), should be paid to Nelson Enterprises (Timber) Company Limited, a HK company within their respective agreed periods.' The Hainan Higher People's Court in its Request for Instructions to SPC states that: *'recognising and enforcing a debt that was already determined to be invalid or nonexistent in the court of the enforcement State and the resulting legal and social consequences should be seen as violating that enforcement State's public policy.* Thus it constitutes the legal ground for refusing recognition and enforcement of foreign arbitral awards under Article V(2) of the New York Convention'.[40] Yet the SPC disagreed and ruled that the Hainan court should not refuse recognition and enforcement based on public policy violation.

Second, when a foreign tribunal and PRC courts have different views on the validity of an arbitration agreement, it seems that PRC courts take into consideration of the timing when a foreign tribunal renders its award: is the foreign award rendered before or after the PRC courts rule that same arbitration agreement is invalid? In the *Reply of the Supreme People's Court to the Request for Instructions Re Application of Castel Electronics Pty Ltd. for Recognition and Enforcement of an Foreign Arbitral Award* (the *Castel* case),[41] the SPC clearly indicated that:

> The arbitral awards were made on 23 December 2010 and 27 January 2011; while the PRC court's ruling that the arbitration agreement in dispute was invalid was rendered on 20 December 2011. It is obvious that the arbitral awards were made before the PRC's court ruling became effective. Moreover, TCL company did not raise any jurisdictional objection during the arbitral proceedings on the grounds that the underlying arbitration agreement was invalid. Instead, TCL company submitted counterclaims to the arbitral tribunal, which accordingly confirmed the validity of the arbitration agreement and its jurisdiction. This is in compliance with the arbitration law and arbitration rules of the seat of arbitration and does not violate the PRC's judicial sovereignty. .... In this case, the inconsistency/conflict existing between the foreign arbitral award and effective PRC court ruling about the validity of the same arbitration clause nevertheless did not suffice to constitute violation of the public policy of this country.

In contrast, in the *Wicor* case,[42] where Wicor Holding AG applied with the Jiangsu Taizhou Intermediate People's Court for the recognition and enforcement of

---

40. *Ibid.*
41. (2013) Min-Si-Ta-Zi No. 46, 10 October 2013.
42. Jiangsu Taizhou Intermediate People's Court Civil Ruling (2015) Tai-Zhong-Shang-Zhong-Shen-Zi No. 00004, 2 June 2016. Before Jiangsu Higher People's Court rendered its Civil Ruling (2012) Su-Shang-Wai-Xia-Zhong-Zi No 0012 that the arbitration agreement was invalid, it had reported the case to the SPC. *See* SPC's Reply to the Jiangsu Higher People's Court at: Reply of the Supreme People's Court on Request for Instructions on Sino-foreign Joint Venture Contract Dispute between Taizhou Hope Investment Co., Ltd. and Wicor Holding AG, (2012) Min-Si-Ta-Zi No. 6, 1 March 2016.

18295/CKY arbitral awards respectively rendered on 18 July 2014 and 27 November 2014 by the ICC International Court of Arbitration in Hong Kong, the Jiangsu Taizhou Intermediate People's Court held that:

> When Jiangsu Higher People's Court had heard another dispute between Wicor Holding AG and Taizhou Hope Investment Co., Ltd. arising from the 'Sino-foreign Taizhou Huawei Insulation Materials Co. Ltd. Joint Venture Contract', it held on 11 December 2012 in its Civil Ruling (2012) Su-Shang-Wai-Xia-Zhong-Zi No 0012 that the arbitration agreement in dispute was invalid. This Civil Ruling has come into force. However, the arbitrator rendered the arbitral award under the condition precedent that the arbitral agreement was valid. Enforcing the arbitral award in Mainland China would contravene with the above effective Court Ruling and thus, violate the social and public interest. Therefore, this court held that the arbitral award should not be enforced; pursuant to Article 7.3 of the 'SPC's Arrangement Concerning Mutual Enforcement of Arbitral Awards Between the Mainland and the Hong Kong Special Administration Region' and Article 154 paragraph 1 item (11) of the SPC's Civil Procedure Law, the court has decided not to enforce the 18295/CKY arbitral awards respectively rendered on 18 July 2014 and 27 November 2014 by the ICC International Court of Arbitration.

In light of the author's comparative analysis of the *Hemofarm* case, *Mitsui* case, *Castel* case and *Wicor* case, if the content of an arbitral award negates or opposes to a PRC court judgment or ruling, then depending on the circumstances of each case, the PRC court may, but not necessarily, refuse to recognise and enforce such an award on the basis of PRC public policy violation. The court may reach different decisions in individual cases.

Third, the *Liupanshui* case, *Chao Lai Xin Sheng* case and *Leaf Confectionery* case all relate to the scope of the PRC court's jurisdiction and the respect for it. The *Castel* case and *Wicor* case also indirectly related to the scope of the PRC court's jurisdiction as it involved different decisions by the arbitral tribunal and the PRC court on the validity of an arbitration clause. The difference between these cases is that, the *Liupanshui* case, *Chao Lai Xin Sheng* case and *Leaf Confectionery* case all concerned the issue of whether foreign elements were involved, as disputes without foreign elements cannot be submitted to arbitration by arbitration institutions outside the PRC's territory. In the author's opinion, this is a very important feature which warrants all comprehensive discussions in section 5.3 of this chapter. By contrast, the circumstances in the *Castel* case and *Wicor* case were different, as one of the parties involved in both cases were foreign companies and thus, there were foreign elements in both cases.[43] Therefore, the *Castel* case and *Wicor* case did not involve the submission of dispute without foreign element to arbitration outside the PRC's territory.

---

43. In the *Castel* case, Castel Electronics Pty Ltd. is an Australian company and in the *Wicor* case, Wicor Holding AG is a Swiss company.

Chapter 5: Mainland China's Departure from International Consensus

5.2.2 *Louis Dreyfus* Case: Arbitral Tribunal's Misconception of Whether There Exists Significant Gaps Between PRC Laws and Their Practical Application

5.2.2.1 *Case Summary*

In the Reply of the Supreme People's Court on Request for Instructions Re Application of Louis Dreyfus Commodities Asian Co., Ltd. for Recognition and Enforcement of Arbitration Award No. 3980 of International Federation of Oils, Seeds & Fats Associations (the *Louis Dreyfus* case),[44] the Federation of Oils, Seeds and Fats Associations (FOSFA) made an award concerning a contract for the sale of soybeans between Louis Dreyfus (Louis Dreyfus Commodities Asian Co., Ltd.) and Fuhong (Guangdong Fuhong Edible Oil Co. Ltd.) on 29 August 2007 in London. The award states:[45] 'There is a very significant gap between the stipulation of PRC laws and their application in practice, the details relating to PRC law provisions are ultimately not very important. Chinese laws and regulations are complex regardless of viewing them from which angle. Just as any supervisory system can influence certain international sale and purchase contract, what matters to the parties is not how the local laws should be interpreted, but how these laws are applied in practice.'

Upon Louis Dreyfus' application for this award's recognition and enforcement, the Zhanjiang Intermediate People's Court responded to the above statement in the award: 'the reasons in that award severely challenge the authoritativeness of the laws and regulations of this country and violate the public policy of this country'. The case was reported to the Guangdong Higher People's Court, in which the majority of the collegiate bench agreed with the Zhanjiang court and held that 'the arbitral award's negative assessment and misinterpretation of the law of this country infringe upon the authoritativeness of the laws and regulations of this country and violate the public policy of this country, consequently falling within the grounds for non-recognition and non-enforcement in Article V(2)(b) of the New York Convention'. By contrast the minority of the collegiate bench stated: 'although the arbitrator made improper assessment of the law of this country, however the consequences of recognising and enforcing this award would not lead to a violation of this country's public policy, thus the award does not violate the public policy of this country'.

After the case was reported to the SPC, the SPC stated,[46] 'the arbitrator believed that there exists significant gaps between the stipulation and the practical application of PRC laws, but such misconception may not cause the award's recognition and enforcement to be contrary to PRC public policy. Hence there is insufficient evidence for refusing to recognize and enforce this award on the basis of public policy'.

---

44. (2010) Min-Si-Ta-Zi No. 48, 10 October 2010.
45. The discussions in this arbitral award were cited from Guangdong Higher People's Court's Request for Instructions Re Application for Recognition and Enforcement of a Foreign Arbitration Award Concerning Louis Dreyfus Commodities Asian Co., Ltd. and Guangdong Fuhong Edible Oil Co. Ltd., (2009) Yue-Gao-Fa-Min-Si-Ta-Zi No. 10, 20 June 2010.
46. *Supra* n. 44.

5.2.2.2 Comment

As the *Louis Dreyfus* case demonstrates, even if the arbitral award contains comments such as 'a very significant gap exists between the stipulation of PRC laws and their application in practice', and even though the SPC regards such comments as 'misconception', the SPC may not necessarily regard the enforcement of such award as being contrary to PRC public policy.

5.2.3 *Guangxia Culture* Case: Arbitral Tribunal's Disapproval of PRC Administrative Decisions

5.2.3.1 Case Summary

Although the *Guangxia Culture* case concerned the non-enforcement of a *foreign-related* award rather than recognition and enforcement of a *foreign* award, its comparison and contrast with the *Hemofarm* case concerning recognition and enforcement of a foreign award warrant further analysis.

In the Reply of the Supreme People's Court on the Non-enforcement of an Arbitral Award concerning Shenzhen Guangxia Culture Industry Company, Ningxia Islamic International Trust and Investment Company, Shenzhen Xingqing Electronics Company and Misuer Co., Ltd.,[47] CIETAC rendered an award on 30 July 1996 (No. 0271 of 1996) on the joint venture dispute between Guangxia (Shenzhen Guangxia Culture Industry Company), Ningxia (Ningxia Islamic International Trust and Investment Company), Xingqing (Shenzhen Xingqing Electronics Company) and Misuer (Misuer Co., Ltd.). The award ordered the three applicants (Guangxia, Ningxia and Xingqing) to pay USD 1.6 million to the respondent (Misuer) with interest at an annual rate of 8% in case of overdue payment. The tribunal dismissed the other claims from both sides and ordered the applicants to pay the arbitration fees of CNY 20,950 and the respondent to pay the arbitration fees of CNY 145,800 for its counterclaim and actual costs.

On 9 September 1996, the three applicants (Guangxia, Ningxia and Xingqing) applied to the Beijing Second Intermediate People's Court to set aside the award on the grounds of procedural and substantive errors. On 29 July 1997, the Beijing court suspended the revocation proceedings and notified CIETAC to re-arbitrate, because the three applicants were unable to present their case in the arbitral proceedings for reasons not attributable to the applicants. On 30 June 1998, CIETAC made a new award to maintain its previous award (Mao-Zhong-Cai-Zi No. 0271 of 1996) and stipulated that this new award constituted a part of the original award. After this new award came into effect, Misuer applied to the Shenzhen Intermediate People's Court for enforcement. The three applicants applied respectively to the Beijing Second Intermediate People's Court and Shenzhen Intermediate People's Court for non-enforcement and

---

47. Reply of the Supreme People's Court on the Non-enforcement of an Arbitral Award Concerning Guangxia Culture Industry Company, Ningxia Islamic International Trust and Investment Company, Shenzhen Xingqing Electronics Company and Misuer Co., Ltd., (2000) Zhi-Jian-Zi No. 96-2, 20 April 2002.

Chapter 5: Mainland China's Departure from International Consensus

revocation of the award, which were both unsuccessful. The Shenzhen Intermediate People's Court then made a ruling to seize the applicants' relevant property. The three applicants appealed to the SPC.

In their appeal the applicants raised both substantive and procedural defects. The alleged substantive defects are unrelated to public policy and therefore omitted from discussion. The alleged procedural defects primarily relate to page 26 of the arbitral award:[48]

> In the opinion of this arbitral tribunal, the applicants obtained a capital verification report inconsistent with the facts through improper means, and filed a request with the relevant government department for change of shareholders based thereon. The aforesaid administrative decision made by the relevant government department was the result of tortious acts of the applicants and in no way of an isolated administrative act, so the applicants cannot escape the tortious liability they should assume on the excuse of an administrative act of an administrative organization.

In addition to substantive defects, the applicants raised various serious procedural defects including lack of jurisdiction, specifically the Shenzhen Administration for Industry and Commerce's notice to Misuer on 26 August 1992 about Misuer's breach of contract due to its failure to make capital contribution, followed by the Shenzhen Administration for Industry and Commerce's decision on 3 November 1992 to disqualify Misuer as shareholder of the joint venture company. They argued that such administrative acts were within the Shenzhen Administration for Industry and Commerce's scope of authority and were in accordance with the law. Nonetheless the arbitral tribunal disregarded these administrative decisions by deciding that Misuer had complied with its contribution obligations.

On 27 October 2000, the Enforcement Office of the SPC (later renamed as Enforcement Bureau of the SPC)[49] established a panel of judges to discuss the case. The panel unanimously held that the award's enforcement should be refused because the arbitral tribunal had no right to deny administrative decisions made by the administrative authorities in accordance with the law; the tribunal arbitrated beyond its authority and violated PRC public policy. Yet the SPC subsequently decided to have another panel discussion on 17 July 2001 due to national concern over this case. The panel found that the arbitral tribunal exceeded the scope of arbitration and the award should be refused enforcement under Article 260 (currently Article 274) of the PRC Civil Procedure Law. In order to prudently address the views of other authorities and departments, including the Federation of Returned Overseas Chinese, the panel recommended referral to the SPC's Judicial Committee for further consideration.

---

48. Excerpted from Reply of the Supreme People's Court on the Non-enforcement of an Arbitral Award Concerning Guangxia Culture Industry Company, Ningxia Islamic International Trust and Investment Company, Shenzhen Xingqing Electronics Company and Misuer Co., Ltd. (2000) Zhi-Jian-Zi No. 96-2, 20 April 2002.
49. Notice of the Supreme People's Court Regarding Renaming the Enforcement Office of Supreme People's Court to the Enforcement Bureau, Fa-Fa (2008) 31, 8 October 2008.

On 4 March 2002 the SPC's Judicial Committee in its 1217th meeting deliberated and ruled against enforcing the award, because the subject matter of this case was tort liability, which was not within the arbitral tribunal's jurisdiction pursuant to the CIETAC Arbitration Rules, and because the arbitral tribunal exceeded its authority by negating the decisions made by the administrative authorities. In its Reply of the Supreme People's Court on the Non-enforcement of an Arbitral Award concerning Shenzhen Guangxia Culture Industry Company, Ningxia Islamic International Trust and Investment Company, Shenzhen Xingqing Electronics Company and Misuer Co., Ltd., the SPC pointed out the following two procedural defects in the award:[50]

> Firstly, the arbitrated matter in the arbitral award was beyond the scope of arbitration. The arbitral award (1996) Mao-Zhong-Cai-Zi No. 0271 of CIETAC confirmed that Misuer Company had fulfilled its obligation of contribution to the joint venture company, which factually denied the conclusion of the Shenzhen Administration for Industry and Commerce that Misuer Company failed to make contribution as per the time limit and amount under the Joint Venture Contract and therefore breached the contract; and at the same time, violated the decision of the Shenzhen Municipal People's Government on cancellation of the shareholder eligibility of Misuer Company. If a joint venture company deems that a shareholder fails to make contribution in full, it may, according to its by-laws and other relevant provisions, apply to the relevant administrative department for the replacement or cancellation of eligibility of the shareholder, and the administrative organ may make an administrative decision according to law after examination. *An arbitral tribunal shall not be entitled to rule on the legality of an administrative decision legally made by an administrative organ. In accordance with Article 260 [currently Article 274] paragraph 1 item (4) of the Civil Procedure Law, the matter arbitrated by the said arbitral tribunal was beyond the scope of arbitration, and the arbitral tribunal had no authority to arbitrate the matter at issue.*
>
> Secondly, the contents of the arbitral award violated the arbitration rules. Article 2 of the Arbitration Rules of the China International Economic and Trade Arbitration Commission provides that 'The China International Economic and Trade Arbitration Commission independently and impartially resolves, by means of arbitration, disputes arising from international or foreign-related economic and trade transactions of a contractual or non-contractual nature.' As one may see, the cases arbitrated by arbitral tribunals are limited to civil and commercial disputes of a contractual or non-contractual nature, and arbitral tribunals do not have the authority to arbitrate cases involving tort disputes. The arbitral tribunal in this case held in the award that the specific administrative acts of the government departments were results of tortious acts of the three applicants; that is to say, it deemed that the replacement of shareholders by the joint venture company with the approval of the governmental departments was a tort. Accordingly, it made an award that the three applicants should assume tort liability. The aforesaid award of the arbitration tribunal clearly violated the relevant provisions of the Arbitration Rules of the China International Economic and Trade Arbitration Commission on jurisdiction.

---

50. Cited from Reply of the Supreme People's Court on the Non-enforcement of an Arbitral Award Concerning Shenzhen Guangxia Culture Industry Company, Ningxia Islamic International Trust and Investment Company, Shenzhen Xingqing Electronics Company and Misuer Co., Ltd, *supra* n. 44.

Chapter 5: Mainland China's Departure from International Consensus

Accordingly, the SPC's Reply explicitly stated:[51] 'The Shenzhen Intermediate People's Court shall revoke its Ruling (1998) Shen-Zhong-Fa-Jing-Er-Chu-Zi No. 97 and at the same time, make a ruling not to enforce the award (1996) Mao-Zhong-Cai-Zi No. 0271 of CIETAC.' The SPC also instructed the Guangdong Higher People's Court:[52] 'After receipt of this Reply, please immediately urge the Shenzhen Intermediate People's Court to act according to the opinions expressed in this Reply and report the execution of this Reply.' This shows the SPC did not refuse the award's enforcement on the grounds of 'contrary to social and public interest', but did so on the grounds that the arbitral tribunal arbitrated matter 'beyond the scope of arbitration' and the 'contents of the arbitral award violated the arbitration rules'.

5.2.3.2 *Comment*

In the *Guangxia Culture* case, the Shenzhen Administration for Industry and Commerce cancelled Misuer's shareholder eligibility for failure to make contribution in accordance with the time limit and amount specified in the JVC, but the arbitral tribunal ruled that Misuer had fulfilled its contribution obligation and effectively denied the decision of the Shenzhen Administration for Industry and Commerce. The SPC once had two different views on which grounds for non-enforcement in Article 274 of the PRC Civil Procedure Law should apply.

One view is that the arbitral tribunal had no right to deny administrative decisions and no authority to arbitrate the disputed matter, and it also violated PRC public policy, thus falling with Article 274 paragraph 1 item (4) and paragraph 2. This was the unanimous decision reached by the panel of judges at the SPC Enforcement Office on 27 October 2000.

The other view is that Article 274 paragraph 1 item (4) regarding lack of authority to arbitrate was applicable. This view was ultimately adopted by the SPC's Judicial Committee.

In comparison, the contents of the SPC's Reply in the *Hemofarm* case can be divided into two parts. The first half stated that the arbitral tribunal '*went beyond the applicable scope of the arbitration clause in the Joint Venture Contract*' by hearing and deciding on the disputes regarding the lease agreement between Yongning and the joint venture company. The second half held that: 'The relevant Chinese courts had previously issued property preservation orders and entered judgments regarding the lease disputes between Jinan Yongning Pharmaceutical Co., Ltd. and the joint venture company, Jinan-Hemofarm Pharmaceutical Co., Ltd. Given this, the ICC International Court of Arbitration's hearing and ruling on the same lease disputes between Yongning and the joint venture company, Jinan-Hemofarm Pharmaceutical Co., Ltd., *infringed the judicial sovereignty of the PRC and the jurisdiction of the PRC courts*. The recognition and enforcement of the ICC award No. 13464/MS/JB/JEM should be refused under Articles V(1)(c) and (2)(b) of the New York Convention.' The SPC ultimately refused

---

51. *Supra* n. 44.
52. *Ibid.*

the ICC award's enforcement on the grounds of public policy violation, without using the grounds in Article V(1)(c) of the New York Convention about the award containing 'decisions on matters beyond the scope of the submission to arbitration'. Hence it has been suggested that the *Hemofarm* case could have used the grounds of exceeding the scope of arbitration in Article V(1)(c) of the New York Convention to refuse enforcement, without the need to rely on the public policy ground in Article V(2)(b) of the New York Convention.[53] Nevertheless, Justice Xiaolong Lu (President of the SPC Fourth Tribunal) and Justice Xifu Yu (from the Shandong Higher People's Court involved in this case) both stated:[54] 'The cautious use of public policy means that public policy should neither be misused nor be unused. The New York Convention entitles the enforcement court or other authorities to refuse recognition and enforcement of foreign arbitral awards on the ground of contravention of the enforcement State's public policy. When this happens, the enforcement court or other authorities should righteously use this public policy ground in the New York Convention to protect the interests of the enforcement State and its people. Doing so does not harm the enforcement State's authority and image at all, as it is truly implementing the New York Convention's obligations and safeguarding the system of international commercial arbitration.' Thus the SPC invoked Article V(1)(c) together with Article V(2)(b) of the New York Convention in the *Hemofarm* case.

5.2.4 Summary

The following four conclusions stem from the analysis of the relevant cases (*Hemofarm*, *Mitsui*, *Castel*, *Wicor*, *Louis Dreyfus*, and *Guangxia Culture*) in section 5.2 of this chapter:

(1) The arbitral tribunal's general comment in a foreign award that 'there is a significant gap between the stipulation and practical application of PRC law provisions' (e.g., the *Louis Dreyfus* case) may not cause the PRC court to conclude that such award's enforcement would violate PRC public policy.
(2) Arbitral decisions that are different from or even opposite to the administrative decisions on specific cases (e.g., the *Guangxia Culture* case) also may not prompt the PRC court to conclude that a foreign-related award's enforcement would violate PRC social and public interest. Yet it does not necessarily follow that the protection given by the SPC to administrative decisions is weaker than the protection given to judicial sovereignty. Although the SPC in the *Guangxia Culture* case did not refuse enforcement of the foreign-related award for reason of contravening social and public interest, the SPC

---

53. Cited from *supra* n. 25, at 405.
54. *Ibid.*

Chapter 5: Mainland China's Departure from International Consensus

clarified:[55] 'An arbitral tribunal shall not be entitled to rule on the legality of an administrative decision legally made by an administrative organ.' Thus the foreign-related award's enforcement was refused on the grounds that 'the arbitrated matter was beyond the scope of arbitration' under the current Article 274 paragraph 1 item (4) of the PRC Civil Procedure Law.

(3) Arbitral awards that are contrary to specific decisions by the PRC courts (e.g., the *Mitsui* case, *Castel* case and *Hemofarm* case) seem to engender inconsistent views within the SPC depending on the circumstances of each case. In the *Castel* case, where the foreign arbitral award was made before the Zhongshan Intermediate People's Court ruled that the arbitration agreement in dispute was invalid. The SPC held that: 'the inconsistency existing between the foreign arbitral award and effective PRC court ruling about the validity of the same arbitration clause nevertheless did not suffice to constitute violation of the PRC's public policy'. However, in the *Wicor* case, where the Jiangsu Higher People's Court held that the arbitration agreement in dispute was invalid before the Hong Kong awards were made, the Taizhou Intermediate People's Court held that: '[e]nforcing the arbitral award in Mainland China would contravene with the above effective Court Ruling and thus, violate the social and public interest.'

(4) In the *Mitsui* case, the content of the arbitral award upheld a debt that was previously held to be invalid by PRC courts, yet the SPC was against refusing this award's enforcement on the basis of PRC public policy violation. On the other hand, in the *Hemofarm* case, the SPC held that the arbitral tribunal infringed 'the PRC's judicial sovereignty and the PRC courts' jurisdiction' by hearing and ruling on the lease disputes that were already decided by the PRC courts, thus refusing the award's enforcement for reason of PRC public policy violation. As extrapolated from the *Hemofarm* case, if the content of an award is not only contrary to specific PRC court decisions but the award has also determined and even criticised specific PRC court decisions with comments that such decided matters belong to the arbitral tribunal's jurisdiction and should be submitted to arbitration, then the PRC courts would regard such award as infringing the PRC's judicial sovereignty and the PRC courts' jurisdiction.[56] Such award's enforcement would violate PRC public policy and should therefore be refused under Article V(2)(b) of the New York Convention. As will be seen in the following section 5.3 of this Chapter, the *Liupanshui* case, *Chao Lai Xin Sheng* case and *Leaf Confectionery* case[57] present similar views on the scope of the PRC's judicial sovereignty.

---

55. Cited from Reply of the Supreme People's Court on the Non-enforcement of an Arbitral Award Concerning Shenzhen Guangxia Culture Industry Company, Ningxia Islamic International Trust and Investment Company, Shenzhen Xingqing Electronics Company and Misuer Co., Ltd, *supra* n. 44.
56. Terminology adopted from the SPC's Reply in the *Hemofarm* case, *supra* n. 21.
57. For details of the *Liupanshui* case and the *Leaf Confectionary* case, *see* Ch. 3 s. 3.2.1.3.

5.3 PROTECTION OF PRC'S JUDICIAL SOVEREIGNTY AND JURISDICTION: IN CASES WITHOUT FOREIGN ELEMENTS, PARTIES' AGREEMENTS ON FOREIGN ARBITRATION INSTITUTION OR FOREIGN ARBITRAL SEAT ARE INVALID

The PRC's loss of consular jurisdiction in the nineteenth century may be regarded as one of the most humiliating events in the PRC's modern history.[58] The PRC courts' protection and sensitivity with respect to jurisdiction over foreign-related cases are therefore unsurprising. Safeguarding the PRC's judicial sovereignty and the PRC courts' jurisdiction entails invaliding agreements which submit arbitration to institutions outside the PRC's territory or which do not specify any arbitral seat in cases with foreign elements. Violation of such requirement would result in the PRC courts' invalidation of arbitration agreement on the ground of public policy violation or the PRC court's refusal to recognise and enforce awards made by arbitral tribunals or institutions outside the PRC's territory on the ground of public policy violation.

5.3.1 *Liupanshui* Case, *Chao Lai Xin Sheng* Case and *Leaf Confectionery* Case

In the *Liupanshui* case the SPC stated:[59]

> The mechanisms for resolving civil and commercial disputes which occurred within the territory of a country is a matter of that country's judicial sovereignty and is also part of that country's public policy. The contracting parties shall only be allowed to agree upon mechanisms to the extent permitted by the prevailing laws of that country. Any agreement made arbitrarily which deviates from or goes beyond the scope permitted by the laws of that country shall be deemed invalid due to a violation of the public policies of that country.

As the parties in the *Liupanshui* case of domestic arbitration submitted their disputes to arbitration by the HKIAC, an arbitration institution located outside of the territory of Mainland China rather than a 'foreign' arbitration institution, the SPC stated that 'even within a sovereign nation, public policy considerations should also be assessed in the context of different legal jurisdictions'. According to the SPC:

> Article 255 of the PRC Civil Procedure Law provides:[60] 'Where, for disputes involving foreign economic and trade activities or international transportation or maritime activities, the parties have included an arbitration clause in the contracts or have reached a written arbitration agreement after a dispute arose to refer such

---

58. Bilateral conventions concerning Consular Jurisdiction between the PRC and foreign countries in modern times began with the Treaty of Peace, Friendship and Commerce between Her Majesty the Queen of Great Britain and Ireland and the Emperor of China in 1843 (Art. 13), followed by the Treaty of Wanghia (Peace, Amity and Commerce between the United States of America and the Chinese Empire) in 1844 (Art. 25) and the Treaty of Tien-Tsin between the Queen of Great Britain and the Emperor of China in 1858 (Art. 17), etc.
59. (2010) Min-Er-Zhong-Zi No. 86. For details of the *Liupanshui* case, *see* Ch. 3 s. 3.2.1.
60. Currently Art. 271 of the PRC Civil Procedure Law.

disputes to an international arbitration institution of the People's Republic of China or any other arbitral institution for arbitration, the parties shall not institute an action in a people's court.' Its reference to 'any other arbitral institution' can be understood as arbitration institutions situated outside Mainland China, and its legislative purpose is to confirm that parties to foreign-related civil disputes and with arbitration agreement cannot litigate in the PRC people's courts. Meanwhile, Article 255 of the PRC Civil Procedure Law has also made it clear that only for disputes arising from foreign-related economic, trade, transportation or maritime activities which involve foreign elements, may the parties concerned enter into an arbitration agreement or arbitration clause to submit the dispute for arbitration to an foreign-related arbitration institution of the People's Republic of China or to other arbitration institution. Article 128 (2) of the PRC Contract Law also provides that '[p]arties to a foreign-related contract may apply to a Chinese arbitration institution or other arbitration institution for arbitration'. Again this confirms the principle that only parties to civil cases involving foreign elements may select arbitration institutions outside the territory of Mainland China. In line with these legislative provisions, *if the parties to non-foreign-related disputes have agreed to submit their disputes to arbitration institutions outside the territory of Mainland China, then such an agreement would exceed beyond the permitted legal parameters and would not be valid.* Although the parties' arbitration agreement in this case specified a dispute resolution mechanism and agreed to arbitration by an arbitration institution outside the territory of Mainland China, such agreement is nevertheless invalid because this case is not a foreign-related civil case.

In summary, the SPC in the *Liupanshui* case clearly stated that an arbitration agreement between parties in non-foreign-related civil cases which submits disputes to arbitration by institutions outside the territory of Mainland China would be void because of public policy violation.

According to some scholars,[61] if the parties in a domestic arbitration without any foreign elements choose to arbitrate outside the territory of Mainland China, then for the same reasons, the PRC courts are likely to refuse the resulting arbitral award's recognition and enforcement on the basis of public policy violation. Such type of cases already exists in practice, an example of which is the *Chao Lai Xin Sheng* case (concerning and application by Beijing Chao Lai Xin Sheng Sports and Leisure Co., Ltd. for recognition and enforcement of a foreign arbitral award).[62] This case did not involve any foreign elements and the arbitral award was made by KCAB. The Beijing Second Intermediate People's Court refused to recognise and enforce the arbitral award on the grounds of invalidity of arbitration agreement and violation of public policy under Article V(1)(a) and (2)(b) of the New York Convention. The Shanghai Second Intermediate People's Court in the *Leaf Confectionary* case also adopted the same view.[63] Nevertheless, the Shanghai court did not invalidate the relevant arbitration

---

61. Jingzhou Tao, *Arbitration Law and Practice in China* 121–122 (3rd ed., Wolters Kluwer 2012).
62. Beijing Second Intermediate People's Court Civil Ruling (2013) Er-Zhong-Min-Te-Zi No. 10670, 20 January 2014.
63. For details of the *Leaf Confectionary* case, see Ch. 3 s. 3.2.1.

agreement, because this case did involve a foreign element as one of the parties (named Hanguang Huang) held Malaysian citizenship.

5.3.2 Substantive Differences Between Domestic Arbitration and Foreign-Related Arbitration

Section 3.2.2.1 of Chapter 3 describes the background and criteria for differentiating between domestic arbitration and foreign-related arbitration (such as the existence of foreign elements). According to the SPC, if the parties agree to submit their disputes to an arbitration institution outside the territory of Mainland China or to arbitrate outside the territory of Mainland China in the absence of any foreign elements, then the parties' arbitration agreement would be invalid by virtue of public policy violation. If the parties apply for the PRC courts' recognition and enforcement of the resultant arbitral award, the PRC courts are likely to refuse such application on the basis of public policy violation. The following significant differences explain why the SPC highly values the distinction between domestic arbitration and foreign-related arbitration.

5.3.2.1 Parties to Domestic Arbitration Cannot Submit Disputes to Foreign Arbitration Institutions

It may be recalled that the middle paragraph of Article 128 of the PRC Contract Law[64] provides that '[p]arties to a foreign-related contract may apply to a Chinese arbitration institution or other arbitration institution for arbitration'; while Article 271 of the PRC Civil Procedure Law provides, 'Where, for disputes involving foreign economic and trade activities or international transportation or maritime activities, the parties have included an arbitration clause in the contracts or have reached a written arbitration agreement after a dispute arose to refer such disputes to an international arbitration institution of the People's Republic of China or any other arbitral institution for arbitration, the parties shall not institute an action in a people's court.' An inverse interpretation of the preceding provisions is that parties in domestic cases cannot submit their disputes to arbitration by institutions outside the territory of Mainland China. In addition, the SPC expressly states in its Guide on Foreign-related Commercial and Maritime Trial:[65] 'If domestic parties submit disputes regarding a contract or property rights without any foreign elements to foreign arbitration institutions, the people's courts should regard such an arbitration agreement as invalid.'

Examples of the PRC judicial practice in this regard include the previously mentioned *Liupanshui* case, *Chao Lai Xin Sheng* case and *Leaf Confectionary* case.

---

64. Contract Law of the People's Republic of China, Order of the President of the PRC No. 15, promulgated on 15 March 1999, effective from 1 October 1999.
65. Exiang Wan (editor in chief), the Civil Fourth Tribunal of the Supreme People's Court (ed.), *Answers to Practical Questions on Foreign-Related Commercial and Maritime Trials (I)*, in 7 *Guide on Foreign-Related Commercial and Maritime Trial* 64–65 (People's Court Press 2004).

Chapter 5: Mainland China's Departure from International Consensus

5.3.2.2 Parties to Domestic Arbitration Cannot Seat Their Arbitration Outside the Territory of Mainland China?

Unlike the legal bases for the proposition that parties to domestic arbitration cannot submit disputes to arbitration institutions outside the territory of Mainland China (i.e., the middle paragraph of Article 128 of the PRC Contract Law and Article 271 of the PRC Civil Procedure Law), there are no clear legal bases for the proposition that parties to domestic arbitration cannot agree on an arbitral seat outside the territory of Mainland China.[66] On 31 December 2003, the SPC published 'Provisions of the Supreme People's Court on Handling Foreign-related Arbitration and Foreign Arbitration (draft issued for soliciting public opinions)' through the *People's Court Daily* and the SPC's website.[67] Clause 20 of the Provisions explicitly listed 'domestic parties agreeing to submit disputes without any foreign elements to foreign arbitration' as one of the grounds for invalidating an arbitration agreement, if so requested by one of the parties. Such an express provision was nevertheless absent from the SPC's subsequent publication of its Interpretation of Certain Issues Relating to the Application of the PRC Arbitration Law in 2006.[68]

Yet express provisions can be seen in some local judicial documents. For instance, Article 17 of the Jiangsu Higher People's Court's Opinions on Certain Issues Concerning Judicial Review of Civil and Commercial Arbitration expressly states:[69] 'if the parties agree to submit civil and commercial disputes involving no foreign elements to arbitration by a foreign arbitration institution or in a foreign seat, such an arbitration agreement is invalid'. Similarly, in the Jiangsu Higher People's Court's Third Civil Tribunal's Understanding and Advice on How to Apply the SPC's Interpretation of Certain Issues Relating to the Application of the PRC Arbitration Law, paragraph 3(2) regarding 'the criteria for verifying arbitration agreement's validity' states:[70] 'Pursuant to Article 257 of the PRC Civil Procedure Law and Article 65 of the PRC Arbitration Law,

---

66. Kun Fan, *Arbitration in China: A Legal and Cultural Analysis* 26 (Hart Publishing 2013): This provision (Art. 128 of the *PRC Contract Law*) creates doubts as to whether domestic arbitrations can be seated outside China.
    Jingzhou Tao, *Arbitration Law and Practice in China* 121 (3rd ed., Kluwer Law International 2012): 'in practice, it might be problematic for the parties in a domestic arbitration to choose to arbitrate outside the territory of China'.
67. On 31 December 2003, the SPC published a document through the *People's Court Daily* and the website of the SPC for public consultation on certain provisions for dealing with foreign-related and foreign arbitration. Although this is not a legal document that has officially entered into force, it is nevertheless authoritative in practice, as some lower courts have directly referred to it while some English literature also specifically addresses its content. *See*, e.g., Daniel R. Fung & Shengchang Wang (ed.), *Arbitration in China: A Practical Guide* 769–782 (Sweet & Maxwell 2004).
68. Fa-Shi (2006) No. 7, 23 August 2006.
69. Jiangsu Higher People's Court's Decision to Amend Its Opinions on Certain Issues Concerning Judicial Review of Civil and Commercial Arbitration, passed by the twenty-first meeting of the Jiangsu Higher People's Court's Judicial Committee in 2010 (2010) Su-Gao-Fa-Shen-Wei No. 11, dated 6 September 2010.
70. Cited from the Civil Third Tribunal of Jiangsu Higher People's Court, the Civil Third Tribunal of Jiangsu Higher People's Court's Understanding and Application of 'Interpretation of the Supreme People's Court concerning Some Issues on Application of the Arbitration Law of the People's Republic of China', 62(2) Beijing Arbitration 167–179 (2007).

only foreign-related disputes can be submitted to foreign arbitration institution or arbitration in a foreign seat. Thus the people's courts should regard an arbitration agreement under which the parties agree to submit their disputes involving no foreign elements to arbitration by foreign arbitration institution *or arbitration in a foreign seat* as invalid.'

The PRC courts have indeed held such an arbitration agreement to be invalid. In a case concerning a management agreement between an international company and a hotel management company dated 28 April 1998,[71] clause 27.2 of the agreement provides that any dispute or claim arising from or in connection with this agreement or any breach shall be finally resolved by arbitration. If the arbitral proceedings are initiated by the international company, the seat of arbitration should be Sydney, Australia. In November 2003, the international company commenced proceedings in a Higher People's Court against the management company for its loss arising from the management company's failure to manage the company in accordance with the management agreement. The international company requested the court to terminate the management agreement, evict the management company from the hotel and order the management company to compensate its economic loss and litigation costs. The management company raised jurisdictional objection within the prescribed time limit and applied for dismissal of the court proceedings which were beyond the court's jurisdiction. The court at first instance dismissed the jurisdictional objection on the basis of invalid arbitration agreement, as this was not a foreign-related case involving foreign elements and the parties simply specified the arbitral seat without a clear agreement on the arbitration commission in clause 27 of their agreement. On appeal by the management company, the court confirmed that the court at first instance had jurisdiction over this case, which was a domestic civil commercial dispute without any foreign elements, and therefore the parties' arbitration agreement to seat the arbitration outside the PRC's territory was invalid.

5.3.2.3 *Only Parties to Foreign-Related Arbitration Can Stipulate Foreign Laws to Govern Their Arbitration Agreements*

With respect to the law applicable to determining an arbitration agreement's validity, Article 16 of the Interpretation of the Supreme People's Court Concerning Some Issues on Application of the Arbitration Law of the PRC states:[72] 'The examination of the validity of a foreign-related arbitration agreement shall be governed by the laws agreed upon between the parties concerned; if the parties concerned did not agree upon the applicable law but have agreed upon the seat of arbitration, the law at the arbitration seat shall apply; if the parties have not chosen the law and the arbitral seat has not been chosen or is unclear, the applicable law is the law of the forum.' Moreover, Article 18 of the Law of the PRC on Choice of Law for Foreign-related Civil Relationships

---

71. Cited from http://www.pkulaw.cn/case, PKU Law No. CLI.C. 283908. Unfortunately this database did not specify the court, case number, judgment date and other information.
72. Fa-Shi (2006) No. 7, promulgated on 23 August 2006, effective from 8 September 2006.

provides:[73] 'The parties concerned may choose the laws applicable to arbitration agreement by agreement. If the parties do not choose, the laws at the place of the arbitration institution or of the arbitration shall apply.' The order of determining the applicable law for an arbitration agreement's validity prescribed by these provisions applies to foreign-related arbitration only, as PRC law governs domestic arbitration. There are some unique PRC law provisions regarding an arbitration agreement's validity, such as requiring 'a designated arbitration commission' as one of the mandatory particulars in an arbitration agreement (Article 16 paragraph 2 item (3) of the PRC Arbitration Law).[74] The majority of other countries do not have such a legislative requirement. Thus the issue of whether or not the parties can agree on a foreign law as the applicable law for their arbitration agreement has important ramifications in practice.

5.3.2.4 The Law Governing Substantive Matters in Domestic Arbitration is PRC Law

According to Article 126 paragraph 1 of the PRC Contract Law:[75] 'Parties to a foreign-related contract may select the applicable law for resolution of a contractual dispute, except as otherwise provided by law.' This is commonly understood to mean that substantive matters in non-foreign-related cases are always governed by PRC law and that the parties cannot agree on a governing law other than the law of Mainland China.[76] For example, in an appeal case concerning disputes arising from a loan agreement between Miaokang Zhang and Taizhou Qianjin Motorcycle Parts Co., Ltd., Jiangsu Higher People's Court upheld a lower court's decision and confirmed that 'this

---

73. Order of the President of the PRC No. 36, promulgated on 28 October 2010, effective from 1 April 2011.
74. For the PRC law provisions and judicial decisions on determining the validity of arbitration agreements, *see* Helena Hsi-Chia Chen, *Regulations and Cases Concerning Validity of Arbitration Agreements in Mainland China*, 91 Arbitration 92–126 (2010).
75. According to Art. 126 para. 2 of the PRC Contract Law, the phrase 'except as otherwise provided by law' in Art. 126 para. 1 includes (but is not limited to): 'Chinese-foreign equity joint venture contract, Chinese-foreign contractual joint venture contract, or a contract for Chinese-foreign exploration and development of natural resources which is performed within the territory of the People's Republic of China', the parties cannot agree on non-PRC laws to govern these contracts despite the involvement of foreign elements.
    With respect to civil and commercial disputes involving Taiwan, the SPC has specifically published *Provisions of the Supreme People's Court on the Application of Law in the Trial of Taiwan-Related Civil and Commercial Cases* in 2010 (Fa-Shi (2010) No. 19, promulgated on 27 December 2010 and effective from 1 January 2011), Art. 1 paras 1 and 2 of the Provisions state: 'When hearing commercial cases involving Taiwan, the people's court may apply the law that it determines applicable to civil law in Taiwan according to the law and judicial interpretation on the principles of choice of law.'
76. 'This (Article 126 of the *PRC Contract Law*) is commonly understood to mean that non-foreign-related arbitrations are always governed by Chinese law.' *See* Kun Fan, *Arbitration in China: A Legal and Cultural Analysis* 26 (Hart Publishing 2013).

case does not involve any foreign element, consequently there is no question about the choice of law applicable to the parties' rights and obligations, as these should undoubtedly be governed by PRC law'.[77]

5.3.2.5 Parties to Foreign-Related Arbitration Have More Freedom in Choice of Arbitrators

Although the PRC Arbitration Law does not expressly require the parties to select their arbitrators from a list of arbitrators, in the past the PRC arbitration institutions had always implemented the so-called closed or mandatory panel or list system, meaning that when parties submit their disputes to a particular arbitration institution, the parties can only select from that arbitration institution's panel of arbitrators and cannot appoint arbitrators who are not on the panel.[78] This system has been criticised both within and outside the PRC.[79] One of CIETAC's amendments to its arbitration rules in 2005 is the adjusted version of the closed list system: the parties may appoint arbitrators who are not on the panel by mutual agreement and with the confirmation of CIETAC's chairperson. To a certain degree this amendment has overcome the limitations of the closed list system by giving parties the authority to appoint arbitrators who are not on the panel.[80] The Shanghai International Economic and Trade Arbitration

---

77. Civil Judgment of Jiangsu Higher People's Court (2010) Su-Shang-Wai-Zhong-Zi No. 0039, 28 July 2010. Similar court opinions are numerous, including: in the Appeal Concerning Disputes Arising from a Loan Guarantee Agreement between Shantou City Commercial Bank Huashan Branch and Kuncai Chen, Guangdong Higher People's Court held that the guarantee disputes between the Bank and Kuncai Chen did not involve any foreign elements and the law of Mainland China shall govern: please see Guangdong Higher People's Court's Civil Judgment (final judgment), (2004) Yue-Gao-Fa-Min-Si-Zhong-Zi No. 278, 7 December 2004; in the Appeal Concerning Disputes Arising from a Sample Sales Contract between Jiangsu Jiahong International Trading Corp. Ltd. and Jiangxi Jishui Jiasheng Leather Factory, Jiangsu Huaian Intermediate People's Court held that: 'The relevant contract was between PRC legal persons and performed within the PRC's territory; it did not involve any foreign element and, therefore, the international trade usage is not applicable in this case.' Please see Jiangsu Huaian Intermediate People's Court's Civil Judgment (final judgment), (2011) Huai-Zhong-Shang-Zhong-Zi No. 0077, 13 April 2011.
78. Examples include the earlier editions of the CIETAC Arbitration Rules before the 2005 amendments (2000 and 1998 editions, etc.).
79. For example, Jerome A. Cohen recommended CIETAC to amend the mandatory list system and adopt a more liberal approach instead: Cohen, *Time to Fix China's Arbitration*, Far Eastern Economic Review (2005) Jan./Feb. Prof. Lianbin Song also suggested a system of recommended list instead of mandatory list, please see Lianbin Song, *From Ideology to Rules – Some Issues of Concern When Amending Arbitration Law*, in *Law Report on Commercial Arbitration Law*, vol. 1, 100 (Jian Han & Yifei Lin eds, Citic Publishing House 2005).

    Yet some scholars adopt a different view: 'Although allowing the parties to select arbitrators outside the list can maximize the parties' right in relation to arbitrator appointment, however hasty implementation of this method in the current PRC environment of inadequate credibility and legal system may not achieve the intended results and may in fact be counterproductive, as some malicious parties may use it to interfere with and sabotage the arbitral proceedings. Thus it is recommended that the amendment to the *PRC Arbitration Law* can temporarily omit this issue.' See Zhanjun Ma, *New Comments on Arbitration Law Amendment* 100 (Law Press 2011).
80. The original text used by Shengchang Wang is 'giving the parties the power to appoint arbitrators who are not on the list'. Please see Shengchang Wang, *Introduction to the*

Chapter 5: Mainland China's Departure from International Consensus

Commission (Shanghai International Arbitration Center) Arbitration Rules also provide that:[81] 'Where the parties have agreed to appoint arbitrators from outside of the Panel of Arbitrators, the arbitrator(s) so appointed by the parties or nominated according to the agreement of the parties may act as co-arbitrator, presiding arbitrator or sole arbitrator after the appointment has been confirmed by the Chairman of SHIAC in accordance with the law.'

Yet not all PRC arbitration institutions have adopted similar amendments, as some institutions continue to use the closed list system, including Shanghai Arbitration Commission[82] and Xiamen Arbitration Commission,[83] etc.

Some arbitration institutions have different provisions for 'domestic arbitration' and 'foreign-related arbitration'. For example, the BAC's Arbitration Rules provide that parties to domestic arbitration shall choose arbitrators from the panel of arbitrators maintained by the BAC,[84] whereas parties to foreign-related arbitration can select arbitrators outside the panel of arbitrators maintained by the BAC with the BAC's confirmation.[85] Pursuant to such arbitration rules, the parties to foreign-related arbitration have more freedom to select their arbitrators than the parties to domestic arbitration.

5.3.2.6 *The Grounds for Revocation and Non-enforcement Differ Between Domestic Arbitral Awards and Foreign-Related Arbitral Awards*[86]

There are different PRC law provisions for revocation and non-enforcement of domestic arbitral awards and foreign-related arbitral awards, as listed below:[87]

Amendment of CIETAC Arbitration Rules, 96 Arbitration and Law 36 (2005). The author believes a more proper wording should be 'giving the parties the authority to appoint arbitrators who are not on the list'.

81. Article 21 of Shanghai International Economic and Trade Arbitration Commission (Shanghai International Arbitration Center) Arbitration Rules (effective from 1 January 2015).
82. Article 26 para. 2 of the Shanghai Arbitration Commission Arbitration Rules (effective from 1 January 2013) provides: 'The parties concerned shall appoint the members of an arbitration tribunal from the list of arbitrators or the list of arbitrators on specialties established by the Arbitration Commission.'
83. Article 16 para. 3 of the Xiamen Arbitration Commission Arbitration Rules (effective from 1 May 2007) provides: 'The arbitrator(s) shall be appointed or designated from the Panel of Arbitrators provided by this Commission.'
84. Article 18 of the Beijing Arbitration Commission Arbitration Rules (effective from 1 April 2015).
85. *Ibid.*, Art. 62 para. 2.
86. For the different grounds for annulment and non-enforcement of domestic awards and foreign-related awards under the PRC legal system, *see also*: Helena Hsi-Chia Chen, *A Comparative Study on the Arbitration Law on Both Sides of the Taiwan Strait (Part II)*, 97 Arbitration 43–45 (2013).
87. One commentator has recommended the adoption of a 'single-track system' as part of amending the PRC Arbitration Law: 'Since the current arbitration institutions in the PRC can also deal with foreign-related cases and in light of this double-track system, it would be extremely unfair to have different judicial review standards for assessing awards made by the same arbitration institution depending on whether there are foreign elements involved.'; *see* Yanming Huang, *Research on Judicial Supervision over Commercial Arbitration – From the Perspective of the Practice of Judicial Supervision over Commercial Arbitration by Shanghai Second Intermediate People's Court*, 71 Beijing Arbitration 152, 157 (2010).

- Revocation of domestic arbitral awards: Article 58 of PRC Arbitration Law.
- Non-enforcement of domestic arbitral awards: Article 63 of PRC Arbitration Law; Paragraphs 2 and 3 of Article 237 of PRC Civil Procedural Law.
- Revocation of foreign-related arbitral awards: Article 70 of PRC Arbitration Law.
- Non-enforcement of foreign-related arbitral awards: Article 71 of PRC Arbitration Law and Article 274 of PRC Civil Procedure Law.

A comparison of the grounds for revocation and non-enforcement of domestic awards and foreign-related awards reveals that a party may apply for revocation or non-enforcement of domestic awards on the following two grounds: '[t]he evidence on which the award is based was forged' and '[t]he other party has withheld the evidence which is sufficient to affect the impartiality of the arbitration'.[88] Yet there are no equivalent or comparable grounds for revocation or non-enforcement of foreign-related awards.

5.3.2.7 *Reporting System is Applicable to Foreign-Related Arbitration*

Through the SPC's Notification of Certain Issues Relating to the People's Courts' Dealing with Foreign-Related and Foreign Arbitration in 1995[89] and SPC's Notification of Certain Matters Relating to the People's Courts' Revocation of Foreign-Related Arbitral Awards and Article in 1998,[90] the SPC established the so-called Reporting System for three situations: determination of validity of foreign-related arbitration agreements; revocation or non-enforcement of foreign-related arbitral awards; and recognition and enforcement of foreign arbitral awards. The following discussions relate to foreign-related arbitration.[91]

---

88. One of the important arbitration-related amendments to the PRC Civil Procedure Law in 2012 is to replace the grounds for non-enforcement from the former Art. 213 of the 2007 version (para. 2 item (4) re 'the main evidence for finding the facts is insufficient' and item (5) re 'there is an error in the application of the law') to the current Art. 237 (para. 2 item (4) re '[t]he evidence on which the award is based was forged' and item (5) re '[t]he other party has withheld the evidence which is sufficient to affect the impartiality of the arbitration'). The grounds for revocation and non-enforcement of domestic awards are now consistent: *see* Helena Hsi-Chia Chen, *The Impact of the 2012 Amendments to the Civil Procedure Law of the People's Republic of China on the Arbitration Regime in China*, 6 International Arbitration Law Review 248 (2012).
89. Fa-Fa (1995) No. 18, promulgated on 28 August 1995.
90. Fa (1998) No. 40, promulgated on 23 April 1998.
91. On the other hand, the second point of the SPC's Notification of Certain Issues Relating to the People's Courts' Dealing with Foreign-Related and Foreign Arbitration states: '[w]here one of the parties applies to the people's court to enforce a foreign-related arbitral award or to recognise and enforce a foreign arbitral award, and if the people's court considers that the foreign-related arbitral award falls within one of the grounds stipulated in Art. 260 of the PRC Civil Procedure Law, or if the foreign arbitral award does not comply with the provisions in the New York Convention or the principle of reciprocity, then the people's court shall report to the higher people's court in its locality for review before making any decisions. If the higher people's court agrees with non-enforcement or refusal of recognition and enforcement, it shall further report to the SPC. The court may render a ruling of non-enforcement or refusing recognition and enforcement only after it receives the SPC's reply.'

Chapter 5: Mainland China's Departure from International Consensus

With respect to determining the validity of foreign-related arbitration agreements, the first point in the SPC's Notification of Certain Issues Relating to the People's Courts' Dealing with Foreign-Related and Foreign Arbitration provides:[92] 'For cases concerning economic trade or maritime disputes that are foreign-related or involve Hong Kong, Macau or Taiwan, if the parties have stipulated arbitration clauses in their contracts or have subsequently reached arbitration agreements, and if the people's court regards the arbitration clause or arbitration agreement as invalid, nullified or unenforceable due to uncertainty, the people's court shall report the case to the higher people's court in its locality before deciding to accept the case. If the higher people's court agrees with the people's court's decision, the higher people's court shall report its advice to the SPC. The courts may temporarily refrain from accepting the case before the SPC's reply.' This requirement only applies to foreign-related arbitration agreements (including those that involve Taiwan, Hong Kong or Macau) and does not apply to arbitration agreements without any foreign elements.

With respect to revocation and non-enforcement of foreign-related arbitral awards, the above-mentioned SPC's Notifications of 1995 and 1998 provide that, if a party requests for revocation or non-enforcement of a foreign-related award and the people's court finds that the award falls within the grounds for revocation or non-enforcement, the people's court shall report the case to the higher people's court in its locality before deciding to refuse enforcement, revoke the award or notify the arbitral tribunal to re-hear the case. If the higher people's court agrees with non-enforcement, revocation or re-hearing by the arbitral tribunal, the higher people's court shall further report its advice to the SPC and wait for the SPC's Reply before deciding to refuse enforcement, revoke the award or notify the arbitral tribunal to re-arbitrate the case. Again this requirement only applies to foreign-related arbitral awards and does not apply to domestic arbitral awards. By contrast, revocation and non-enforcement of domestic arbitral awards are 'single final rulings', as they are not subject to any appeal pursuant to Article 154 of the PRC Civil Procedure Law.[93]

5.3.2.8 *Different Court Levels for Determining Applications for Preservation of Evidence and Property*

According to Article 46 of the PRC Arbitration Law, if a party to domestic arbitration applies for preservation of evidence after the request for arbitration, the arbitration institution shall submit this application to 'the basic people's court in the place where the evidence is located'. Yet in cases of foreign-related arbitration, Article 68 of the PRC Arbitration Law requires the arbitration institution to submit applications for preservation of evidence after requests for arbitration to 'the intermediate people's court' in the place where the evidence is located. Thus the court levels for processing applications for preservation of evidence differ between domestic arbitration and foreign-related arbitration. In addition, Article 81 paragraph 2 of the PRC Civil Procedure Law

---

92. Fa-Fa (1995) No. 18, promulgated on 28 August 1995.
93. Article 154 of PRC Civil Procedure Law.

was inserted in 2012 to address applications for preservation of evidence 'before instituting an action or applying for arbitration'. Nevertheless the different court levels as prescribed in Articles 46 and 68 of the PRC Arbitration Law should also apply to applications for preservation of evidence before arbitration.

On the other hand, the parties' applications for property preservation in domestic arbitration shall be submitted by the arbitration institution to 'the basic people's court' in the party's domicile or the property's location, whereas applications in foreign-related arbitration shall be submitted by the arbitration institution to 'the intermediate people's court' in the party's domicile or the property's location (*see* Articles 11 and 12 of the SPC's Several Provisions on Certain Issues Relating to Enforcement by the People's Courts (For Trial Implementation)).[94] Article 272 of the PRC Civil Procedure Law also provides: 'Where a party applies for a preservation measure, the foreign-related arbitration institution of the People's Republic of China shall submit the party's application to the intermediate people's court at the place of domicile of the respondent or at the place where the respondent's property is located.' Furthermore, Article 101 paragraph 1 of the PRC Civil Procedure Law was inserted in 2012 to address the parties' applications for property preservation before applying for arbitration. In light of Article 272, such applications should also be submitted to the different court levels as prescribed in the above-mentioned Articles 11 and 12 of the SPC's Several Provisions on Certain Issues Relating to Enforcement by the People's Courts.

It should be clarified that, although applications for evidence and property preservation are decided by different courts depending on whether the arbitration is domestic or foreign-related, the same court level (i.e., the intermediate people's courts) determines applications for revocation and non-enforcement of both domestic awards and foreign-related awards.[95] Furthermore, regardless of the distinction between domestic arbitration and foreign-related arbitration, the same court level (i.e., the intermediate people's courts) also determines the validity of arbitration agreements.[96]

---

94. Fa-Shi (1998) No. 15, 8 July 1998.
95. Regarding revocation of arbitral awards, Art. 58 of the PRC Arbitration Law expressly provides: 'A party may apply for setting aside an arbitration award to the *intermediate people's court* in the place where the arbitration commission is located...' [emphasis added].

    Regarding non-enforcement of arbitral awards, the applicant for enforcement submits the relevant evidence to the court and the *intermediate people's court* is the court of enforcement (*see* Art. 29 of the Interpretation of the Supreme People's Court concerning Some Issues on Application of the Arbitration Law of the People's Republic of China, (2006) Fa-Shi No. 7, 23 August 2006): 'a party's application for enforcing arbitral award will be determined by the intermediate people's court in the place where the party against whom the enforcement is sought is domiciled or where the property subject to enforcement is located'.) It follows that the intermediate people's court also determines non-enforcement of arbitral awards.
96. *See* Art. 12 paras 1 and 2 of the Interpretation of the Supreme People's Court Concerning Some Issues on Application of the Arbitration Law of the People's Republic of China (Fa-Shi (2006) No. 7, 23 August 2006), which provide: '(1) A party's application to the people's court for confirming the validity of arbitration agreement will be determined by the *intermediate people's court* in the place where the arbitration institution is located. If the arbitration agreement is unclear about the arbitration institution, the application will be determined by the *intermediate people's court* in the place where the arbitration clause was executed or the applicant is domiciled. (2) An application for confirming the validity of foreign-related arbitration agreement will be

5.4 SUMMARY

Before the Reporting System's implementation, local courts were more likely to abuse 'social and public interest' to protect the interests of their localities or specific industries, as appropriately illustrated by the widely criticised *Dongfeng* case. The SPC's replies demonstrate that the Reporting System has been effective in reducing such abuse. An example is the *Shin-Etsu* case, in which the Jiangsu Higher People's Court was inclined to refuse a foreign award's recognition and enforcement on the basis of public policy violation in order to protect the interests of a specific industry. However upon reporting to the SPC, the SPC did not support this approach. It can also be seen from the *Baosheng* case concerning the enforcement of a foreign-related award that the SPC interprets 'social and public interest' more narrowly than the Anhui Higher People's Court. Indeed the *Shin-Etsu* case and the *Baosheng* case clearly demonstrate the Reporting System's effectiveness in preventing the lower courts' implementation of local protectionism through an excessively wide application of 'public policy' or 'social and public interest'. Consequently, 'despite the strong scepticism expressed by foreign scholars' with regard to Chinese notion of "social and public interest", it seems that it rarely leads to the non-enforcement of foreign-related, Greater China and foreign awards'.[97]

As seen from the three case analyses in section 5.2 of this chapter, the SPC is very concerned with 'the PRC's judicial sovereignty and the PRC courts' jurisdiction', and may regard an arbitral award's enforcement as contrary to PRC 'public policy' if that award infringes upon 'the PRC's judicial sovereignty and the PRC courts' jurisdiction'. When an arbitral award's content differs from court judgments, the SPC has nevertheless adopted different views depending on the circumstances of each case (e.g., the *Hemofarm* case, *Mitsui* case, *Castel* case and *Wicor* case). However, if the content of an award is not only contrary to specific PRC court decisions but the award has also determined and even criticised specific PRC court decisions with the view that such decided matters belong to the arbitral jurisdiction and should be submitted to arbitration (e.g., the *Hemofarm* case), then the PRC courts would regard such foreign award as infringing the PRC's judicial sovereignty and the PRC courts' jurisdiction. The SPC in the *Liupanshui* case, the Beijing Second Intermediate People's Court in the *Chao Lai Xin Sheng* case and the Shanghai Second Intermediate People's Court in the *Leaf Confectionary* case also exemplify the same approach to safeguarding the PRC courts' jurisdiction.

One of the distinguishing features of the PRC arbitration law is that the PRC courts maintain certain degree of control over domestic arbitration through the legal framework for distinguishing domestic arbitration from foreign-related arbitration. In areas of substantive law, only PRC law can govern domestic arbitration. In areas of

---

determined by the *intermediate people's court* in the place where the arbitration institution is located, or where the arbitration agreement was executed, or where the applicant or the respondent is domiciled.' [emphasis added]

97. Clarisse von Wunschheim, *The Setting Aside and Enforcement of Awards in China*, in *Chinese Arbitration Law* 385–386 (Peter Yuen, Damien McDonald & Arthur X. Dong ed., LexisNexis 2015).

procedural law, PRC law also exclusively governs the procedures of domestic arbitration. In terms of appointment of arbitrators, PRC law imposes certain restrictions on such appointment. The PRC courts' strict differentiation between domestic arbitration and foreign-related arbitration is understandable after understanding the different laws and regulations that govern domestic arbitration and foreign-related arbitration. If the parties to domestic arbitration purport to evade the legal framework for domestic arbitration through private agreement, such as submitting their disputes to arbitration by a foreign arbitration institution or in a foreign seat outside the PRC's territory, then the SPC would use 'public policy' as a sword to invalidate such an arbitration agreement, or to refuse the resultant award's recognition and enforcement upon the parties' application. In other words, the application of 'public policy' in such kind of cases assists with maintaining the distinction between domestic arbitration and foreign-related arbitration, a legal framework with distinctive Chinese characteristics. Hence the interpretation and application of 'public policy' under Article V(2)(b) of the New York Convention in such kind of cases are also flavoured with such Chinese characteristics.

CHAPTER 6
Conclusion

Although 'public policy' is an uncertain legal concept, internationally there is substantial consensus on the core meaning of 'public policy' in Article V(2)(b) of the New York Convention, as can be seen from the history and drafting process of international conventions, discussions by internationally renowned scholars, relevant court precedents, the efforts and research reports of ILA,[1] and a comparative study on the major countries' legislative provisions. The following conclusions about the PRC courts' interpretation and application of 'public policy' and the comparable 'social and public interest' in the last twenty years arise from an in-depth study of the PRC's relevant legal system, legislative provisions, judicial interpretations and scholarly discussions together with a comprehensive observation of all the relevant PRC cases that have been published or can be ascertained by the author.

First, in terms of regulatory terminology, 'social and public interest' is the traditional term used in the PRC's legal system. The use of the term 'public policy' only began after the New York Convention took effect in the PRC. In addition, it can be seen from the relevant judicial interpretations issued by the SPC that the SPC basically follows certain principles in the choice of terminology – namely, the term 'public policy' is used only in circumstances involving the New York Convention.[2] In contrast, the term 'social and public interest' is used in relation to the PRC court's enforcement of arbitral awards made in Hong Kong, Macau or Taiwan. Furthermore, the term 'social

---

1. Please see s. 2.5 of Ch. 2 for the International Law Association's initial report (Taiwan conference in 1998), 'Interim Report on Public Policy as a Bar to Enforcement of International Arbitral Awards' (London conference in 2000), and 'Final Report on Public Policy as a Bar to Enforcement of International Arbitral Awards' (New Delhi conference in 2002).
2. The reference to 'public policy' in relation to the enforcement in Mainland China of arbitral awards made in Hong Kong and Macau was also in consideration of the fact that Hong Kong and Macau were subject to the application of the New York Convention before their return to the PRC.

and public interest' is also used in relation to the revocation or non-enforcement of domestic arbitral awards or foreign-related arbitral awards.[3]

The second conclusion concerns the question of whether there is any difference in the meaning or connotation of 'public policy' and 'social and public interest', as well as whether there is any difference in their interpretation and application in the PRC's judicial practice. Most scholars opine that, in terms of context, 'social and public interest' has a wider meaning and is more uncertain than 'public policy'. As observed and discovered from specific precedents of the people's courts in Mainland China, the people's courts' interpretation of 'social and public interest' in cases concerning the revocation and non-enforcement of domestic arbitral awards is distinctly wider than the SPC's interpretation of 'public policy' in cases concerning the recognition and enforcement of foreign arbitral awards. This demonstrates that the SPC understands and is mindful that the 'public policy' stipulated in Article V(2)(b) of the New York Convention is 'international'. The standards and criteria for interpreting and applying 'public policy' in cases concerning the recognition and enforcement of foreign arbitral awards should be different from the standards and criteria for interpreting and applying 'social and public interest' in cases concerning the revocation and non-enforcement of domestic arbitral awards. This also simultaneously evidences that the Reporting System has performed considerable function.

It is worth noting that, pursuant to the SPC's Arrangement Concerning Mutual Enforcement of Arbitral Awards Between the Mainland and Hong Kong Special Administrative Region as well as the SPC's Arrangement Concerning Mutual Recognition and Enforcement of Arbitral Awards Between the Mainland and Macau Special Administrative Region, the people's courts may refuse to enforce arbitral awards made in Hong Kong or Macau if they find that such awards' enforcement would violate 'the Mainland China's social and public interest'. However, it cannot be found from a comparative observation of the cases to date that the SPC's interpretation and application of 'public policy' in cases concerning the recognition and enforcement of foreign arbitral awards is any different from the SPC's interpretation and application of 'social and public interest' in cases concerning the enforcement of arbitral awards made in Hong Kong.[4] In other words, before the signing of the SPC's Arrangement Concerning Mutual Enforcement of Arbitral Awards Between the Mainland and Hong Kong Special Administrative Region, scholars in Hong Kong had raised their concerns about the terminological imbalance as Article 7 paragraph 3 stipulates that the enforcement of the award may be refused if the court of the Mainland holds that the enforcement of the arbitral award in the Mainland would be contrary to the public interest of the Mainland, or if the court of the Hong Kong Special Administrative Region decides that the enforcement of the arbitral award in Hong Kong would be contrary to

---

3. For discussions on the inconsistencies between the PRC's Civil Procedure Law and Arbitration Law concerning whether 'violation of social and public interest' can be a ground for revocation or non-enforcement of domestic arbitral awards or foreign-related arbitral awards, *see* s. 3.2.2.2 of Ch. 3.
4. To date the author has not seen any reply from the SPC with respect to the recognition and enforcement of arbitral awards made in Macau.

the public policy of the Hong Kong Special Administrative Region.[5] Nevertheless, we have not seen any difference or inconsistency in the interpretation and application of these two terms by the SPC from more than ten years of judicial practice since the implementation of the SPC's Arrangement Concerning Mutual Enforcement of Arbitral Awards Between the Mainland and Hong Kong Special Administrative Region on 1 February 2000.

In the author's opinion, the more appropriate understanding in light of the above is that: although 'public policy' and 'social and public interest' are distinctive in purely literal terms: 'public policy' is narrower whereas 'social and public interest is broader, the real distinction, as observed from judicial practice, may not stem from the regulatory terminology of 'public policy' or 'social and public interest', but from the types of cases in which the PRC courts interpret and apply 'public policy' and 'social and public interest'. In cases concerning the enforcement of arbitral awards made in Hong Kong, Macau or Taiwan, although the relevant regulatory terminology is 'social and public interest', the SPC's criteria for determination is very similar to (if not the same as) the criteria for determination in cases of applying 'public policy' in New York Convention's Article V(2)(b) to the recognition and enforcement of foreign arbitral awards. By contrast, in circumstances where 'social and public interest' is also used as the regulatory terminology, the people's court's interpretation of 'social and public interest' in cases concerning non-enforcement of domestic arbitral awards is clearly wider than the people's court's interpretation of 'social and public interest' in cases concerning non-enforcement of foreign-related arbitral awards.

Third, to date the author has not seen any cases in which the people's courts refused the recognition and enforcement of arbitral awards made in Taiwan on the grounds of 'violation of social and public interest'. Nonetheless, from a comparison between the New Provisions (the Provisions of the Supreme People's Court on Recognition and Enforcement of the Arbitral Awards of the Taiwan Region) and the Old Provisions (on the SPC's Provisions on the People's Courts' Recognition of Taiwan Courts' Civil Judgments repealed on 1 July 2015, Article 19 of which stipulated its application to the recognition of Taiwan Region's institutional arbitral awards) together with the SPC's Arrangement Concerning Mutual Enforcement of Arbitral Awards Between the Mainland and Hong Kong Special Administrative Region and the SPC's Arrangement Concerning Mutual Recognition and Enforcement of Arbitral Awards Between the Mainland and Macau Special Administration, it can be seen that several stipulations in the Old Provisions are inapplicable to the recognition and enforcement of arbitral awards. In addition, Article 19 of the Old Provisions merely referred to 'Taiwan Region's institutional arbitral awards' and did not include ad hoc arbitral awards made in Taiwan, which was in contrast (and significant imbalance) with the two Arrangements concerning arbitral awards (institutional and ad hoc) made in Hong Kong and Macau. Thus the Old Provisions had much room for improvement, requiring overall rearrangement such as prescribing individually specific provisions for

---

5. *See* s. 3.1.2 of Ch. 3. *See also* Xianchu Zhang, *The Agreement Between Mainland China and the Hong Kong SAE on Mutual Enforcement of Arbitral Awards: Problems and Prospects*, 29 Hong Kong Law Journal 463, 476 (1999).

the enforcement and recognition of arbitral awards made in Taiwan. Fortunately, the SPC had acknowledged these problems and implemented the New Provisions as from 1 July 2015, which address and resolve these problems.

Fourth, observing from a temporal viewpoint, an excessively broad interpretation of 'social and public interest' in the name of maintaining social and public interest but in fact carrying out local protectionism did exist in the early PRC judicial practice. Subsequently the SPC commenced to proceed with various adjustments from a systematic approach, such as establishing centralised jurisdiction and the Reporting System for the four main types of cases concerning 'validity of foreign-related arbitration agreements', 'non-enforcement of foreign-related arbitral awards', 'revocation of foreign-related arbitral awards' and 'recognition and enforcement of foreign arbitral awards' to allocate the cases reported from the relevant lower courts to the SPC's Fourth Civil Tribunal. The entire systematic design of centralised jurisdiction, Reporting System and allocation of cases to the SPC's Fourth Civil Tribunal has indeed performed its functions effectively. Many cases in which the lower courts found, on the grounds of violation of social and public interest or public policy, that the arbitration agreement should be invalid, or the foreign-related arbitral award should be revoked or refused enforcement, or the foreign arbitral award should be refused recognition and enforcement have, upon reporting to the SPC, been decided in accordance with the SPC's different opinion that the specific circumstances did not constitute violation of social and public interest or public policy to invalidate the arbitration agreement, to revoke or refuse enforcement of the foreign-related arbitral award or to refuse the recognition or enforcement of the foreign arbitral award.[6]

Fifth, the entire systematic design assists with unifying the people's court's opinions on the one hand while assisting with eradicating local protectionism on the other hand. In 2009 Professor Exiang Wan, the SPC's Deputy President at the time, stated during an international academic symposium about the New York Convention's fiftieth anniversary commemoration and judicial challenges:[7] '[s]ome cases have already expressed that the SPC has at least clarified the following circumstances which may not necessarily constitute violation of the PRC's social and public interest: (1) impacts on mere department or local interests; (2) violation of the PRC's individual mandatory legal provisions.' While there may be different views on the issue of whether or not local protectionism has been eradicated completely, there is nevertheless more consensus on the point that 'violation of the PRC's mandatory legal

---

6. Using the SPC's review of the lower courts' application of the New York Convention to the recognition and enforcement of foreign arbitral awards as case illustration, Justice Guixiang Liu and Justice Hongyu Shen of the SPC's Fourth Civil Tribunal stated: 'The statistics of case reporting indicate that the SPC's agreement with the lower courts is less than 50%. On the one hand this explains that procedurally, the Reporting System has performed its supervisory function of controlling and unifying judicial approaches, while on the other hand this illustrates that some differences in the textual understanding of the New York Convention still remain within the various courts awaiting further clarification and unification.' *See* Guixiang Liu & Hongyu Shen, *Recognition and Enforcement of Foreign Arbitral Awards in China: A Look Back on a Decade of Court Practices*, 79 Beijing Arbitration 1, 24 (2012).
7. Exiang Wan, *Judicial Practice with Regards to the New York Convention in China*, 276 Journal of Law Application 4, 6 (2009).

Chapter 6: Conclusion

provisions cannot completely equate with violation of the PRC's public policy', a point which the SPC has repeatedly clarified in the *Mitsui* case and *ED&F Man* case, etc.

Sixth, the above-mentioned systemic design in further coordination with the Supreme People's Court Gazette, Guide on Foreign-Related Commercial and Maritime Trial and other periodicals publish, from time to time, the SPC's opinions concerning the interpretation and application of 'social and public interest' and 'public policy' in these types of cases that 'have representative significance' and 'provide certain guidance'.[8] These greatly improve the transparency of the people's courts' opinions and thereby enhance the predictability of 'public policy' in Mainland China.

Seventh, to date the *Tom Hulett* case is the only case in which the SPC refused to enforce a foreign-related arbitral award on the grounds of the 'violation of social and public interest'. Many scholars are critical of the SPC's opinion in this case. As the SPC has not refused the enforcement of foreign-related arbitral awards on the grounds of violation of social and public interest in more than ten years since its reply in the *Tom Hulett* case in 1997 (which was shortly after the implementation of the Reporting System on 28 August 1995[9]), it can be reasonably inferred that the SPC has adopted a more cautious approach to interpret the meaning of 'violation of social and public interest' as stipulated in Article 274 paragraph 2 of the PRC Civil Procedure Law in this type of cases.

Eighth, a comparison between the cases concerning the SPC's interpretation and application of 'public policy' in New York Convention's Article V(2)(b) with international consensus on this provision reveals that the SPC's opinions are basically and substantially consistent with the international consensus. Such consistency manifests in the following aspects:

(1) The international consensus is that 'public policy' as stipulated in Article V(2)(b) of the New York Convention is the public policy of the 'enforcement State'. As demonstrated by the relevant PRC cases ascertained by the author, all the people's courts considered the public policy of the PRC (as the enforcement State) when applying Article V(2)(b) of the New York Convention.
(2) However, another international consensus is that 'public policy' as stipulated in Article V(2)(b) of the New York Convention is still limited by the requirement of 'internationality'. The SPC upholds the same view, as observed from the specific precedents of the people's courts in Mainland China.
(3) The enforcement courts may jointly consider the merits of the parties' claims and the arbitral tribunal's decisions rather than confining to the content of remedies granted by the arbitral tribunal. As observed from the precedents of

---

8. Article 2 para. 2 of the Administrative Measures for the Proclamation of Document of Judgment by the Supreme People's Court stipulates that 'court documents with representative significance and provide certain guidance are published in the People's Court Daily or Gazette from time to time'. *See* Fa-Ban-Fa [2000] No. 4, promulgated and implemented on 15 June 2000.
9. This refers to the SPC's Notification Of Certain Issues Relating to the People's Courts' Dealing with Foreign-Related and Foreign Arbitration, Fa-Fa [1995] No. 18, promulgated and implemented on 28 August 1995.

the people's court of Mainland China, the people's courts also uphold the same view in cases of determining whether or not to recognise and enforce foreign arbitral awards by jointly reviewing and considering the merits of the parties' claims and the arbitral tribunal's decisions.

(4) 'Public policy' as stipulated in Article V(2)(b) of the New York Convention applies in exceptional circumstances only. It can be seen from precedents of the people's court of Mainland China such as *GRD Minproc* case, *Louis Dreyfus* case and *Western Bulk* case, etc. that the SPC adopts the same approach.

(5) With respect to procedural violations, applying Article V(1)(b) or (d) of the New York Convention should suffice, rather than interpreting 'public policy' in Article V(2)(b) as including 'procedural public policy'. Precedents of the people's court of Mainland China demonstrate that the SPC adopts the same approach of only invoking Article V(1)(b) or (d) of the New York Convention (where these circumstances existed) to refuse the recognition and enforcement of foreign arbitral awards without invoking 'public policy' as stipulated in Article V(2)(b).

(6) Violation of mandatory administrative regulations or departmental rules does not necessarily constitute violation of 'public policy' as stipulated in Article V(2)(b). The SPC also upholds the same view, as can be seen from precedents of the people's court of Mainland China such as the *Mitsui* case and *ED&F Man* case, etc.

Ninth, as shown by the comprehensive analysis of the *Tom Hulett* case, the first and only PRC case to date which refused a foreign arbitral award's recognition and enforcement since the New York Convention took effect in the PRC, the SPC is very concerned with 'the judicial sovereignty of the PRC and the jurisdiction of the PRC courts', and may find the arbitral tribunal's reasoning in the arbitral award as infringing the PRC's sovereignty and the PRC courts' jurisdiction. A joint observation of the *Hemofarm* case, *Louis Dreyfus* case and *Guangxia Culture* case especially reveals the SPC's high degree of attention given to the PRC's sovereignty and the PRC courts' jurisdiction.

Tenth, by reviewing the SPC's reasoning in the *Hemofarm* case and *Liupanshui* case together with the Beijing Second Intermediate People's Court's reasoning in the *Chai Lai Xin Shen* case and the Shanghai Second Intermediate People's Court's reasoning in the *Leaf Confectionery* case while understanding the distinction between domestic arbitration and foreign-related arbitration in the PRC's legal regime for arbitration, we can appreciate how the PRC courts, through the interpretation of 'public policy' in the *Liupanshui* case, *Chai Lai Xin Shen* case and *Leaf Confectionery* case, etc. to maintain this PRC-specific legal framework of distinguishing between domestic arbitration and foreign-related arbitration. Thus the interpretation and application of 'public policy' in Article V(2)(b) of the New York Convention in such kind of cases are also flavoured with such Chinese characteristics.

Bibliography

1. International Law Association Report

The Final Report on Public Policy as a Bar to Enforcement of International Arbitral Awards, presented at the International Law Association's seventieth Conference held in New Delhi, India on 2-6 April 2002.
The Interim Report on Public Policy as a Bar to Enforcement of International Arbitral Awards, presented at the International Law Association's sixty-ninth Conference held in London in 2000.

2. Books Published in English

Alan Redfern & Martin Hunter, *Law and Practice of International Commercial Arbitration* (4th ed., 2004).
Albert Jan van den Berg, *The New York Arbitration Convention of 1958 – Towards a Uniform Judicial Interpretation* (1981).
Andrew Jefferies, *Arbitration in the PRC: Enforcement Issues*, in *Arbitration in China: A Practical Guide* (Daniel R. Fung & Shengchang Wang ed., 2004).
Anthony Aust, *Modern Treaty Law and Practice* (2nd ed., 2007).
Anton G. Maurer, *Public Policy Exception Under the New York Convention: History, Interpretation and Application* (2012).
Chinese Arbitration Law (Peter Yuen, Damien McDonald & Arthur X Dong eds, 2015).
Comparative Arbitration Practice and Public Policy in Arbitration (Pieter Sanders ed., 1987).
Concise International Arbitration (Loukas A Mistelis ed., 2010).
David St. John Sutton, Judith Gill & Mathew Gearing, *Russell on Arbitration* (24th ed., 2015).
Enforcement of Arbitration Agreements and International Arbitral Awards: The New York Convention in Practice (Emmanuel Gaillard & Domenico di Pietro eds, 2008).
Gary B. Born, *International Arbitration: Law and Practice* (2012).
Gary B. Born, *International Commercial Arbitration* (2nd ed., 2014).
Herbert Kronke et al., *The New York Convention: Recognition and Enforcement of Foreign Arbitral Awards* (2010).

Bibliography

ICCA's Guide to the Interpretation of the 1958 New York Convention (ICCA ed., 2011).
Jingzhou Tao, *Arbitration Law and Practice in China* (3rd ed., 2012).
Kun Fan, *Arbitration in China: A Legal and Cultural Analysis* (2013).
Managing Business Disputes in Today's China: Duelling with Dragons (Michael Moser ed., 2007).
New Horizons for International Commercial Arbitration and Beyond (Albert Jan van den Berg ed., Kluwer Law International 2005).
Nigel Blackaby et al., *Redfern and Hunter on International Arbitration* (2009).
Pervasive Problems in International Arbitration (Loukas A. Mistelis & Julian D.M. Lew eds, 2006).
Philip J. McConnaughay & Thomas B. Ginsburg, *International Commercial Arbitration in Asia* (2nd ed., 2006).
Simon Greenberg, Christopher Kee & J. Romesh Weeramantry, *International Commercial Arbitration: An Asia-Pacific Perspective* (2011).
The New York Convention: Convention on the Recognition and Enforcement of Foreign Arbitral Awards of 10 June 1958 – Commentary (Reinmar Wolff ed., 2012).
Thomas E. Carbonneau, *The Law and Practice of Arbitration* (5th ed., 2014).
Ulf Linderfalk, *On the Interpretation of Treaties. The Modern International Law as Expressed in the 1969 Vienna Convention on the Law of Treaties* (2007).
Vienna Convention on the Law of Treaties: A Commentary (Oliver Dörr & Kirsten Schmalenbach eds, 2012).
Shengchang Wang, *Enforcement of Foreign Arbitral Awards in the People's Republic of China, in Improving the Efficiency of Arbitration Agreements and Awards: 40 Years of Application of the New York Convention* (Albert Jan van den Berg ed., 1999).
Yearbook Commercial Arbitration XXXII (Albert Jan van den Berg ed., Kluwer Law International 2007).

3. Dissertation in English

Winnie (Jo-Mei) Ma, *Public Policy in the Judicial Enforcement of Arbitral Awards: Lessons for and from Australia* (2005) (Unpublished Ph. D. Dissertation, Bond University) (on file with the author and also available at: http://epublications.bond.edu.au/theses/ma/).

4. Books Published in Chinese in Taiwan

楊崇森（等著）（2012年3版4刷），《仲裁法新論》，台北：中華仲裁協會。
Chung-Sen Yang et. al., *New Study on Arbitration Act* (3rd ed., CAA, Taipei 2012).
薛西全（2011），《兩岸仲裁法理論與實務》，新北市：弘揚圖書有限公司。
Hsi-Chuan Hsueh, *Cross-Strait Arbitration Law: Theory and Practice* (Hong-Yang Publishing 2011).
林俊益（編著）（2008），《大陸與香港仲裁判斷在台灣之認可裁判輯》，台北：中華仲裁協會。

Jiun-Yi Lin, *Collection of Taiwan Court Judgments Concerning Recognition of Arbitral Awards Made in Mainland China and Hong Kong* (CAA, Taipei 2008).

林俊益（2001），《仲裁法之實用權益》，台北：永然文化出版股份有限公司。
Jiun-Yi Lin, *Practice of Arbitration Act* (Yung-Ran Culture Publishing Inc. 2001).

陳煥文（1993），《兩岸商務糾紛及仲裁實務》，台北：永然文化出版股份有限公司。
John Huan-Wen Chen, *Cross-Strait Commercial Disputes and Arbitration Practice* (Yung-Ran Culture Publishing Inc. 1993).

陳煥文（2002，2版），《仲裁法逐條釋義（增訂再版）》，台北：崗華傳播事業有限公司。
John Huan-Wen Chen, *Interpretation of the Arbitration Act (the Second edition)* (2nd ed., Khan Lee Enterprise 2002).

吳光明、俞鴻玲（2013），《國際商務仲裁理論與發展》，台北：翰蘆圖書出版有限公司。
Kuan-Ming Wu & Hong-Lin Yu, *Theories and Development of International Commercial Arbitration* (Hanlu Publishing 2013).

理律法律事務所（著），陳長文、李家慶（主編）（2012），《兩岸投資保障和促進協議與兩岸商務投資糾紛解決機制》，台北：五南圖書出版股份有限公司。
Lee and Li, Attorneys-at-Law, Charng-Ven Chen & Chai-Ching Lee (eds), *Cross-Strait Bilateral Investment Protection and Promotion Agreement and Cross-Strait Commercial Investment Dispute Resolution Mechanisms* (Wu-Nan Book Inc. 2012).

5. Books Published in Chinese in Mainland China

譚兵（主編）（1995年），《中國仲裁制度研究》，北京：法律出版社。
Bing Tan (ed.), *Research on Chinese Arbitration Legal System* (Law Press 1995).

張斌生（主編）（2010，第4版），《仲裁法新論》，廈門：廈門大學出版社。
Binsheng Zhang (ed.), *Arbitration Law and Practice* (4th ed., Xiamen University Press 2010).

最高人民法院中國應用法學研究所（編）（2000），《人民法院案例選（民事卷）（下）（1992－1999合訂本）》，北京，中國法制出版社。
Chinese Institute of Applied Jurisprudence (ed.), *Selection of People's Courts' Cases (Civil Cases) (Part II) (1992–1999 combined)* (China Legal Publishing House 2000).

中國國際經濟貿易仲裁委員會（編）（2010），《〈紐約公約〉與國際商事仲裁的司法實踐》，北京：法律出版社。
CIETAC (ed.), *Judicial Practice of New York Convention and International Commercial Arbitration* (Law Press 2010).

中國國際經濟貿易仲裁委員會華南分會（編）（2006），《涉外仲裁司法審查》，北京：法律出版社。
CIETAC South China Sub-Commission (ed.), *Judicial Review of the Foreign-Related Arbitration* (Law Press 2006).

程德鈞（1992），《涉外仲裁與法律 第一輯》，北京：中國人民大學出版社。
Dejun Cheng, *Foreign-Related Arbitration and Law*, vol. 1 (China Renmin University Press 1992).

Bibliography

程德鈞、王生長、康明（1993），《國際慣例和涉外仲裁實務》，北京：中國青年出版社。
Dejun Cheng, Shengchang Wang & Ming Kang, *International Practice and Foreign-Related Arbitration* (China Youth Press 1993).

侯登華（2012），《仲裁協議法律制度研究－意思自治視野下當事人權利程序保障》，北京：知識產權出版社。
Denghua Hou, *Research on Legal Framework of Arbitration Agreements – Protection of Parties' Procedural Rights under Party Autonomy* (Intellectual Property Publishing House 2012).

最高人民法院民事審判第四庭（2004），〈涉外商事海事審判實務問題解答（一）〉，萬鄂湘（主編），最高人民法院民事審判第四庭（編），《涉外商事海事審判指導》，2004年1輯（總第7輯），頁45-83，北京：人民法院出版社。
Exiang Wan (editor in chief), the Civil Fourth Tribunal of the Supreme People's Court (ed.), *Answers to Practical Questions on Foreign-Related Commercial and Maritime Trials (I)*, in 7 Guide on Foreign-Related Commercial and Maritime Trial 64-65 (People's Court Press 2004).

袁發強（主編）（2011），《中國商事仲裁機構現狀與發展趨勢研究》，上海：復旦大學出版社。
Faqiang Yuan (ed.), *Commercial Arbitration Institutions in China: Current Status and Trends* (Fudan University Press 2011).

李廣輝、王瀚（2011），《仲裁法》，北京：對外經濟貿易大學出版社。
Guanghui Li & Han Wang, *Arbitration Law* (University of International Business and Economics Press 2011).

宋航（2000），《國際商事仲裁的承認與執行》，北京：法律出版社。
Hang Song, *Recognition and Enforcement of International Commercial Arbitral Awards* (Law Press 2000).

蔡虹、劉加良、鄧曉靜（2011，第2版），《仲裁法學》，北京：北京大學出版社。
Hong Tsai, Jialiang Liu & Xiaojing Deng, *Arbitration Law* (2nd ed., Peking University Press 2011).

楊弘磊（2006），《中國內地司法實踐視角下的〈紐約公約〉問題研究》，北京：法律出版社。
Honglei Yang, *A Study on the New York Convention – From the Perspective of Judicial Practice in Mainland China* (Law Press 2006).

李虎（2000），《國際商事仲裁裁決的強制執行－特別述及仲裁裁決在中國的強制執行》，北京：法律出版社。
Hu Li, *Enforcement of the International Commercial Arbitral Award, with Special Reference to the Enforcement of Arbitral Awards in the P. R. China* (Law Press 2000).

韓健、林一飛（主編）（2005），《商事仲裁法律報告》，第1卷，北京：中信出版社。
Jian Han & Yifei Lin (eds), *Law Report on Commercial Arbitration Law*, vol. 1 (Citic Publishing House 2005).

韓健（2000），《現代國際商事仲裁法的理論與實踐》，北京：法律出版社。
Jian Han, *Theory and Practice of Modern International Commercial Arbitration* (Law Press 2000).

趙健（2000），《國際商事仲裁的司法監督》，北京：法律出版社。
Jian Zhao, *Research on Judicial Supervision over International Commercial Arbitration* (Law Press 2000).

劉景一、喬世明（1997），《仲裁法理論與適用》，北京：人民法院出版社。
Jingyi Liu & Shiming Qiao, *Arbitration Law: Theory and Application* (People's Court Press 1997).

宋連斌（主編）（2010），《仲裁法》，武漢：武漢大學出版社。
Lianbin Song (ed.), *Arbitration Law* (Wuhan University Press 2010).

宋連斌（主編）（2005），《仲裁理論與實務》，長沙：湖南大學出版社。
Lianbin Song (ed.), *Theory and Practice of commercial Arbitration* (Hunan University Press 2005).

宋連斌（2000），《國際商事仲裁管轄權研究》，北京：法律出版社。
Lianbin Song, *A Study of Jurisdictional Problems in International Commercial Arbitration* (Law Press 2000).

韓健、林一飛（主編）（2005），《商事仲裁法律報告（第1卷）》，北京：中信出版社。
Law Report on Commercial Arbitration Law, vol. 1 (Jian Han & Yifei Lin eds, Citic Publishing House 2005).

國家法官學院、中國人民大學法學院（編）（2012），《中國審判案例要覽（2010年商事審判案例卷）》，第71例：〈阿姆龍鋼鐵有限公司申請執行雲南鎳鈷礦業有限公司等仲裁裁決案（對在香港特別行政區作出的仲裁裁決不予執行）〉，北京：中國人民大學出版社。
National Judges College & Renmin University of China Law School (eds), *An Overview of Chinese Court Cases (Volume of Commercial Judgments 2010), Case No. 71: Amlon Metals Ltd's Application for Enforcement of an Arbitral Award against Yunnan Nickel and Cobalt Co., Ltd. (Non-recognition of an Arbitral Award made in Hong Kong)* (China Renmin University Press 2012).

楊良宜、莫世傑、楊大明（2006），《仲裁法－從1996年英國仲裁法到國際商務仲裁》，北京：法律出版社。
Philip Liangyee Yang, Shijie Mo & Daming Yang, *Arbitration Law – From the Arbitration Act 1996 of the United Kingdom to International Commercial Arbitration* (Law Press 2006).

李雙元、徐國建（主編）（1998），《國際民商新秩序的理論建構—國際私法的重新定位與功能轉換》，武漢：武漢大學出版社。
Shuangyuan Li & Guojian Xu (eds), *Construction of the Theory of a New International Civil and Commercial Order – Repositioning and Changing the Function of Private International Law* (Wuhan University Press 1998).

中國國際仲裁商事仲裁年度報告（2014）課題組（2015），《中國國際仲裁商事仲裁年度報告（2014）》，北京：中國仲裁法學研究會。
Task Team of the Annual Report on International Commercial Arbitration in China (2014), *Annual Report on International Commercial Arbitration in China* (2014), (China Academy of Arbitration Law 2015).

江偉（主編）（2012），《仲裁法》，北京：中國人民大學出版社。

Bibliography

Wei Jiang (ed.), *Arbitration Law* (China Renmin University Press 2011).

齊湘泉（2010），《外國仲裁裁決承認及執行論》，北京：法律出版社。

Xiangquan Qi, *Study on the Recognition and Enforcement of Foreign Arbitral Awards* (Law Press 2010).

石現明（2011），《國際商事仲裁當事人權利救濟制度研究》，北京：人民出版社。

Xianming Shi, *Studies on the Remedies for the Parties' Rights Injured in International Commercial Arbitration* (China Renmin University Press 2011).

劉曉紅（主編）（2009），《國際商事仲裁專題研究》，北京：法律出版社。

Xiaohong Liu (ed.), *A Monographic Study on International Commercial Law* (Law Press 2009).

喬欣（主編）（2011），《和諧文化理念視角下的中國仲裁制度研究》，廈門：廈門大學出版社。

Xin Qiao (ed.), *Research on Chinese Arbitration – From the Perspective of Harmony Culture* (Xiamen University Press 2011).

杜新麗（2009），《國際商事仲裁理論與實踐專題研究》，北京：中國政法大學出版社。

Xinli Du, *International Commercial Arbitration Theory and Practice* (China University of Political Science and Law Press 2009).

趙秀文（2012，第3版），《國際商事仲裁法》，北京：中國人民大學出版社。

Xiuwen Zhao (ed.), *International Commercial Arbitration Law* (3rd ed., China Renmin University Press 2012).

趙秀文（2010），《國際商事仲裁法原理與案例教程》，北京：法律出版社。

Xiuwen Zhao, *International Commercial Arbitration Law Principles and Case Textbook* (Law Press 2010).

趙秀文（2010），《國際商事仲裁現代化研究》，北京：法律出版社。

Xiuwen Zhao, *International Commercial Arbitration Modernization Research* (Law Press 2010).

高言、劉璐（1996），《仲裁法理解適用與案例評析》，北京：人民法院出版社。

Yan Gao & Lu Liu, *Understanding and Application of Arbitration Law and Case Analysis* (People's Court Press 1996).

林一飛（2005），《國際商事仲裁法律與實務》，北京：中信出版社。

Yifei Lin, *International Commercial Arbitration Law and Practice* (Citic Publishing House 2005).

林一飛（2008），《仲裁裁決抗辯的法律與實務》，武漢：武漢大學出版社。

Yifei Lin, *Law and Practice of Challenges to Arbitral Awards* (Wuhan University Press 2008).

蘇澤林、景漢朝（主編）（2011），《立案工作指導》，2011年1輯•總第28輯，人民法院出版社。

Zelin Su & Hanchao Jing (ed.), *Guide on Case-Filing*, 2011(1), vol. 28 (People's Court Press 2011).

馬占軍（2011），《仲裁法修改新論》，北京：法律出版社。

Zhanjun Ma, *New Comments on Arbitration Law Amendment* (Law Press 2011).

6. Periodicals Published in English

Andrew de Lotbinière McDougall, *Emerging Dilemmas in International Economic Arbitration – International Arbitration and Money Laundering*, 20 American University International Law Review 1021 (2005).

Andrew I. Okekeifere, *Public Policy and Arbitrability under the UNCITRAL Model Law*, 2 International Arbitration Law Review 70 (1999).

Audley Sheppard, *Whether It Would Be Contrary to English Public Policy to Enforce a Foreign Arbitral Award Because of Illegality*, 1(5) International Arbitration Law Review N78 (1998).

ChristopherB. Kuner, *The Public Policy Exception to the Enforcement of Foreign Arbitral Awards in the United States and West Germany Under the New York Convention*, 7 Journal of International Arbitration 71 (1990).

Catherine Kessedjian, *Transnational Public Policy*, in International Arbitration 2006: Back To Basics? 857–870 (Albert Jan van den Berg ed., 2007).

Chang-fa Lo, *Principles and Criteria for International and Transnational Public Policies in Commercial Arbitration*, 1(1) Contemporary Asia Arbitration Journal 67 (2008).

Christopher S. Gibson, *Arbitration, Civilization and Public Policy: Seeking Counterpoise Between Arbitral Autonomy and the Public Policy Defense in View of Foreign Mandatory Public Law*, 113 Penn State Law Review 1227 (2009).

David P. Roney, *Switzerland: Swiss Federal Supreme Court Holds Competition Law is not Part of Public Policy*, 9(4) International Arbitration Law Review N49 (2006).

Dharmendra Rautray, *India: Choice of Foreign Law and Public Policy in India*, 11(4) International Arbitration Law Review N59 (2008).

Ewan Brown, *Illegality and Public Policy – Enforcement of Arbitral Awards in England: Hilmarton Limited v. Omnium de Traitement et de Valorisation S.A*, 3(1) International Arbitration Law Review 31 (2000).

Friven Yeoh & Yu Fu, *The People's Courts and Arbitration – A Snapshot of Recent Judicial Attitudes on Arbitrability and Enforcement*, 24(6) Journal of International Arbitration 635 (2007).

Haris P. Meidanis, *Public Policy and Ordre Public in the Private International Law of the EU: Traditional Positions and Modern Trends*, 30 European Law Review 95 (2005).

Helena Hsi-Chia Chen, *A Review of the Taiwanese Court's Ruling on Ad Hoc Arbitral Awards*, 20(1) Asian Pacific Law Review 89 (2012).

Helena Hsi-Chia Chen, *The Impact of the 2012 Amendments to the Civil Procedure Law of the People's Republic of China on the Arbitration Regime in the China*, 2012(6) International Arbitration Law Review 247 (2012).

Homayoon Arfazadeh, *In the Shadow of the Unruly Horse: International Arbitration and the Public Policy Exception*, 13 American Review of International Arbitration 43 (2002).

Bibliography

James D. Fry, *Désordre Public International under the New York Convention: Wither Truly International Public Policy*, 8 Chinese Journal of Internationl Law 81 (2009).

Jay R. Sever, *The Relaxation of Inarbitrability and Public Policy Checks on U.S. and Foreign Arbitration: Arbitration out of Control?*, 65 Tulane University Law School Law Review 1661 (1991).

Karl-Heinz Böckstiegel, *Public Policy as a Limit to Arbitration and its Enforcement*, 2(1) Dispute Resolution Internationl (IBA Journal of Dispute resolution, Special Issue 2008, The New York Convention – 50 Years) 123 (2008).

Kun Fan, *Prospects of Foreign Arbitration Institutions Administering Arbitration in China*, 28(4) Journal of Internationl Arbitration 343 (2011).

Lanfang Fei, *Public Policy as a Bar to Enforcement of International Arbitral Awards: A Review of the Chinese Approach*, 26(2) Arbitration International 301 (2010).

Lanming Zhao, *Enforcement of ICC Award Refused on Public Policy Grounds*, 14(2) IBA Arbitration News 18 (2009).

Mark A. Buchanan, *Public Policy and International Commercial Arbitration*, 26 American Business Law Journal 511 (1988).

May Lu, *The New York Convention on the Recognition and Enforcement of Foreign Arbitral Awards: Analysis of the Seven Defenses to Oppose Enforcement in the United States and England*, 23 Arizona Journal of International and Comparative Law 747 (2006).

Michael Pryles, *Reflections on Transnational Public Policy*, 24(1) Journal of International Arbitration 1 (2007).

Paul Tan, *Public Policy in Singapore: An Unruly Horse Rears its Head – AJT v AJU*, 13(6) International Arbitration Law Review 234 (2010).

Peter Molife & Hong-lin Yu, T*he Impact of National Law Elements on International Commercial Arbitration*, 4(1) International Arbitration Law Review 17 (2001).

Pilar Perales Viscasillas, *Case Law on the Recognition and Enforcement of Arbitral Awards Under the UNCITRAL Model Law on International Commercial Arbitration*, 8(5) International Arbitration Law Review 191 (2005).

Robert Pé & Michael Polkinghorne, *Two Steps Forward, One Step ... Sideways-Recent Developments in Arbitration in China*, 25(3) Journal of International Arbitration 407 (2008).

W. Michael Reisman, *Law, International Public Policy (So-Called) and Arbitral Choice in International Commercial Arbitration*, in International Arbitration 2006: Back to Basics? 849–856 (Albert Jan van den Berg ed., 2007).

Xianchu Zhang, *The Agreement Between Mainland China and the Hong Kong SAR on Mutual Enforcement of Arbitral Awards: Problems and Prospects*, 29 Hong Kong Law Journal 463 (1999).

Xianming Shi, *Amlon Dilemma: Another Hilmarton Nightmare in International Commercial Arbitration*, 10 (3) Canadian Social Science 29 (2014)

Xiusong Xing, *Foreign Arbitral Award Refused Recognition and Enforcement on Public Policy Grounds*, dated 4 February 2010, *available at*: http://www.internationallawoffice.com/newsletters/detail.aspx?g=203daa53-a49e-4f6a-9696-a440907e47e2 (accessed 4 May 2017).

7. Periodicals Published in Chinese in Taiwan

Audley Sheppard（2000）、傅崑成（譯），〈以公共政策（public policy）為理由拒絕執行外國仲裁判斷之研究〉，《仲裁》，56期，頁33–61。
Audley Sheppard, Kuenchen Fu (translated), *Public Policy as a Ground for Refusing Enforcement of Foreign Arbitral Awards*, 56 Arbitration 33-61 (2000).

王欽彥（2011），〈我國只有機構仲裁而無個案（ad hoc）仲裁？—最高法院99年度台抗字第358號裁定背後之重大問題—〉，《台灣法學雜誌》，171期，頁193–198。
Chin-Yen Wang, *Has Taiwan Only Institutional Arbitration but no Ad Hoc Arbitration? A Serious Mistake behind Formosan Supreme Court Case 2010-Tai-Kang-Zi No. 358*, 171 Taiwan Law Journal 193–198 (2011).

黃居正（2011），〈印度領土通行地役權案：國際法的法源、習慣國際法、區域性習慣國際法〉，《台灣法學雜誌》，169期，頁93–98。
Chu-Cheng Huang, *Right of Passage over Indian Territory, Merits, Judgment of 12 April, 1960, ICJ Reports 1960 p. 6*, 169 Taiwan Law Journal 93–98 (2011).

陳希佳、張詩芸（2015），〈淺談對賭協議〉，《台商張老師》，196期，頁7。
Helena Hsi-Chia Chen & Alison Shih-Yun Chang, *A Nutshell on VAM Agreements*, 196 Master Chang Monthly 7 (2015).

陳希佳（2012），〈兩岸仲裁法比較研究（上）〉，《仲裁》，96期，頁73–103。
Helena Hsi-Chia Chen, *A Comparative Study on the Arbitration Law on Both Sides of the Taiwan Strait (Part I)*, 96 Arbitration 73–103 (2012).

陳希佳（2013），〈兩岸仲裁法比較研究（下）〉，《仲裁》，97期，頁30–63。
Helena Hsi-Chia Chen, *A Comparative Study on the Arbitration Law on Both Sides of the Taiwan Strait (Part II)*, 97 Arbitration 30–63 (2013).

陳希佳（2011），〈探討我國法院關於非機構（adhoc）仲裁判斷的裁判—臺灣高等法院99年度非抗字第122號民事裁定及其可能的影響〉，《仲裁》，93期，頁26–41。
Helena Hsi-Chia Chen, *A Review of the Taiwanese Court's Ruling on Ad Hoc Arbitral Awards—Comment on Taiwan High Court's Ruling: 99 Fei-Kang-Zi No. 122 and Its Possible Impacts*, 93 Arbitration 26–41 (2011).

陳希佳（2014），〈後投保協議時代的兩岸商務仲裁—以兩岸投保協議第十四條第四款前段之解釋與適用為中心〉，《臺北大學法學論叢》，92期，頁137–185。
Helena Hsi-Chia Chen, *Commercial Arbitration after the Cross-Strait Bilateral Investment Protection and Promotion Agreement-Focused on the Interpretation and Application of Article 14.4 of the Cross-strait Bilateral Investment Protection and Promotion Agreement*, 92 NTPU Law Review 137–185 (2014).

陳希佳（2010），〈大陸關於認定仲裁協議效力的規定與實務見解〉，《仲裁》，91期，頁95–126。
Helena Hsi-Chia Chen, *Regulations and Cases Concerning Validity of Arbitration Agreements in Mainland China*, 91 Arbitration 95–126 (2010).

陳希佳（2013），〈二〇一二年中國大陸民事訴訟法修訂對其仲裁制度之影響〉，《月旦民商法》，41期，頁96–106。

Helena Hsi-Chia Chen, *The Impact of the 2012 Amendments to the Civil Procedure Law of the People's Republic of China on the Arbitration Regime in the China*, 41 Cross-Strait Law Review 96–106 (2013).

海基會（2012），〈兩岸投資保障和促進協議Q&A〉，《兩岸經貿》，2012年9月號。

Straits Exchange Foundation, *Cross-Strait Bilateral Investment Protection and Promotion Agreement Q&A*, Straits Business Monthly (September 2012).

8. Periodicals Published in Chinese in Mainland China

呂炳斌（2010），〈論外國仲裁機構到我國境內仲裁的問題—兼析我國加入《紐約公約》時的保留〉，《法治研究》，2010年10期，頁71－74。

Bing-bin Lv, *Reflection on Foreign Arbitral Institution to Arbitrate in Our Country- Reservations Made by the PRC When Acceding to the New York Convention*, 2010 (10) Research on Rule of Law 71-74 (2010).

馬德才（2010），〈《紐約公約》中的公共政策性質之辨〉，《法學雜誌》，2010年4期，頁69－72。

Decai Ma, *Analysis About the Character of the Public Policy in New York Convention*, 2010(4) Law Science Magazine 69-72 (2010).

萬鄂湘、夏曉紅（2010），〈中國法院不予承認及執行某些外國仲裁裁決的原因—《紐約公約》相關案例分析〉，《武大國際法評論》，13卷2期，頁1－47。

Exiang Wan & Xiaohong Xia, *Reason for the Refusals of the Recognition and Enforcement of Foreign Arbitral Awards in Chinese Courts - New York Convention Case Studies*, 13(2) International Law Review of Wuhan University 1-47 (2010).

萬鄂湘、于喜富（2007），〈我國仲裁司法監督制度的最新發展—評最高人民法院關於適用仲裁法的司法解釋〉，《法學評論》，141期，頁73－79。

Exiang Wan & Xifu Yu, *The Latest Development of Judicial Supervision over Arbitration in the PRC—Comment on the Supreme People's Court's Judicial Interpretations Concerning the Application of Arbitration Law*, 141 Law Review 73-79 (2007).

萬鄂湘（2009），〈《紐約公約》在中國的司法實踐〉，《法律適用》，276期，頁4－6。

Exiang Wan, *Judicial Practice with Regards to the New York Convention in China*, 276 Journal of Law Application 4-6 (2009).

高薇（2010），〈論訴訟與仲裁關係中的既判力問題〉，《法學家》，2010年6期，頁153－163。

Wei Gao, *Res Judicata in Relationship Between State Courts and Arbitral Tribunals*, 6 The Jurist 153-163 (2010).

劉貴祥、沈紅雨（2012），〈我國承認和執行外國仲裁裁決的司法實踐述評〉，《北京仲裁》，79輯，頁1－24。

Guixiang Liu & Hongyu Shen, *Recognition and Enforcement of Foreign Arbitral Awards in China: A Look Back on a Decade of Court Practices*, 79 Beijing Arbitration 1-24 (2012).

毛海波（2011），〈我國司法實踐對國際商事仲裁'公共政策'的理解與適用〉，《仲裁研究》，26輯，頁52－58。

Haibo Mao, *Understanding and Application of Public Policy in International Commercial Arbitration in the Context of Chinese Judicial Practice*, 26 Arbitration Study 52-58 (2011).

宋航（1999），〈中國涉外仲裁裁決的執行—實踐中的問題〉，《仲裁與法律通訊》，4期，頁7－18。

Hang Song, *Enforcement of Foreign-Related Arbitral Awards in China—Issues in Practice*, 4 Arbitration and Law Communication 7-18 (1999).

陳希佳（2016），〈兩岸相互執行仲裁判斷與調解協議的現況與展望〉，《中國國際私法與比較法年刊（2014）》第十七卷，頁188－206。

Helena Hsi-Chia Chen, *The Current Status and Future Possible Developments with regards to Cross-Strait Mutual Recognition and Enforcement of Arbitration Awards and Mediated Settlement Agreements*, 17 Chinese Yearbook of Private International and Comparative Law 188－206 (2016).

楊弘磊（2009），〈人民法院涉外仲裁司法審查情況的調研報告〉，《武大國際法評論》，9卷1期，頁304－321。

Honglei Yang, *Report on the Judicial Review of International Arbitration in Chinese Courts*, 9(1) International Law Review of Wuhan University 304-321 (2009).

杜煥芳（2006），〈從實例看中國涉外仲裁裁決撤銷的完善〉，《仲裁與法律》，第100輯，頁95－107。

Huanfang Du, *The Reform of the Revocation of Foreign-Related Arbitral Awards in China: From a Practice Perspective*, 100 Arbitration and Law 95-107 (2006).

詹慧娟（2009），〈《紐約公約》第5條中公共政策與正當程序條款的適用〉，《北京仲裁》，69輯，頁21－36。

Huijuan Zhan, *The Application of Public Policy and Due Process of Article V of New York Convention*, 69 Beijing Arbitration 21-36 (2009).

趙健（1998），〈論公共秩序與國際商事仲裁裁決的承認與執行〉，《仲裁與法律通訊》，6期，頁14－24；亦刊載於：《中國國際私法與比較法年刊》第2卷，頁378－398。

Jian Zhao, *On the Public Order and the Recognition and Enforcement of International Commercial Arbitral Awards*, 6 Arbitration and Law Communication 14-24 (1998); also available at: 2 Chinese Yearbook of Private International and Comparative Law 378-398 (1999).

宋連斌、趙健（2001），〈關於修改1994年中國《仲裁法》若干問題的探討〉，《國際經濟法論叢》第4卷，頁597－617。

Lianbin Song & Jian Zhao, *Analysis on Amendments to Arbitration Act 1994*, 4 Journal of International Economic Law 597-617 (2001).

宋連斌、王珺（2011），〈國際商會在中國內地仲裁：准入、裁決國籍及執行—由寧波中院的一份裁定談起〉，《西北大學學報（哲學社會科學版）》，41卷3期，頁154－161。

Lianbin Song & Jun Wang, *On Authorization, Nationality and Enforcement of ICC Awards Made in Mainland China: Reflections from the Ningbo Intermediate Court's Ruling*, 41(3) Journal of Northwest University (Philosophy and Social Sciences Edition) 154-161 (2011).

宋連斌（1999年），〈我國內地承認和執行臺灣地區仲裁裁決的若干問題探討〉，《中國國際私法與比較法年刊》第2卷，頁399－408。

Lianbin Song, *A Probe into Some Issues on Recognition and Enforcement of Taiwan's Arbitral Awards in Mainland China*, 2 Chinese Yearbook of Private International and Comparative Law 399-408 (1999).

宋連斌（2004），〈理念走向規則：仲裁法修訂應注意的幾個問題〉，《北京仲裁》，52輯，頁1-19。

Lianbin Song, *Approaches to the Revision of the Arbitration Act 1994: Ideas Into Rules*, 52 Beijing Arbitration 1-19 (2004).

楊玲（2013），〈中國承認與執行仲裁裁決－以「涉外商事海事審判指導」（二〇〇一至二〇一一年）為考察對象〉，《月旦法學》，218期，頁133-145。

Ling Yang, *Recognition and Enforcement of Arbitral Awards in China – Based on 'Guide on Foreign-Related Commercial and Maritime Trial' from 2001 to 2011*, 218 The Taiwan Law Review 133-145 (2013).

劉喬發（2004），〈我國對外國仲裁裁決的承認和執行〉，《涉外商事海事審判指導》，總第7輯，頁178-184。

Qiaofa Liu, *Recognition and Enforcement of Foreign Arbitral Awards in the PRC*, 7 Guide on Foreign-Related Commercial and Maritime Trial 178-184 (2004).

符啟林、羅晉京（2007），〈論社會公共利益和經濟法〉，《河北法學》，2007年7期，頁21-25。

Qilin Fu & Jinjing Luo, *Social Public Interests and Economic Law*, 2007(7) Hebei Law Review 21-25 (2007).

王生長(2005)，〈關於修訂《中國國際經濟貿易仲裁委員會仲裁規則》的說明〉，《仲裁與法律》，96輯，頁32-38。

Shengchang Wang, *Introduction to the Amendment of CIETAC Arbitration Rules*, 96 Arbitration and Law 32-38 (2005).

王生長（1999），〈中國仲裁法講座〉，《仲裁與法律通訊》，1999年11月增刊，頁23。

Shengchang Wang, *Lectures on Chinese Arbitration Law*, Arbitration and Law Communication 23 (November 1999).

王生長(1999)，〈外國仲裁裁決在中國的承認與執行〉，陳安主編，《國際經濟法論叢》第2卷，頁509-510。

Shengchang Wang, *Recognition and Enforcement of Forward Arbitral Awards in China*, in An Chen, 2 Journal of International Economic Law 509-510 (1999).

最高人民法院民四庭（2010），〈關於涉外商事案件集中管轄制度的實施情況及完善對策的調研報告〉，《涉外商事海事審判指導》，21輯，頁216-225。

The Fourth Civil Tribunal of the Supreme People's Court, *An Investigation Report on the Enforcement of Centralized Jurisdiction of Foreign-Related Commercial Cases and Reforms*, 21 Guide on Foreign-Related Commercial and Maritime Trial 216-225 (2010).

趙維東(2011)，〈從《紐約公約》在亞洲國家的實施看國際商事仲裁中的公共秩序〉，《仲裁研究》，27輯，頁54-60。

Weidong Zhao, *See the Public Policy of International Trading Arbitration – From 'New York Convention' in Asian Countries' Implementation*, 27 Arbitration Study 54-60 (2011).

顧維遐（2010），〈我們信賴仲裁嗎？—關於中國仲裁研究的英文文獻綜述〉，《北京仲裁》，72輯，頁1-26。

Weixia Gu, *In Arbitration We Trust…Not? – A Review of English Literatures on the Study of Arbitration in China*, 72 Beijing Arbitration 1-26 (2010).

顧維遐（2009），〈香港與內地仲裁裁決司法審查制度的借鑒和融合〉，《法學家》，2009年4期，頁106‐117。

Weixia Gu, *Judicial Review of Arbitral Awards in Hong Kong and the Mainland: Lessons and Convergence Between Two Jurisdictions in China*, The Jurist 106-117 (2009).

張憲初（2010），〈澳門對中國民商事區際司法協助發展的貢獻及其特色〉，《比較法研究》，2010年3期，頁93‐104。

Xianchu Zhang, *The Contribution of the Macau SAR to the Developments of Regional Judicial Assistance in Civil and Commercial Matters and Its Characteristics*, 2010(3) Journal of Comparative Law 93-104 (2010).

尹翔（2009），〈論我國法院對《紐約公約》裁決的承認與執行〉，《河北法學》，27卷7期，頁19‐22。

Xiang Yin, *The Recognition and Enforcement of the Arbitral Award Manifested in the New York Convention by the Courts in China*, 27(7) Hebei Law Review 19-22 (2009).

齊湘泉（2009），〈嘉能可公司申請承認及執行英國倫敦金屬交易所仲裁裁決案法律問題探析兼評最高人民法院《關於英國嘉能可有限公司申請承認和執行英國倫敦金屬交易所仲裁裁決一案請示的复函》，《仲裁研究》，20輯，頁85‐98。

Xiangquan Qi, *On the Legal Issues Concerning Application for Recognition and Enforcement of London Metal Exchange Arbitral Award by Glencore International AG – Concurrently on the Supreme Court's Official Reply for this Case*, 20 Arbitration Study 85-98 (2009).

劉曉紅（2011），〈海峽兩岸仲裁裁決相互認可與執行制度之檢視與修正〉，《法學》，2011年12期，頁86‐94。

Xiaohong Liu, *Scheme of Mutual Recognition and Enforcement of Cross-Strait Arbitral Awards: Examination & Revision*, 12 Law Science 86-94 (2011).

張瀟劍、韓輝（2010），〈有哪些仲裁研究值得關注？—2009年中文法學期刊仲裁研究論文綜述〉，《北京仲裁》，72輯，頁27‐47。

Xiaojian Zhang & Hui Han, *A Review on Articles Concerning Arbitration Study from Chinese Legal Journals in 2009*, 72 Beijing Arbitration 27-47 (2010).

高曉力（2009），〈我國法院對國際商事仲裁裁決進行司法審查過程中運用公共政策分析〉，《涉外商事海事審判指導》，18輯，頁195‐228。

Xiaoli Gao, *Analysis of the PRC Courts' Application of Public Policy in Judicial Review of International Commercial Arbitral Awards*, 18 Guide on Foreign-Related Commercial and Maritime Trial 195-228 (2009).

葛行軍（2003），〈關於仲裁裁決在執行中存在的有關問題－最高人民法院執行辦主任葛行軍在2003年仲裁員實務研討會上的發言〉，《仲裁與法律》，6期：總89期，頁18‐28。

Xingjun Ge, *Issues Arising from Enforcement of Arbitral Awards – Talk by Justice Xingjun Ge, the Chair of the Enforcement Division of the Supreme People's Court at Arbitrators' Seminar on Practical Issues 2003*, 89 Arbitration and Law 18-28 (2003).

杜新麗（2005），〈論外國仲裁裁決在我國的承認與執行－兼論《紐約公約》在中國的適用〉，《比較法研究》，2005年4期，頁98‐109。

Xinli Du, *Theory on the Recognition and Enforcement of Foreign Arbitral Award in China – Theory on Applying the New York Arbitration Convention of 1958 to China*, 2005(4) Journal of Comparative Law 98–109 (2005).

趙秀文（2006），〈中國《仲裁法》與建設社會主義和諧社會－為記念我國《仲裁法》實施十週年而作〉，《仲裁與法律》，101輯，頁5－28。

Xiuwen Zhao, *Chinese Arbitration Law and Construction of Harmonious Society under Socialism – Commemoration of the Tenth Anniversary of the PRC Arbitration Law's Implementation*, 101 Arbitration and Law 5–28 (2006).

趙秀文（2005），〈論ICC國際仲裁院裁決在我國的承認與執行〉，《法學》，2005年6期，頁67－72。

Xiuwen Zhao, *Recognition and Enforcement of an ICC Arbitral Award in the PRC*, 6 The Jurist 67–72 (2005).

趙秀文（2009），〈從永寧公司案看公共政策作為我國法院拒絕執行仲裁外國仲裁裁決的理由，《法學家》，4期，頁98－105。

Xiuwen Zhao, *Refusing Recognition and Enforcement of Foreign Arbitral Awards on the Ground of Public Policy from the Case of Yongning Corporation*, 4 The Jurist 98–105 (2009).

趙秀文（2009），〈中國仲裁市場對外開放研究〉，《政法論壇》，27卷6期，頁69－78。

Xiuwen Zhao, *The Research of the Opening of China Arbitration Market*, 27(6) Tribune of Political Science and Law June 69–78 (2009).

崔學杰、何云（2010），〈論涉及違反管理性強制性規範的合同所作出的外國仲裁裁決的承認和執行－利夫糖果（上海）有限公司申請承認和執行新加坡國際仲裁中心仲裁裁決案評析〉，《北京仲裁》，72輯，頁152－159。

Xuejie Cui & Yun He, *On Recognition and Enforcement of Foreign Arbitral Awards Reached from Contracts Violating Management and Compulsory Regulations – Comment on the Case of Leaf Candy Limited Corporation of Shanghai's Application of Recognition and Enforcement of the Arbitral Award given by SIAC*, 72 Beijing Arbitration 152–159 (2010).

黃雁明（2010），〈商事仲裁司法監督－以上海市第二中級人民法院商事仲裁司法監督的實踐為視角〉，《北京仲裁》，71輯，頁142－159。

Yanming Huang, *Research on Judicial Supervision over Commercial Arbitration – From the Perspective of the Practice of Judicial Supervision over Commercial Arbitration by Shanghai Second Intermediate People's Court*, 71 Beijing Arbitration 142–159 (2010).

黃亞英（2010），〈解釋和適用《紐約公約》的國際標準〉，《法學雜誌》，2010年10期，頁6－11。

Yaying Huang, *Analysis About the International Standard of Paraphrase and Application of New York Convention*, 2010(10) Law Science Magazine 6–11 (2010).

黃亞英（2007），〈外國仲裁裁決論析—基於《紐約公約》及中國實踐的視角〉，《現代法學》，29卷1期，頁124－131。

Yaying Huang, *Foreign Arbitral Award: In Perspective of the New York Convention and the Judicial Practice of China*, 2007(1) Modern Law Science 124–131 (2007).

林一飛（2009），〈外國仲裁裁決的承認與執行：中國二十年的司法實踐〉，《國際經濟法學刊》，第16卷第1期，頁30－51。

Yifei Lin, *Recognition and Enforcement of Foreign Arbitral Award: 20 Years' Judicial Practice in China*, 16(1) Journal of International Economic Law 30-51 (2009).

田玉璽（2004），〈也談仲裁裁決的司法審查〉，《北京仲裁》，51輯，頁6-12。

Yuxi Tian, *Comment on Domestic Judicial Review on Arbitration*, 51 Beijing Arbitration 6-12 (2004).

費宗禕（2007），〈費宗禕先生談仲裁法的修改〉，《北京仲裁》，62輯，頁1-4。

Zongyi Fei, *Comment on the Revision of the Arbitration Act by Fei Zong Yi*, 62 Beijing Arbitration 1-4 (2007).

9. Periodicals Published in Chinese in Macau

賴建國（2012），〈澳門仲裁法制修改研究〉，《行政：澳門公共行政雜誌》第25卷，總第95期，頁63-81，澳門特別行政區政府行政公職局出版。

Jianguo Lai, *Amendment of the Macao Arbitration System*, 95 Administracao: Revista de Administracao Publica de Macau 63-81 (2012).

10. Periodicals Published in Japanese in Japan

中村達也（2010），〈JCAAの仲裁判断の承認・執行を拒否した中国裁判所の判断の問題点〉，《国際商事法務》，38巻5期，頁628-634。

Tatsuya Nakamura, *Couple Questions Concerning PRC Court's Decision to Refuse Recognition and Enforcement of JCAA's Arbitral Award*, 38(5) International Business Law and Practice (Kokusai - Shoji - Homu) 628-634 (2010).

Table of Cases

Table of Cases

Form 4-1

No.	Name	Matter Number	Date Issued	Companies Involved
	最高人民法院關於申請人 Castel Electronics Pty Ltd. 申請承認和執行外國仲裁裁決一案請示的復函 Reply of the Supreme People's Court to the Request for Instructions on Application by Castel Electronics Pty Ltd for Recognition and Enforcement of a Foreign Arbitral Award	(2013)民四他字第46號 Supreme People's Court (2013) Min-Si-Ta-Zi No. 46	2013年10月10日 10 October 2013	
	廣東省高級人民法院申請人 Castel Electronics Pty Ltd. 申請承認和執行外國仲裁裁決一案的請示 Guangdong Higher People's Court's Request for Instructions on Application by Castel Electronics Pty Ltd for Recognition and Enforcement of a Foreign Arbitral Award	(2012)粵高法仲復字第7號 Guangdong Higher People's Court (2012) Yue-Gao-Fa-Zhong-Fu-Zi No. 7	2013年7月10日 10 July 2013	
1.	中山中院民事裁定書 Guangdong Zhongshan Intermediate People's Court Civil Ruling	(2009)中中法民四初字第3號 Guangdong Zhongshan Intermediate People's Court Civil Ruling (2009) Zhong-Zhong-Fa-Min-Si-Chu-Zi No. 3	2011年10月20日 20 October 2011	Castel電子公司 TCL空調器（中山）有限公司 Castel Electronics Pty Ltd. TCL Air Conditioner (Zhongshan) Co Ltd.

Form 4-1

No.	Name	Matter Number	Date Issued	Companies Involved
	最高人民法院關於韋斯頓瓦克公司申請承認與執行英國仲裁裁決案的請示的復函 Reply of the Supreme People's Court on Request for Instructions Re Application by Western Bulk Pte Ltd. for the Recognition and Enforcement of an English Arbitral Award	(2012)民四他字第12號 Supreme People's Court (2012) Min-Si-Ta-Zi No. 12	2012年5月21日 21 May 2012	
2.	天津市高級人民法院關於韋斯頓瓦克公司申請承認與執行英國仲裁裁決案的請示 Tianjin Higher People's Court's Request for Instructions Re Application by Western Bulk Pte Ltd. for the Recognition and Enforcement of an English Arbitral Award	(2011)津高民四他字第4號 Tianjin Higher People's Court (2011) Jin-Gao-Min-Si-Ta-Zi No. 4	2012年3月19日 19 March 2012	韋斯頓瓦克公司 北京中鋼天鐵鋼鐵貿易有限公司 Western Bulk Pte Ltd. Beijing Zhonggang Tiantie Iron & Steel Trading Co., Ltd.
3.	最高人民法院關於路易達孚商品亞洲有限公司申請承認和執行國際油、種子和脂肪協會作出的第3980號仲裁裁決請示一案的復函 Reply of the Supreme People's Court on Request for Instructions Re	(2010)民四他字第48號 Supreme People's Court (2010) Min-Si-Ta-Zi No. 48	2010年10月10日 10 October 2010	

Table of Cases

Form 4-1

No.	Name	Matter Number	Date Issued	Companies Involved
	Application by Louis Dreyfus Commodities Asian Co., Ltd. for Recognition and Enforcement of Arbitration Award No. 3980 of International Federation of Oils, Seeds & Fats Associations			
	廣東省高級人民法院關於路易達孚商品亞洲有限公司與廣東富虹油品有限公司申請承認和執行外國仲裁裁決一案的請示 Guangdong Higher People's Court's Request for Instructions Re Application for Recognition and Enforcement of a Foreign Arbitration Award Concerning Louis Dreyfus Commodities Asian Co., Ltd. and Guangdong Fuhong Edible Oil Co. Ltd.	(2009) 粵高法民四他字第10號 Guangdong Higher People's Court (2009) Yue-Gao-Fa-Min-Si-Ta-Zi No. 10	2010年6月20日 20 June 2010	路易達孚商品亞洲有限公司 廣東富虹油品有限公司 Louis Dreyfus Commodities Asian Co., Ltd. Guangdong Fuhong Edible Oil Co. Ltd.

Table of Cases

Form 4-1

No.	Name	Matter Number	Date Issued	Companies Involved
	最高人民法院關於申請人天瑞酒店投資有限公司與被申請人杭州易居酒店管理有限公司申請承認仲裁裁決一案的請示報告的復函 Reply of the Supreme People's Court on Request for Instructions Re Recognition of the Arbitral Award in the Case of Tianrui Hotel Investment Co., Ltd. (Petitioner) v. Hangzhou Yiju Hotel Management Co., Ltd. (Respondent)	(2010)民四他字第18號 Supreme People's Court (2010) Min-Si-Ta-Zi No. 18	2010年5月18日 18 May 2010	
4.	浙江省高級人民法院關於申請人民天瑞酒店投資有限公司與被申請人杭州易居酒店管理有限公司申請承認仲裁裁決一案的請示報告 Zhejiang Higher People's Court's Request for Instructions Re Recognition of the Arbitral Award in the Case of Tianrui Hotel Investment Co., Ltd. (Petitioner) v. Hangzhou Yiju Hotel Management Co., Ltd. (Respondent)	(2010)浙商外他字第3號 Zhejiang Higher People's Court (2010) Zhe-Shang-Wai-Ta-Zi No. 3	2010年3月15日 15 March 2010	天瑞酒店投資有限公司 杭州易居酒店管理有限公司 Tianrui Hotel Investment Co., Ltd. Hangzhou Yiju Hotel Management Co., Ltd.

Table of Cases

Form 4-1

No.	Name	Matter Number	Date Issued	Companies Involved
	最高人民法院關於GRD Minproc有限公司申請承認並執行瑞典斯德哥爾摩商會仲裁院仲裁裁決一案的請示的復函 Reply of the Supreme People's Court on Request for Instructions Re Application by GRD Minproc Limited for Recognition and Enforcement of the Arbitration Award of Arbitration Institute of the Stockholm Chamber of Commerce	(2008)民四他字第48號 Supreme People's Court (2008) Min-Si-Ta-Zi No. 48	2009年3月13日 13 March 2009	
5.	上海市高級人民法院關於GRD Minproc有限公司申請承認並執行瑞典斯德哥爾摩商會仲裁院仲裁裁決一案的請示 Shanghai Higher People's Court's Request for Instructions Re Application by GRD Minproc Limited for Recognition and Enforcement of the Arbitration Award of Arbitration Institute of the Stockholm Chamber of Commerce	(2008)滬高民四（商）他字第2號 Shanghai Higher People's Court (2008) Hu-Gao-Min-Si (Shang)-Ta-Zi No. 2	2008年8月18日 18 August 2008	GRD Minproc 有限公司 上海飛輪實業有限公司 GRD Minproc Limited Shanghai Flyingwheel Industry Co., Ltd.

214

Table of Cases

Form 4-1

No.	Name	Matter Number	Date Issued	Companies Involved
	最高人民法院關於不予承認和执行国际商會仲裁院仲裁裁決的請示的復函 Reply of the Supreme People's Court to a Request for Instructions on the Non-Recognition and Non-Enforcement of an Arbitral Award of the ICC International Court of Arbitration	(2008)民四他字第11號 Supreme People's Court (2008) Min-Si-Ta-Zi No. 11	2008年6月2日 2 June 2008	濟南海慕法姆製藥有限公司 濟南永寧製藥股份有限公司 Hemofarm DD MAG國際貿易公司 蘇拉麼媒體有限公司 Jinan-Hemofarm Pharmaceutical Co., Ltd. Jinan Yongning Pharmaceutical Co., Ltd. Hemofarm DD MAG Intertrade Holding DD Suram Media Ltd
6.	山東省高級人民法院關於不予承認和執行國際商會仲裁院仲裁裁決的請示 Shandong Higher People's Court's Request for Instructions on the Non-Recognition and Non-Enforcement of an Arbitral Award of the ICC International Court of Arbitration	(2007)魯民四他字第12號 Shandong Higher People's Court (2007) Lu-Min-Si-Ta-Zi No. 12	2008年1月30日 30 January 2008	
7.	最高人民法院《關於不予承認日本商事仲裁協會東京04－05號仲裁裁決的報告》的復函 Reply of the Supreme People's Court on the Report of Non-Recognition of Arbitration Award No. 04-05 (Tokyo) of Japan Commercial Arbitration Association	(2007)民四他字第26號 Supreme People's Court (2007) Min-Si-Ta-Zi No. 26	2008年3月3日 3 March 2008	日本信越化學工業株式會社 江蘇中天科技股份有限公司 Shin-Etsu Chemical Co., Ltd. Jiangsu Zhongtian Technology Co., Ltd.

Table of Cases

Form 4-1

No.	Name	Matter Number	Date Issued	Companies Involved
	江蘇省高級人民法院關於不予承認日本商事仲裁協會東京04-05號仲裁裁決的報告 Jiangsu Higher People's Court's Report of Non-Recognition of Arbitration Award No. 04-05 (Tokyo) of Japan Commercial Arbitration Association	(2007)蘇民三他字第0002號 Jiangsu Higher People's Court (2007) Su-Min-San-Ta-Zi No. 0002	2007年5月25日 25 May 2007	
	最高人民法院關於馬紹爾群島第一投資公司申請承認和執行英國倫敦臨時仲裁庭仲裁裁決案的復函 Reply of the Supreme People's Court on Application of First Investment Corp. of the Marshall Islands for Recognition and Enforcement of Arbitration Award of an Ad Hoc Arbitration Tribunal in London	(2007)民四他字第35號 Supreme People's Court (2007) Min-Si-Ta-Zi No. 35	2008年2月27日 27 February 2008	馬紹爾群島第一投資公司 福建省馬尾造船股份有限公司 福建省船舶工業集團公司 First Investment Corp (Marshall Island) Fujian Mawei Shipbuilding Ltd. Fujian Shipbuilding Industry Group Company Limited
8.	廈門海事法院民事裁定書 Xiamen Maritime Court's Civil Ruling	(2006)廈海法認字第1號 Xiamen Maritime Court Civil Ruling (2006) Xia-Hai-Fa-Ren-Zi No. 1	2008年5月11日 11 May 2008	

Form 4-1

No.	Name	Matter Number	Date Issued	Companies Involved
	最高人民法院關於對海口中院不予承認和執行瑞典斯德哥爾摩商會仲裁院仲裁裁決請示的復函 Reply of the Supreme People's Court on the Request for Instructions on the Non-Recognition and Non-Enforcement of an Arbitral Award of the Arbitration Institute of the Stockholm Chamber of Commerce	(2001)民四他字第12號 Supreme People's Court (2001) Min-Si-Ta-Zi No. 12	2005年7月13日 13 July 2005	
9.	海南省高級人民法院《關於對海口中院"瑞典斯德哥爾摩商會仲裁院第060/1999號仲裁裁決書不予承認和執行案"審查意見的請示報告》 Hainan Higher People's Court's Request for Instructions on the Hainan Haikou Intermediate People's Court's Non-Recognition and Non-Enforcement of No. 060/1999 Arbitral Award of the Arbitration Institute of the Stockholm Chamber of Commerce	(2001)瓊經復字第1號 Hainan Higher People's Court (2001) Qiong-Jing-Fu-Zi No. 1	2001年4月5日 5 April 2001	日本三井物產株式會社 海南省紡織工業總公司 海南瓊海滌綸廠 Mitsui & Co., Ltd. Hainan Textile Industry General Corporation Hainan Qionghai Polyester Factory

Table of Cases

Form 4-1

No.	Name	Matter Number	Date Issued	Companies Involved
	最高人民法院關於ED&F曼氏（香港）有限公司申請承認和執行倫敦糖業協會仲裁裁決案的復函 Reply of the Supreme People's Court on Request for Instructions Re Application by ED&F (Hong Kong) Co., Ltd. for Recognition and Enforcement of the Arbitral Award of the Sugar Association of London	(2003)民四他字第3號 Supreme People's Court (2003) Min-Si-Ta-Zi No. 3	2003年7月1日 1 July 2003	
10.	北京市高級人民法院關於對ED&F曼氏（香港）有限公司申請承認及執行倫敦糖業協會第158號仲裁裁決一案的請示 Beijing Higher People's Court's Request for Instructions Re Application by ED&F (Hong Kong) Co., Ltd. for Recognition and Enforcement of the No. 158 Arbitral Award of the Sugar Association of London	京高法(2003)7號 Beijing Higher People's Court (2003) Jing-Gao-Fa No. 7	2003年1月15日 15 January 2003	曼氏（香港）有限公司 中國糖業酒類集團公司 ED&F Man (Hong Kong) Co., Ltd. China National Sugar & Alcohol Group Corp.

Form 4-2

No.	Name	Matter Number	Date Issued	Companies Involved
1.	阿姆龍鋼鐵有限公司申請執行雲南鎳鈷礦業有限公司等仲裁裁決案 雲南省昆明市中級人民法院 Amlon Metals Ltd.'s Application for Enforcement of the Arbitral Award Concerning Yunnan Nickel and Cobalt Co., Ltd. and Others Yunnan Kunming Intermediate People's Court	(2008)昆非執字第48-1 號 Yunnan Kunming Intermediate People's Court (2008) Kun-Fei-Zhi-Zi No. 48-1	執結日期 2009年11月10日 The Enforcement Proceedings closed on 10 November 2009	阿姆龍鋼鐵有限公司 雲南鎳鈷礦業有限公司 昆明鐵路局進出口有限公司 Amlon Metals Ltd. Yunnan Nickel and Cobalt Co., Ltd. Kunming Railway Bureau Import and Export Corporation
2.	最高人民法院關於舟山中海糧油工業有限公司申請不予執行香港國際仲裁中心仲裁裁決一案的請示復函 Reply of the Supreme People's Court on Request for Instructions Re Application by Zhoushan Zhonghai Cereals & Oils Industry Co., Ltd. for Non-Enforcement of Arbitration Award of Hong Kong International Arbitration Centre	(2009)民四他字第2號 Supreme People's Court (2009) Min-Si-Ta-Zi No. 2	2009年3月18日 18 March 2009	
	浙江省高級人民法院《關於舟山中海糧油工業有限公司申請不予執行香港國際仲裁中心仲裁裁決一案的請示報告》 Zhejiang Higher People's Court's Request for Instructions Re	(2007)浙執他字第4號 Zhejiang Higher People's Court (2007)	2008年12月15日	來寶資源有限公司 舟山中海糧油工業有限公司 Noble Resources Pte Ltd. Zhoushan Zhonghai Cereals & Oils Industry Co., Ltd.

Table of Cases

Form 4-2

No.	Name	Matter Number	Date Issued	Companies Involved
	Application by Zhoushan Zhonghai Cereals & Oils Industry Co., Ltd. for Non-Enforcement of the Arbitral Award of Hong Kong International Arbitration Centre	Zhe-Zhi-Ta-Zi No. 4	15 December 2008	
	最高人民法院關於香港享進糧油食品有限公司申請執行香港國際仲裁中心仲裁裁決案的復函 Reply of the Supreme People's Court Re Application by Head Choice Cereals, Oils & Foodstuffs Limited for Enforcement of the Arbitral Award of Hong Kong International Arbitration Centre	(2003)民四他字第9號 Supreme People's Court (2003) Min-Si-Ta-Zi No. 9	2003年11月14日 14 November 2003	
3.	安徽省高級人民法院關於對香港國際仲裁中心仲裁裁決香港享進糧油食品有限公司與安徽糧油食品進出口（集團）公司買賣合同糾紛案不予執行的請示 Anhui Higher People's Court's Request for Instructions Re the Non-Enforcement of the Arbitral Award of Hong Kong International Arbitration Centre on Dispute Over the Sales Contract Between Head Choice Cereals, Oils & Foodstuffs Limited and Anhui Cereals Oils & Foodstuffs I/E (Group) Corp.	(2003)皖執他字第01號 Anhui Higher People's Court (2003) Wan-Zhi-Ta-Zi No. 01	[日期不詳] [Date unknown]	香港享進糧油食品有限公司 安徽糧油食品進出口（集團）公司 海南高富瑞工貿有限公司 Head Choice Cereals, Oils & Foodstuffs Limited Anhui Cereals Oils & Foodstuffs I/E (Group) Corp. Hainan Gao Fu Rui Industry and Trade Co., Ltd.

Form 4-3

No.	Name	Matter Number	Date Issued	Companies Involved
1.	最高人民法院關於深圳市廣夏文化實業總公司、寧夏伊斯蘭國際信託投資公司、深圳興慶電子公司與密蘇爾有限公司仲裁裁決不予執行案的復函 Reply of the Supreme People's Court on the Non-enforcement of an Arbitral Award concerning Shenzhen Guangxia Culture Industry Company, Ningxia Islamic International Trust and Investment Company, Shenzhen Xingqing Electronics Company and Misuer Co., Ltd.	(2000)執監字第96-2號 Supreme People's Court (2000) Zhi-Jian-Zi No. 96-2	2002年4月20日 20 April 2002	深圳市廣夏文化實業總公司 寧夏伊斯蘭國際信託投資公司 深圳興慶電子公司 密蘇爾有限公司 Shenzhen Guangxia Culture Industry Company Ningxia Islamic International Trust and Investment Company Shenzhen Xingqing Electronics Company Misuer Co., Ltd.
2.	最高人民法院關於北京市第一中級人民法院不予執行美國製作公司和湯姆胡萊特公司訴中國婦女旅行社演出合同糾紛仲裁裁決請示的批復 Reply of the Supreme People's Court on the Non-enforcement of an Arbitral Award on Dispute Over the Performance Contract among USA Productions, Tom Hulett & Associates and China Women Travel Service	他(1997)35號 Supreme People's Court (1997) Ta No. 35	1997年12月26日 26 December 1997	

Table of Cases

Form 4-3

No.	Name	Matter Number	Date Issued	Companies Involved
	北京市高級人民法院《關於同意北京市第一中級人民法院不予執行美國製作公司、湯姆胡萊特公司訴中國婦女旅行社演出合同仲裁裁決請示的請示》 Beijing Higher People's Court's Request for Instructions on the Non-enforcement of an Arbitral Award on Dispute Over the Performance Contract among USA Productions, Tom Hulett & Associates and China Women Travel Service	京高法(1996)239號 Beijing Higher People's Court (1996) Jing-Gao-Fa No. 239	[日期不詳] [Date unknown]	美國製作公司 湯姆胡萊特公司 中國婦女旅行社 USA Productions Tom Hulett & Associates China Women Travel Service
3.	廣東省湛江市中級人民法院民事裁定書 Guangdong Zhanjiang Intermediate People's Court Civil Ruling	(1996)湛中法執字第1號 Guangdong Zhanjiang Intermediate People's Court (1996) Zhan-Zhong-Fa-Zhi-Zi No. 1	1998年12月30日 30 December 1998	
4.	最高人民法院函 Reply of the Supreme People's Court	[函號不詳] [Reply Letter number unknown]	1992年11月6日 6 November 1992	

222

Form 4-3

No.	Name	Matter Number	Date Issued	Companies Involved
				開封市東風服裝廠 河南省服裝進出口 （集團）有限公司 大進國際貿易 （香港）有限公司
	河南省鄭州市中級人民法院民事裁定書 Henan Zhengzhou Intermediate People's Court Civil Ruling	［案號不詳］ [Docket number unknown]	1992年9月28日 28 September 1992	Dongfeng Clothing Factory of Kaifeng Henan Clothing Import & Export (Group) Company Advancetex International Trading (H.K.) Co. Ltd.

Table of Cases

Form 4-4

No.	Name	Matter Number	Date Issued	Companies Involved
	六盤水恒鼎實業有限公司與張洪興採礦權轉讓合同糾紛管轄權異議案 最高人民法院民事裁定書 Objection to the Jurisdiction over Disputes arising from the Mining Right Transfer Agreement between Liupanshui Hidili Industry Co., Ltd. and Zhang Hongxing Supreme People's Court Civil Ruling	(2010)民二終字第86號 Supreme People's Court (2010) Min-Er-Zhong-Zi No. 86	2010年8月26日 26 August 2010	六盤水恒鼎實業有限公司 Liupanshui Hidili Industry Co., Ltd.

Index

A

Administrative decision
  Guangxia (see *Guangxia Culture* case)
  shareholder eligibility, 141
  tortious acts, 140
Administrative regulation
  Chinese, 110, 118
  mandatory, 95, 107, 110, 112, 117, 128, 192
  prohibited business operation, 110, 119
  social and public interest, 49
Anti-dumping, 125, 126, 152, 153
Appointment of arbitrators
  foreign-related arbitration, 180, 181
  by parties, 22, 133
  proper notice, 51, 104, 154
  restrictions, 186
  sole, 106, 109, 133
Approval
  administrative authorities, 108–110
  commercial activities, 118, 130
  competent authority, 108, 109, 130
  and enforcement of arbitral awards, 46, 48
  explanation, 46
  governmental departments, 141
  joint venture company, 170
  Macau's arbitral awards, 43
  Ministry of Culture's scope of, 143, 151
  and registration, 93–95, 128, 148

  Taiwan Region's arbitral awards, 43, 48
  term, 46, 47
ARATS. *See* Association for Relations Across the Taiwan Straits (ARATS)
Arbitrability, 5, 16
Arbitral award. *See* Award
Arbitral tribunal
  ad hoc, 42
  arbitration agreement disputes, 113–115
  arbitration proceedings, 105, 153
  award, 152, 154
  composition, 50–52, 105, 106
  decisions, 87, 98, 100–102, 107, 120, 124, 139, 159, 164, 191, 192
  error in merits or applicable laws, or unfair outcomes, 90–93
  interpretation, 90
  procedural public policy, 103
  proceedings, 19, 128
  protection of PRC's judicial sovereignty and jurisdiction
    Guangxia Culture case, 168–173
    Hemofarm case, 156–166
    Louis Dreyfus case, 167–168
  quality of the disputed equipment, 100
  re-arbitration, 56, 58, 73
  remedies, 98
  requirement of, 22
  revoke, award, 183

Index

scope of arbitration and jurisdiction, 140, 141
Arbitration
 ad hoc, 4, 34, 40, 104, 127
 agreement, 5, 7, 28, 37, 38, 50–56, 58–60, 68, 69, 76, 77, 89, 105, 113, 115, 128, 131, 138, 144–147, 152, 160, 165, 166, 173–179, 182–184, 186, 190
 domestic (*see* Domestic arbitration)
 foreign-related (*see* Foreign-related arbitration)
Arbitration Commission
 Beijing Arbitration Commission (BAC), 69, 91, 181
 Hainan Arbitration Commission, 92, 96, 97
 Kunming Arbitration Commission, 91
 Shanghai Arbitration Commission, 181
 Xiamen Arbitration Commission, 181
 Xiangtan Arbitration Commission, 96
 The Arbitration Institute of the Stockholm Chamber of Commerce (SCC), 93, 95, 100–102, 108, 112, 122, 123, 128
Arbitration institution
 domestic, 54
 foreign (*see* Foreign arbitration institution)
 foreign-related (*see* Foreign-related arbitration institution)
Arbitration proceedings
 arbitral award, 42, 105, 128
 arbitral tribunal, 19, 133, 162
 ICC arbitration, 157
 New York Convention, 154
 substantive public policy, 104
Association for Relations Across the Taiwan Straits (ARATS), 4
Award
 domestic (*see* Domestic arbitral award)
 foreign arbitral, 1, 4–8, 11, 12, 14–17, 19, 21, 23–25, 27, 28, 30–39, 43–46, 48, 49, 53, 56, 58–60, 70, 71, 73, 82, 86, 87, 89, 90, 93, 95, 97–99, 103–106, 108, 113–146, 156, 165, 172, 173, 179, 182, 188–190, 192
 foreign-related arbitral (*see* Foreign-related arbitral award)
 non-domestic, 1, 36–38

B

Baosheng case, 155–156, 185
Basic principles of law
 concepts of, 84
 and fundamental social interest, 112
 Mainland China, 39, 45
 and moral ethics, 74
 PRC's, 31–35
 violation, 77, 102, 114
Bifurcated system, 60

C

Castel case, 113, 165, 166, 172, 173, 185
CCOIC. *See* China Chamber of International Commerce (CCOIC)
Centralised jurisdiction, 5, 28, 53–54, 190
Chao Lai Xin Sheng case, 59, 60, 65, 147, 166, 173–176, 185
Cheng-Ren (承認), 4, 43, 46
China Chamber of International Commerce (CCOIC), 30
China International Economic and Trade Arbitration Commission (CIETAC), 61, 62, 64, 69, 76, 77, 79, 80, 139, 140, 143, 148, 150, 151, 155, 168, 170, 171, 180
China Maritime Arbitration Commission (CMAC), 61
Chinese court, 9, 99, 114, 123, 158, 161, 171

Index

CIETAC. *See* China International Economic and Trade Arbitration Commission (CIETAC)
CMAC. *See* China Maritime Arbitration Commission (CMAC)
Commercial reservation, 31
Contracting States
  ad hoc arbitral awards, 34
  Art. V(2)(b), New York Convention, 16, 17, 19, 33, 89
  non-Contracting States, 32–34
  re-examination, public policy, 1
  restriction, 89
Convention on the Execution of Foreign Arbitral Awards, 14

D

Dignity, 34
Domestic arbitral award
  civil procedure law, 70
  vs. foreign arbitral awards, 35–39
  PRC's arbitration law, 70
  violation, social and public interest, 80–81
Domestic arbitration
  foreign arbitration institutions, 176
  PRC law, 179–180
  territory of Mainland China, 177–178
Domestic arbitration institution, 54
Domestic award. *See* Domestic arbitral award
Dongfeng case, 148–149
'Dual-track' or 'bifurcated' system, 60
Duferco case, 37

E

ECOSOC. *See* United Nations Economic and Social Council (ECOSOC)
ED&F Man case
  enforcement, 97, 107, 108
Escape mechanism
  ex officio, 1, 16, 74, 80, 83, 104, 105

Exceptional
  escape device, 18
  foreign arbitral awards, 89
  private international law, 88
  public policy
    Art. V(2)(b), New York Convention enforcement, foreign arbitral awards, 99
    PRC judicial practice, 99–103
    restriction, 98
  State's local laws, 18
Executive Yuan, 46, 47

F

Foreign arbitration institution, 32–36, 38, 40–42, 53, 54, 69, 144, 160, 174, 176–178, 186
Foreign arbitral award. *See* Award
Foreign debt guarantee, 93–95
Foreign elements
  foreign-related arbitration, 62
  national arbitral awards, 70
Foreign-related arbitral award
  vs. domestic arbitral awards, 181–182
  and foreign-related institutional arbitral awards, 55, 60–70, 72, 73, 79
  revocation of, 55–57
  social and public interest, 71–78
Foreign-related arbitration
  CIETAC, 61
  vs. domestic arbitration (*see* Domestic arbitration)
  reporting system, 182–183
Foreign-related arbitration agreement
  reporting system, 54
  validity of, 55
Foreign-related arbitration institution, 51, 61, 62, 64, 146, 175
Foreign-related civil case, 59, 62, 146, 147, 175
Foreign-related civil relationship, 63, 66, 67, 83, 94, 95, 178

Index

Foreign-Related Commercial and Maritime Trial, 8, 33, 34, 82, 83, 94, 176, 191
Foreign-related institutional arbitral award, 55, 60-70, 72, 73, 79
Fourth Civil Tribunal, SPC's
 centralised jurisdiction, 53-54
 functions, 57
 reporting system, 54-57
Fundamental principles
 fundamental principles of the law, 15, 16
 procedural, 21
 substantive, 21, 106

G

Geneva Convention, 14, 15
Good morals
 public policy/public order, 25
 and social order, 26
GRD Minproc case, 93, 119, 192
Guangxia Culture case, 139, 168-172, 192

H

Hemofarm case, 123, 147, 156-166, 168, 171-173, 185, 192
Higher People's Court
 Anhui Higher People's Court, 79, 137, 138, 155, 185
 Beijing Higher People's Court, 79, 97, 108, 130, 142
 Guangdong Higher People's Court, 77, 113, 115, 116, 167, 171
 Hainan Higher People's Court, 128, 164, 165
 Henan Higher People's Court, 149
 Jiangsu Higher People's Court, 68, 124-126, 131, 152-154, 166, 173, 177, 179, 185
 Shandong Higher People's Court, 123, 124, 157-159, 161-163, 172
 Shanghai Higher People's Court, 63, 68, 101, 119, 120
 Tianjin Higher People's Court, 102, 114, 115
 Yunnan Higher People's Court, 134
 Zhejiang Higher People's Court, 110, 117, 134, 136
Hong Kong
 arbitration institution, 59
 Arbitration Ordinance, 48
 authorities, 8
 courts, 48
 currency, 128, 165
 enforcement of arbitral awards, 70, 82, 105
 extra-territorial arbitral awards, 49
 foreign parties, 4
 HKIAC (*see* Hong Kong International Arbitration Centre (HKIAC))
 HKSAR (*see* Hong Kong Special Administrative Region (HKSAR))
 international commercial arbitration, 69
 judicial review, arbitral awards, 68
 recognition and enforcement of awards, 25, 28, 29, 39-45, 48
 stock exchange, 65
 validity, foreign-related arbitration agreements, 55
Hong Kong International Arbitration Centre (HKIAC), 58, 105-106, 112, 133-139, 174
Hong Kong Special Administrative Region (HKSAR), 39, 41, 44, 45, 48, 67, 69, 106, 112, 131, 134, 166, 188, 189

Index

I

ICAC. *See* The International Commercial Arbitration Court at the Chamber of Commerce and Industry of the Russian Federation (ICAC)
ILA. *See* International Law Association (ILA)
Interim measures, 32
Intermediate People's Court
  Beijing First Intermediate People's Court, 108, 150
  Beijing Fourth Intermediate People's Court, 65
  Beijing Second Intermediate People's Court, 76, 91, 92, 147, 168, 175, 185, 192
  Beijing Third Intermediate People's Court, 77
  Chengdu Intermediate People's Court, 102, 103
  Dongying Intermediate People's Court, 65
  Fuzhou Intermediate People's Court, 112, 113
  Haikou Intermediate People's Court, 92, 95, 107, 108, 112, 128
  Hainan First Intermediate People's Court, 96, 97
  Hangzhou Intermediate People's Court, 109, 110, 117
  Hefei Intermediate People's Court, 138, 155
  Jinan Intermediate People's Court, 124, 157, 159
  Kunming Intermediate People's Court, 91, 105, 131, 132
  Nanjing Intermediate People's Court, 74, 75
  Nantong Intermediate People's Court, 126, 152
  Ningbo Intermediate People's Court, 37, 38, 136
  Shanghai First Intermediate People's Court, 66, 101, 120
  Shanghai Second Intermediate People's Court, 59, 60, 69, 74, 75, 111, 147, 175, 185, 192
  Shenzhen Intermediate People's Court, 74, 77, 168, 169, 171
  Suzhou Intermediate People's Court, 68, 80
  Taizhou Intermediate People's Court, 64, 131, 165, 166, 173
  Wuxi Intermediate People's Court, 37, 38
  Xiangtan Intermediate People's Court, 96
  Yueyang Intermediate People's Court, 81
  Zhanjiang Intermediate People's Court, 79, 115, 116, 143, 151, 167
  Zhengzhou Intermediate People's Court, 78, 143, 149
  Zhongshan Intermediate People's Court, 113, 173
The International Commercial Arbitration Court at the Chamber of Commerce and Industry of the Russian Federation (ICAC), 24
Internationality, 87, 89–97, 191
International Law Association (ILA), 11–13, 103, 187
International obligations, 21–23, 86

J

Japan Commercial Arbitration Association (JCAA), 124, 152–154, 156
Judicial review
  arbitral awards, 68
  Art. V(2)(b), New York Convention, 45
  civil and commercial arbitration, 68
  foreign arbitration, 158
  foreign-related arbitration, 8
  process, 53
Judicial sovereignty
  infringement, 59

Index

nation's, 58
and PRC courts' jurisdiction
  Hemofarm case
    perspectives, 38
Jurisdiction
  arbitral tribunal, 140
  arbitration institution, 145
  centralised, 5, 28, 53–54
  CIETAC's scope, 64
  civil and commercial cases, 68
  contract, 58, 144
  enforcement of awards, 1
  and judicial sovereignty (*see* Judicial sovereignty)
  legal, 8
  personal, 137
  PRC courts, 123, 147
  PRC law, 95

K

Korean Commercial Arbitration Board (KCAB), 175

L

LCIA. *See* London Court of International Arbitration (LCIA)
Leaf Confectionary case, 59, 60, 111, 175, 176, 185
Legislative Yuan, 46, 47
Liupanshui case, 58–60, 65, 144, 147, 166, 173–176, 185, 192
Lois de police, 21, 22
London Court of International Arbitration (LCIA), 105, 109, 117, 119
Louis Dreyfus case, 102, 115, 116, 167–168, 172, 192

M

Macau
  applicable laws, 67
  foreign arbitral awards, 45, 49
  foreign parties, 4
  laws and regulations, 8
  recognition and enforcement of awards, 25, 28, 29, 40–44, 48
  Special Administrative Region (*see* Macau Special Administrative Region)
  validity, foreign-related arbitration agreements, 55
Macau Special Administrative Region
  arbitral awards, PRC, 44
  arbitration laws and regulations, 41
  arbitrators, 41
  choice of law, foreign-related civil relationships, 67
  mutual recognition and enforcement of arbitral awards, 40, 41, 48
  violation, social and public interest, 188
Mainland China
  arbitration institutions, 69, 70, 145, 146
  basic principles of law/social and public interest, 40
  civil arbitral awards, 41
  judicial sovereignty and jurisdiction, PRC (*see* Protection of PRC's judicial sovereignty and jurisdiction)
  mutual recognition and enforcement of awards, 25, 39–41, 45, 46, 48, 106, 131, 134, 138, 188, 189
  non-enforcement of an arbitral award, 142
  people's courts, 8, 9, 188, 191, 192
  predictability, public policy, 191
  protection of departmental/local interests
    Baosheng case, 155–156
    Dongfeng case, 148–149
    Shin-Etsu case, 152–154
    Tom Hulett case, 150–152
  social and public interest, 39, 44, 74, 85
  and Taiwan, 47
Mandatory Laws

Germany, 89
PRC, 93–95
violation
 registering foreign debt guarantees, 93–95
 State's public policy, 87, 106–146
Mediated settlement agreement, 42, 96
Mitsui case, 95, 97, 107, 128, 164, 166, 173, 183, 191, 192
Mutual recognition and enforcement of arbitral awards, 40, 41, 48, 188, 189

N

National and social interest, PRC, 28, 30–35, 49
National sovereignty
 control, 2
 and dignity, 34
 infringement, 102, 114
 violations, 83
New York Convention
 Art. V, 1, 13, 108
 Art. V(1)(b), 22, 37, 38, 103–105, 115, 125, 128, 152–154, 156, 172, 175, 192
 Art. V(2)(b), 1–5, 11–14, 16–19, 27, 31, 33, 44, 45, 49, 58–60, 82, 86–90, 97–99, 101–105, 110, 114, 115, 117, 119, 120, 123, 125, 130, 147, 153, 154, 164, 167, 172, 173, 186–89, 191, 192
Non-enforcement of foreign-related arbitral awards
 Art. V(2)(b), New York Convention, 60
 Art. 71, PRC Arbitration Law, 78, 182
 Art. 274, PRC Civil Procedure Law, 182
 Baosheng case, 155, 156
 foreign-related arbitration, 182, 183
 judicial review process, 53
 limitations, 7
 opinions of the court, 139–146
 procedural regulations, 53
 social and public interest, 28, 79, 82, 189
Non-recognition and non-enforcement of foreign arbitral awards, 7, 8, 16, 22, 56, 59, 60, 95, 103–106, 108, 112, 113, 123, 124, 128, 152, 156, 158, 167
Notification
 lower courts, 32, 35
 PRC's accession, New York Convention, 34
 SPC's, 43, 54, 55

O

Ordre Public. *See* Public order

P

PRC Arbitration Law
 provisions, New York Convention, 29
 recognition and enforcement of arbitral awards
  difference, 40–48
  Hong Kong, 39
  Macau, 40
  Taiwan, 39
 recognition and enforcement of foreign arbitral awards
  after PRC's accession to the New York Convention, 31–39
  before PRC's accession to the New York Convention, 30–31
 social and public interest (*see* Social and public interest)
PRC Civil Procedure Law
 amendment, 32, 33
 arbitration institution, 35
 and Arbitration Law, 59–81
 Art. 81, 183
 Art. 118, 162
 Art. 154, 183
 Art. 204, 27, 30–34, 49
 Art. 255, 145, 174, 175

Index

Art. 257, 177
Art. 260, 56, 169
Art. 260(2), 149, 155
Art. 269, 32, 33, 108
Art. 271, 59, 176, 177
Art. 272, 184
Art. 274, 155, 171, 173, 182, 191
Art. 283, 36
litigation costs, 163
and New York Convention, 35
recognition and enforcement of arbitral awards, 32
social and public interest, 28, 50–53
violation, 96, 97
PRC Contract Law, 49, 59, 146, 175–177, 179
Protection of PRC's judicial sovereignty and jurisdiction
  differences, domestic arbitration and foreign-related arbitration, 176–184
  Liupanshui, Chao Lai Xin Sheng and *Leaf Confectionery* cases, 174–176
  violation, arbitral tribunal's disapproval of PRC administrative decisions, *Guangxia Culture* case, 168–173
  Hemofarm case, 156–166
  Louis Dreyfus case, 167–168
Public interest
  PRC Arbitration Law (*see* PRC Arbitration Law)
  and social (*see* Social and public interest)
Public order
  Acts Disrupting Public Order and Punishment, 29
  and good morals, 25, 83
  Macau, 40
  and PRC Constitution, 29
  and public policy, 13–14, 23, 85
  reservation, 71, 82, 83
  social and public interest, 84, 85
  violation, 93
Public policy

domestic, 4, 19, 20, 24, 44, 89, 90, 186
international, 4, 17–21, 24–25, 88–98
parallel provisions of, 25
procedural, 2, 22, 87, 103–106, 192
and public order (*see* Public order)
really international, 4
substantive, 2, 87, 104, 106
transnational public policy, 4, 17, 18, 20, 87, 88
truly international public policy, 4, 17–21, 88
Public policy rules. *See Lois de police*
Public sentiments (guo-qing), 143, 151

R

Re-arbitration, 56, 58, 73, 81
Reciprocity
  principle of reciprocity, 28, 30, 32, 33, 35, 49, 55, 73
  reservation, 31, 34–36
Recognition and enforcement of foreign arbitral awards
  after PRC's accession to New York Convention, 31–39
  Art. IV(h), Draft Convention, 15
  Art. V(2)(b), New York Convention, 12, 89, 104, 130, 189, 192
  before PRC's accession to New York Convention, 30–31
  domestic arbitral awards, 93
  Mainland China, 45
  PRC's public policy, 27, 90
  Shin-Etsu case, 152
  social and public interest, 82
Ren-ke (認可), 4, 45, 46
Reply, SPC's, 8, 14, 43, 56, 58, 65, 73, 77, 79, 93, 97, 101, 102, 104, 107, 108, 112–115, 117, 119, 123, 124, 127, 128, 130, 134, 137, 139, 143, 149–154, 156, 158, 163–166, 168, 170, 171, 183, 191
Reporting system
  multi-tiered reporting system, 68

232

revocation, foreign-related arbitral awards, 56–57
social and public interest (*see* Social and public interest)
Revocation of foreign-related arbitral awards
reporting system, 56–57
social and public interest, 70–81
SPC's Fourth Civil Tribunal, 190
Revoke, 38, 56, 73, 75–77, 79, 91, 92, 107, 171, 183, 190

S

Safety valve, 11, 16, 17, 99
SCC. *See* The Arbitration Institute of the Stockholm Chamber of Commerce (SCC)
Shanghai International Arbitration Center (SHIAC), 181
Shanghai International Economic and Trade Arbitration Commission, 180–181
Shin-Etsu case, 124, 152–154, 156, 185
Singapore International Arbitration Centre (SIAC), 59, 69, 111
Social and public interest
application of foreign laws, 82–83
Arbitration Law of the People's Republic of China, 28, 50–53, 70, 71
centralised jurisdiction, 53–54
Civil Procedure Law of the People's Republic of China, 28, 50–53, 70, 71
controversy, 84
differences, Arbitration Law and Civil Procedure Law
foreign-related arbitral awards, 60–70
foreign-related institutional arbitral awards, 60–70
non-enforcement of foreign-related arbitral awards, 70–81

revocation of foreign-related arbitral awards, 70–81
domestic arbitral awards, 48
foreign-related arbitral award, 150
Fourth Civil Tribunal, SPC's, 57
interpretation, SPC's, 28
legislations, PRC, 2
local protectionism, 85, 149
Mainland China, 112
PRC cases, 82
reporting system
enforcement of foreign-related institutional arbitral awards, 55
revocation of foreign-related arbitral awards, 55–57
validity of foreign-related arbitration agreements, 55
violation, 45, 48, 85, 90, 92, 105
Social ethics, 29, 49
Social order, 26, 103, 110, 119
Social public order, 29
Standing Committee of National People's Congress (NPCSC), 13, 14, 31, 49
Straits Exchange Foundation (SEF), 4
Supreme People's Court of the People's Republic of China (SPC), 5–8, 14, 28, 29, 31–35, 37–45, 47, 48, 53–60, 62, 65–68, 72–73, 77, 79, 82, 88, 93–95, 97–102, 105, 107, 108, 110, 111, 131, 140, 147, 149–156, 158, 159, 161–165, 167–172, 174, 176, 177, 182–184
Supreme People's Court Gazette, 8, 191

T

Taiwan
Arbitration Law, 14, 25, 45
civil court judgments, 43
institutional arbitral awards, 42, 45, 189
recognition and enforcement of arbitral awards, 39, 45, 189
related civil and commercial case, 68
region (*see* Taiwan Region)

Index

Taiwan Arbitration Law, 14, 25, 45
Taiwan Region, 39–43, 45, 48, 68, 69, 189
Taiwan-related civil and commercial cases, 67, 68
Tianjin Maritime Court, 115
Tom Hulett case, 150–152, 191, 192

U

UNCITRAL Model Law, 18, 24, 88
United Nations Economic and Social Council (ECOSOC), 15
Unruly horse, 1, 98

V

Validity of arbitration agreements, 38, 56, 175
Value Adjustment Mechanism (VAM), 112
Variable Interest Entity (VIE), 112
Vienna Convention on the Law of Treaties (VCLT), 11, 12
Violation
   arbitral tribunal's
      Guangxia Culture case, 168–172
      Hemofarm case, 156–166
      Louis Dreyfus case, 167–168

award's, 96–97
criminal law, 16
enforcement of State's Mandatory Laws
   international consensus, 106–107
   PRC judicial practice, 107–146
enforcement State's public policy, 99
lois de police/public policy rules, 22
mandatory laws, registering foreign debt guarantees, 93–95
national and social interest, 30
PRC's public policy, 58, 59, 99, 105, 173, 176
social and public interest, 45, 48, 71–81, 85, 90, 150, 189–191
substantive/procedural public policy, 2, 22, 103

W

Western Bulk case, 93, 114, 192
Wicor case, 131, 165, 166, 173, 185

Y

Yongning, 123, 124, 157–164, 171

Z

Züblin case, 37, 38